NORTHERN CALIFORNIA
CABINS & COTTAGES

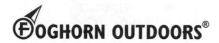

FOGHORN OUTDOORS®

NORTHERN CALIFORNIA

CABINS & COTTAGES

Great Lodgings with Easy Access to Outdoor Recreation

Stephani & Tom Stienstra

AVALON
TRAVEL

FOGHORN OUTDOORS:
NORTHERN CALIFORNIA
CABINS & COTTAGES

First Edition

Stephani & Tom Stienstra

Published by
Avalon Travel Publishing
5855 Beaudry Street
Emeryville, CA 94608, USA

Text © 2002 by Stephani & Tom
Stienstra.
All rights reserved.
Maps and illustrations
© 2002 by Avalon Travel Publishing, Inc.
All rights reserved.

Please send all comments, corrections,
additions, amendments, and critiques to:

FOGHORN OUTDOORS:
NORTHERN CALIFORNIA
CABINS & COTTAGES

AVALON TRAVEL PUBLISHING
5855 BEAUDRY ST.
EMERYVILLE, CA 94608, USA

email: atpfeedback@avalonpub.com
website: www.foghorn.com

Printing History
1st edition—April 2002
5 4 3 2 1

Some photos and illustrations are used by permission
and are the property of the original copyright owners.
Photographs used on pages 1, 27, 71, 103, 153, 177, 219, 245, 289, 315, 337 © Tom Stienstra
Photographs of individual cabins and cottages are courtesy of establishment,
except where otherwise credited.

ISBN: 1-56691-378-0
ISSN: 1538-053X

Editor: Marisa Solís
Series Manager: Marisa Solís
Copy Editor: Emily Lunceford
Proofreader: Mia Lipman
Research Assistant: Ryan Bacchia
Graphics Coordinators: Melissa Sherowski, Laura VanderPloeg
Production: Laura VanderPloeg, Alvaro Villanueva
Designer: Alvaro Villanueva
Map Editor: Olivia Solís
Cartographers: Chris Folks, Kat Kalamaras, Mike Morgenfeld, Suzanne Service
Indexer: Marisa Solís

Front cover photo: © La Playa Hotel

Back cover photo: The Ahwahnee Hotel © Chambers Lorenz Design/Kasparovitch Photography

Distributed by Publishers Group West

Printed in the United States by R.R. Donnelley

ABOUT THE AUTHORS

Stephani and **Tom Stienstra** have adventured across California for years—hiking, boating, and fishing—searching for the best of the outdoors and writing about it. Tom is the outdoors writer for the *San Francisco Chronicle* and has been twice honored with the Presidents Award by the Outdoors Writers Association of America as the national Outdoor Writer of the Year for the newspaper division. Stephani's extensive travels are highlighted by climbing the West's highest summits, including Mt. Whitney, Shasta, and Half Dome. Tom and Stephani are the authors of the popular new book, *Foghorn Outdoors: Washington Camping.* They live with their two sons in the "State of Jefferson," and can be reached directly on the Internet at www.TomStienstra.com, where their other books are available.

COURTESY OF STEPHANI STIENSTRA

© KURT ROGERS

CONTENTS

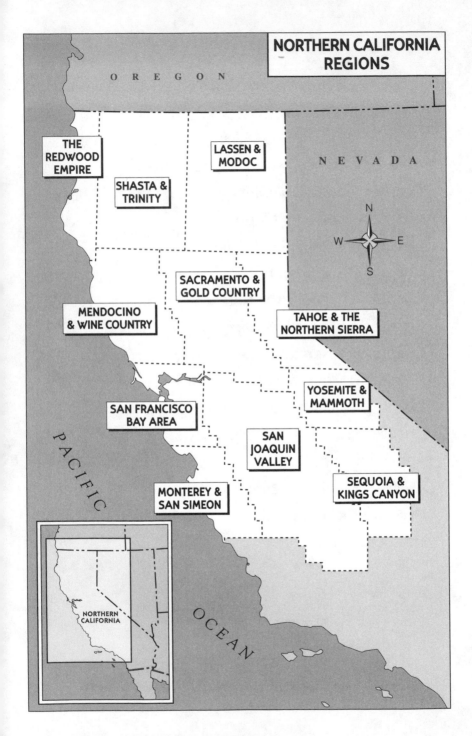

NORTHERN CALIFORNIA REGIONS

OREGON

THE REDWOOD EMPIRE

LASSEN & MODOC

NEVADA

SHASTA & TRINITY

N
W   E
S

SACRAMENTO & GOLD COUNTRY

MENDOCINO & WINE COUNTRY

TAHOE & THE NORTHERN SIERRA

SAN FRANCISCO BAY AREA

YOSEMITE & MAMMOTH

SAN JOAQUIN VALLEY

PACIFIC

MONTEREY & SAN SIMEON

SEQUOIA & KINGS CANYON

OCEAN

NORTHERN CALIFORNIA

MAPS

DEFINING
CABINS AND COTTAGES

The purpose of this book is to provide a resource of cabins and cottages, from romantic to rustic, that are available for rent in Northern California. The territory covered spans from San Simeon to Mount Whitney in the south and all the way north to the Oregon border.

Recreational opportunities that are available near each cabin are also featured. With the array of outdoor activities in Northern California, you can enjoy many things, including beachcombing for sea shells, hiking to a gorgeous lookout, fishing for trout, or soaking in mineral hot springs. The result is a book that features opportunities for outdoor recreation by day, with a roof over your head—plus separate walls and privacy—by night. Our goal is to put the best of Northern California right in your hands, whether for a one-night getaway or a full vacation.

Each cabin or cottage listed in this guidebook provides self-contained, stand-alone lodging. They range from luxurious cottages and vacation home rentals to rustic tent cabins and yurts. Many are part of a resort, lodge, ranch, campground, or rental company. Each lodging is a separate building or unit, and would be suitable for couples, families, or singles who want more privacy than at a bed-and-breakfast and more personality than at a typical hotel or motel. The cabins and cottages in this guide are constructed from a variety of materials, including pine logs, redwood, canvas, and in rare cases, fiberglass, such as for luxury yachts that can be rented at their moorings in San Francisco and Oakland.

Each listing in *Foghorn Outdoors: Northern California Cabins & Cottages* is located in or near a major outdoor recreation area, including five national parks: Redwood, Lassen Volcanic, Yosemite, Sequoia, and Kings Canyon. In addition, the length of the Pacific coast from San Simeon to Oregon is also featured, along with the Sierra Nevada and its foothills, and the Sacramento and San Joaquin valleys.

Foghorn Outdoors: Northern California Cabins & Cottages provides everything you need for an enjoyable weekend getaway or a week-long vacation centered around outdoor recreation, with a cabin or cottage—or yurt, chalet, or yacht—that's right for you.

HOW TO USE THIS BOOK

Foghorn Outdoors: Northern California Cabins & Cottages is divided into 11 chapters: The Redwood Empire, Shasta & Trinity, Lassen & Modoc, Mendocino & Wine Country, Sacramento & Gold Country, Tahoe & the Northern Sierra, San Francisco Bay Area, Yosemite & Mammoth, Monterey & San Simeon, San Joaquin Valley, and Sequoia & Kings Canyon. This book is designed to be as user-friendly as possible. Navigating this guide can be done easily in two ways:

1. If you know the general area you want to visit, turn to the map at the beginning of that chapter. Each cabin listing is identified on the map by number. You can then determine which cabins are at or near your destination. In addition, opposite the map is a chapter table of contents that lists each lodging in the chapter by map number and the page number it's profiled on.

2. If you know the name of the lodging facility you want to stay at, or the name of the surrounding geographical area or nearby feature (town, national or state park or forest, mountain, lake, river, etc.), look it up in the index beginning on page 369 and turn to the corresponding page.

ABOUT THE CABIN PROFILES

Each featured cabin includes an introduction to the lodging facility and what it has to offer. This usually includes an overview of the grounds, units, facilities, and amenities. There is also a discussion of the recreation opportunities available on-site or within a short drive. These feature hiking, biking, boating, fishing, wildlife watching, and other activities.

The practical information you need to plan an enjoyable trip is broken down further into the following categories:

Facilities — This section lists the number of cabins or cottages available and their furnishings. It may include information on bedrooms, bathrooms, showers, and cooking or kitchen facilities. In some cases, these facilities are serviced daily. In others, they can be extremely limited, or not available. Other amenities may include fireplace, hot tub, air-conditioning, and heating, as well as facilities available on the property, such as swimming pool, restaurant, and picnic area.

Bedding — This section details whether linens and towels are provided, and if not, what you should bring to sleep comfortably.

Reservations and rates — This section notes whether reservations are required or recommended. It also details the rates for each cabin, which can change according to cabin size, amenities, time of week, and time of year. Also included are additional fees for extra persons or pets, whether package deals are available, or if the cabin is open seasonally. The prices for each listing were checked twice before publication; regardless, rates can change without notice at any time. It's always best to call the cabin ahead of time to verify rates.

ABOUT THE ICONS

The icons in this book are designed to provide at-a-glance information on activities that are available on-site or nearby each listing. Some icons have been selected also to represent facilities available or services provided. They are not meant to represent every activity or service, but rather those that are most significant.

 — Hiking trails are available.

 — Biking trails or routes are available. Usually this refers to mountain biking, although it may represent road cycling as well. Refer to the text for that cabin for more detail.

 — Swimming opportunities are available.

 — Fishing opportunities are available.

 — Boating opportunities are available. Various types of vessels apply under this umbrella activity, including motorboats, canoes, kayaks, sailboats, personal watercrafts, and row boats. Refer to the text for that cabin for more detail, including mph restrictions and boat ramp availability.

 — Beach activities are available. This general category may include activities such as beachcombing, surfing, and volleyball. Refer to the text for that cabin for more detail on what's allowed.

 — Winter sports are available. This general category may include activities such as downhill skiing, cross-country skiing, snowshoeing, snowmobiling, snowboarding, and ice skating. Refer to the text for that cabin for more detail on which sports are available.

 — Hot or cold springs are available.

 — Pets are permitted. Lodging facilities that allow pets may require a deposit, nightly fee, or for the pet to be on a leash. Cabins may also restrict pet size or behavior, and in all cases, prohibit pets from being left unattended. Refer to the text for that cabin for more specific instruction or call the cabin in advance.

— The cabin or cottage is especially popular with families. Typically this is because it has activities nearby that are suitable. These include a playground or play area, swimming pool, ocean beach, lake with a wading or swimming beach, or family-oriented skiing or snow play. At these kid-friendly cabins, you won't have to travel far to keep the youngsters entertained.

 — Wheelchair access is provided. Not all cabins at a facility may be wheelchair accessible, but if at least one is, the cabin will receive this icon. Refer to the text for that cabin for more detail or call the cabin in advance.

ABOUT THE RATINGS

Every lodging option in this book is rated on two scales.

Luxury rating — This scale of **1** to **5** rates the comfort level of the cabin, from primitive to luxurious, respectively. While we realize this is relatively arbitrary, there are basic guidelines that were followed in determining these ratings. For example, a tent cabin without bathrooms nor running water will receive a **1** or **2**. That doesn't mean that you can't have the perfect vacation here. All it means is you might have to carry your water from a nearby fountain and be prepared to use chemical toilets. Likewise, a cottage with well-furnished bathroom, fireplace, hot tub, king-size bed, and down comforts will probably rank **4** or **5**. But, that doesn't guarantee the perfect vacation; the cabin may be close to a noisy highway, the management may not be friendly, or the recreation options may be an hour's drive away.

In other words, the luxury rating does not predict the quality of your trip, which can be determined by many factors, including weather, but simply the level of furnishings available. Many people desire more primitive settings, and others would never settle for anything less than a **4**, regardless of cost.

Recreation rating — This scale of **1** to **5** rates the quality and variety of nearby recreation activities. We expect that users of this guidebook are interested in the outdoors and seek a cabin experience that is coupled with recreation opportunities. This scale does not rate the level of recreation expertise needed to participate in them. The rating instead is based primarily on how *accessible* the activities are to you. A low rating does not mean a quality vacation is not available, but rather that you may need to drive to reach the activity destination.

ABOUT THE MAPS

Each chapter in this book begins with a map of the area featured. Every cabin profile in the chapter is noted by a number on the map. These points are placed as precisely as possible, but the scale of these maps often makes it difficult to pinpoint a cabin's exact location. We advise that you purchase a detailed map of the area, especially if it is new to you.

OUR COMMITMENT

We are committed to making *Foghorn Outdoors: Northern California Cabins & Cottages* the most accurate, thorough, and enjoyable guide to cabin and cottage rentals in Northern California. Each ranch, campground, inn, and resort featured in this book has been carefully reviewed and accompanied by the most up-to-date information available. Be aware, however, that with the passing of time, some of the rates listed herein may have changed, facilities may have been upgraded (or downgraded), and changes in weather may close cabins or the roads leading to them. With these possibilities in mind, or if you have a specific need or concern, it's best to call the location ahead of time.

If you would like to comment on the book, whether it's to suggest a cabin or cottage we overlooked or to let us know about any noteworthy experience—good or bad—that occurred while using *Foghorn Outdoors: Northern California Cabins & Cottages* as your guide, we would appreciate hearing from you. Please address correspondence to:

Foghorn Outdoors:
Northern California Cabins & Cottages,
   First Edition
Avalon Travel Publishing
5855 Beaudry Street
Emeryville, CA 94608
U.S.A

email: atpfeedback@avalonpub.com

If you decide to send us an email, please put "Northern California Cabins & Cottages" in the subject line. Thanks.

None of the cabins and cottages featured in this book have paid to be included. The cabins and cottages were researched and selected by the authors and profiled at their discretion.

FINDING YOUR OWN GOLDEN POND

The idea for this book first came after watching one of our favorite movies, *On Golden Pond*.

It seemed to us that many people want to find their own Golden Pond, that is, a little cabin, cottage, or chalet in a beautiful spot—sometimes romantic, sometimes amid great recreation opportunities—and always a private hideaway. We searched across the state in hopes of finding every cabin and cottage rental from San Simeon to Mt. Whitney, and then across Northern California up to Oregon. We included a few bonus spots, such as a moored yacht at San Francisco's Fisherman's Wharf and even a few fire lookouts in remote national forests. The result is a collection that ranges from some of the most luxurious and expensive accommodations available to some of the most primitive and cheap, as well as everything in between. Perhaps in these pages, you can find your own Golden Pond.

Northern California Cabins and Cottages was a perfect book to co-author, with each of us providing a special emphasis. Stephani often detailed the quality of facilities, while Tom often described the nearby outdoors recreation opportunities.

The book features some of the most beautiful landscape on earth. Each region offers something compelling and unique, providing everyone with the opportunity for a stellar getaway. The outdoors is good for the soul. Adventures can refresh the spirit. And the experience can be enhanced greatly by staying in a cabin or cottage. In fact, we can't think of a enjoying a better time in California than spending the day hiking, boating, fishing, or sight-seeing and spending the night in a little cottage or cabin.

Who knows, maybe you will find your own Golden Pond.

—Stephani & Tom Stienstra

CHAPTER 1

The Redwood Empire

*V*isitors come from around the world to the Redwood Empire
for one reason: to see the groves of giant redwoods, the
tallest trees in the world. On a perfect day in the redwoods
here, refracted sunlight beams through the forest canopy,
creating a solemn, cathedral-like effect. It feels as if you are
standing in the center of the earth's pure magic.

But the redwood forests are only one of the attractions to this
area. The Smith River canyon, Del Norte and Humboldt Coasts,
and the remote edge of the Siskiyou Wilderness in Six Rivers
National Forest all make this region like none other in the world.

On sunny days in late summer, some visitors are incredulous
that so few people live in the Redwood Empire. The reason why
is the same one that explains why the trees grow so tall: rain in
the winter—often for weeks at a time—and fog in the summer. If
the sun does manage to appear, it's an event almost worthy of
calling the police to say you've spotted a large, yellow
Unidentified Flying Object. So most folks are content to just visit.

In our opinion, three stellar areas should be on your must-see
list for outstanding days of adventure here: the redwood parks
from Trinidad to Klamath River, the Smith River Recreation
Area, and the Lost Coast.

We've hiked every trailhead from Trinidad to Crescent City.
The hikes here feature some of the best adventuring in Northern
California. A good place to start is Prairie Creek Redwoods State
Park, where you can see fantastic herds of Roosevelt elk. Then
head over to the beach by hiking Fern Canyon, where you walk
for 20 minutes at the bottom of a canyon adjacent to vertical

walls covered with ferns, and then continue north on the Coastal Trail, where you'll pass through pristine woodlands and fantastic expanses of untouched beaches. All the trails through the redwoods north of the Klamath River are winners; it's just a matter of matching up your level of ambition to the right hike.

The Smith River Recreation Area is equally gorgeous. The Smith is one of the last major free-flowing rivers in America. Wild, pristine, and beautiful, it's set in a series of gorges and bordered by national forest. The centerpiece is Jedediah Smith State Park and its grove of monster-sized redwoods. South Fork Road provides an extended tour into Six Rivers National Forest along the South Fork Smith River, with the option of visiting many of the largest trees in Jedediah Smith State Park. The turnoff is located on U.S. 199 just northeast of the town of Hiouchi. Turn right, cross two bridges, and you will arrive at a fork in the road. Turning left at the fork will take you along the South Fork Smith River and deep into Six Rivers National Forest. Turning right at the fork will take you to a series of trailheads for hikes into redwoods. Of these, the best is the Boy Scout Tree Trail.

The Lost Coast is often overlooked by visitors because of the difficulty in reaching it; your only access is via a slow, curvy road through the Mattole River Valley, past Petrolia, and out to a piece of coast. The experience is like being in suspended animation—your surroundings peaceful and pristine, with a striking lack of people. One of the best ways to capture the sensation is to drive out near the mouth of the Mattole, then hike south on the Coast Trail long enough to get a feel for the area.

Compared to other regions in California, this corner of the state is somewhat one-dimensional. The emphasis here is solely on exploring the redwoods and the coast, and to some extent, fishing. Most of the cabins here are designed with that in mind; they're basic, rustic (with a few noteworthy exceptions), and among the most economical in the state.

Carter House Inns in Eureka ranks at the top of the luxury scale. It's a romantic getaway with an emphasis on fine cuisine and upscale lodging. Other high-quality spots include View Crest Lodge and Bishop Pine Lodge.

For beach and ocean lovers, White Rock Resort has park model cabins with beach frontage, and Casa Rubio Bed and Breakfast has similar frontage and beach access.

On the opposite end of the spectrum are two primitive and remote lodgings: Bear Basin Lookout and the adjoining Pierson Cabin. Both are operated by the Forest Service and served as a former fire lookout station.

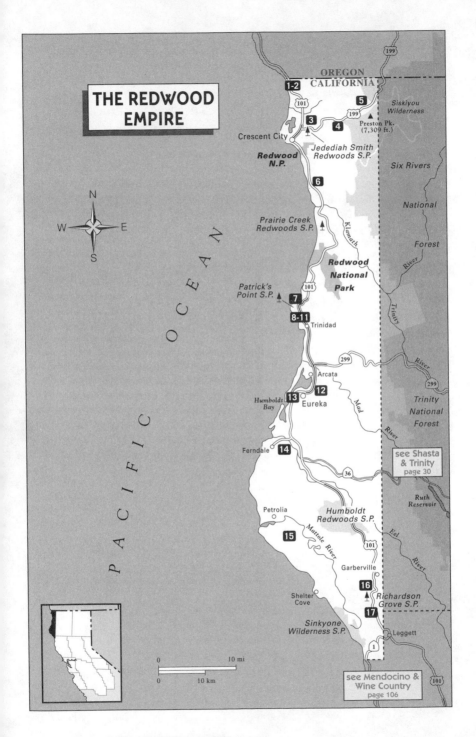

THE REDWOOD EMPIRE

OREGON
CALIFORNIA

1-2

5

101

3

4

Preston Pk.
(7,309 ft.)

199

Siskiyou
Wilderness

Crescent City

Redwood
N.P.

Jedediah Smith
Redwoods S.P.

Six Rivers

6

National

N
W E
S

Prairie Creek
Redwoods S.P.

Redwood
National
Park

Forest

Klamath River

Patrick's
Point S.P.

7

101

8-11

Trinidad

299

Arcata

299

12

Mad River

Humboldt
Bay

13

Eureka

Trinity

Trinity
National
Forest

River

Ferndale

14

36

see Shasta
& Trinity
page 30

Ruth
Reservoir

Petrolia

Humboldt
Redwoods S.P.

15

Mattole River

Eel River

101

Garberville

16

Richardson
Grove S.P.

Shelter
Cove

17

Sinkyone
Wilderness S.P.

Leggett

1

0   10 mi
0   10 km

see Mendocino &
Wine Country
page 106

P A C I F I C   O C E A N

CHAPTER 1
THE REDWOOD EMPIRE

1. WHITE ROCK RESORT

Here's an example of a new breed of cabin rentals, and it's in a class of its own. Built in 1999, these little cabins are packed full of amenities and seem much larger than their approximate 500- to 600-square-foot size. Inside there's a bedroom, sleeping loft, kitchen, full bath, and small living area with a cathedral ceiling.

Luxury rating: 4

Recreation rating: 3

Del Norte Coast, off U.S. 101 in Smith River

Situated on a low bluff or sand dune, the cabins are spaced fairly close together in two rows facing the ocean. The smaller cabins are closest to the ocean, while the larger units, with fireplaces, are in the second row. Each cabin has its own deck with spa and landscaping. A walking path to the beach is located between cabins three and four.

When you arrive, the smell of freshly baked bread usually fills the air. It's part of the resort's service, and the management says they really want you to feel at home. If the bread doesn't do the trick, maybe the complimentary bottle of wine, champagne, or sparkling cider will get you into vacation mode.

The design of these cabins makes them ideal for groups. You want a good set-up for the family? You got it. You want to go fishing with your buddies? It works. You want romance? There's potential.

For details about the area, refer to the next listing for Casa Rubio Bed and Breakfast.

Facilities: White Rock Resort has 21 cabins that sleep four adults or one family. Each cabin has a bathroom with shower/tub, fully equipped kitchen, and deck with spa. Some units have fireplaces. Cable television, VCR, stereo, and complimentary bottle of wine, champagne, or sparkling cider are provided. Laundry facilities are available, and a restaurant is within walking distance. Barbecues are available on request. The resort is suitable for children. One cabin is designated for smokers. Pets are not allowed.

Bedding: Linens and towels are provided.

Reservations and rates: Reservations are recommended during the summer. Rates are $109 to $135 per night for an oceanfront cabin, $135 to $160 for an ocean-view cabin. There is a 10 percent discount for seven days or more. For more than four people, $15 per person per day is charged. There is a two-night minimum on weekends and three-night minimum on holidays. Major credit cards are accepted.

Directions: From Crescent City, drive north on U.S. 101 for approximately 20 miles to within .25 mile of the Oregon-California border. The resort is on the left.

Contact: White Rock Resort, 16800 U.S. 101 North, Smith River, CA 95567; 707/487-1021 or 888/487-4659, fax at 707/487-1063; website: www.white rockresort.com.

White Rock Resort

2. CASA RUBIO BED AND BREAKFAST

Panoramic ocean views and easy beach access are the highlights here. With each lodging unit varying greatly in size and amenities, you can tailor your stay according to the number of people in your group and their needs. Each cabin or house is stocked with either croissants or muffins, juice, and coffee. And if you stay for at least three days, you'll receive a free dinner at Rubio's Restaurant in Brookings, Oregon. In case you're wondering, it's only a 10-minute drive north to get there.

Luxury rating: 3

Recreation rating: 3

Pacific Coast, off U.S. 101 in Smith River

Casa Rubio is on Pelican Bay, which forms at the mouth of the Winchuk River, right on the California-Oregon border. You'll probably see plenty of seagulls, seals, and otters during your stay. Whale watching traditionally starts in mid-December and continues through spring. The best times to see these magnificent mammals are the periods between storms, when the skies clear, the wind dies, and the ocean calms. These conditions seem to arrive each year around Christmas and New Year's, then again in mid-March and April.

Surfing is available north of the property. The beach is just a short walk from your cabin, through a well-kept garden. And, of course, there are plenty of fishing opportunities since you're in one of the best angling areas in California. There's superb steelhead fishing on the Smith River during the winter, and giant-sized salmon to be had during the fall. Take your pick.

Facilities: Casa Rubio has one cabin, along with a studio, suite, and a "nest," set just to the south of the main house; all vary in size and amenities. All lodgings have a full bathroom, and two units have fully equipped kitchens. Barbecues are available on request. Most units have a deck, and the largest house has a woodstove. Continental breakfast is provided. The facility is suitable for children. No smoking is allowed. Female dogs are allowed with prior permission.

Bedding: Linens and towels are provided.

Reservations and rates: Reservations are recommended during the summer. Rates are $68 to $98 per night, with a discount after five days. Additional persons are $10 per night per person, and children under age five are free.

Directions: From Crescent City, drive north on U.S. 101 for approximately 20 miles to Crissey Road, within 800 feet of the Oregon-California border. Turn left and drive a short distance to the resort on the right.

Contact: Casa Rubio Bed and Breakfast, 17285 Crissey Road, Smith River, CA 95567; 707/487-4313 or 800/357-6199; website: www.casarubio.com.

Casa Rubio Bed and Breakfast

3. CRESCENT CITY REDWOODS KOA CABINS

This KOA campground features 18 camping cabins, most of which are set in redwoods. These little log cabins typically have a bunk bed on one side and a queen bed on the other. Each cabin has electric

heat and an electrical outlet, but you bring the rest: sleeping bag, pillow, and anything else you require for a good night's sleep.

Compared to many other KOAs, this one has fewer amenities, with no swimming pool or hot tub. But it is set in an ideal location: two miles from Redwood National Park and a 10-minute drive from Jedediah Smith State Park and the Smith River National Recreation Area on U.S. 199. It's also less than a 10-minute drive south on U.S. 101 to Crescent City, where there is a harbor with boat launch, expansive beach, and, of course, seafood restaurants.

One of the area's prettiest driving tours begins by heading east on U.S. 199 to Hiouchi. Continue one mile to the turnoff for South Fork Road. Turn right, cross over two bridges, then turn left on

Luxury rating: 2

Recreation rating: 4

Redwood Empire, off U.S. 101 near Crescent City

South Fork Road. This pretty two-laner heads deep into national forest, running right along the beautiful South Fork Smith River for 20 miles. It extends beyond to the remote headwaters of the South Fork Smith, at the edge of some of California's wildest remaining country accessible by car.

Facilities: Crescent City Redwoods KOA has 18 cabins, 44 tent spaces, and 50 sites for RVs with full hookups. Each cabin has primitive beds, electric heat, a barbecue, and deck. A restroom with showers, coin laundry, and a small store are available. Leashed pets are allowed, but not in the cabins.

Bedding: No linens are provided; you must bring a sleeping bag and pillow.

Reservations and rates: Reservations are recommended (call 800/562-3403). The fees are $43 for a one-room cabin, $49 for a two-room cabin.

Directions: From Eureka, take U.S. 101 north to Crescent City. Continue on U.S. 101 five miles north of town. One mile past the junction with U.S. 199, look for the well-signed KOA entrance on the right (east) side of the road.

Contact: Crescent City Redwoods KOA, 4241 U.S. 101 North, Crescent City, CA 95531; 707/464-5744, website: www.koa.com. For steelhead fishing information, contact Smith River Outfitters, 707/487-0935.

Crescent City Redwoods KOA Cabins

4. BEAR BASIN LOOKOUT & PIERSON CABIN

© USDA FOREST SERVICE

Luxury rating: 1

Recreation rating: 4

Six Rivers National Forest, off U.S. 199 near Gasquet

The Bear Basin Lookout & Pierson Cabin are rented as a pair, set in the northwestern corner of California in remote Del Norte County, deep in Six Rivers National Forest near the little-traveled Siskiyou Wilderness and the spectacular Smith River National Recreation Area. The view from the lookout is fantastic. A sea of conifers seems to stretch into infinity in all directions. The view is best into Gasquet Flat and the headwaters of the Smith River Canyon.

Unlike other Forest Service lookouts available for rent, this one comes with a very rustic cabin. The bonus of a cabin means you won't have the light intrusion problem that wakes sleepers so early in the summer months at the other lookouts. Don't take that for granted. At other lookouts, you sleep encased in what feels like a giant glass rectangle, so there is no hiding from the sun once dawn arrives. At this spot, you've got some buffer.

Be certain to bring everything you need. This is very primitive; after all, you're sitting on a remote mountaintop. No running water is available or much of anything else, and it's a long drive to any supplies. Make sure you're equipped with all the basics: sleeping bag, water, and food. A bonus is that you can bring your dog.

Though the Forest Service hopes to have this lookout and cabin available for rent year-round, note that in winter, this is often one of the rainiest places in the Lower 48. Camp 6, a local designated weather station a short distance away from the Bear Basin Lookout, documented a record 257 inches of rain in 1983; thanks to El Niño, this was the most rainfall in one season ever recorded in the continental United States.

Nearby recreation is outstanding in Bear Basin and the surrounding region, including Doe Flat, Bucks Lake, Devils Punchbowl, Clear Creek, and Wilderness Falls.

Facilities: The Big Basin Lookout & Pierson Cabin are rented as a pair. Pierson Cabin has an outside bathroom. No water is provided, and no showers are available. Leashed pets are allowed.

Bedding: Beds are available, but you must bring your own sleeping bag.

Reservations and rates: Reservations are required. Rates are $75 for the pair.

Directions: From Crescent City, drive north on U.S. 101 for five miles to U.S. 199. Turn east on U.S. 199, drive 17 miles to Gasquet, and look for the Forest Service ranger station on the left (north) side of the road. Folks there will provide you with specific directions to the lookout. From the ranger station, it takes about an hour of driving on dirt Forest Service roads to reach the lookout station; it can take a bit longer for those unfamiliar with Forest Service roads.

Contact: Bear Basin Lookout & Pierson Cabin, Smith River National Recreation Area, Six Rivers National Forest, 1330 Bayshore Way, Eureka, CA 95501; 707/457-3131. The hours of operation for the district office are 8 A.M. to 4:30 P.M., seven days a week, from early June through September. From October through May, the office is closed on weekends.

Bear Basin Lookout & Pierson Cabin

5. PATRICK CREEK LODGE

This place captures the best of California's north woods and water. It is pretty, clean, and more of a little-known getaway spot than anything else.

Luxury rating: 3

Recreation rating: 4

Smith River Recreation Area, off U.S. 199 near Gasquet

After checking in, you drive to the back of the lodge on a curving, rising gravel road, ending at a cottage set well above the lodge in the forest . . . quiet and private. The cottage has two bedrooms, plus a kitchen and a large main room. It is ideal for a large family, buddies on a fishing weekend, or a group of friends using the cabin as headquarters for a Smith River–based vacation.

In addition to this cabin, the lodge offers 15 rooms in various styles in two buildings. There are no telephones or televisions in the rooms, which for many is the ideal for a wooded hideaway.

For a place you can reach by pavement, it is way out there, located near the California-Oregon border on U.S. 199. It is set near the point where Patrick Creek enters the Smith River, one of the last major undammed streams in America. It takes nearly two hours of driving from Eureka to get here, so if you add another 300 miles from San Francisco, you can figure on almost a day of saddle time before you can pull up to the hitching post. The prime adventures here are exploring the Middle Fork Smith River, which is accessed on U.S. 199. There are many pullouts along the river with short trails down to beautiful spots. This is one of the most beautiful river gorges in California that you can reach by car.

Facilities: Patrick Creek Lodge has a two-bedroom cabin and a lodge with four rooms, three two-bedroom suites, two continental rooms, and another building with five motel-style rooms. No telephones are available in the rooms or cabins; telephones are provided in the lodge lobby, and a public pay phone is just outside the entrance. There is a television with satellite hookup in the lodge lobby, as well as in the cabin. An on-site restaurant serves meals daily from 7 A.M. to 10 P.M., and a popular champagne brunch on Sunday from 10 A.M. to 2 P.M. No pets are permitted.

Bedding: Bedding and towels are provided.

Reservations and rates: Reservations are recommended. The fee ranges from $120 to $200 per night for the cabin in the summer, depending on number of people; lodge rooms run $80 to $110. Prices are slightly reduced in the winter.

Directions: From Crescent City, drive north on U.S. 101 for five miles; then turn east on U.S. 199 and drive about 25 miles. Patrick Creek Lodge is located on the north side of the road.

Contact: Patrick Creek Lodge, 13950 U.S. 199, Gasquet, CA 95543; 707/457-3323.

Patrick Creek Lodge

6. CAMP MARIGOLD GARDEN COTTAGES

Camp Marigold is set on three-and-a-half landscaped garden acres bordering redwood forests. The area offers boundless activities and world-famous scenery. It is surrounded by Redwood National Park, towering redwoods, Pacific Ocean beaches, driftwood, agates, fossilized rocks, blackberries, Fern Canyon, Lagoon Creek Park, and the Trees of Mystery. Plus, it's just two miles from the Klamath River.

Luxury rating: 2

Recreation rating: 4

Klamath River, off U.S. 101 near Crescent City

Both rustic cottages and lodge rooms are available. The cottages are rustic but not primitive. The lodge rooms are designed for sleeping and not much else; they're set up to accommodate up to 15 people, and separate restrooms for men and women provide adequate facilities. Collectively, it seems best designed for groups or family meetings. Note that this park also operates an RV camp. This gives the place the feel of being primarily designed as a base of operations for outdoor adventure, rather than a luxurious, romantic getaway.

There are trails on the property, as well as blackberry vines—picking is great in the fall. The nearby Klamath River offers opportunities for fishing for salmon in the fall and eel in the spring. Given your proximity to the Redwood Empire and the Pacific Ocean, you can wander and explore for days. A treat especially for families, the Trees of Mystery lies just a mile south of the cottages. This popular vacationer's rest stop is best known for two things: trees that have been grown in many odd configurations and the dinosaur-sized Paul Bunyan and Babe (the blue ox) statues next to the parking lot. Trees of Mystery has a popular gift shop and a park-like setting.

Remember to bring warm clothing for early- and late-hour outdoor recreation; summers can be foggy here, so pack extra layers during this time as well.

Facilities: Camp Marigold has four cabins and a six-bedroom lodge. One cabin has a full kitchen; the other three have fully equipped kitchenettes. All cabins have modern bathrooms and sleep two to six people. Their group lodge has a fully equipped kitchen and sleeps up to 15 people. Small leashed pets are permitted.

Bedding: Linens are provided.

Reservations and rates: Reservations are recommended. Cabins rent for $48 to $78 per night; the lodge rents for $180 per night for the first 10 people, $5 for each additional person (maximum 15). Major credit cards are accepted. Open year-round.

Directions: From Eureka, drive 60 miles north on U.S. 101 to the campground, which is four miles north of the Klamath River Bridge, on the right side of the road.

Contact: Camp Marigold Garden Cottages, 16101 U.S. 101, Klamath, CA 95548; 707/482-3585 or 800/621-8513.

Camp Marigold Garden Cottages

7. BISHOP PINE LODGE

The Humboldt coast near Trinidad is highlighted by Patrick's Point State Park and its outstanding views, short hikes, and beaches; forests with Sitka spruce, Bishop pine, and redwoods; ocean fishing; whale-watching; and the ease of just leaning against a rock and watching all that water out there.

Bishop Pine Lodge is located near the best of the outdoors, set just a few minutes' drive from both Patrick's Point State Park and the town of Trinidad. The lodge consists of small cottages that are neat and well-kept. Each cottage has a small kitchen, bathroom, and living area/bedroom. Although a television is provided, you can always drape a towel over it, or if it's in a cabinet, you can close the doors.

One element some visitors find off-putting is the cottages' luminous paint job, including front doors that are fire-engine red and bright green. It's also important to note that although the lodge is located *near* the ocean, it is set in the woods. Some newcomers are disappointed to discover no ocean views or a feeling of being close to the ocean.

Luxury rating: 4

Recreation rating: 4

Humboldt Coast, off U.S. 101 in Trinidad

The nearby must-do spots feature the Seascape Restaurant at Trinidad Head, a great beach just north of the parking lot here, and of course, Patrick's Point State Park. The Rim Trail at Patrick's Point follows a two-mile route on the edge of the bluff around three sides of the park; several short cutoff trails take visitors to coastal lookout spots. Among the featured lookout spots are Mussel Rocks, Agate Beach, Rocky Point, Patrick's Point, Abalone Point, and Palmer's Point. We recommend hiking the Rim Trail and exploring all of these side trails, as each provides a different glimpse of this special place.

Facilities: Bishop Pine Lodge has 13 cottages, each a different size with unique interior designs. Most have kitchens and all have bathrooms and telephones. Well-behaved pets are permitted with an additional charge.

Bedding: Bedding, linens, and towels are provided, and a daily maid service is available.

Reservations and rates: Reservations are recommended and are often required in peak months: June, July, and August. Fees range from $80 to $100 per night per couple.

Directions: From Eureka, drive north on U.S. 101 for 20 miles to Trinidad and take the Trinidad exit. At the stop sign, turn left and drive west under the freeway a short distance to Patrick's Point Drive. Turn right on Patrick's Point Drive and drive 1.9 miles to Bishop Pine Lodge on the right side of the road.

Contact: Bishop Pine Lodge, 1481 Patrick's Point Drive, Trinidad, CA 95570; 707/677-3314, fax 707/677-3444; website: www.bishoppinelodge.com.

Bishop Pine Lodge

8. EMERALD FOREST

This campground is set on 12 acres of redwoods with the ocean at Trinidad Head only about a five-minute drive away. It's a nice spot, with friendly folks and an abundance of recreation available nearby.

Luxury rating: 2

Recreation rating: 4

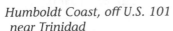

Humboldt Coast, off U.S. 101 near Trinidad

The accommodations are fairly rustic. After all, this is a campground first and foremost, with the cabins provided as a bonus. There is a large recreation hall with a kitchen—great for large families or groups.

The proximity of woods and water provides the reward here. The camp is set amid redwoods on Patrick's Point Drive, only a five-minute drive from Patrick's Point State Park. This drop-dead gorgeous park is famous for the Rim Trail, an easy hike that peeks in and out of the forest onto panoramas of the ocean (see Patrick's Point State Park listing in this chapter).

On the best days, Trinidad is one of the prettiest places on earth. The harbor is gorgeous, with a protected, rock-strewn bay providing a launch point for fishing trips and crabbing. Just to the north of Trinidad Head is a pretty and expansive beach, ideal for walks, and best at low tide when it seems to stretch on forever. The hike to the top of Trinidad Head is also outstanding, with long-distance ocean views; you'll find the trailhead next to Seascape Restaurant, known for its fantastic crab omelets and sandwiches.

Facilities: Emerald Forest has 12 cabins with kitchens. A playground, mini-mart, and coin laundry are available. A recreational hall with fireplace, kitchen, and a seating capacity of 40 is on-site. Leashed pets are permitted, except in the tent sites. An RV campground is on the property.

Bedding: Bedding, linens, and towels are provided, as well as a daily service with a change of towels and trash removal.

Reservations and rates: Reservations are recommended in the summer. Cabins cost $85 to $169 per night, depending on the size of your party; off-season discounts are available. There is a $1 pet fee. Major credit cards are accepted. Open year-round.

Directions: From Eureka, drive north on U.S. 101 for 28 miles to Trinidad. Take the Trinidad exit, turn left at the stop sign, and drive a short distance under the freeway to Patrick's Point Drive. Turn right on Patrick's Point Drive and drive about a mile north to the campground on the right side of the road.

Contact: Emerald Forest, 753 Patrick's Point Drive, Trinidad, CA 95570; 707/677-3554, fax 707/677-0963; website: www.cabinsintheredwoods.com.

Emerald Forest

9. SYLVAN HARBOR RV PARK AND CABINS

Luxury rating: 3

Recreation rating: 4

Humboldt Coast, off U.S. 101 near Trinidad

Sylvan Harbor is most often used as a base camp for anglers. It is designed as an RV park and fish camp, with cleaning tables and canning facilities available both on-site and a short distance from the boat hoist at Trinidad Pier. Since this privately operated park is primarily set up for RVs, the cabins are more of an option than its centerpiece. All three cabins are located in the campground. In the summer, when visitor numbers are highest, RVs may be parked in the area near the cabins. In fall and spring, when RV numbers are low, these spots are usually empty. Each cabin comes with a fully equipped kitchen—everything you need to set up house while you're on vacation. But note the cabins do not have microwaves or electric coffee makers.

Sylvan Harbor is on Patrick's Point Drive, a road lined with towering redwoods, only about a mile outside the small port town of Trinidad. Beauty surrounds Sylvan Harbor on all sides for miles around. Visitors come to enjoy the various beaches, to go agate or driftwood hunting, or to hike the various trails at nearby Patrick's Point State Park.

Facilities: The cabins have kitchens, telephones, cable TV, decks, and gas barbecue grills. Coin laundry, LP gas, multiple fish cleaning tables, three fish smokers, and canning facilities are available. No smoking is allowed. Pets are not permitted.

Bedding: Linens and towels are provided.

Reservations and rates: Reservations are recommended in summer months. Rates are $57 per night or $288 per week for a one-room cabin for two, $3 per additional guest.

Directions: From Eureka, drive north on U.S. 101 for 28 miles to Trinidad. Take the Trinidad exit, turn left at the stop sign, and drive a short distance under the freeway to Patrick's Point Drive. Turn right and drive one mile to the campground.

Contact: Sylvan Harbor RV Park and Cabins, 875 Patrick's Point Drive, Trinidad, CA 95570; 707/677-9988; website: www.sylvanharbor.com.

Sylvan Harbor RV Park and Cabins

10. PATRICK'S POINT STATE PARK

This pretty park is filled with Sitka spruce, dramatic coastal lookouts, and several beautiful beaches, including one with agates, one with tidepools, and another with an expansive stretch of beachfront leading to a lagoon. You can best see all of it from the Rim Trail, which has many smaller side trails to the lookouts and down to the beaches.

Luxury rating: 1

Recreation rating: 4

Trinidad Head, off U.S. 101 near Trinidad

What makes it all work is the cabin and the yurt, unusual features not found in most state parks. The cabin is rustic and primitive. The yurt—though an anomaly in California—has gained popularity in the Pacific Northwest for providing shelter from the winter rain and the summer coastal drizzle. It isn't a luxury, but hey, it'll keep you dry—and in these parts, dry can count for plenty!

The cabin and yurt are located near the Agate Beach campground, set in the northeast section of the park, within walking distance of the trailhead to see the Octopus Trees. Both sleep four. The cabin has heating and a bathroom with a flush toilet. Showers are available nearby. The yurt has a space heater; for bathroom and shower facilities, you use the campground's restroom. The campground is sheltered in the forest, and while it is often foggy and damp in the summer, it is always beautiful.

At the north end of the park, a short hike to see the bizarre Octopus Trees is a good side trip. The trees acquired this name because they grow atop downed logs, leaving their root systems exposed like octopus tentacles. In addition, several miles of pristine beach to the north extend to the lagoons. Interpretive programs are available. Plan on making reservations. The park also boasts a Native American village, constructed by the Yurok tribe, which can be viewed as a historical interpretive exhibit.

Facilities: Patrick's Point State Park has one cabin and one yurt, along with a developed campground for tent camping and RVs. Drinking water, flush toilets, and coin-operated showers are available nearby. Some facilities are wheelchair accessible.

Bedding: Linens and towels are not provided. Visitors should bring their own sheets or sleeping bags.

Reservations and rates: Reservations are recommended; call 800/444-PARK (800/444-7275) or visit the website: www.ReserveAmerica.com. The yurt is $20 per night, the cabin $29 per night, and the campsites $12 per night. Open year-round.

Directions: From Eureka, drive north on U.S. 101 for 22 miles to Trinidad. At Trinidad, continue north on U.S. 101 for 5.5 miles to Patrick's Point Drive. Take that exit, and at the stop sign, turn left and drive .5 mile to the park entrance.

Contact: Patrick's Point State Park; 707/677-3570 or 707/488-5555.

Patrick's Point State Park

11. VIEW CREST LODGE

Most cabins, lodgings, and campgrounds on the Humboldt coast have no ocean view, even though they are located close to the water. View Crest, on the other hand, didn't get its name by accident. Although there is a road to look across, the seven cottages here provide a mix of glimpses and views of the ocean and the coast, each one different from the next. The best? Cottage Number 5, perhaps. Though everybody has their own opinion.

The first thing you notice upon arrival, though, is not the view but the extraordinary landscaping at the entrance. It's so inviting that people let themselves right in. The cabins are clean, comfortable, and fully equipped, including the kitchen. The owners recently added a hot tub to one of the cottages, making it ideal for honeymooners and romantic getaways. Note that some of the cabins are positioned apart from the rest, and some are duplex style.

Luxury rating: 4

Recreation rating: 4

Humboldt Coast, off U.S. 101 in Trinidad

Besides the ocean views and the cute cottages, there is another feature that keeps people coming back time after time: the birds. Hundreds of swallows often perform uncanny flying displays, doing dipsy-doos in a swirling maze just before sunset. Many have nests at the cottages. This aerial display can be your send-off for a great vacation at Trinidad, which may include trips to Patrick's Point State Park one mile north, and farther north to Big Lagoon, Prairie Creek Redwoods State Park, and Redwood National Park.

Finally, while it can be easy to arrange a stay at View Crest during the week, it can be extremely difficult during good-weather weekends. For weekends, book your trip as far in advance as possible.

Facilities: View Crest Lodge has seven cottages made up of separate units and duplexes. Each has a bathroom and a kitchen with cookware and utensils. Most have cable TV and telephones. No smoking is permitted in the cottages. Restaurants, a grocery store, a boat hoist, and fishing trips are available four miles south in Trinidad. An adjacent campground and RV park are available on the property. No pets are permitted.

Bedding: Linens are provided.

Reservations and rates: Reservations are recommended. Cabin rates range from $80 to $160 per night, depending on the size of the cabin, with no minimum stay.

Directions: From Eureka, drive north on U.S. 101 for 20 miles to Trinidad and take the Trinidad exit. At the stop sign, turn left and drive west under the freeway a short distance to Patrick's Point Drive. Turn right on Patrick's Point Drive and drive four miles to View Crest Lodge on the right side of the road.

Contact: View Crest Lodge, 3415 Patrick's Point Drive, Trinidad, CA 95570; 707/677-3393; website: www.viewcrestlodge.com.

View Crest Lodge

12. EUREKA/ARCATA KOA KAMPING KABINS

KOA campgrounds have experienced a rejuvenation across America by offering a more protected camping experience than your usual tent—log cabins in miniature. And the KOA on the Humboldt coast hasn't missed the chance to upgrade. It features six small cabins located along U.S. 101; though near urban facilities, the KOA lies within reasonable driving range of many adventure destinations.

Luxury rating: 2

Recreation rating: 3

Humboldt Coast, off U.S. 101 near Arcata

KOA Eureka is actually located north of Eureka, closer to Arcata, just east of the highway. Its yellow-orange sign is easily visible to passing drivers. You turn in and discover that they have created a park-like feel, with a line of trees along the rear border of the park. The Kamping Kabins (hey, that's the way they're spelled) are small and cute, complete with a little porch and a swinging bench. Each features electricity, heat, and beds. But no linens or blankets are available, so don't forget your sleeping bag or sheets and blankets.

These cabins are prefabricated off-site, and when space is available at a campground, they are then shipped and assembled. That is why they are exactly the same at each KOA throughout the country. So you always know what to expect.

Good hiking is available nearby at Patrick's Point State Park (707/677-3570) and at Redwood National and State Parks (707/464-6101).

Facilities: KOA Eureka has 10 small log cabins and two cottages. The cabins feature a porch with a swing, electric heat, and beds. The cottages have kitchens, bathrooms, and fireplaces. A swimming pool, hot tubs, laundry room, shower facilities, game room, and a small grocery store are available. There are also 25 tent sites and 140 RV sites. Pets are permitted in some log cabins.

Bedding: Linens and towels are not provided; bring a sleeping bag and pillow.

Reservations and rates: Reservations are recommended. Cabin fees are $40 per night; cottages are $120 per night.

Directions: From Eureka, drive four miles north on U.S. 101 and turn right on KOA Drive. If you are coming from Arcata, drive two miles south on U.S. 101 and turn left on KOA Drive.

Contact: KOA Eureka, 4050 North U.S. 101, Eureka, CA 95503; 707/822-4243; website: www.koa.com.

KOA Eureka

13. CARTER HOUSE INNS

Forget rustic. Forget primitive. Forget mosquito repellent. Just remember your wallet because you're going to need it. And, oh, is it worth the price for a special, memorable stay when you want to be pampered. If you're looking for a quiet getaway near exceptional outdoor activities, but you don't want to forgo first-class accommodations and the finest food and wine, then you've hit the jackpot here.

© JOHN SWAIN

Luxury rating: 5

Recreation rating: 4

Eureka, off U.S. 101

Located in Eureka's historic district, alongside Humboldt Bay, Carter House Inns consists of four Victorian structures, including Bell Cottage and Carter Cottage. The cottages have four-poster beds, antique furnishings, double-headed showers, in-room entertainment centers, and honor bars. All inn rooms and cottages include complimentary full breakfast, and afternoon and evening refreshments. The inns' Restaurant 301 holds a Wine Spectator Grand Award and features a wide selection of vintage wine. The garden supplies the restaurant with fresh produce. Carter Inns is considered the finest accommodation in Humboldt County, and the restaurant's food is superb.

Now let's talk about the cottages; that's why they're in this book. Carter Cottage is a completely self-contained unit, luxurious and private, and ideal for a honeymoon or romantic vacation. It is spacious and decorated with bright, sunny colors and a modern flair. Amenities include a deep marble spa tub, two marble fireplaces, private deck with bay view, and a state-of-the-art kitchen. Now get this: One of the inns' chefs, at your request, will prepare and serve you a five- or nine-course dinner, with or without wine selections, right in your cottage. There's an extra fee, of course, but don't you feel pampered?

The other units at Carter House Inns are cottage-like, most accurately described as inn rooms with kitchen facilities. However, Bell Cottage can be rented in its entirety by a group as a single unit. Bell Cottage is a refurbished 1800s structure with three separate suites, each with its own bathroom, marble fireplace, television, VCR, and stereo/CD player. A fully equipped kitchen and other common areas are available within the building.

Carter House rents traditional inn rooms, that is, without kitchen facilities. It's located across the street from the hotel and has five suites, all with private baths. One suite has a whirlpool tub. There are no telephones or televisions.

Facilities: Carter House Inns has one cottage, five cottage rooms, 23 inn rooms, and a restaurant. Accommodations include spacious rooms and full bathrooms; some rooms have in-room entertainment centers, marble fireplaces, and honor bars. Carter Cottage has a fully equipped kitchen. Although children can be accommodated, the inns are more suitable for adults. Pets can lodge in a special pet area, but they are not allowed in the rooms or cottages. No smoking is allowed.

Bedding: Comfy beds, pillows, linens, and towels are provided.

Reservations and rates: Reservations are recommended during the summer. Rates range from $138 to $497 per night, which includes a full gourmet breakfast, wine and hors d'oeuvres in the late afternoon, and evening tea and cookies. For more than two persons, $25 per person per night is charged. Major credit cards are accepted.

Directions: From U.S. 101 southbound in Eureka, turn right (west) on L Street and drive two blocks to the inn's lobby on the right side.

Contact: Carter House Inns, 301 L Street (at 3rd St. in Old Town), Eureka, CA 95501; 707/444-8062 or 800/404-1390, fax 707/444-8067; website: www.carterhouse.com.

Carter House Inns

14. RIVERWALK RV PARK

Luxury rating: 2

Recreation rating: 3

Humboldt Coast,
off U.S. 101 in Fortuna

Location, location, location is what you have here. The park is in fairly close proximity to a number of exceptionally scenic spots and recreational opportunities. And as with horseshoes, close does count here. You're 20 miles from the ocean and Humboldt Bay, and a few miles north of stands of old-growth redwoods in Grizzly Creek Redwood State Park and Humboldt Redwoods State Park. Other side trip options include touring the giant sawmill in Scotia and accessing the nearby Eel River and one of its tributaries, the Van Duzen River. There's a great fishing spot for salmon in October, where the Van Duzen enters the Eel. Please note that the Van Duzen's waters can fluctuate greatly, making it dangerous to enter on occasions when the waters are high; at other times, during low water levels, it may be closed to fishing.

As for the accommodations, Riverwalk offers four one-room cabins and one two-room cabin. The one-room cabins can sleep four, and the two-room cabin sleeps six. They're clean and simple, providing the basic elements you need. The beds are log-frame with foam mattresses. Each has a porch with swing, barbecue, and picnic table. This is also an RV campground.

Facilities: Riverwalk RV Park has four one-room cabins and one two-room cabin. A restroom with showers, group kitchen facilities, a coin laundry, a recreation room, a small store, and modem hookup in the office are available. A pool and spa are open during the summer season. The park is suitable for children. Leashed pets are allowed. No smoking is permitted in the cabins.

Bedding: Linens are not provided, so bring towels and sleeping bags or bedding.

Reservations and rates: Reservations are recommended during the summer. Rates are $30 to $38 per night and $180 to $228 per week for a one-room cabin, $37 to $43 per night and $222 to $258 per week for a two-room cabin. For more than two persons, $2 to $3 per person per night is charged. Children under age four are free. A $75 security deposit is required for pets. Major credit cards are accepted.

Directions: From Eureka, drive 16 miles south on U.S. 101 to the Kenmar/Riverwalk Drive exit. Turn right (west) and drive to the end of the off-ramp. Turn right (west) and drive 0.25 mile to the park entrance on the right.

Contact: Riverwalk RV Park, 2189 Riverwalk Drive, Fortuna, CA 95540; 707/725-3359 or 800/705-5359, fax 707/725-7809; website: www.riverwalkrvpark.com.

Riverwalk RV Park

15. MATTOLE RIVER ORGANIC FARM'S COUNTRY CABINS

There is no place on earth like the Lost Coast, and on the Lost Coast, there is no place like Mattole River Country Cabins. The Lost Coast is located in remote southern Humboldt County, completely isolated and shielded by natural boundaries: the Pacific Ocean to the west, Humboldt redwoods to the east, Bear River Ridge to the north, and the King Mountain Range to the south. The road here is long and twisty, combining dirt, asphalt, and gravel. It's a destination you have to earn.

The coast here is an unusual blend of remote farm country and ranchlands in a river valley that extends to isolated beaches, rocky coastal outcrops, and tidelands where few ever venture. In the center of the Mattole River Valley is the Mattole River Resort,

featuring inexpensive rental cabins, perfectly situated for adventuring on the Lost Coast. The cabins come with small kitchens, so once you've set up camp, you can turn this trip into a do-it-yourself special.

But get this: Even though there are seven cabins, they are numbered 2, 3, 4, 5, 6, 7, and 9; there are no cabins 1 or 8. It's just the way things are out here. The best cabin by far is Number 9. It has a woodburning stove, skylights, decks in the back and front, and is totally secluded and separate from the other units. It is private, quiet, and pretty.

Luxury rating: 3

Recreation rating: 4

Lost Coast, off Mattole Road near Petrolia

In addition to the scenic area drives to the coast, there is excellent hiking and biking in the summer. One good trip for hiking or biking is a drive out to the end of Lighthouse Road, where you'll find a trailhead for the Lost Coast Trail just beyond the Bureau of Land Management's Mattole Campground. From here, take the abandoned jeep trail for three miles out to the Punta Gorda Light Tower—a day trip with superb coastal views.

Facilities: Mattole River Organic Farm's Country Cabins offers seven cabins, each with a bathroom and kitchen. Cookware and utensils are provided. Small grocery stores are located nearby in the towns of Petrolia and Honeydew. Pets are permitted with no extra fee.

Bedding: Bed linens and towels are provided.

Reservations and rates: Reservations are recommended. Cabin rates range from $45 to $100, depending on the number of beds and amount of privacy.

Directions: From San Francisco, take U.S. 101 north past Garberville and Redway to the South Fork Road/Honeydew exit. Take South Fork Road and drive west (it becomes gravel/dirt at different points) for about an hour to Honeydew. In Honeydew, drive over the Mattole River Bridge, turn right on Mattole Road, and drive three miles. Look for the Mattole River Organic Farm's Country Cabins (white cabins, blue trim) on the left side of the road.

Contact: Mattole River Organic Farm's Country Cabins, 42354 Mattole Road, Petrolia, CA 95558; 707/629-3445 or 800/845-4607.

Mattole River Organic Farm's Country Cabins

16. RICHARDSON GROVE RV PARK & FAMILY CAMP

This private camp provides a nearby alternative to Richardson Grove State Park. Here you can enjoy cabin rentals near the state park, known for its grove of giant redwoods and excellent hiking.

Luxury rating: 2

Recreation rating: 4

Redwood Empire, off U.S. 101 near Garberville

Richardson Grove RV Park & Family Camp is family-oriented, with volleyball and basketball courts and horseshoe pits. It is also set up for group outings and religious retreats. In fact, the place is owned and operated by the Northern California/Nevada District Assemblies of God. "We are dedicated to assisting you in impacting lives for Jesus Christ in this beautiful wooded mountain setting," says manager David Rice.

The facilities are fairly rustic, but inexpensive, with four tent cabins that each sleep six and two log cabins that each sleep four. There is also a church dorm that can accommodate up to 30. Though the cabins are small and primitive, they're clean. The park provides a great base camp for a retreat in the dramatic Redwood Empire; note that a large campground for tents and RVs is the major part of the operation.

The adjacent South Fork Eel River may look like a trickle in the summer, but there are some good swimming holes available. It also provides good steelhead fishing in January and February. There is especially good shore fishing access here, as well as to the south in Cooks Valley (check Department of Fish and Game regulations before fishing).

Facilities: Richardson Grove Campground has tent cabins that will sleep up to 30 people and log cabins available that will sleep up to 8 people. Restrooms, showers, an RV dump station, a playground, a coin laundry, a grocery store, LP gas, and ice are available. A kitchen facility with refrigeration and food storage capabilities for large or small groups is also available.

Bedding: No linens or towels are provided. Visitors should bring sleeping bags, pillows, and towels.

Reservations and rates: Reservations are recommended. Cabins rent for $27 per night. Group rates are available. Major credit cards are accepted. Open year-round.

Directions: From the junction of U.S. 101 and Highway 1 in Leggett, drive north on U.S. 101 one mile past Richardson Grove State Park to the camp entrance on the left (west) side of the road.

Contact: Richardson Grove Campground, 75000 U.S. 101, Garberville, CA 95542; 707/247-3380, fax 707/247-9806; website: www.redwoodfamilycamp.com.

Richardson Grove RV Park & Family Camp

17. REDWOODS RIVER RESORT

Woods and water. For many, that's all you need for a vacation setting, and that's what you get here at Redwoods River Resort. The woods are the big redwoods; this area is the southern gateway to the Redwood Empire, which features excellent hiking. The water is the South Fork Eel River, which provides a few hidden swimming holes in summer and fishing for steelhead in winter. In fact, the resort has 3,000 feet of river frontage. A hiking trail leads from the resort to the Eel River, a walk of about 300 yards.

Luxury rating: 3

Recreation rating: 4

Eel River, off U.S. 101 near Leggett

To make it work, many pick Redwoods River Resort. It offers several choices for accommodations, but most pick the well-furnished cabins. The key questions with every cabin include: Is there a bed with fresh sheets? Is there a bathroom with a shower? Is there a kitchen? The answers here are yes, yes, and yes for most of the cabins, and that makes it a winner.

More primitive cabins are also available—what they call camping cabins. The camping cabins provide you the opportunity to save a few bucks by staying in a non-furnished unit and using the resort's campground facilities.

Redwoods River Resort is situated in a 21-acre grove of redwoods on U.S. 101, at an elevation of 700 feet. Richardson Grove Redwoods near Garberville is a must-do side trip. The Lookout Point Loop Trail here provides a tour through giant redwoods culminating at a canyon rim over the South Fork Eel River. Giant redwoods approaching 300 feet tall and an estimated 1,000 years old are the highlights of Richardson Grove, while younger redwoods, fir, and tan oak trees fill out the forest.

Facilities: Redwoods River Resort has six standard cabins, one deluxe cabin, and two camping cabins. There are also eight lodge rooms with kitchenettes. Standard cabins provide bathrooms with showers, fully equipped kitchens, and woodburning stoves, and sleep up to six. The deluxe cabin has the same amenities plus full bathroom. Camping cabins have two sets of bunk beds, and a table, and can sleep up to four. A bathhouse is available. All cabins have barbecues and fire pits and full use of resort facilities. That includes heated swimming pool (summer only), playground, recreation room, mini-mart, coin laundry, group kitchen, evening campfire (summer), and organized summer activities. Firewood is available. Leashed pets are allowed only in two cabins and two lodge rooms during the off-season.

Bedding: Linens and towels are provided in the standard cabins. In the camping cabins, you must bring your own sleeping bag, pillow, and towels.

Reservations and rates: Reservations are recommended. Double occupancy rates for standard and deluxe cabin rentals are $68 to $76 per night, camping cabins are $28 to $30 per night, and lodge rooms are $63 per night in summer. Additional persons for the standard or deluxe cabins are $5.50 per night, and $3.50 per night for the camping cabins in the summer only. Pets, when allowed, are $10 per pet per night. Major credit cards are accepted. Open year-round.

Directions: From the junction of U.S. 101 and Highway 1 in Leggett, drive north on U.S. 101 for seven miles to the campground entrance.

Contact: Redwoods River Resort, 75000 U.S. 101, Leggett, CA 95585; 707/925-6249, fax 707/925-6413; website: www.redwoodriverresort.com.

Redwoods River Resort

CHAPTER 2

Shasta & Trinity

*A*t 14,162 feet, Mt. Shasta rises like a diamond in a field of coal. Its sphere of influence spans a radius of 125 miles, and its shadow is felt everywhere in the region. This area has much to offer with giant Shasta Lake, the Sacramento River above and below the lake, the McCloud River, and the wonderful Trinity Divide country with its dozens of pretty backcountry lakes and several wilderness areas. This is one of the best regions anywhere for an outdoor adventure—especially hiking, fishing, power boating, rafting, and exploring.

In this area, you can rent cabins that are truly set near remote, quiet wilderness, and that offer the potential for unlimited adventures. Of all the regions in this book, this is the easiest one in which to find a cabin in a secluded setting near great recreation opportunities. That is the main reason people visit.

The most upscale lodging is offered by the Mount Shasta Resort, where to play golf you have to wear a shirt with a collar. That rule is something of an anomaly for an area known for great outdoors recreation, one where even the nicest restaurants will allow you to dine in your hiking boots.

There are hundreds of destinations, but the best are Shasta Lake, the Trinity Alps and its surrounding lakes and streams, and the Klamath Mountains, known as "Bigfoot Country" by the locals.

Shasta Lake is one of America's top recreation lakes. It is the one destination that is big enough to handle all who love it. The massive reservoir boasts 370 miles of shoreline, 1,200 campsites, 21 boat launches, 11 marinas, 35 resorts, and numerous houseboat and cabin rentals. A remarkable 22 species of fish live in the lake. Many of the cabin rentals here feature decks with lake views. In addition, getting here is easy—a straight shot off Interstate 5.

At the charmed center of this beautiful region are the Trinity Alps, where lakes are sprinkled everywhere. It's also home to the headwaters for feeder streams to the Trinity River, Klamath River, New River, Wooley Creek, and others. Trinity Lake provides outstanding boating and fishing, and just downstream, smaller Lewiston Lake offers a quiet alternative. One advantage to Lewiston Lake is that it is always full of water, even all summer long, making for a very pretty scene. Downstream of Lewiston, the Trinity River provides low-cost rafting and outstanding shoreline access along Highway 299 for fishing for salmon and steelhead.

The neighboring Klamath Mountains are well known as Bigfoot Country. If you drive up the Forest Service road at Bluff Creek, just off Highway 96 upstream of Weitchpec, you can even find the spot where the famous Bigfoot movie was shot in the 1960s. Well, we haven't seen Bigfoot, but we have discovered tons of outdoor recreation. This remote region features miles of the Klamath and Salmon Rivers, as well as the Marble Mountain Wilderness. Options include canoeing, rafting, and fishing for steelhead on the Klamath River, or hiking into your choice of more than 100 wilderness lakes.

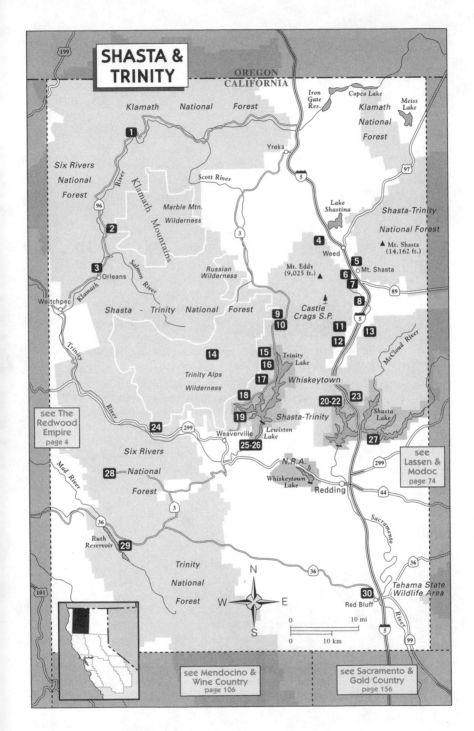

SHASTA &
TRINITY

OREGON
CALIFORNIA

Klamath   National   Forest

1

Six Rivers
National
Forest

River

Klamath

Marble Mtn.
Wilderness

2

Scott River

Yreka

5

Iron
Gate
Res.

Copco Lake

Klamath
National
Forest

Meiss
Lake

Lake
Shastina

Shasta-Trinity

National Forest

▲ Mt. Shasta
(14,162 ft.)

97

3

Orleans

Salmon River

Russian
Wilderness

3

Mt. Eddy
(9,025 ft.) ▲

4

Weed

○ Mt. Shasta

5

6

89

Weitchpec

Klamath

Shasta - Trinity   National   Forest

Castle
Crags S.P.

7

8

5

Trinity

9

10

11

12

13

McCloud River

14

Trinity Alps

Wilderness

15

16

17

18

Trinity
Lake

Whiskeytown

River

19

Shasta-Trinity

20-22   23

Shasta
Lake

27

24

299

Weaverville

Lewiston
Lake

25-26

see The
Redwood
Empire
page 4

Six Rivers

28   National

Forest

3

N.R.A.

Whiskeytown
Lake

Redding

299

44

see
Lassen &
Modoc
page 74

Mud River

36

Ruth
Reservoir

29

Trinity

National

Forest

Sacramento

36

101

N

W ✦ E

S

36

Tehama State
Wildlife Area

30

Red Bluff

River

5

99

0   10 mi

0   10 km

see Mendocino &
Wine Country
page 106

see Sacramento &
Gold Country
page 156

CHAPTER 2
SHASTA & TRINITY

1. BEAR COVE CABINS

Year in and year out, the Klamath River is the best family rafting river in California. It provides a good selection of exciting and safe runs on warm water all summer long. Right in the middle of the best of it is the little-known Bear Cove Cabins, set in the town of Happy Camp in remote northwestern Siskiyou County. Highway 96 fronts the property, with the river just on the other side of the road. The cabins are set along a horseshoe-shaped dirt access road. Though the cabins are relatively close to each other, once you're inside, you can't hear your neighbors.

Luxury rating: 3

Recreation rating: 5

Klamath River, off Highway 96 in Happy Camp

The location is ideal for rafting in inflatable kayaks on the friendly waters of the Klamath River. River Country Rafting (530/493-2207) is located directly across from the property. That is a key part of the experience, since no one comes here to hang out in the cabins. The cabins are designed simply for sleeping in and cooking in and that's about it.

Guides advise that a great first rafting trip for families is to start below a Class III rapid named Otter's Play Pen, then enjoy easy water all the way home to Happy Camp, with some great beaches and swimming holes along the way. It's an easy 15 miles, rated Class I+. For more serious water, there is plenty above and below this section. This area also offers lots of birdlife and river bends.

The fishing for steelhead here is often excellent as well. In mid-August, the first run of what are called half-pounders arrive. These are actually juvenile steelhead ranging from 10 to 16 inches. They are followed by salmon in September and steelhead in the 16- to 22-inch class in October.

Facilities: Bear Cove Cabins has eight cabins. Each has a small kitchen with refrigerator and stove, a double bed, and a television. A telephone is available in the Bear Cove office. Well-behaved pets are permitted.

Bedding: Linens and blankets are provided.

Reservations and rates: Reservations are recommended. The fee is $40 per night, and no minimum stay is required.

Directions: From Redding, drive north on I-5 past the town of Yreka to Highway 96. Take Highway 96 and drive west for 65 miles, passing the town of Seiad Valley, to the town of Happy Camp. Drive to 64715 Highway 96, located on the north side of the road.

From Eureka, drive north on U.S. 101 just past Arcata to the junction with Highway 299. Turn east on Highway 299 and drive to Willow Creek. At Willow

Creek, turn north on Highway 96 and drive 88 miles, passing the town of Clear Creek, to the town of Happy Camp. Drive to 64715 Highway 96, located on the north side of the road.

Contact: Bear Cove Cabins, P.O. Box 534, Happy Camp, CA 96039; 530/493-2677. For rafting trips, contact River Country Rafting, 530/493-2207. For a fishing guide, contact Wally Johnson in Seiad Valley, 530/496-3291.

Bear Cove Cabins

2. MARBLE MOUNTAIN RANCH

This is as much a hideout as a hideaway. Marble Mountain Ranch is set deep in Klamath National Forest along Highway 96, the curving two-laner that runs along the Klamath River. So right off, this spot is extremely remote. Hey, some people think the town of Yreka along I-5 is remote, right? Well, from Yreka, it's another two hours of driving to get to Marble Mountain Ranch. Because of that remoteness, this ranch offers complete, self-contained vacation packages. You not only have the opportunity for cabin lodging, but three meals a day and a major activity each day. The most popular activities are rafting on the Klamath, horseback riding, wilderness pack trips, salmon and steelhead drift-boat fishing, and mountain biking. Put it all together and you may just want to make this your permanent hideout.

Luxury rating: 3

Recreation rating: 5

Klamath River, on Highway 96 near Somes Bar

At Marble Mountain Ranch, all guests share homestyle meals with other guests and staff in the dining facility. Meals are bountiful and include home-baked breads and desserts, salads, vegetables fresh from the garden, and select meats smoked and roasted over native hardwoods. Adventure seeking attracts most people to the ranch for the first time, but it is the meals that often bring them back.

For the price, the cabins are well-equipped. But if you can book the deluxe lodge homes, that's the way to go if you want a more woodsy comfort. The grounds of the ranch feature vegetable gardens and many fruit trees. Swimming is available down the trail at the river or at any of several "secret" swimming holes nearby. This is a great place to bring youngsters; the ranch features a play gym, swings, and a small petting zoo with miniature horses (which they may also ride), miniature goats, and bunnies.

Most summer visitors will arrange at least one day of rafting on the Klamath River. The company Access to Adventure (800/442-6284) offers trips that are "Mild to Wild." That means you can match the trip with the level of white-water excitement you can handle. This section of the Klamath is one of its prettiest, a mix of oak woodlands and conifers. With that mix comes a wide variety of wildlife, outstanding for bird watching.

Facilities: Marble Mountain Ranch has 11 cabins and two deluxe lodge homes. Cabins and lodges vary in size and can accommodate 2 to 10 people. Each cabin provides full bathrooms and fully stocked kitchens. Many have decks and four have woodstoves. A game room and weight room are available. Therapeutic massage is available for a fee. No smoking is allowed. Pets are discouraged.

Bedding: Linens are provided.

Reservations and rates: Reservations are accepted. Rates are $60 per night for a cabin for two and $100 for a home for four with two bedrooms. Rates for lodging, three meals, and a major activity are $160 per day per adult and $100 per day per child. Major credit cards are accepted. Open year-round, weather permitting.

Directions: From Redding, drive north on I-5 to Yreka and Highway 263. Turn north on Highway 263 and drive to Highway 96. Turn west on Highway 96 and drive 63 miles to Happy Camp, then continue another 30 miles to the ranch on the left.

From Eureka, drive north on U.S. 101 just past Arcata to Highway 299. Take Highway 299 east and drive for 50 miles to Willow Creek and Highway 96. Turn north on Highway 96 and drive 47 miles to Somes Bar and continue 7.5 miles to the ranch on the right.

Contact: Marble Mountain Ranch, Somes Bar, 92520 Highway 96, Somes Bar, CA 95568; 530/469-3322 or 800/552-6284, fax 530/469-3357; website: www.marblemountainranch.com. For rafting trips, contact Access to Adventure, 800/552-6284, or River Country Rafting, 530/493-2207.

Marble Mountain Ranch

3. SANDY BAR RANCH CABINS

Sandy Bar Ranch features a collection of little redwood cabins that are set in a valley on national forest land, about a mile from the town of Orleans. They are inexpensive for what you get, with each cabin providing a separate bedroom, a hideaway bed in the living room, and a full kitchen. With a grocery store located about a mile away, cooking can help keep the price of your trip down. A café is located nearby as well. A unique quality of Sandy Bar Ranch is an extensive organic gardening program on the grounds. There is also a fruit tree nursery and homemade crafts. A series of special nursery programs are offered at various times during the year.

Luxury rating: 3

Recreation rating: 5

*Klamath River, off Highway 96
near Orleans*

Sandy Bar Ranch is nestled in a beautiful valley carved out by the Klamath River. It serves as a gateway to the trails and rivers of the Klamath-Siskiyou mountains. This is one place where nature has used a broad brush in its artwork, with beauty touching everything. The Klamath River tumbles around boulders, into gorges, and then flattens into slicks, all framed by a high canyon and bordered by forest. There is an abundance of birdlife, wildlife, and—from late summer through fall—fish, as steelhead and salmon migrate through the area.

In the summer, from April through August, water conditions are perfect for rafting, and in July, the temperatures warm up considerably for swimming. For expert rafters, the nearby Cal Salmon, a tributary to the Klamath River, is one of the best little-known white-water rafting rivers in California. The best put-in spot is near the town Forks of the Salmon. From here, the first five miles are Class II+—and then it really sizzles, with Class IV and V rapids. Last Chance Rapid is a Class V that features a mind-bender of a drop that will have your heart leaving your body for what seems like an eternity.

Facilities: Sandy Bar Ranch has four redwood cabins that sleep four, each with full kitchen and bathroom. Controlled pets are permitted. A grocery store and café are located within a mile.

Bedding: Linens are provided.

Reservations and rates: Reservations are accepted. Cabin rates are $68 per night or $408 per week for two persons. Each additional person is $10 per night. There are discounts for children.

Directions: From Eureka, drive north on U.S. 101 just past Arcata to the junction with Highway 299. Turn east on Highway 299 and drive to Willow Creek. At Willow Creek, turn north on Highway 96 and drive 43 miles, passing the town of Weitchpec, to the town of Orleans. In Orleans, turn left at Ishi Pishi Road and drive .75 mile. Look for Sandy Bar Ranch Cabins on the right side of the road.

Contact: Sandy Bar Ranch, P.O. Box 347, Orleans, CA 95556; 530/627-3379. For rafting, contact Klamath River Outfitters, 530/469-3349.

Sandy Bar Ranch Cabins

4. STEWART MINERAL SPRINGS

In an area where Shasta's fabled Lemurians (tiny, mysterious beings that live in underground caves lined with gold) are said to reign, you probably figured there was a place like Stewart Mineral Springs near Mt. Shasta—a therapeutic retreat with mineral baths, saunas, massage service, and Native American–style purification sweats. Well, if you did, you figured right. But before you laugh it off as some New Age curiosity, consider first that the treatment here actually works. You will leave feeling like a whole new person.

Luxury rating: 3

Recreation rating: 4

Shasta-Trinity National Forest, off I-5 near Weed

Stewart Mineral Springs is located on the northern slope of Mt. Eddy, across the Shasta Valley from giant Mt. Shasta. It's set in the woods on property bordering the Shasta-Trinity National Forest. There are five cabins available, along with dorm rooms, small apartments, and tepees. The cabins are rustic but comfortable and include bedding. The tepees have two cots, but no bedding. Note that the tepees have dirt floors; some guests bring a rug as a flooring cover and air beds. Kitchenettes are provided in the cabins and apartments. There is a small, rustic restaurant on the premises that is open only by advance arrangement for groups staying at the resort.

Stewart Mineral Springs is an old resort—over 100 years old. The cold, streaming Parks Creek flows through the property a short distance from the mineral baths. The magic happens in the combination of hot mineral baths, saunas, or sweats followed by a jump into the cold creek. One of the perpetual challenges here is to go from one to the other. Providing you survive, that is.

Facilities: Stewart Mineral Springs has five cabins, six apartments, three tepees, dorm rooms, an A-frame house, and spaces for tent camping and RVs. Kitchenette facilities are provided in the cabins and apartments. A restaurant, open to groups and seminars only, is located on the premises. Therapeutic mineral baths, massages, saunas, and purification sweats are available. Reservations are not required for mineral baths, but you must have an appointment for a massage or Reiki treatment. Nudity is not promoted but is tolerated if discreet. No smoking is allowed. Pets are not permitted.

Bedding: Linens are provided in the cabins. Linens are not provided in the tepees; be sure to bring a sleeping pad, sleeping bag, and pillow.

Reservations and rates: Reservations are recommended. The fee is $54 per night per cabin and $44 to $74 for an apartment room. Tepees are available at $24 per night double occupancy, with a $5 charge for each additional person to a maximum of five. An A-frame cabin that can sleep 10 is available for $325 per night. The fee for a mineral bath is $17 for guests at Stewart Mineral Springs, $20 for day-use visitors.

Directions: From Redding, drive north on I-5 just past the town of Weed. Take the Edgewood exit, turn left at the stop sign, and drive a short distance (under the freeway) to Old Highway 99. Turn right on Old Highway 99 and drive a short distance to Stewart Springs Road. Turn left and drive four miles to Stewart Springs.

Contact: Stewart Mineral Springs, 4617 Stewart Springs Road, Weed, CA 96094; 530/938-2222, fax 530/938-4283; website: www.starhawk.com.

Stewart Mineral Springs

5. MOUNT SHASTA KOA

The view from the picnic table in front of K1, that is, Kabin 1, as they call it, is a superb panorama of 14,162-foot Mt. Shasta, the prettiest mountain in California. The park-like grounds of Mount Shasta KOA are spacious and set at 3,500 feet in elevation, in the foothills of the old volcano, just on the outskirts of town. The four log-style camping cabins are nestled under trees on the edge of the property. The trees

© STEPHANI STIENSTRA

make it surprisingly intimate, despite this being a big KOA with lots of RV campers located just a few blocks from downtown Mount Shasta. Each cabin has a bunk bed and a queen bed; visitors should bring a sleeping bag and a pillow. Each cabin has electric heat and an electrical outlet. Outside, a barbecue, picnic table, and swing are available. A telephone, restrooms, and showers are available within short walking distance.

Luxury rating: 2

Recreation rating: 4

Mount Shasta, off I-5

A must-do is the drive up the Everitt Memorial Highway to Bunny Flat on Mt. Shasta, where at elevation 6,900 feet, you can scan for miles, highlighted by views of Mt. Lassen, Castle Crags, and the Sacramento River canyon in one direction, and in the other, the main climber's route to the Shasta peak up Avalanche Gulch, past the Thumb and Red Banks.

Facilities: Mount Shasta KOA has four camping cabins (two one-room and two two-room cabins), each with a double bed and bunk bed with mattress. There is electricity. A restroom with showers, a small store, a game room, a swimming pool, a laundry facility, and a dump station are available. There are also 41 RV sites with full hookups and 89 additional spaces for tents and RVs. Leashed pets are permitted.

Bedding: No linens or pillows are provided; bring your sleeping bag.

Reservations and rates: Reservations are accepted. The rates are $40 per night for a one-room cabin, $50 per night for a two-room cabin, $15 per night for tent sites, and $27 per night for RV sites with water, electricity, and sewer hookups.

Directions: From Redding, drive north on I-5 for 58 miles to the town of Mount Shasta. Continue past the first Mount Shasta exit and take the Central Mount Shasta exit. Turn right at the stop sign and drive to the stoplight at Mount Shasta Boulevard. Turn left and drive .5 mile to East Hinckley Boulevard. Turn right on East Hinckley, drive a very short distance, then turn left at the extended driveway entrance to Mount Shasta KOA.

Contact: Mount Shasta KOA, 900 North Mount Shasta Boulevard, Mount Shasta, CA 96067; 530/926-4029; website: www.koa.com.

Mount Shasta KOA

6. MOUNT SHASTA RESORT

This is the kind of place where you expect the finest. That is, the finest in lodging, dining, surrounding natural beauty, and recreation. At Mount Shasta Resort, your expectations are met.

From the moment you drive in, you are put on notice that this is the most deluxe golf club and resort setting open to the public in the region. The first rule is that men have to wear shirts that have collars. Let us tell you, there are guys in Siskiyou County who don't own a shirt with a collar. So right off, you've got a sense that it's something of an exclusive place, and so it is.

Luxury rating: 4

Recreation rating: 5

Mount Shasta, off I-5

The resort is located at the foot of Mt. Shasta. The views from the fairway and from the restaurant are simply stunning, making it one of the prettiest golf courses in Northern California. The course is a professionally-designed 18-hole course situated on 126 acres of forest and rolling terrain, a challenge to amateurs and professionals alike. The trees are very sturdy, ideal for wrapping your golf clubs around after you miss yet another shot. Heh. No, that kind of behavior is not tolerated.

The chalets are fairly new, quite beautiful, and well-furnished. They come in one- and two-bedroom units and include private bathrooms, full kitchens (with cherry-wood cabinetry), living rooms with gas fireplace, television, telephones, and sleeper sofas. And did we mention the tiled entry provides ski racks, coat racks, and storage for golf clubs? Some of the units have their own decks with private hot tubs. The chalets are set amid ponderosa pines across the road from the resort headquarters, within range (but without views) of the north shore of nearby Lake Siskiyou.

Facilities: Mount Shasta Resort has 30 one-bedroom chalets, 20 two-bedroom chalets, and 15 motel-style Woodland rooms. All chalets have furnished bedrooms, bathrooms, and kitchens. Some have decks with private hot tubs. A restaurant, bar, golf course, golf lessons, pro shop, and tennis courts are available on the property. No smoking is allowed. Pets are not permitted.

Bedding: Linens and towels are provided.

Reservations and rates: Reservations for lodging and tee times are recommended (call 800/958-3363). Rates for one-bedroom chalets for two people are $144 to $159, two-bedroom chalets are $190 to $239, and Woodland rooms for two people are $99. A deposit is required. Off-season discount rates are available. Golf, ski, and midweek packages are available. Major credit cards are accepted. Open year-round.

Directions: From the town of Mount Shasta on I-5, take the Central Mount Shasta exit and drive to the stop sign. Turn west and drive a short distance to Old Stage Road. Turn left and drive .25 mile to a Y at W.A. Barr Road. Bear right on W.A. Barr Road and drive to the stop sign. Continue straight for one mile to the signed entrance for Mount Shasta Resort on the left.

Contact: Mount Shasta Resort, 1000 Siskiyou Lake Boulevard, Mount Shasta, CA 96067; 530/926-3030 or 800/958-3367; golf course information, 530/926-3052; website: www.mtshastaresort.com.

Mount Shasta Resort

7. LAKE SISKIYOU RESORT

Native American legend has it that Mt. Shasta was created when the Great Spirit poked a hole in the sky and made a tepee out of the fallen pieces. Sitting at the base of giant Mt. Shasta is Lake Siskiyou—a true jewel. This artificially constructed lake is in one of the prettiest settings in the United States. It was created for the sole purpose of recreation—not to store water for farmers—so while reservoirs in the California foothills get drained, Siskiyou remains full.

Lake Siskiyou Resort provides a huge campground complex that is tucked into the forest so visitors don't get their style cramped. RV rentals, lodging units, and cabins are also available. They are clean and set up to provide an advanced form of camping. That is, you bring your sleeping bag and towels. Many anglers use this as a base camp for a vacation, camping in relative luxury, then fishing at Lake Siskiyou.

Virtually in the shadow of Mt. Shasta, Lake Siskiyou is almost always full and offers a variety of recreation options. From the resort, the lake is within walking distance and provides a swimming beach protected by a buoy line and cool, clean water. An excellent boat ramp is available and a 10-mph speed limit is strictly enforced and keeps the place quiet. In the summer months, the lake gets a lot of traffic from swimmers, sunbathers, and anglers.

Luxury rating: 2

Recreation rating: 5

Mount Shasta, off I-5

Facilities: Lake Siskiyou Resort has 11 RV rentals and 24 lodging units available, including cabins. A campground with both RV sites and tent sites is on the property nearby. Drinking water, flush toilets, showers, playground, propane, grocery store, coin laundry, and RV dump station are available. There are also marinas, boat rentals (canoes, kayaks, motorized boats), free boat launching, fishing dock, fish-cleaning station, beach, and a banquet room. A free movie plays every night in the summer. Some facilities are wheelchair accessible. Smoking is permitted in the RVs only. The pet policy is under review; call first.

Bedding: Linens and towels are not provided. Bring your own sleeping bag, pillow, and towel.

Reservations and rates: Reservations are recommended. RVs rent for $50 to $85 per night. Lodging cabins are $85 to $105 per night. It costs $4 for each additional vehicle per night. Major credit cards are accepted. Open April through October, weather permitting.

Directions: From the town of Mount Shasta on I-5, take the Central Mount Shasta exit and drive to the stop sign. Turn west and drive a short distance to Old Stage Road. Turn left and drive .25 mile to a Y at W.A. Barr Road. Bear right on W.A. Barr Road and drive past Box Canyon Dam. Two miles farther, turn right at the entrance road for Lake Siskiyou Campground and Marina and drive a short distance to the entrance station.

Contact: Lake Siskiyou Campground and Marina, P.O. Box 276, Mount Shasta, CA 96067; 530/926-2618 or 888/926-2618; website: www.lakesis.com.

Lake Siskiyou Resort

8. CAVE SPRINGS/ DUNSMUIR CABINS

Dunsmuir Cabins are located in the town of Dunsmuir, about an hour's drive north of Redding, and are set in different locations near the Upper Sacramento River. They include a variety of units, ranging from California box construction cabins to guest homes along the river. Some are small and rustic, others are upscale and gorgeous with decks overlooking the water. All have full kitchens and larger units have televisions. The best way to get started on this trip is to call the owner, Louie Dewey, at 530/235-2721, and discuss what best fits your expectations.

Luxury rating: 3

Recreation rating: 4

Upper Sacramento River, off I-5 in Dunsmuir

The main attraction here is the Upper Sacramento River. In July 1991, the river was the site of the worst inland toxic spill in the history of California. A Southern Pacific freight train derailed at Cantara Loop, just north of Dunsmuir, and sent a tanker full of poison into the river. As the poison oozed downstream, everything in its path was killed across 38 miles of river from Cantara Loop to the headwaters of Shasta Lake.

In the time since that catastrophe, what is known as the "Genesis Effect" has taken place. The aquatic food web of the river was reestablished, from algae to caddis larvae, and this provided the foundation for the recovery of the trout fishery. It is once again considered one of the best trout streams in America, and is easily accessible from the adjacent interstate highway. The trout population has now stabilized, providing not only a stellar fishery, but an example of how nature reversed a human-caused cataclysm—and in that sense, it is considered a living laboratory.

The recovery effort has put Dunsmuir Cabins back in business as the best place to stay along the Sacramento River for visitors who want to fish, explore, hike, or even kayak this now famous trout stream.

Hikes are available nearby at Castle Crags State Park, and of course, at Mt. Shasta to the north and in the nearby Eddy Range to the west. There are several excellent driving tours as well. The best three include: one, from south of Dunsmuir, take the Castle Crags

State Park exit and drive past the state park and continue up the mountain for awesome views of the Crags; two, from within the town of Mount Shasta, take the Central Mount Shasta exit and continue up the Everitt Memorial Highway all the way to Panther Flat at 7,400 feet elevation; and three, from Dunsmuir, drive to Lake Siskiyou and turn left for the drive up to Castle Lake, set at 5,450 feet, for incredible views of Mt. Shasta to the east.

Facilities: Dunsmuir Cabins come in a wide variety of lodging styles, from box construction cabins to guest homes along the river. Cabins include full kitchens. Pets are permitted.

Bedding: Linens and towels are provided.

Reservations and rates: Reservations are recommended. Rates range from $35 to $170 per night.

Directions: From Redding, drive 52 miles north on I-5 to Dunsmuir. Take the Central Dunsmuir exit, which feeds onto Dunsmuir Avenue. Continue to 4727 Dunsmuir Avenue.

Contact: Dunsmuir Cabins, 4727 Dunsmuir Avenue, Dunsmuir, CA 96025; 530/235-2721 or 888/235-2721; website: www.cavesprings.com. For fishing guide/tour service, contact Jack Trout Flyfishing International & Mt. Shasta Scenic Tours, 530/926-4540; website: www.MtShasta.com. For fishing supplies and information, contact Ted Fay Fly Shop, 530/235-2969; or Dunsmuir Flyfishing Company, 530/235-0705.

Cave Springs/Dunsmuir Cabins

9. RIPPLE CREEK CABINS

Sure, there are a ton of cabin rentals in the vicinity of Trinity Lake. But each one is unique, and so it is at Ripple Creek Cabins.

This resort is located in the Trinity River Valley, about a 20-minute drive north of Trinity Lake. The cabins are nestled along a creek in a forest setting. On the inside, the cabins are well-furnished with a knotty-pine interior, often with a potbellied woodstove—a nice touch. Each cabin is different in its design, but all provide the goodies a family needs: bedrooms, bathrooms, kitchens, and living rooms. Considering the relative remoteness of the place, most visitors find the accommodations far better than expected. For many, this is what a cabin-based vacation should be, both inside and out.

This area is very popular for hiking, with many outstanding trips in the vicinity. Our personal favorite is the all-day hike to Mt.

© JOHN BAGLEY

Luxury rating: 3

Recreation rating: 4

Shasta-Trinity National Forest,
off Highway 3 near Trinity Lake

Eddy (elevation 9,025 feet). It offers one of the most outstanding views anywhere in Northern California. On the climb up, you pass Deadfall Lakes, the rise up the back side of Mt. Eddy. Only in your last steps to the top does Mt. Shasta suddenly come into view to the east, a moment you will never forget. A detailed story about our hike to the Eddy summit is available for guests at Ripple Creek.

But there are many other options, including a series of wilderness trailheads along Highway 3, as well as along Coffee Creek Road nearby to the south. See the guidebook *Foghorn Outdoors: California Hiking* for other trails in the area. A map of Shasta Trinity National Forest is also a must.

Facilities: Ripple Creek has six cabins and one large group cabin. Each cabin is unique. Bathrooms with showers, fully-stocked kitchens, woodstove, and electric heat are provided. Each cabin has a private yard, picnic table, and barbecue. Laundry facilities, recreation room, play area with volleyball, badminton, and horseshoes are available nearby. A country store is four miles away. No smoking is allowed. Pets are permitted, but pet owners are requested to bring pet beds.

Bedding: Linens and towels are provided.

Reservations and rates: Reservations are recommended. The double-occupancy rate is $94 per night and $590 per week. For four persons, the rate is $145 per night. Off-season discounts are available. There is a charge of $10 per pet per stay. Major credit cards are accepted.

Directions: From Redding, turn west on Highway 299 and drive 40 miles to Weaverville and Highway 3. Turn north on Highway 3 and drive 40 miles (just past Coffee Creek Road) to Eagle Creek Loop. Turn left and drive 1.5 miles to the Ripple Creek Cabins entrance on the right.

Contact: Ripple Creek Cabins, Route 2, Box 4020, Trinity Center, CA 96091; 530/266-3505. For a map, ask for Shasta-Trinity National Forest and send $6 to U.S. Forest Service, Attn: Map Sales, P.O. Box 587, Camino, CA 95709; 530/647-5390, fax 530/647-5389; or visit the website: www.r5.fs.fed.us/visitorcenter. Major credit cards are accepted.

Ripple Creek Cabins

10. ENRIGHT GULCH CABINS

Enright Gulch Cabins is a settlement of deluxe housekeeping cabins and motel units located a short distance to the north of giant Trinity Lake (think fishing, swimming, boating, and waterskiing), as well as wilderness trailheads for day hikes to Boulder Creek, Lake Eleanor, and up Swift Creek. These are the main recreation draws. The historical significance of the area provides a special perspective to a vacation.

Luxury rating: 3

Recreation rating: 4

Trinity Lake, off Highway 3 near Trinity Center

Enright Gulch received its name when it was patented as a Placer gold mine in 1877. During the construction of Trinity Dam in the late 1950s, houses from the small community of Stringtown (which was later buried under the waters of Trinity Lake) were moved onto the property among the cedar, fir, and pines next to the small creek that flows through the area.

That is how this resort was created. The place has a history like no other cabin rental resort in California.

These cabins now offer not only a bit of history, but also an oasis of comfort, peace, and privacy in a natural setting. The one potential drawback is that because of the sloping curves of the access road, medium to large boats cannot be trailered in. Boat owners looking for a headquarters for a Trinity Lake adventure should make sure they can trailer their boats in and out of the resort without a problem, or find other lodging closer to the lake.

There are two unique attractions nearby: Carrville Dredger Pond (for fishing) and Alpen Cellars (for wine-tasting). Carrville Dredger Pond is less than a half-mile from Enright Gulch. It's fed by year-round springs, it's stocked regularly with rainbow trout, and it's open to fishing all year. Alpen Cellars, a top winery, is a short drive from the resort. Visitors are always welcome for wine-tasting.

Facilities: Enright Gulch Cabins has four cabins that sleep two to eight persons. There are also motel-style rooms. A fully-stocked kitchen, heat, and deck with barbecue are provided. No smoking is allowed. Pets are permitted but must be attended at all times.

Bedding: Linens and towels are provided.

Reservations and rates: Reservations are recommended (call 888/383-5583). The double-occupancy rate is $80 per day or $490 per week for a one-bedroom cabin, and $90 per day or $570 per week for a two-bedroom cabin; it's $5 per day or $30 per week for each additional person. Pets are $10 per day or $30 per week. There is a $100 deposit. Major credit cards are accepted.

11. PINE-GRI-LA

Folks around here try to keep Pine-Gri-La a secret. For instance, we were asked not to print the specific directions to their cottage rentals. In fact, the owners do not give out the directions to the public, but provide them only to those who have reserved a stay. That's because the cottages are extremely hidden and charming, ideal both for a family adventure getaway or a romantic hideaway. The owners want to keep it that way. So no one will be driving by, peeking in the windows, or trying to get a preview of the place.

Luxury rating: 4

Recreation rating: 5

On Upper Sacramento River, off I-5 near Castella

The rentals are located roughly in the vicinity of Castle Crags State Park near Castella, 45 miles north of Redding. The cottages are set in the only privately occupied parcel in the Trinity Divide country of the Shasta-Trinity National Forest, roughly a 25-minute drive from I-5. So what you have here is a high-mountain wildland— yet with a gorgeous cottage to stay in as a launch point for your vacation. That's right, all the comforts of home in the wilderness.

The three cottages are named Skylight, Country Chalet, and Deluxe, and all have full kitchens and decks with gorgeous views. These cottages are custom-built mountain cabins. They are not motel units, park model units, RV cabins, or residential houses. They are built for privacy and sleeping comfort. Your only "neighbors" are deer and bears strolling about the tall firs, the pines, and the wildflowers— and the trout doing laps in the nearby lakes. The Trinity Divide is loaded with trout. Gray Rocks, Castle Crags, and Mt. Shasta loom over the landscape. There are also three sleeping cabins that can be rented to accommodate large groups.

One more note: The owners told us they often sleep in the cottages to judge and assure the quality of each. The real reason, we later figured, is so they too can feel like they're on a stellar vacation.

Facilities: Pine-Gri-La has three customized cottages that can sleep between 2 and 10 persons, and a small lodge. The cottages have full kitchens, heat, and decks. The deluxe unit has a fireplace. There are also three sleeping cabins available to accommodate additional persons in your party. Dinners are available for purchase. No smoking is allowed. Pets are not permitted. Families are welcome.

Bedding: Linens and pillows are provided.

Reservations and rates: Reservations are recommended. The base rate is $125 to $150 per night for cabins sleeping 2 to 10, with a $10 fee for each person over 6 years old. Sleeping cabins, which accommodate between 5 and 11 people, are $75 per person. Major credit cards are accepted. Open year-round.

Directions: From Redding, drive north on I-5 for 45 miles to Castella and the Castle Crags State Park exit. Take that exit and drive a short distance to the stop sign. Turn left and drive under the highway underpass and continue .25 mile to the gas station/store on the left. Turn left and park, a pay phone is available. Phone 530/235-4466 for specific directions to your cottage.

Contact: Pine-Gri-La, P.O. Box 100, Castella, CA 96017; 530/235-4466; website: www.shastacabins.net. For a map, ask for Shasta-Trinity National Forest and send $6 to U.S. Forest Service, Attn: Map Sales, P.O. Box 587, Camino, CA 95709; 530/647-5390; fax 530/647-5389; or visit the website: www.r5.fs.fed.us/visitorcenter. Major credit cards are accepted.

Pine-Gri-La

12. BEST IN THE WEST RESORT

Luxury rating: 3

Recreation rating: 4

Upper Sacramento River, off I-5 near Castella

This park is set in the Upper Sacramento River Canyon, within close range of excellent fly fishing for rainbow trout. The lay of the park is split by a small road, with the cabins on one side and an RV park on the other. The RV park is landscaped with shaded sites and lawns. The proximity to Castle Crags State Park, the Sacramento River, and Mt. Shasta makes the location a winner.

The Best in the West Resort is a small resort situated among pines, cedars, and firs. The cabins are arranged around a courtyard alongside little Mears Creek. A short walk will bring you to the forests, birds, animals, and wildflowers. Azaleas scent the air in spring and blackberries abound in late summer. As with all the camps, cabins, and cottages in the Sacramento River Canyon, passing trains are common and can alarm those with heightened sensibilities. Others say they don't even hear the trains, and in fact, some say the sound of the trains is comforting.

The Upper Sacramento River is again becoming one of the best trout streams in the west, with easy and direct access off an interstate highway. The trout population has recovered since the devastating spill from a train derailment that occurred in 1991. The Sims area provides access to some of the better spots for trout fishing, particularly from mid-May through July. The technique that works best here is nymphing with a Copper John and Prince Nymph and short-lining with a strike indicator.

In the spring, from April through mid-June, this is also a great section for rafting, with several Class III runs in the vicinity. The town of Mount Shasta, 20 miles to the north, has golf courses and restaurants. If you want to literally get away from it all, there is a trailhead about three miles east on Sims Flat Road which climbs along South Fork, including a terrible, steep, one-mile section near the top, eventually popping out at Tombstone Mountain.

Facilities: Best in the West Resort has five cabins with one or two bedrooms with queen-size beds. The cabins sleep six to eight people and have a full bath, deck, woodburning stove, television, and fully-equipped kitchen. An RV campground is also on the property, but separated by a small road. Restrooms, hot showers, cable TV, coin laundry, and a playground are available. Pets and smoking are allowed. The cabins are not wheelchair accessible.

Bedding: Linens and towels are provided.

Reservations and rates: Reservations are accepted. Cabins cost $45 to $65 per night. Open year-round.

Directions: From Redding, drive north on I-5 for about 40 miles to the Sims Road exit. Take the Sims Road exit and drive one block west on Sims Road to the campground on the left.

Contact: Best in the West Resort, 26987 Sims Road, Castella, CA 96017; 530/235-2603; website: www.eggerbestwest.com.

OTHER CABINS AND COTTAGES NEARBY:

• Castle Crags River Resort, 29429 Castella Loop, P.O. Box 70, Castella, CA 96017-0070; 530/235-0081; website: www.castlecrags.com.

Best in the West Resort

13. GIRARD RIDGE LOOKOUT

The views are simply eye-popping from Girard Ridge, set at 4,809 feet above the Sacramento River canyon: You look straight across the canyon and down at the granite spires of Castle Crags, across to Gray Rocks, and north to Mt. Shasta. The lookout is perched on the west shoulder of the ridge, backed by fir trees, so it isn't completely exposed. It's located near Dunsmuir (north of Redding) directly to the east of I-5. The dirt Forest Service Road up here crosses the Pacific Crest Trail (a good hiking option) less than two miles from the lookout, and is a great, though aggressive, mountain bike route. Behind the lookout station you can explore a bit amid the trees. On the ridge, facing east, you can catch a glimpse of yet another view: a silhouette of Mt. Lassen.

© MT. SHASTA RANGER DISTRICT

Luxury rating: 1

Recreation rating: 4

Castle Crags, off I-5 near Dunsmuir

The views from the lookout are the primary reward here, along with great hiking and challenging but satisfying biking. The lookout itself is very primitive—no running water and no cooking facilities. That means you need to bring everything, just like on a camping trip. There is a vault toilet available nearby.

A suggestion is to get to bed early, or bring some kind of eye mask to block the bright sunlight of dawn. The lookout is walled by glass, and that means exposure to sunlight. It is very bright, and for those who are sensitive to light, it is impossible to sleep much past 5:45 or 6 A.M. in the summer months. In the winter, the place is buried deep in snow, and therefore is closed. It usually becomes accessible in late April or early May.

Facilities: Girard Ridge Lookout has an outside vault toilet. Beds are available, but you must bring your own sleeping bag. No water is provided and no kitchen facilities are available. Leashed pets are allowed.

Bedding: No linens are provided. Bring a sleeping bag and pillow.

Reservations and rates: Reservations are required. The fee is $35 per night.

Directions: From Redding, drive north on I-5 for 40 miles near Castle Crags to the Soda Springs exit. Take that exit and head east on Soda Springs Road. From this point on, follow the detailed directions provided when your reservation is confirmed and you are provided the combination to the locked gate.

Contact: Shasta-Trinity National Forest, McCloud District, 530/964-2184.

Girard Ridge Lookout

14. TRINITY MOUNTAIN MEADOW RESORT

If you want children to learn to love the wilderness and have a great outdoor experience, this is one of the best places imaginable to bring them. That is because Mountain Meadow Resort is like a wilderness retreat, set at the edge of the Trinity Alps Wilderness near the Coffee Creek Trailhead. All meals are provided, you sleep in a snug cabin, a solar-heated swimming pool with a gorgeous view is available, and special programs and meals are set up for kids. So for many families, this is the ideal getaway.

Luxury rating: 2

Recreation rating: 4

Coffee Creek, off Highway 3 near Trinity Alps

The cabins are on the rustic side but make a good fit for the location. Hey, any cabin that has a bed, linens, shower, and towels gets a gold star when considering the comfort factor, even if it is set on the edge of never-never land.

The resort is set for children to enjoy a variety of crafts and activities that are scheduled throughout the week. An early dinner for children is supervised by staff and followed by organized games. That means the adult dinner hour is quiet and private. That's right, parents get some down time from being parents. This doesn't mean there aren't plenty of family activities available. The whole family can participate in volleyball, badminton, horseshoes, and sing-alongs by the campfire.

A real plus is the swimming pool. There are sun chairs set with dramatic panoramas of the surrounding canyon and mountain country. Even though this is the mountains, it can get hot here, and jumping in that swimming pool—especially with the surrounding scenery—is often euphoric.

For ambitious hikers, the nearby Coffee Creek Trailhead provides a wilderness hike to the beautiful Caribou Lakes. This is an all-day trip, nine miles one-way to the first lake. However, it's best done in three days, backpacking style, with a rest day in the middle at a base camp to explore and swim in the three lakes.

Facilities: Trinity Mountain Meadow Resort has 10 cabins and a small lodge. The cabins have beds and bathrooms. A deck with a barbecue is available. There is no kitchen; three meals a day are provided, including a separate early dinner for children. A swimming pool, laundry facilities, recreation room, and small bar are available. Smoking is permitted. No pets are allowed. The resort is especially designed for families.

Bedding: Linens and towels are provided.

Reservations and rates: Reservations are recommended (call 530/462-4617). Rates for cabins for two people are $735 per week; lodge rooms for two people are $570 per week. An additional fee of $510 per person per week for more than two persons is charged. Child rates are available. Daily rates are sometimes available for $122 for two per day for cabins, $95 per day for two for lodge rooms. Rates include three meals per day. No credit cards are accepted. Open in summer, with opening and closing dates determined by the weather.

Directions: From Redding, turn west on Highway 299 and drive 40 miles to Weaverville and Highway 3. Turn north on Highway 3 and drive 38 miles (past Trinity Lake) to Coffee Creek Road. Turn left and drive 20 miles to Trinity Mountain Meadow Resort near the end of the road.

Contact: Trinity Mountain Meadow Resort, Star Route 2, Box 5700, Trinity Center, CA 96091; 530/462-4677.

Trinity Mountain Meadow Resort

15. BONANZA KING RESORT

Bonanza King Resort is located on eight acres in a mountain meadow setting of pines, fur, and cedar along Coffee Creek. Right there is one reason why some overlook it. The other reason is that once most visitors to the area reach Trinity Lake, they stay; few head onward just beyond the lake and turn left on Coffee Creek Road. Yet this is where Bonanza King Resort is hidden. So, you get a good deal of privacy if you go the extra mile.

The housekeeping cabins are fully equipped and well-maintained—and have heat. The cabins are spaced apart from each other, and each has its own front yard, backyard, and driveway. The grounds are covered with plenty of green grass, edged by flower beds, and border Coffee Creek and a national forest filled with a sea of conifers. You'll be within close proximity of Trinity Lake, as well as several outstanding

Luxury rating: 3

Recreation rating: 4

Coffee Creek, off Highway 3 near Trinity Lake

trailheads for day trips to wilderness lakes. The property also offers a playground for kids.

Nearby Coffee Creek is a mountain stream fed by snow from the Trinity Alps. This is stocked with trout by the Department of Fish and Game, and there are a few swimming holes as well. If you drive up Coffee Creek, there are sections where boulders are piled high along the river. These are mining tailings from the gold rush days, kind of like a living history lesson.

Many other adventures await nearby. Trinity Lake is only three miles to the south, the Coffee Creek Trailhead for access to the Trinity Alps Wilderness is 20 minutes at the end of Coffee Creek Road, and there are several other trailheads along both Coffee Creek Road nearby Highway 3; see the guidebook *Foghorn Outdoors: California Hiking* for details.

In the winter, the surrounding mountains provide good cross-country skiing and snowshoeing. It's a good thing that Bonanza King Resort is open year-round.

Facilities: Bonanza King Resort has seven cabins that sleep from three to seven people. All have bedrooms, bathrooms with showers, furnished kitchens, living rooms, and heat. A porch with barbecue and picnic table is provided. A washing machine and clothesline are available. A country store and café are nearby. Volleyball, badminton, a basketball hoop, horseshoes, croquet, and Ping-Pong are available. No smoking is allowed. Pets are not permitted.

Bedding: Linens and towels are provided.

Reservations and rates: Reservations are recommended. Double-occupancy rates range from $75 to $90 per day and $525 to $630 per week. There is a $10 per day per person charge for extra guests; children under three are free. Additional persons in tents or campers are not permitted. There is a two-night minimum. A deposit is required for reservations. Special arrangements are required for check-in after 6 P.M. Major credit cards are accepted. Open year-round, weather permitting.

Directions: From Redding, turn west on Highway 299 and drive 40 miles to Weaverville and Highway 3. Turn north on Highway 3 and drive 38 miles (past Trinity Lake) to Coffee Creek Road. Turn left and drive .5 mile to the resort on the left.

Contact: Bonanza King Resort, HC 2, Box 4790, Trinity Center, CA 96091; 530/266-3305.

Bonanza King Resort

16. WYNTOON RESORT

This huge resort is an ideal family vacation destination. Set in a wooded area covering 90 acres on the north shore of Trinity Lake, it provides opportunities for fishing, boating, swimming, and waterskiing, with lake access within walking distance. The lake sits at the base of the dramatic Trinity Alps, one of the most beautiful regions in Northern California.

Luxury rating: 3

Recreation rating: 5

Trinity Lake, off Highway 3 near Trinity Center

The cottages are clean and well furnished, with air-conditioning and heaters. For some, the area can seem hot and a bit dusty, so air conditioners get a lot of use in summer—along with nearby Trinity Lake.

Trinity Lake is California's third-largest reservoir, yet because of the long drive required for most to reach it, it receives far less use than the other big recreation lakes in California, such as Shasta, Oroville, Folsom, New Melones, Pine Flat, and Kaweah. The 145 miles of shoreline feature hundreds of secluded coves and beaches. During the summer, water surface temperatures rise to a comfortable 80°F and even higher, ideal for water sports.

The backdrop for all of this is the Trinity Alps Wilderness, a huge wildland covering more than 500,000 acres and best known for pristine lakes and high alpine ridges. There are excellent day hikes nearby that are routed into the edge of the wilderness and are featured in the guidebook *Foghorn Outdoors: California Hiking*.

Though most visitors come between the 4th of July and Labor Day weekends, the spring and fall are outstanding times. Wildflowers can be brilliant in the area from mid-April through May, and in the fall, the autumn foliage peppers the hills with color.

Facilities: Wyntoon Resort has 19 one- and two-bedroom housekeeping cottages that include fully equipped kitchens and air-conditioning. A swimming pool, horse corral, clubhouse with kitchen, and a recreation pavilion (with video games and bingo on Wednesday nights during the summer) are available. Shuffleboard, bicycle rentals, a children's playground, and a store are also available. An RV and tent campground is also located on the property. Some facilities are wheelchair accessible. Leashed pets are permitted.

Bedding: Linens and towels are provided.

Reservations and rates: Reservations are recommended (call 800/715-3337). The double-occupancy rate is $95 to $145 per night, with discounts for weekly stays. The fee per pet is $10 plus $8 per night. Major credit cards are accepted. Open year-round.

Directions: From Redding, turn west on Highway 299 and drive to Weaverville at Highway 3. Turn north on Highway 3 and drive to Trinity Lake. At Trinity Center, continue .5 mile north on Highway 3 to the resort.

Contact: Wyntoon Resort, P.O. Box 70, Trinity Center, CA 96091; 530/266-3337 or 800/715-3337, fax 530/266-3820; website: wyntoonresort.com.

Wyntoon Resort

17. PINEWOOD COVE

This is a privately operated camp with full boating facilities at Trinity Lake. Its location is a highlight, with its own boat dock and small marina. That means this is the kind of place you tow a boat to, set up camp in one of the cabins, then enjoy yourself for a week on the lake—boating, skiing, swimming, fishing, or exploring the many hidden coves and shoreline points. The elevation is 2,300 feet.

© MIKE NICHOLS

The park has a full spectrum of offerings for lodging, with park-model cabins, trailers, and an A-frame cabin, along with campsites for tents and RVs on the property.

Trinity Lake is huge at 17,000 acres. It's big enough to provide plenty of room for all types of water sports. Yet it is sufficiently remote that large numbers of boaters almost never descend on the place. The lake's warm surface temperatures make it a haven for families with youngsters desiring water recreation. It warms up by late June, and by mid-summer can be like a giant bathtub, great for tubing.

Luxury rating: 2

Recreation rating: 4

Trinity Lake, off Highway 3 near Trinity Center

One frustrating element is that after light winters, the lake can be subject to drawdowns, especially in August. Most of the water is sent via an underground pipe over to the Sacramento Valley, where it is exported to points south. That means less water for Trinity and a lot of bare, exposed shore in some years.

But it is a big lake, and once you're on the water, the levels matter little, as there is still plenty of lake to explore. The fishing is often good, including some of California's best fishing for smallmouth bass in late winter and spring, and good prospects for rainbow trout in late spring and summer. In winter, the place is virtually abandoned.

Facilities: Pinewood Cove has six park-model cabins, one A-frame cabin, and six trailer rentals. Kitchens are provided. An RV park, campground, and marina are on the property. Restrooms, showers, coin laundry, RV dump station, a recreation room, a grocery store, a boat dock with 32 slips, a beach, and boat rentals are available. Some facilities are wheelchair accessible. Leashed pets are permitted.

Bedding: Pillows are provided but linens and towels are not. Bring your own bedding or a sleeping bag.

Reservations and rates: Reservations are recommended in the summer. For park model cabins, the rate is $700 per week for four people (these can sleep six); for the A-frame, the rate is $75 per night or $525 per week for up to five people. Major credit cards are accepted. Open mid-April through October.

Directions: From Redding, turn west on Highway 299 and drive to Weaverville. In Weaverville, turn right (north) on Highway 3 and drive 14 miles to the campground entrance on the right.

Contact: Pinewood Cove Campground, 45110 State Highway 3, Trinity Center, CA 96091; 530/286-2201 or 800/988-5253.

Pinewood Cove

18. TRINITY ALPS RESORT

We've heard a few cases where romantic cottage getaways can require reservations a year or more in advance. That is almost never the case for cabin rentals set up for family summer vacations, that is, except for a few rare exceptions—and Trinity Alps Resort is one of those exceptions.

Luxury rating: 2

Recreation rating: 5

Near Trinity Lake, off Highway 3 at Stuart Fork

Reservations are often needed a year in advance to get a cabin here, and if you want a vacation during prime time—from 4th of July through Labor Day weekend—well, you usually have to sign up on a waiting list and hope for a cancellation. There's a reason for this. Everything is designed at Trinity Alps Resort as the ultimate, fun, camp vacation. In other words, you show up and turn off the outside world for a week.

The resort is big—43 cabins on 90 acres. It is located on Stuart Fork, a pretty stream that pours out of the Trinity Alps, just 1.5 miles from Trinity Lake. There is a lot of action all the time. Every night, there could be a game of bingo, a talent show, or square dancing.

If the cabins appear rustic when you first arrive, it's because they were built in the 1920s. The interiors have been remodeled, of course. While they provide the basic necessities for a week's stay—beds, kitchen, bathroom with shower, and some with a small living room—

many just bring their sleeping bags, pillows, and towels (or rent linens from the resort) and use the cabins as a base camp for exploring the area and hanging out at the lake. In fact, five of the cabins are set right above swimming holes on Stuart Fork. These cabins are named Kern, Lassen, Modoc, Tehama Lake, and Solano.

The nearby outdoor recreation is outstanding, of course. The Stuart Fork arm of Trinity Lake often provides excellent trout fishing, and the lake is outstanding for all water sports, especially waterskiing. In addition, if you drive another mile to Bridge Camp at the end of Trinity Alps Road, there is a trailhead that provides access to the Trinity Alps Wilderness, used mostly by overnight backpackers.

Facilities: Trinity Alps Resort has 43 cabins and apartment-style lodge rooms. Beds, kitchens with oven and refrigerator, and bathrooms with showers are provided. A restaurant, barbecue, and community center with nightly activities are available nearby. Smoking and pets are permitted.

Bedding: Linens and towels are not provided. Bring a sleeping bag or rent linens for $20 from the resort. Be sure to bring a towel.

Reservations and rates: Reservations are required. Rates range from $695 per week for four persons to $1,050 for up to 10 persons. Apartments for four cost $545. Credit cards are not accepted. Discounts are available during the off-season. Pets are free.

Directions: From Redding, turn west on Highway 299 and drive to Weaverville and Highway 3. Turn right (north) on Highway 3 and drive 15 miles to the Stuart Fork Bridge and Trinity Alps Road. Turn left and drive 1.5 miles to the resort.

Contact: Trinity Alps Resort, 1750 Trinity Alps Road, Trinity Center, CA 96091; 530/286-2205.

Trinity Alps Resort

19. TRINITY LAKE RESORT

Trinity Lake Resort is still better known as Cedar Stock Resort, its former name. By any title, it features excellent housekeeping cabins sized to sleep from 4 to 12 people, ideal for a vacation at Trinity Lake.

Luxury rating: 3

Recreation rating: 4

Trinity Lake, off Highway 3 near Trinity Center

Trinity Lake is a giant reservoir set at the foot of the Trinity Alps that is sometimes overlooked from being in the shadow of its even bigger brother, Shasta Lake, north of Redding. It is a great lake for boating, waterskiing, swimming, and fishing by virtue of quiet water and few speedboats. With 145 miles of shoreline, it is big enough to provide plenty of room for every type of user. To stay out of the northwest winds, most water-skiers prefer the sheltered western shoreline. Yet bass fishers prefer the hidden fingers and coves along the eastern shoreline, so they almost never get in each other's way.

If hiking is a favorite activity, there is a trailhead to the Trinity Alps Wilderness located nearby the resort. It's not a trail for novices, though. In order to reach the wilderness lakes, you'll be headed uphill and it will take a few days.

The cabins here are available by the week from mid-June through early September, when families usually visit the lake. Special two-day deals are available from April to June, when anglers are more apt to visit. Major discounts are available during the off-season.

With the new owners comes new service, and that now includes sheets, pillows, and towels with your rental. The cabins provide a stove with oven, sink, and small refrigerator; it's a good idea to bring a large ice chest so you have plenty of room for produce and beverages. All cabins are equipped with cookware, plus a nearby barbecue. A restaurant, grocery store, marina, and boat ramp are all close at hand.

Facilities: Trinity Lake Resort has housekeeping cabins sized to sleep between 4 and 12 persons. A kitchen, bathroom, cookware, and dishes are provided, and a barbecue is available nearby. A restaurant, grocery store, marina, boat rentals, and launch ramp are available. Pets are permitted with an additional $40 cleaning fee.

Bedding: Linens and towels are provided.

Reservations and rates: Reservations are often required during summer. Fees vary according to the time of year. From June 1 to September 3, a two-person cabin rents for $455 per week. From April 1 to June 15, a four-person cabin rents for $350 for two nights and includes a fishing boat and $25 credit toward dinner. In the off-season, a four-person cabin rents for $50 per night or $350 per week.

Directions: From I-5 at Redding, turn west on Highway 299, drive over Buckhorn Summit, and continue to Weaverville. In Weaverville, turn right on Highway 3 and drive about 15 miles to Cedar Stock Road. Turn right on Cedar Stock Road and drive a short distance to the resort office.

Contact: Trinity Lake Resort, 45810 State Highway 3, Trinity Center, CA 96091; 530/286-2225 or 800/982-2279, fax 530/286-2665.

Trinity Lake Resort

20. TSASDI RESORT CABINS

The first thing most people want to know about this place is how to say Tsasdi. It is pronounced Sauz-dee, and is believed to be a Wintu Indian word that means "white mountain."

Luxury rating: 4

Recreation rating: 5

Shasta Lake, off I-5 near Lakehead

This is a beautiful resort set near the head of Shasta Lake. It includes a gorgeous deck overlooking the lake, a swimming pool, beautiful rooms, and cabins with private decks and picnic tables—all within close range of Shasta Lake. Don't get the idea that these are lakeside cabins; there is no such thing at giant Shasta Lake. These cabins are set on a hillside about 100 feet above the water, but there is direct lake access via a stairway that leads down to it.

The 20 cabins offer views of the Sacramento River arm of Shasta Lake. The cabins are in good shape, with knotty-pine walls and air-conditioning. The cabins are always clean and well maintained by owners who live here year-round. A bonus here is that if you have your own boat, you can dock it here for free as long as you stay.

Shasta Lake is the number-one boating recreation lake in California. It is a huge lake, with 370 miles of shoreline and five major lake arms. Shasta can have a surface temperature of 80°F, which has given the lake a reputation as best for hot weather, warm water, gobs of suntan lotion, and lots of fun.

An overlooked bonus is that fall is one of the more beautiful times to visit, when the hillsides are brought to life by the autumn colors and there is relief from the summer heat.

Facilities: Tsasdi Resort has 20 air-conditioned cabins sized at one, two, and three bedrooms; all feature bathrooms, fully equipped kitchens, cable television, decks with a picnic table, and barbecues. A swimming pool is available. Free boat slips and a boat ramp are nearby. A grocery store is located in the town of Lakehead. There are no boat rentals at Tsasdi's, although they can be found nearby at Antlers, Lakeshore, or Sugarloaf Marinas. Pets are permitted.

Bedding: Linens and towels are provided.

Reservations and rates: Reservations are recommended. Cabin rates are by the week in the summer, ranging from $735 for a cabin that sleeps four and $1,400 for one that sleeps nine, to $1,470 for a modular home that sleeps 12. In the off-season, it is possible to rent a cabin by the night for as low as $65. Boat docking is free.

Directions: From Redding, drive 24 miles north on I-5 to the town of Lakehead. At Lakehead, take the Lakeshore/Antlers exit. At the stop sign, turn left, drive under the freeway and arrive at Lakeshore Drive. Turn left on Lakeshore

Drive and drive two miles, then look for the sign for Tsasdi Resort on the right side of the road.

Contact: Tsasdi Resort, 19990 Lakeshore Drive, Lakehead, CA 96051; 530/238-2575 or 800/995-0291. For a trout fishing guide, call Gary Miralles at 530/275-2278.

Tsasdi Resort Cabins

21. SUGARLOAF COTTAGES RESORT

Sugarloaf Cottages Resort has some of the most loyal patrons in Northern California. To these people, Sugarloaf is like a second home for a vacation every year. Same time, same place, right down to the same cottage. If you want to join in the fun, it is critical to make your reservation very early, as soon as possible. Often there is space available for summer beginning in January, and that is when you must strike.

Luxury rating: 4

Recreation rating: 5

Shasta Lake, off I-5 near Lakehead

The reason for the consistent bookings is that Sugarloaf provides a great escape adjacent to Shasta Lake. All of the cottages are near the lake shore. The two-bedroom townhouse cottages face the lake, and the three-bedroom, two-bath cottages have panoramic views of the lake. They are very cozy and beautiful inside, with A-frame style bedrooms paneled with knotty pine. They come loaded. You pretty much need to bring nothing except your toothbrush.

Sugarloaf is located on the upper end of Shasta Lake, on the Sacramento River arm, a short drive from I-5 at Lakehead. Boat docking, free with a cottage rental, is within short walking range of the cottages. This is a great spot for trout fishing and bass fishing, as well as a preeminent destination for all water sports.

Facilities: Sugarloaf Cottages Resort has 15 cottages in one-, two-, and three-bedroom layouts. Air-conditioning, full all-electric kitchens, bathrooms with showers, and televisions are provided. Laundry service is available. The lodge with a swimming pool is nearby. A marina with boat launch, boat moorings, boat rentals, gas, houseboats, and a store with tackle shop and bait are available. Free moorage with cottage rental. Volleyball, basketball, horseshoes, and a tire swing are available nearby. Pets and smoking are permitted.

Bedding: Linens and towels are provided.

Reservations and rates: Reservations are recommended. The weekly rates range from $735 for a cabin for two persons to $1,645 for up to 12 persons. Pets are allowed with a $5 fee. Major credit cards are accepted. Open year-round, weather permitting.

Directions: From Redding, drive north on I-5 to Lakehead and the Lakeshore/Antlers Road exit. Take that exit to Lakeshore Road. Turn left and drive three miles to the resort entrance on the left. Turn left and drive to the cottages on the left.

Contact: Sugarloaf Cottages Resort, 19667 Lakeshore Drive, P.O. Box 768, Lakehead, CA 96051; 530/238-2448 or 800/953-4432; website: www.shastacabins.com.

Sugarloaf Cottages Resort

22. LAKESHORE INN & RV

Some of the best views of Shasta Lake are from the Lakehouse Cottage here at Lakeshore Inn & RV. The cottage features a balcony that provides a beautiful lookout of the Sacramento River arm of Shasta Lake. The rest of the property is a mini-village, with rustic cabins and an RV park. The cabins are extremely popular. If you want to stay, make your reservation as early as possible, because by mid-June, everything is often reserved for the rest of the summer.

Luxury rating: 3

Recreation rating: 4

Shasta Lake, off I-5 near Lakehead

The grounds are sprinkled with ponderosa pines and oaks, but the big draw here is Shasta Lake, California's number-one recreation lake. A nearby boat ramp and private marina are available. Shasta Lake is a massive reservoir with 370 miles of shoreline, 1,200 campsites, 21 boat launches, 11 marinas, houseboat rentals, and 35 resorts. In addition, getting here is easy, a straight shot off I-5. A remarkable 22 species of fish live in these waters, with bass, crappie, and trout providing the best results.

This is the one place where there is plenty of room for everybody. Even on the most crowded weekends, with thousands of boats on the water, it seems like a giant party with everybody happy, lathering up with sunscreen, and drinking lots of liquids. If you want to escape the festivities, just head into one of the quiet coves; there are thousands of them.

Facilities: Lakeshore Inn & RV has seven one-bedroom cabins and three two-bedroom cabins with fully equipped kitchenettes, private bathrooms with showers, and cable available for television (but you must bring your own television set). Roll-a-ways are available for additional persons. The Lakehouse Cottage sleeps six and has a full kitchen, lawn with a picnic table and fire pit, barbecue and an RV site attached. Leashed pets are permitted. An RV park, large swimming pool, bar (open weekends), restaurant, store, playground, picnic area, game room, hot showers, laundry facilities, dump station, and wheelchair-accessible restrooms (at the main lodge) are available nearby. Family barbecues are held on Sunday during the summer from 5 P.M. to 9 P.M. Live music is scheduled most weekends. A marina and boat rentals are available nearby.

Bedding: Linens and towels are provided.

Reservations and rates: Reservations are required (summers often fill in advance). Rates are $75 to $95 per night ($160 for lakeside). A three-day minimum stay is required in summer with advance reservations. Off-season discounts are available. Major credit cards are accepted. Open year-round.

Directions: From Redding, drive north on I-5 for 24 miles to the Lakeshore-Antlers Road exit in Lakehead. Take that exit, turn left at the stop sign, and drive under the freeway to Lakeshore Drive. Turn left on Lakeshore Drive and drive one mile to the park.

Contact: Lakeshore Inn & RV, 20483 Lakeshore Drive, Lakehead, CA 96051; 530/238-2003 or 888/238-2003 (in California only), fax 530/238-2832; website: www.shastacamping.com.

Lakeshore Inn & RV

23. ANTLERS RESORT

Luxury rating: 3

Recreation rating: 5

Shasta Lake, off I-5 near Lakehead

Antlers Resort is a great place on Shasta Lake. The cabins are in a rustic setting amid oaks and pines. They are beautifully furnished and include decks that overlook the lake. For many visitors, that's all they need for a vacation getaway.

But that's just the start. The resort is located on the Sacramento River arm of the lake near the town of Lakehead, a short drive from I-5. This is a great spot for waterskiing and all other water sports, as well as fishing. Getting on the water in a boat is the appeal that usually brings vacationers here.

For out-of-towners, the first thing you will likely notice when arriving for a summer vacation is the heat. Afternoon temperatures in the 90s and low 100s are common here. You might wonder if you can take a full week of it. Stop your wondering. For starters, all the cabins are air-conditioned, and you've got the lake right next to you. Shasta Lake is like a giant swimming pool in the summer, with surface temperatures ranging from 75°F to 82°F, perfect for water play, swimming, and all boating.

The cabins here are designed with pine interiors, and come clean and fully furnished. You can even see the lake and marina from the picture windows—as well as from the decks with barbecues. The lodge is equally nice, with a dining room, pool table, and a small bar.

Antlers has successfully dealt with the one big problem here, lake drawdowns in late summer, by installing a floating marina system where the marina and docks move up and down the shore according to water levels. Boat launching and parking are easy and ample, respectively.

Facilities: Antlers Resort has 11 cabins in one-, two-, and three-bedroom layouts. Air-conditioning, full all-electric kitchens, showers, private decks with barbecue, and televisions are provided. Laundry service is available. The on-site lodge has a swimming pool, dining room, bar, and pool table. A marina with boat launch, boat moorings, boat rentals, gas, houseboats, and a store with tackle shop and bait are available. A boat mechanic is available. Pets are permitted but must be attended at all times. Smoking is permitted.

Bedding: Linens and towels are provided.

Reservations and rates: Reservations are recommended. Cabin rates are $875 per week for a one-bedroom cabin that sleeps six, $1,341 for a two-bedroom cabin that sleeps 10, and $1,574 for a three-bedroom cabin that sleeps 12. Discounts are available September 4 to June 15. Small boat moorage costs $14. Pets cost $5. Major credit cards are accepted. Open year-round, weather permitting.

Directions: From Redding, drive north on I-5 for 25 miles to Lakehead and Antlers Road. Take that exit and continue a short distance to Antlers Road. Turn right at Antlers Road and drive (it curves to the left) until the road dead-ends at Antlers Resort.

Contact: Antler's Resort, 20679 Antlers Road, P.O. Box 140, Lakehead, CA 96051; 530/238-2553 or 800/238-3924, fax 530/238-2340; website: www.shasta-lakevacations.com.

OTHER CABINS AND COTTAGES NEARBY:

• Fawndale Lodge & RV Resort, 15215 Fawndale Road, Redding, CA 96003; 530/275-8000, 530/275-1863, or 800/338-0941; website: http://members.aol.com/fawnresort.

• Premier RV Resort, 280 North Boulder Drive, Redding, CA 96003; 530/246-0101 or 800/562-0899; website: www.premier rvresort.com.

Antlers Resort

24. STEELHEAD COTTAGES

Money can make a difference, especially if you don't plan on spending much, yet want a first-class vacation. There's a place on the Trinity River that solves this dilemma, where you can stay in a cabin at night and play in the river by day for as little as $48 per night. And an extra $28 will get you an inflatable kayak for a day on the Trinity River, including all gear and a shuttle ride, from Bigfoot Rafting.

Luxury rating: 3

Recreation rating: 4

Trinity River, off Highway 299 near Big Flat

The cabins here are set on the northeast side of the highway, across the road from the river, on a half moon–shaped driveway. They are well-furnished and clean and comfortable, with the grounds sprinkled with pines. It is walking distance to a small beach along the river.

In the summer, many visitors take advantage of the excellent rafting. You get a chance at pure exhilaration doing a sport that is far easier to learn and safer than most people believe. In a survey we conducted of rafting companies in the west, this trip at Big Flat on the Trinity River turned out to be the least expensive among hundreds of white-water adventures.

Near Big Flat, the Trinity is a "pool-and-drop" river. That is, it consists of long, deep pools sprinkled with sudden riffles and drops, making it perfect for rafting. Class II and III rapids such as Hell Hole, The Slot, Zig-Zag, Fishtail, Pinball, and others occur every five minutes or so, providing short bursts of thrill, then short rests to regain your composure. Most of the rapids are Class II, nothing serious, just fun and ideal for youngsters. For a river trip with a cottage, this is the cheapest deal around.

Fishing on the Trinity River is free, with a current state license, of course. A bonus is that this area has many of the best spots on the entire river for fishing from shore. This is the appeal of Big Flat, a little one-store settlement along Highway 299, about an hour-and-a-half drive either way from Eureka or Redding.

Facilities: Steelhead Cottages has five cabins, each with a full bathroom, kitchen, and propane heat. Picnic tables and barbecues are available, and a fish-cleaning station, horseshoe pits, a small grocery store, and a restaurant are nearby. A fish smoker is also available. Call for details regarding pet policies.

Bedding: Linens and towels are provided.

Reservations and rates: Reservations are recommended from August through November. Cottages rent from $48 per night for two to $76 per night for four.

Directions: From I-5 at Redding, turn west on Highway 299 and drive through

Weaverville, continuing for 23 miles to Big Flat. Look for Steelhead Cottages on the right side of the road.

If you are coming from U.S. 101 at Eureka, drive north to Arcata. Just past Arcata, turn east on Highway 299 and drive through Willow Creek, continuing for 40 miles to Big Flat. Look for Steelhead Cottages on the left side of the road.

Contact: Steelhead Cottages, 408 State Highway 299W, Junction City, CA 96048; 530/623-6325 or 800/742-3785. For rafting information, phone Bigfoot Rafting at 530/629-2263.

OTHER CABINS AND COTTAGES NEARBY:

• Trinity Canyon Lodge and Resort, 27025 Highway 299 West, Junction City, CA 96048; 530/623-6318

• Bigfoot Campground and RV Park, P.O. Box 98, Junction City, CA 96048; 530/623-6088 or 800/422-5219; website: www.bigfootrvcabins.com

Steelhead Cottages

25. LAKEVIEW TERRACE RESORT

Luxury rating: 3

Recreation rating: 5

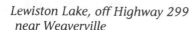

Lewiston Lake, off Highway 299 near Weaverville

Lewiston Lake has just about everything. It's a treasure of a lake—surrounded by alpine beauty, always full, good for trout fishing, set near Trinity Alps, and with cabins for lodging. But it is what Lewiston does not have—loud, high-powered jet boats—that makes it most special. A 10-mph speed limit guarantees quiet water, making your experience at Lewiston intimate and tranquil, yet retaining prospects for great adventure. This makes Lewiston Lake an ideal place for a small boat, especially a canoe. When you paddle across the lake, the conifer-lined mountain slopes can reflect on the lake surface, with the only sound being the dipping of paddles, leaving little whirlpools with every stroke. From the far shore of the lake, you can see the snow-covered Trinity Alps.

It has become a popular destination for fly fishers casting near the tules near Lakeview Terrace. There can be an impressive surface rise near sunset here, so good that fly fishers will drive long distances for the chance to cast to it.

And if you are out on the lake, whether in a canoe, one of the rental boats, or even a float tube, not once will you cringe at the far-off roar of a high-powered V-8 engine echoing across the lake, followed a moment later by the arrival of a speedboat barreling in your direction at 50 mph. It won't happen because there are none. There never will be. Lewiston Lake will always be quiet and peaceful.

Lakeview Terrace has cabins sized at one, two, three, and four rooms, along with an adjacent resort and RV park. There is also a swimming pool and a small coin laundry on-site. The cabins are distant enough from the RV park to provide privacy. Each cabin has a picnic table and a barbecue, making them fine for evening celebrations after a day of fishing. They are little, red with green roofs, and have clean interiors.

Facilities: Each Lakeview Terrace cabin has one or more bedrooms, living room, dining area, fully equipped kitchen, and bathroom with shower. Picnic tables with barbecues are provided nearby. Beach mooring is available with boat and motor rentals. A swimming pool, and a coin laundry are available. Call for details regarding pet policies.

Bedding: Linens and towels are provided.

Reservations and rates: Reservations are required. Fees range from $60 to $120 per day or $378 to $756 per week, depending on the size of the cabin and number of people in your party.

Directions: From I-5 at Redding, turn west on Highway 299, drive over Buckhorn Summit and continue for five miles to the Lewiston-Trinity Center turnoff. Turn right on Trinity Dam Boulevard, drive about 10 miles (five miles past Lewiston), and look for Lakeview Terrace Resort on the left side of the road.

Contact: Lakeview Terrace Resort, HC 01, Box 250, Lewiston, CA 96052; 530/778-3803, fax 530/778-3960; website: www.lakeviewterraceresort.com.

Lakeview Terrace Resort

26. TRINITY RIVER LODGE RV RESORT

In some rural areas, the nearby locations become a more important consideration than the luxury level of accommodations. Trinity River Lodge RV Resort is one of those places.

Its location is everything—set along the Trinity River near the town of Lewiston, yet just a short drive north to Lewiston Lake or a bit farther to giant Trinity Lake. River or lake, take your pick. There are also several outstanding hiking trailheads available within a half-hour's drive.

Luxury rating: 2

Recreation rating: 4

Trinity River, off Highway 3 near Lewiston

This is not a luxury-style romantic hideaway, but primarily a family and outdoor enthusiast's campground that provides the bonus opportunity of renting a furnished trailer for the night. The park has shaded green lawns sprinkled with maples and the adjacent natural beauty of the Trinity River—all set amid forested mountains. Wildlife is often abundant here, with deer roaming the grounds daily. Eagles, osprey, herons, and ducks are frequently seen flying past. For anglers, the adjacent Trinity River can provide excellent fishing opportunities for brown trout, and in the fall, for migrating salmon and steelhead.

In addition, there is excellent low-cost rafting available nearby, ideal for families, with the rapids rated Class I and Class II. There are also golf courses nearby.

Facilities: Trinity River Lodge RV Resort has three furnished trailers and one cabin. Cable television is available. The resort is designed primarily as a campground with restrooms, hot showers, coin laundry, a recreation room, a library, a clubhouse, a recreation field, a store, and horseshoes available. Some facilities are wheelchair accessible. There is lake fishing less than 10 minutes away. Leashed pets are permitted.

Bedding: Linens and towels are provided.

Reservations and rates: Reservations are recommended. The fee is $90 per night per cabin. Major credit cards are accepted. Open year-round.

Directions: From Redding, go west on Highway 299, drive over Buckhorn Summit, and continue for five miles to County Road 105. Turn right on County Road 105 and drive four miles to Lewiston. Turn right at Trinity Dam Boulevard and drive six miles, crossing the Trinity River. Just after the bridge, turn left on Rush Creek Road and drive to the campground on the left.

Contact: Trinity River Lodge RV Resort, P.O. Box 137, Rush Creek Road, Lewiston, CA 96052; 530/778-3791 or 800/761-2769; website: www.trinityrivercampground.com.

Trinity River Lodge RV Resort

27. SILVERTHORN RESORT

Shasta Lake is so giant, with 370 miles of shoreline, that each lake arm can feel like a different lake. Silverthorn Resort can offer a remote launch point for your Shasta vacation because it's located on the relatively distant Pit River arm of the lake.

Luxury rating: 3

Recreation rating: 5

Shasta Lake, off Highway 299 near Bella Vista

Silverthorn Resort is well known among those who love Shasta for its array of deluxe houseboats, lake cabins, and location near excellent fishing and boating. There are a variety of cabins to choose from. Each offers a cozy yet rustic atmosphere. They come complete with kitchen conveniences, covered patios, gas barbecues, and more. Though set in the pines, the cabins are within walking distance of the marina and a restaurant. Cabin 7 has a fantastic view of Shasta Lake, and Cabin 8 has a breathtaking view from the large second story deck. In addition, Cabin 3 is wheelchair accessible.

But sooner or later, you will see the houseboats here that have everybody on the lake gawking and talking. These are among the most luxurious houseboats ever built and available to the public, including several that have 1,500 square feet of cabin and deck space and will sleep 16. One even has a tub!

Silverthorn is also the place of legends. Merle Haggard, the great country singer, once owned the resort and had a giant houseboat built that included a hole in the floor next to the dining table—so he could fish while eating dinner!

The Pit River arm of Shasta Lake hides many secrets. The calm, clear water in front of the resort, though, is well known as a great site for waterskiing. Upstream there is a five-mph speed limit that protects quiet water for excellent fishing for bluegill, crappie, and catfish; it's probably the best area of the lake for panfish. The immediate vicinity of Silverthorn is good in the spring for bass and trout as well.

Facilities: Silverthorn Resort has eight cabins with layouts for two to eight people. One is wheelchair accessible. Air-conditioning, bedrooms, all-electric kitchens, bathrooms with showers, and televisions are provided. Houseboat rentals range from $2,390 per week for 10 people to $5,490 per week for 16 people, depending on the size and furnishings. Off-season discounts are available. A marina with boat launch, boat moorings, boat rentals, houseboats, and a store with tackle shop and bait are available. A recreation room and pizza pub with pool table, video games, Ping-Pong, and music is available nearby. Pets and smoking are permitted.

Bedding: Linens and towels are provided.

Reservations and rates: Reservations are recommended. Rates for cabins range from $105 to $245 per night and $650 to $1,500 per week, depending on size and number of people. A three-night minimum is required. Major credit cards are accepted. Open year-round.

Directions: From Redding, turn east on Highway 299 and drive 7.5 miles to Bella Vista and Dry Creek Road. Turn left on Dry Creek Road and drive nine miles to a Y in the road. Bear left at the Y and continue to Silverthorn Resort.

Contact: Silverthorn Resort, P.O. Box 1090, Bella Vista, CA 96008; 530/275-1571 or 800/332-3044; website: www.silverthornresort.com.

Silverthorn Resort

28. ZIEGLER'S TRAILS END

Where the heck is Hyampom?

Isn't that the point?

This hideout is literally in the middle of nowhere, but you already knew that. The nearest place of note is Hayfork. No, that is not one of those pointy-tooled objects with a long handle known as a pitchfork. Hayfork is actually a town. Like we said, isn't that the point?

Luxury rating: 2

Recreation rating: 4

Shasta-Trinity National Forest, off Highway 3 in Hyampom

By now you have probably figured out that this isolated retreat is set up primarily for disappearing from the world. Some people also go fishing, hunting, or exploring around in the nearby river.

Ziegler's Trails End is set near the South Fork Trinity River on the edge of remote Shasta-Trinity National Forest, about 50 miles west of Redding. Each cabin has an individual character and is decorated accordingly. The resort grounds are landscaped with shade and fruit trees, flowers and shrubs, and a picnic area. The entire property has a laid-back, country feel. A swimming hole and beach on the river lie within walking distance.

This is a good area for viewing wildlife, especially ospreys, bald eagles, and blue herons cruising the stream. The area is something of a fishing and hunting retreat, with guide services available in season.

We'll tell you something else. If you are looking to avoid a sheriff trying to serve you with a subpoena, he or she will never find you out here.

Facilities: Ziegler's Trails End has seven cabins in one- or two-room layouts. Air-conditioning, full kitchens, bathrooms with showers, and televisions are provided. A barbecue, breakfast service, pool table, and VHS movies are available. A general store is nearby. Pickup from Hyampom Airport is available with advance arrangement. No smoking is allowed in the cabins. Pets are permitted.

Bedding: Linens and towels are provided.

Reservations and rates: Reservations are recommended. The rates range from $50 per night for two persons to $600 per week for six persons. It costs $10 for each additional person. Major credit cards are accepted. Open year-round, weather permitting.

Directions: From Redding, drive west on Highway 299 for 25 miles to Douglas City and Highway 3. Turn left (south) on Highway 3 and drive 24 miles to Hayfork and Hyampom Road. Turn right and drive 24 miles to the resort.

Contact: Ziegler's Trails End, P.O. Box 150, Hyampom, CA 96046; 530/628-4929 or 800/566-5266; website: www.zieglerstrailsend.com.

Ziegler's Trails End

29. LITTLEFIELD RANCH CABINS

It's a winding, seemingly unending drive on Highway 36 way out here, but you end up in one of the most remote cabin settings in California. Littlefield Ranch Cabins is backed up against Six Rivers National Forest, just across a pasture (about 400 yards) from Mad River. There is a path that starts near Cabin 3 that is routed into remote forest country, although there is no real destination, just "out there." To get an idea of how remote this area is, take the drive up the nearby Forest Service Road to the top of South Fork Mountain, where you'll be treated to great views in all directions of this region of isolated western Trinity County.

Luxury rating: 2

Recreation rating: 4

Ruth Lake, off Highway 36 near Ruth

One of the unique elements of Littlefield Ranch is that it was built in the 1930s to house loggers. The cabins have been restored with antique touches. Each has a small yard with trees set near a vintage barn. The cabins come in one- to three-bedroom configurations.

Ruth Lake is a primary attraction, located just two miles from Littlefield Ranch. It's the only lake of any consequence within decent driving range of

Eureka. This is a long, narrow lake set at an elevation of 2,800 feet. There is a free boat ramp, and the Ruth Lake Marina rents fishing boats along with houseboats, pontoon boats, and ski boats.

Facilities: Littlefield Ranch has four cabins with one, two, or three bedrooms. All have bathrooms and kitchens with cookware, utensils, and woodburning stoves. Patio tables and barbecues are provided. Boat rentals are available at Ruth Lake, two miles away; reservations can be made through the ranch or through the marina. A grocery store is one mile away. Call for details regarding pet policies.

Bedding: Linens are provided in only one cabin. Bring your sleeping bag and pillow if you reserve any of the other cabins.

Reservations and rates: Reservations are preferred. Cabin rates range from $65 per night for a one-bedroom cabin to $95 per night for a three-bedroom cabin that sleeps 10 people. Boat rentals can be arranged at Ruth Lake Marina, 707/574-6524.

Directions: From Red Bluff, turn west on Highway 36 and drive about 60 miles (about 10 miles past the town of Forest Glen). Turn left at the sign for Ruth Lake and drive 18 miles to the town of Ruth. Continue one mile past the Ruth Store and look for Littlefield Ranch on the left side of the road (just past the Ruth District Forest Service office).

From San Francisco, drive north on U.S. 101 about 250 miles. At Alton, turn east on Highway 36 and drive about 50 miles to just past the town of Mad River. Turn right at the sign for Ruth Lake and drive 18 miles to the town of Ruth. Continue one mile past the Ruth Store and look for Littlefield Ranch on the left side of the road (just past the Ruth District Forest Service office).

Contact: Littlefield Ranch, Rural Route, Box 600, Ruth, CA 95526; 707/574-6689.

Littlefield Ranch Cabins

30. CAMP DISCOVERY

When the gates at the Red Bluff Diversion Dam on the Sacramento River are closed, it creates Lake Red Bluff, where waterskiing, bird watching, hiking, and fishing are popular activities. This occurs from April through early September every year. In mid-September, the gates at the dam are opened, draining the lake. Overnight, it is transformed again to the Sacramento River. This allows salmon and steelhead to migrate unimpeded through the area.

Luxury rating: 1

Recreation rating: 3

Lake Red Bluff/Sacramento River, off I-5 near Red Bluff

Created by the Red Bluff Diversion Dam, Lake Red Bluff has become a backyard swimming hole for local residents during the summer, when the temperatures reach the high 90s and low 100s almost every day.

Adjacent to Lake Red Bluff are the headquarters for Camp Discovery, a visitor information center, where visitors check in when they arrive. This also includes a fish-viewing station, where you can occasionally see migrating salmon passing up the fish ladders to get past the Red Bluff Diversion Dam. Camp Discovery contains a series of campsites, group camps, and picnic areas, plus six screened cabins operated by the Forest Service. It's popular for groups to reserve the cabins, which together provide space for up to 48 people. Staying at the cabins, however, isn't much different than camping: You are responsible for bringing everything you need.

There are no beaches at Lake Red Bluff, but there is a large grassy area on the west bank where people sunbathe and swim. This is the only practical area for wading and swimming because the water temperatures are far lower out on the main lake body. Only the hardy few who can tolerate cold water try swimming here, though many will attempt a quick dip in summer to cool off from the 100-degree temperatures. Waterskiing is popular at Lake Red Bluff, as this area is often less windswept than the wide-open lakes set in the foothills, making its flat surface ideal for waterskiing. However, many will avoid risking a fall because of the stunning shock of the cold water.

Facilities: Camp Discovery has six screened cabins that can each accommodate a maximum of eight people. Drinking water, showers, vault and flush toilets, two boat ramps, a fish-viewing plaza, and two covered eating areas that will accommodate up to 100 people are available. In the group camp area, there are two large barbecues, electrical outlets, lockable storage, five large picnic tables, a comfort station with showers and sinks, and an amphitheater.

Bedding: No linens (nor beds) are provided. Bring a sleeping pad or air mattress plus a sleeping bag.

Reservations and rates: Reservations are required. The fee per night is $100 for up to 50 people, $150 for 51 to 75 people, and $200 for 76 to 100 people. Open April through October.

Directions: From I-5 at Red Bluff, turn east on Highway 36 and drive 100 yards to the first turnoff at Sale Lane. Turn right (south) on Sale Lane and drive .5 mile to the campground at the end of the road.

Contact: Camp Discovery, Lake Red Bluff, Mendocino National Forest, Corning Work Station, CA; 530/824-5196.

Camp Discovery

CHAPTER 3

Lassen & Modoc

*M*t. Lassen and its awesome volcanic past seem to cast a shadow everywhere you go in this region. At 10,457 feet, the mountain's domed summit is visible for more than 100 miles in all directions. It blew its top in 1914, with continuing eruptions through 1918. Although now dormant, the volcanic-based landscape dominates Lassen's vast sphere of influence.

In terms of lodging, many resorts are remodeling and upgrading their cabins and cottages, and new operations are opening with quality accommodations in appealing settings. There are lodges here that are set up for the high-end fly-fishing crowd and others that are just one step above camping.

The top cabins include those at Drakesbad Guest Ranch—the epitome of what many desire in this area—as well as Burney Mountain Guest Ranch and Lava Creek Lodge. Drakesbad, for example, is the only place in the region where visitors get stellar accommodations and meals in a setting on the edge of wilderness in a national park. (The place is often completely booked far in advance.) A number of cabin rentals designed as fish-camp lodges surround Lake Almanor, the highlight of which is Lassen View Resort. One of the most economical deals is at Eagle Lake Cabins, especially for anglers with their own boats who are determined to catch large trout.

Of all the areas covered in this book, this region has the least number of romantic getaway spots. It caters instead primarily to outdoors enthusiasts. And Lassen is one of the best places to lace up the hiking boots or spool new line on a reel. It's often off the radar scope of vacationers, making it one of the few national parks where you can enjoy the wilderness in relative solitude.

Lassen Volcanic National Park is easily explored along the main route, the Lassen Park Highway. Along the way, you can pick a few trails for adventure. The best hikes are the Summit Climb (moderate to challenging), best done first thing in the morning, and Bumpass Hell (easy and great for kids) to see the sulfur vents and boiling mud pots. Another favorite for classic alpine beauty is the Shadow Lake Trail.

Unique features of the area include its pumice boulders, volcanic rock, and spring-fed streams from the underground lava tubes. The highlights include the best still-water canoeing and fly fishing at Fall River, Big Lake, and Ahjumawi State Park. Access at Ahjumawi is by canoe or powerboat only, and you can arrange it through Lava Creek Lodge, featured in this chapter.

Nearby is Burney Falls State Park, along with the Pit River and Lake Britton, which together make up one of Northern California's best recreation destinations for families. This is also one of the best areas for fly fishing, especially at Hat Creek, Pit River, Burney Creek, and Munzanita Lake. For more beautiful settings, you can visit Lake Almanor and Eagle Lake, both of which provide cabin rentals and excellent fishing and boating recreation.

And there's more. In remote Modoc County, you'll find Lava Beds National Monument and the South Warner Wilderness. Lava Beds is a stark, pretty, and often lonely place. It's sprinkled with small lakes full of trout, is home to large-antlered deer that migrate in after the first snow (and after the hunting season has closed), and features a unique volcanic habitat with huge flows of obsidian (dark, smooth, natural glass formed by the cooling of molten lava) and dacite (gray, craggy volcanic flow). Lava Beds National Monument boasts 445 caves and lava tubes, including the 6,000-foot Catacomb tunnel. Nearby is pretty Medicine Lake, formed in a caldera, which provides good trout fishing, hiking, and exploring.

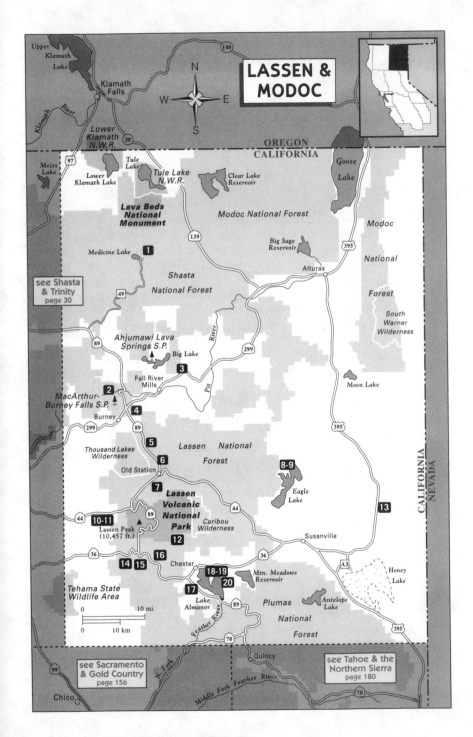

OREGON
CALIFORNIA

Upper
Klamath
Lake

Klamath
Falls

Klamath River

Lower
Klamath
N.W.R.

Meiss
Lake

Lower
Klamath Lake

Tule
Lake

Tule Lake
N.W.R.

Clear Lake
Reservoir

Goose
Lake

**Lava Beds
National
Monument**

Modoc National Forest

Modoc

National

Forest

Big Sage
Reservoir

Alturas

Medicine Lake

1

see Shasta
& Trinity
page 30

Shasta

National Forest

South
Warner
Wilderness

*Ahjumawi Lava
Springs S.P.*

River

Big Lake

3

Moon Lake

Fall River
Mills

Pit

MacArthur-
Burney Falls S.P.

2

4

Burney

5

Lassen   National

Thousand Lakes
Wilderness

6

Forest

8-9

Old Station

*Eagle
Lake*

13

7

**Lassen
Volcanic
National
Park**

10-11

Lassen Peak
(10,457 ft.)

*Caribou
Wilderness*

12

Susanville

A3

Honey
Lake

14 **15**

16

Chester

Tehama State
Wildlife Area

18-19

Mtn. Meadows
Reservoir

20

17

*Lake
Almanor*

Antelope
Lake

0   10 mi

Plumas

0   10 km

Feather River

National

Forest

see Sacramento
& Gold Country
page 156

N. Fork

Quincy

see Tahoe & the
Northern Sierra
page 180

Chico

Middle Fork Feather River

CALIFORNIA
NEVADA

CHAPTER 3
LASSEN & MODOC

1. LITTLE MOUNT HOFFMAN LOOKOUT

In spite of its remoteness, this lookout station has proved to be one of the most popular cabin-style rentals in California. Upon arrival, the scenery will simply astonish you. Looking north, you get a sweeping view of Lava Beds National Monument and beyond to Mount McLaughlin in Oregon. To the east is Big Glass Mountain, and to the south is Lassen Peak. To the west, of course, is Mount Shasta, the most dramatic photo opportunity available here. It is simply breathtaking and you will never forget it. And all these world-class views are provided without a difficult hike.

 © SHASTA CASCADE WONDERLAND ASSOCIATION

Luxury rating: 1

Recreation rating: 4

Medicine Lake, off Highway 89 in Shasta-Trinity National Forest

This lookout is perched at 7,309 feet atop Little Mount Hoffman. It's a 10-minute drive to Medicine Lake and the nearby Lava Beds National Monument. When you add it up, you have the perfect recipe for a getaway: isolation, quiet, beauty, and nearby recreation.

Staying at Little Mount Hoffman Lookout is like primitive camping; there is no running water, but cushioned sleeping platforms and an outside vault toilet are provided. You climb a ladder to gain entry to the lookout, once used to spot the smoke of forest fires. Once inside, you are encased by four picture windows for a true 360-degree view.

The appeal is the view, the remoteness, and the proximity of Medicine Lake (three miles) and the Lava Beds. The biggest problem here—and it's not that big—is that some campers visiting Medicine Lake will make the short drive up to the lookout to enjoy the view; then upon seeing people inside the lookout, will mistakenly think they are Forest Service fire spotters. So you might get some surprise visitors asking you questions like, "How do you get a job like this?" Once or twice, hey, no problem. But if a Boy Scout Troop shows up and wants a guided tour, well, it can get in the way of your vacation.

Nearby Medicine Lake provides excellent fishing for brook trout and the opportunity for boating and swimming, though the water is cold. It is a unique spot where the lake has been formed in the caldera of a volcano at an elevation of 6,700 feet.

It is also a lot of fun to explore the dacite and glass flows of the

Lava Beds. It is easy walking and rock climbing, ideal for families. The full expanse of the Lava Beds features 445 caves and lava tubes, including the 6,000-foot Catacomb.

At one time, there were 600 lookouts on national forest land. Many have decomposed into oblivion, with only 174 still standing. Of those, 55 are still in use as lookouts—and seven have been transformed for public use. In the winter, the place is buried deep in snow. It usually becomes accessible by Memorial Day Weekend.

Facilities: Little Mount Hoffman Lookout has an outside vault toilet available. Beds are available. No water or kitchen facilities are provided. Leashed pets are allowed.

Bedding: You must bring your own sleeping bag and pillow.

Reservations and rates: Reservations are required. The fee is $35 per night. Major credit cards are accepted.

Directions: From Redding, turn north on Interstate 5 and drive 56 miles to the exit for Highway 89/McCloud. Bear right on Highway 89 and drive 28 miles to Bartle. Just past Bartle, turn left (northeast) on Powder Hill Road (Forest Road 49) and drive 31 miles (it becomes Medicine Lake Road) to the Medicine Lake and campground turnoff. Turn left on the campground road, then bear right and drive past several campgrounds (on your left) and continue to Headquarters Campground. Continue straight (Headquarters Campground will be on your left) on the Mount Hoffman access road and drive three miles to the summit.

Contact: Shasta-Trinity National Forest, McCloud District, 530/964-2184. For a map, ask for a map of Modoc National Forest and send $6 to U.S. Forest Service, Attn: Map Sales, P.O. Box 587, Camino, CA 95709; 530/647-5390, fax 530/647-5389; or visit the website: www.r5.fs.fed.us/visitorcenter

Little Mount Hoffman Lookout

---

2. CLARK CREEK LODGE

At one time, the cabins at Clark Creek Lodge served as the hideouts of a variety of nefarious and celebrated characters, from gangster Al Capone during the bootleg whiskey days to former heavyweight boxing champ Jack Dempsey. More recently, people from the Bay Area have used it as their hideaway rather than their hideout, taking advantage of the privacy, fishing and boating at adjacent Lake Britton, enjoying the fantastic waterfall walk at nearby McArthur-Burney Falls State Park, and hiking and fly fishing along the Pit River.

The lodge mixes a lot of the old with

Luxury rating: 3

Recreation rating: 4

Lake Britton, off Highway 89 near Burney

a little of the new. New owners arrived in 2001 and the place is looking better. The old includes the lodge headquarters, built in 1921, and many of the cabins. The new includes a steak/seafood restaurant and bar. Put them together and you'll discover how two different worlds can ride the same orbit.

The cabins are rustic enough for the lodge owners to allow pets (not on the beds), but all have showers and most have at least small refrigerators. They don't have kitchens, so visitors learn to make do for food; some end up half-starved at the restaurant for dinner. The rooms do not have televisions, radios, or telephones.

Lake Britton is a very pretty, emerald-green lake. At its headwaters, the lake narrows with steep sides, providing dramatic beauty. Then it opens into a wide expanse perfect for fishing, especially for trout in spring and fall and for smallmouth bass and crappie in early summer. The boat ramp at McArthur-Burney Falls State Park offers boat rentals of many varieties, including aluminum boats with motors, canoes, and paddleboats.

The park is better known, however, for its 129-foot waterfall, which is wide and cascading, with miniature waterfalls oozing out of the adjacent moss-lined walls. It's a dramatic sight year-round and is especially awesome in the early summer. There is a great lookout of the waterfall from the Burney Falls Trail.

Another nearby adventure for hikers as well as fly fishers is possible along the Pit River below the dam at Lake Britton. It is an excellent fishing area, where trout will rise to a carefully presented caddis fly. Anglers should note, however, that the wading can be slippery, deep, and tricky, and your casts must have a light touch with precision to inspire consistent rises. We've seen some people just give up, sit down on a rock, and watch the water run by.

Facilities: Clark Creek Lodge has five cabins of various sizes with bathrooms and propane heat. There are no kitchens, but cabins are equipped with refrigerators, microwaves, and coffeemakers. Barbecue facilities are available. A boat ramp is located nearby at the state park. A dinner restaurant and full bar is on the property; it opens at 5 P.M. and is closed on Monday. Pets are permitted.

Bedding: Linens and towels are provided.

Reservations and rates: Reservations are accepted, and the phone is attended during the evening. Cabin rates range from $65 to $100 per night, with a two-night minimum stay on three-day holiday weekends.

Directions: From Redding, turn east on Highway 299 and drive to the junction of Highway 299 and Highway 89. Turn left (north) on Highway 89 and drive 10 miles, past McArthur-Burney Falls State Park and Lake Britton to North Clark Creek Road. Turn left on North Clark Creek Road and drive 2.5 miles to Clark Creek Lodge on the right side of the road.

Contact: Clark Creek Lodge, 36333 Clark Creek Road, Burney, CA 96013; 530/335-2574; website: www.clarkcreeklodge.com.

Clark Creek Lodge

3. LAVA CREEK LODGE

Here's a great spot that is missed by many. It's on Eastman Lake at 3,280 feet in elevation, right next to one of the California's least known state parks, Ahjumawi Lava Springs. A great appeal is some of California's best fly fishing on nearby Fall River, which attracts skilled anglers from across the West.

Luxury rating: 3

Recreation rating: 4

Fall River, off Highway 299 near Fall River Mills

The lodge offers direct access to the park and its network of hiking trails. Why is this so special? Normally, the only way you can access the park is by boat from Big Lake and waterways such as Eastman Lake, Fall River, Big Lake, and a series of other smaller, slow-moving, spring-fed rivers, all linked and accessible only by boat. Because this network of connected waterways is surrounded by private land, public access is very poor. It also means these lakes are relatively unknown outside of the region. The only way to reach the state park waters is by boat, launching at a primitive and obscure boat ramp, or through the better-known Lava Creek Lodge. Therefore, it is one of the best places to kayak or canoe in Northern California. You can explore for days.

Ahjumawi means "where the waters come together," named by Pit River Native Americans who inhabit the area near the confluence of several rivers, creeks, and lakes. Together these waters form one of the largest freshwater springs in the world. It is clear and slow-flowing, perfect for fly fishing for giant native rainbow trout—or canoeing quietly waiting to spot a bald eagle perched nearby on a pine.

What you'll see here is primeval beauty with springs flowing from the lava along the shoreline. A lot of the land is covered by lava flows, including large areas of jagged black basalt, along with lava tubes and spattercone and conic depressions. Eastman Lake and Big Lake are brilliant aqua in some shallow areas, and the place is so quiet you can hear the hordes of mosquitoes swarming around. Fall River is a spring-fed stream that appears almost still, with pristine, clear water and tremendous hatches of insects that inspire large numbers of elusive 20-inch trout.

At the lake, fishing is good for bass, with big trout in the springs area. Canoeing is great here, and if you're out paddling, be on the lookout for nesting areas for bald eagles, ospreys, and blue herons. It's a great opportunity for bird watching.

The lodge has been renovated and caters to a diverse crowd—anglers, couples, families, and groups. About half come for the stellar fishing, the other half for boating, canoeing, and bird watching. For romance, try Cabins 11 or 12, which include vaulted beam ceilings, cedar paneling, and modern, oversize showers. Cabins 13 through 15 are more rustic, with barnwood paneling. Families and groups prefer Cabins 16 and 17, both two-bedroom units. The bunkhouse was added in 2001; it sleeps four and has a large bathroom, a refrigerator, a microwave, and a wet bar. And by the way, the dinners here are just out-of-this-world sumptuous, especially on Mexican night.

This place is one-of-a-kind. There is almost zero public access to this area. That alone makes Lava Creek a great choice.

Facilities: Lava Creek Lodge has eight cabins, eight lodge rooms, and a bunkhouse. There are no kitchen facilities, but a restaurant and lounge are available. Each cabin has a bathroom with shower and covered porch; some units are air-conditioned. A boat launch and rentals for boats, kayaks, and canoes are available.The lodge is suitable for children. Call for details regarding pet policies. No smoking is permitted. Some facilities are wheelchair accessible.

Bedding: Linens, pillows, and towels are provided.

Reservations and rates: Reservations are recommended, and there is usually at least a three-month waiting list. The fees are $70 per night for one person, $80 per night for two persons, $90 per night for three persons, $100 per night for four persons, and deluxe units are $120 per night. The bunkhouse is $20 per person per night. Continental breakfast is $6, full breakfast is $10, lunch is $8, and dinner is $20. Major credit cards are accepted. Open April through November.

Directions: From Redding, drive east on Highway 299 to Burney and continue for 17 miles to Glenburn Road. Turn left and drive five miles to McArthur Road. Turn right and drive .2 mile to the church. Bear left at the church (it's still McArthur Road) and drive 1.9 miles to Island Road. Turn right and drive three miles to the lodge at the end of the road.

Contact: Lava Creek Lodge, #1 Island Road, Fall River Mills, CA 96028; 530/336-6288, fax 530/336-1087.

Lava Creek Lodge

4. BURNEY MOUNTAIN GUEST RANCH

Those who love to fly-fish should apply here. Horseback riders and hikers can check in as well. This is a modern guest ranch on 120 acres that caters to people from around the world who come mainly for some of the best fishing in California. It's not a western dude ranch at all; it's a fishing, horseback riding, and hiking resort that caters to adults. You surely won't find hayrides and a petting zoo.

Luxury rating: 3

Recreation rating: 4

Hat Creek, off Highway 299 in Burney

Burney Mountain Guest Ranch opened in 1998 with two newly-built duplex units (each housing two "cabins") and two suites in a house, which together can accommodate up to 12 guests at once. The cabins are surrounded by Shasta National Forest, and the rates include all meals and fishing. What you get here is friendly, personalized service and a low-key atmosphere.

The cedar-sided cabins are situated alongside a casting pond, about 20 feet apart. The 400-square-foot cabins have white-painted walls and are tastefully decorated. Each has a private bathroom with shower and tub. There are no kitchen facilities, since meals are provided in the lodge.

A day's activities might include fishing in nearby Hat Creek, Pit River, or Fall River. Professional fishing guides are available, and average about $195 for a half day. If you don't want to fish, you can hike or ride horseback on trails that lead into Shasta National Forest. The Pacific Crest Trail is a popular choice. Regular rides are available to beautiful 129-foot Burney Falls and Baum Lake; an extra fee is charged for riding.

The ranch owners say no one should get bored here because they ensure that every guest has an opportunity to participate in the activities that they enjoy. For instance, couples often split up for the day, with one going fishing and the other going riding, bird watching, or merely relaxing and reading; then they meet up again at dinner.

Facilities: Burney Mountain Guest Ranch has four cabins, each with bathroom and porch. There are no kitchen facilities, but complimentary meals are provided in the lodge. There are also two suites in the main house. Fishing guides and horseback riding guides are available for a fee. The ranch is not suitable for children. Pets are not allowed. No smoking is permitted.

Bedding: Linens and towels are provided, and there is daily maid service.

5. RIPPLING WATERS RESORT

You wouldn't think a little resort on the side of the highway in a remote part of California would have a full house all summer, would you? Wrong. You better have reservations or you can forget about staying here. The attraction? It's shaded, it's pretty, there's good fishing right next to the resort on Hat Creek, and it's fairly close to a lot of great getaways.

Luxury rating: 3

Recreation rating: 4

Hat Creek, off Highway 89

Rippling Waters Resort borders Lassen National Forest and is within easy walking distance of a secluded section of Hat Creek. Three smaller creeks run through the property and guests have use of a private pond. If this isn't enough for you, within 20 miles are the Pit River, Fall River, Lake Britton, Baum Lake, McArthur-Burney Falls State Park, the lava tubes at Subway Caves, and Thousand Lakes Wilderness. You have almost an endless supply of fishing and hiking options here.

Each cabin is different, set among tall pines and cedars, and some are along Hat Creek. Cabin 1 is probably the most popular because it's creekside and has the best bathroom, with a tub and shower. Cabin 2 is a close second, with a private deck overlooking the creek. Cabin 5 has a bedroom door that opens to the creek, a feature many people like. Cabin 6 has a carport and trellised deck with barbecue, and although it is farthest from the creek, it's the most secluded cabin.

The elevation here is 3,700 feet, and while most summer days are warm and sunny, here's a hint about winter: they provide flannel sheets. What does that tell you? It's butt-cold in winter, that's what.

Facilities: Rippling Waters Resort has six studio or one-bedroom cabins with fully equipped kitchens, including microwave and coffeemaker, and full bathrooms with shower. Most cabins have a deck, woodstove, and living room. Barbecues are provided, but bring your own charcoal. A trout pond, a small gift shop, fishing supplies, a play area for children, horseshoes, basketball, and a banquet room are available. The resort is suitable for children. Call for details regarding pet policies. No smoking is permitted.

Bedding: Linens are provided. Bring your own towels.

Reservations and rates: Reservations are required. The fee is $75 to $155 per night for two persons; the seventh night is free. For additional persons, $15 per person per night is charged. Children ages five and under are free. With a reservation, a two-night minimum stay (three nights on holiday weekends) is required. Major credit cards are accepted.

Directions: From Redding, drive east on Highway 299 to Burney and continue for five miles to the junction with Highway 89. Turn right (south) on Highway 89 and drive 14 miles to the resort on the left.

Contact: Rippling Waters Resort, 16242 Highway 89, Hat Creek, CA 96040; 530/335-7400; website: www.ripplingwaters.com.

Rippling Waters Resort

6. PADILLA'S RIM ROCK RESORT

Padilla's Rim Rock Resort is named after the Hat Creek Rim of the northern Lassen volcanic plateau country, but is better known for its proximity to Hat Creek and Lassen Volcanic National Park. Hat Creek is a fine

trout stream, well-stocked along Highway 89 to the north, with access points from several Forest Service camps along the road. But some people staying in cabins at Padilla's Rim Rock Resort just walk right across the street and start fishing. Note that the special wild trout section of Hat Creek, entirely catch-and-release using artificial lures with single barbless hooks, is located off Highway 299.

Luxury rating: 3

Recreation rating: 4

Near Lassen Volcanic National Park, off Highway 44 near Old Station

If hiking is your thing, Lassen Park, of course, is famous for its great trails, ported thermal activity, wilderness lakes, and the two-hour (one-way) Lassen summit climb, which offers an outstanding view to the north of Mount Shasta. The resort is located 14 miles from the northern park entrance at Manzanita Lake.

The cabins at Padilla's Rim Rock Resort run the gamut when it comes to quality. Two new log cabins are really quite nice and come completely furnished with everything but towels. The others range from fair to decent, including a few old cabins that are on what some would call the rustic side. But even these do fine if you're just looking for a notch up from a campground.

A little country store fronts the property, a cute place that the owners call "the biggest little store in Shasta County." A lot of trips have been salvaged thanks to that store, because no matter what you forget, it is likely to have it.

Facilities: Padilla's Rim Rock Resort has 10 cabins of varying sizes and ages. Bathrooms and kitchens with cookware and utensils are provided. Six lodge rooms are also available. A small grocery store is on the property. Call for details regarding pet policies.

Bedding: Linens are provided. Bring your own towels.

Reservations and rates: Reservations are accepted. Cabin rates range from $48 to $95 per night, depending on the size and age of cabin. Discounted weekly rates are also available. Lodge rooms are $38 per night.

Directions: From Redding, take Highway 44 east for 48 miles to the junction with Highway 44/89. Turn left (north) on Highway 44/89 and drive 14 miles to Old Station. Continue for two miles and look for Padilla's Rim Rock Resort on the right side of the road.

Contact: Padilla's Rim Rock Resort, 13275 Highway 89, Old Station, CA 96071; 530/335-7114. For fishing information, phone Vaughn's Sporting Goods in Burney at 530/335-2381.

Padilla's Rim Rock Resort

7. HAT CREEK RESORT

The major pastime here is fishing for trout—rainbows, brookies, and browns—in Hat Creek. You see, the Department of Fish and Game makes regular plants on Hat Creek along Highway 89 throughout the summer, and that keeps the fishing enthusiasts coming.

Luxury rating: 3

Recreation rating: 4

Hat Creek, off Highway 44/89 in Old Station

If fishing is not your passion, the Pacific Crest Trail runs right next to Hat Creek Resort and provides hiking options; you can go this way or you can go that way. Ten miles from the property is the northern entrance to Lassen Volcanic National Park, a must-see with plenty of hiking (including the Mt. Lassen summit climb) and exploring to do, as well as catch-and-release fishing at Manzanita Lake.

The 10 cabins at Hat Creek Resort are situated among tall pines and next to a grassy area, with Hat Creek flowing by. Cabins 3A and 4A sit right along the creek and are the most popular because of the creek views. Cabin 7 is the most private and is aptly nicknamed The Honeymoon Cottage; it's located behind the lodge and features a forest setting. The resort is located on 20 acres and is adjacent to Lassen National Forest.

Facilities: Hat Creek Resort has 10 cabins and seven lodge rooms. Cabins range from studios to three-bedrooms and can accommodate up to eight persons. Each has a fully equipped kitchen and bathroom with shower. There are no telephones or televisions. A barbecue, laundry facilities, badminton, horseshoes, complimentary wagon rides on weekends, and a restaurant and store are available. The resort is suitable for children. Pets are allowed, and smoking is permitted.

Bedding: Linens and towels are provided.

Reservations and rates: Reservations are recommended. The double-occupancy rate is $66 to $112 per night per cabin; the seventh night is free. Lodge rooms are $49 to $62 per night. Additional persons are charged $7 per person per night. There is a two-night minimum. Major credit cards are accepted.

Directions: From Redding, drive east on Highway 44 to the junction with Highway 89 (near the entrance to Lassen Volcanic National Park). Turn north on Highway 89 and drive about 12 miles to the resort entrance on the right side of the road. If you reach Old Station, you have gone one mile too far.

Contact: Hat Creek Resort, P.O. Box 73, 12533 Highway 44/89, Old Station, CA 96071; 530/335-7121.

Hat Creek Resort

8. EAGLE LAKE CABINS

With every blessing, there seems to come a curse. So it is at Eagle Lake. This lake has big trout, real big: 18- to 20-inchers on average, with five-pounders pretty common. The documented lake record was a smidgen over 11 pounds, and there are reports of even bigger fish. That is the blessing. The curse? It's the wind. It can really howl out here on the edge of the high desert in Lassen County, whipping huge yet shallow Eagle Lake to a froth, a common enough event to earn the respect of nearly every visitor.

What to do? No problem. You go and hide out in your cabin until the wind dies down—which will likely be the next morning—and then head out again. You'll book your cabin through Heritage Land Company, which operates a rental business from the little town of Spaulding Tract, set on the western shore of the lake. The 45 cabins available for rent include bathrooms, kitchens, and propane heat. Some of the cabins have views of the lake. No linens or towels are

Luxury rating: 3

Recreation rating: 4

Eagle Lake, off Highway A1 in Spaulding

provided, so you should bring a sleeping bag, pillow, and plenty of towels, or you'll be in a heck of a fix. Think of your stay here as being more like a fish camp than anything else.

The boat ramp is located only a half-mile from the cabins, making it a snap to get from bed to the lake. It's a good thing, too, because with that wind, you need to be out very early. Get out at dawn, get your fishing done, and get the heck off the water. Though there are days when it never blows (most commonly in the fall), in summer your fishing day is often over by 10 A.M. By 10:30 A.M., you're fishing on borrowed time. By 11 A.M., you're a fool. And by noon, if you're still out there and the wind is roaring, we'll start praying we don't have to fish you out of Davy Jones's locker.

Note that the fishing season at Eagle Lake is different from other areas of California. It runs from Memorial Day weekend through December 31.

Facilities: There are 45 cabins in various sizes, each with a bathroom and kitchen. Cooking utensils, dishes, and silverware are provided. A boat ramp is available 0.5 mile away. A small store is located at a nearby RV park and grocery stores are available in Spaulding Tract and Stones Landing.

Bedding: No bedding or towels are provided. Bring your own sleeping bag and towels.

Reservations and rates: Reservations are required. Cabin fees range from $50 to $125 per night, depending on the size of the cabin. Weekly rates are also available.

Directions: From Redding, drive east on Highway 44 to Highway 44/89. Turn right on Highway 44/89 and drive 45 miles to Highway 36. Continue east on Highway 36 for about four miles to County Road A1. Turn left on County Road A1 and drive to Spaulding on the shore of Eagle Lake. In Spaulding, turn right on Spaulding Road and drive 1.5 miles. Look for the sign for Heritage Land Company on the right side of the road.

Contact: Eagle Lake Cabins (Heritage Land Company), 686-920 Spaulding Road, Eagle Lake, CA 96130; 530/825-2131, fax 530/825-2139; website: www.eaglelakeheritage.com.

Eagle Lake Cabins

9. EAGLE LAKE RV PARK & CABINS

Eagle Lake RV Park & Cabins has become something of a headquarters for anglers in pursuit of Eagle Lake trout, which typically range 18 to 22 inches, the largest average trout of any lake in California. A nearby boat ramp provides access to Pelican Point and Eagle Point, where the fishing is often best in the summer. A full-service store on the premises is a great plus—and the owners have a way of stocking just what you need for your trip but forgot to bring. That also means no special trips into town for supplies are necessary. No worrying, just vacation time: lounging beside Eagle Lake, maybe catching a big trout now and then. Resident deer can be like pets here on late summer evenings, including bucks with spectacular racks. One night here, our boys, Jeremy and Kris, were stunned to see a pair of bucks with spectacular antlers walk right past as if these wild animals were tame.

Luxury rating: 2

Recreation rating: 4

Eagle Lake, off Highway A1 near Spaulding

The cabin rentals range such a wide spectrum in accommodations—from a primitive camping cabin to an all-furnished cabin—that the luxury rating should actually be 2, 3, and 4 because no one single number does the place justice. In short, there are two camping cabins (no heating nor plumbing) that can sleep up to four, one fully-furnished house that can sleep up to eight (heating, plumbing, and electricity included), one studio (with shower but without bedding) that sleeps up to four, one trailer (with shower but without bedding) that sleeps four, and one fully-furnished mobile home that sleeps four.

Eagle Lake is the second-largest natural lake in California; it borders the high desert on the edge of the Great Basin. It offers long-distance views, crystal-clear water, and native trout that are beyond compare. One downer: The wind typically howls here most summer afternoons. So get out on the water at first light, catch your fish early, and then enjoy the rest of the day exploring the area.

Facilities: Eagle Lake RV Park & Cabins has two camping cabins, one house, one studio, one trailer, and one mobile home. The house and mobile home are fully furnished, including bedding, kitchen facilities, and satellite television. There is a separate area on the property for RVs and another for tents only. Restrooms, showers, coin laundry, a sanitary disposal station, a grocery store, a recreation room, and a boat ramp are available. Leashed pets are permitted.

10. KOA LASSEN/SHINGLETOWN

This is a 12-acre KOA campground that offers its cute Kamping Kabins as a lodging option. Set at 3,900 feet in the foothills of Mt. Lassen near Shingletown, the KOA's proximity to Lassen Volcanic National Park, Burney Falls, and Hat Creek make this camp a popular spot.

Luxury rating: 1

Recreation rating: 4

Lassen Volcanic National Park, off Highway 44 in Shingletown

The small log cabins basically provide a private sleeping space. In other words, you bring a sleeping bag, pillow, food, and anything else you need. What they provide is four walls, a roof, an electrical outlet, and a heater (if needed).

The best thing about this KOA is its location, not its ambience. It doubles as a popular RV park, often filling in the summer. The cabins are set a fair distance from the camping area, and once inside a cabin, it is private and quiet. All facilities are within nearby walking distance. But the bottom line here is that it is primarily an RV park. The cabins are a bonus, along with the location. It's 14 miles from the entrance of Lassen Volcanic National Park, nearby Hat Creek provides trout fishing along Highway 89, and just inside the Highway 44 entrance station at Lassen Volcanic National Park is Manzanita Lake, providing fishing and hiking.

There's no prettier lake that you can reach by car in Lassen Volcanic National Park than Manzanita Lake, located just beyond the entrance station at the western boundary of the park. An easy hike here traces the shoreline of this pretty lake at a 5,950-foot elevation and is easily accessible from either the parking area just beyond the entrance station or from the campground. A good side trip is across the road to Reflection Lake, a small and also beautiful lake; including this one in your hike only adds about half a mile to the trip. Note that the fishery at Manzanita Lake is managed as a special wild trout fishery. That means there are no stocks. It also means that bait and hooks with barbs are prohibited. Instead, use artificials only with single, barbless hooks. Most anglers here are fly fishers, fishing from float tubes or prams.

Facilities: KOA Lassen/Shingletown has four camping cabins (three one-room cabins and one two-room cabin). Each cabin has primitive beds, electric heat, barbecue, and deck. A restroom with showers, coin laundry, a heated swimming pool, and a small store are available. Volleyball, horseshoes, a playground, and a petting zoo are available nearby. Pets are not permitted. Smoking is not allowed.

Bedding: No linens are provided. You must bring a sleeping bag and pillow.

Reservations and rates: Reservations are recommended (call 800/562-3403). The rate is $40 per night for two per one-room cabin and $55 for a two-room cabin. Open year-round.

Directions: From Redding, turn east on Highway 44 and drive to Shingletown. In Shingletown, continue east for four miles and look for the KOA sign.

Contact: KOA Lassen/Shingletown, 7749 KOA Road, Shingletown, CA 96088; 530/474-3133; website: www.koa.com or www.shingletown.com.

11. MILL CREEK PARK

Mill Creek Park is set up primarily for RVs, but has an area with small cabins and another with tent sites. It's small and intimate,

Luxury rating: 2

Recreation rating: 4

Lassen Volcanic National Park, off Highway 44 in Shingletown

the owners are friendly and helpful, and they'll tell you that is exactly how they plan on keeping it. The elevation is 4,000 feet, and the place is set amid towering pines and large oaks on the western slopes of Mt. Lassen. The proximity to Lassen Volcanic National Park represents a key attraction.

Mill Creek Park covers 15 acres and includes a great two-acre pond for fishing for bass or trout, as well as a pretty stream and a small waterfall. There are some easy walking trails on the property as well. With luck, you might catch a glimpse of some of the local wildlife that abounds in the area, including deer, sometimes black bears, and the rare antelope.

The cabins are rustic but cheap, and since the draw here is good hiking and fishing, most visitors don't mind. The four cabins are set in the middle of a small campground which has seven tent sites and 16 RV sites. All cabins have heating (two with propane, two with electric) and two have bathrooms. For the two cabins that do not have bathrooms, it is only a 15-foot walk to bathrooms. Each cabin also has a barbecue. For groups and families, a group picnic area with a massive barbecue is available across a meadow, about a quarter-mile away. The road up to it is easy and wheelchair-accessible.

The park is 14 miles from the entrance to Lassen Volcanic National Park and Manzanita Lake. Another popular getaway is the drive on Highway 89 past the foot of Mt. Lassen to the steaming mud pots, called Bumpass Hell. In addition, nearby Grace and Nora Lakes are rich in local history, including the ruins of a castle built by a local land baron many years ago, and Lake Macumber and Lake Almanor provide good fishing for bass and trout.

Facilities: Mill Creek RV Park has four cabins, two with bathrooms. A laundry room, a group picnic area, a fishing pond, and a creek are available nearby. Leashed pets are permitted.

Bedding: Linens and towels are not provided. Bring your sleeping bag, pillow, and towels.

Reservations and rates: Reservations are recommended and a deposit is required. The rate is $35 for cabins without bathrooms and $50 for cabins with bathrooms; the seventh night is free. Major credit cards are accepted. Open year-round.

Directions: From Redding, drive east on Highway 44 to Shingletown. In Shingletown, continue east on Highway 44 for two miles to the campground.

Contact: Mill Creek Park, Shingletown, P.O. Box 267, Shingletown, CA 96088; 530/474-5384, fax 530/474-1236; website: www.millcreekrvpark.com.

Mill Creek Park

12. DRAKESBAD GUEST RANCH

This is it. The kind of place you've fantasized about: a quintessential, picture-perfect rustic lodge with cabins located in one of the most

beautiful meadows in California, secluded and low-key. This place really exists. At 5,700 feet in elevation, it's Drakesbad Guest Ranch.

There's just one problem: It takes about two years to get a reservation—unless you get lucky and happen to squeeze in at the last minute because someone else canceled their trip, which occurs occasionally each summer.

This place is unique in every way. Once you book a stay, expect rustic, modest accommodations on a guest ranch built in the late 1800s. It has been updated, of course, and is well-furnished, cozy, and peaceful. The meals are also excellent. Finding these qualities in such a remote setting always comes as a pleasant surprise to newcomers. After all, the road in is long, twisty, and dusty, and the place is set

Luxury rating: 2

Recreation rating: 5

Lassen Volcanic National Park, off Highway 89 near Chester

on the edge of wilderness in a remote sector of a national park. That is why many celebrities have stayed here; the lodge provides a genuine hideaway where you aren't bugged by anything. In addition, the management is first-class, with a focus on quality of service.

All meals are provided in the lodge's dining room; vegetarian meals are available. Barbecues take place every Wednesday. Since there's no electricity in the cabins, kerosene lamps and propane heat are used. Leave your electrical appliances at home. But do bring your swimsuits—Drakesbad Guest Ranch was named for the warm water hot springs that fill the pool. The springs keep the pool temperature toasty all summer.

The ranch has horse stables and daily guided rides are provided for an extra fee. Fly fishing and lessons in nearby Hot Springs Creek are also available; you can buy a fishing license at the ranch.

The hiking is unusual and fairly easy, with the highlight a 4.4 mile round-trip walk to Devils Kitchen. The trail leads directly from the lodge. You'll encounter steaming vents and boiling mud pots and fumaroles. For safety reasons, it is illegal to walk off the trail in this area.

So, don't you feel lucky?

© THE CALIFORNIA PARKS CO.

Facilities: Drakesbad Guest Ranch has four cabins, eight bungalows, one duplex, and six lodge rooms. There are no kitchen facilities, but the lodge provides three meals a day that are included in your rental rate. All units include a toilet and sink. Some have a shower, and a bathhouse is available. A pool, a restaurant, laundry facilities, horseback riding and lessons, fly fishing guide and lessons, volleyball, table tennis, horseshoes, badminton, and croquet are available. A canoe is available at Dream Lake, a five-minute walk from the lodge. The ranch is suitable for children. No pets are allowed. Smoking is permitted.

Bedding: Linens and towels are provided and there is daily maid service.

Reservations and rates: Reservations are required and there is at least a two-year waiting list. The rate is per person, but based on double occupancy of adults, with additional charges for extra people, but that charge varies according to whether the extra guest is a child or an adult. The rate is $108 to $153 per adult per night or $648 to $945 per adult per week. For ages 2 to 11, the fee is $70 per night or $420 per week. Additional persons are $91 to $104 per night. All prices include three meals a day. A $10 national park entrance fee is added to each reservation. Holders of a Golden Eagle Pass or Lassen Volcanic National Park annual pass will be waived the $10 entrance fee. Open early June to mid-October, weather permitting.

Directions: From Red Bluff, take Highway 36 east for 44 miles to the junction with Highway 89 (do not turn left on Highway 89 to Lassen Volcanic National Park entrance, as signed). Continue east on Highway 36/89 to Chester. In Chester, turn left (north) on Feather River Drive (Warner Valley Road). Drive .75 mile to County Road 312. Bear left and drive six miles to Warner Valley Road. Turn right and drive 11.5 miles to the resort. Note: The last 3.5 miles are unpaved.

Contact: Drakesbad Guest Ranch, 2150 North Main Street, Suite 5, Red Bluff, CA 96080; 530/529-1512, fax 530/529-4511; website: www.drakesbad.com. From June to October, you can reach the lodge by contacting an AT&T operator and asking for Drakesbad #2 toll station, 530 area code.

Drakesbad Guest Ranch

13. SPANISH SPRINGS RANCH

From our vantage points in the saddles, we could just make out the silhouette of a lone rider on horseback. Our horses let out a few snorts. "Good horsey," we each pleaded. But no amount of "good horseys" could calm them. We scanned across the ranch. We were alone. Then the horses snorted again. Nervous. They seemed to recognize this lone rider. Who could it be? A lone outlaw gunman? Nope. It turned out to be the guy who feeds them every night at the ranch.

The ranch, in this case, was Spanish Springs Ranch, a huge spread in northeastern California's Madeline Plains, high-desert sagebrush country where there are still miles and miles to roam on horseback, cows to tend, and steaks to eat. This is cowboy country.

We rode in and dismounted, attempting to walk as if our butts didn't hurt, and then sauntered into the ranch house. After our prodigious appetites had been satisfied with giant T-bone steaks, our group broke up to get a little shut-eye. Some stayed in log cabins, others in suites with kitchenettes, and still others in private rooms in the bunkhouse. In the darkness, we were just about to drift off to sleep when we began to consider the business of tomorrow.

Luxury rating: 3

Recreation rating: 5

Ravendale, off U.S. 395 near Susanville

What to do? We could roam off to find a herd of antelope. We could do some fishing. We could go for a trail ride, maybe head up the hills for a panoramic view of the high desert.

In the fall, during the waterfowl season, Spanish Springs provides an excellent location for hunting geese. This is also when the major cattle drives and horse drives are scheduled (lasting six nights and seven days), when it really does feel something like the Old West, complete with sore butt. Other possible activities include a hay-wagon ride, archery, trapshooting, swimming, and tennis. Overnighters and trail riders are always welcome.

Facilities: Spanish Springs Ranch has four log cabins, 14 suites with kitchenettes, six duplex units, and three private rooms in a bunkhouse. Bathrooms are provided, but kitchens are not available except in the suites. All meals are provided ranch-style. The ranch is suitable for children. Leashed pets are allowed at the main ranch but not at the working cattle ranch.

Bedding: Linens are provided.

Reservations and rates: Reservations are accepted. Cabin rates are $145 per night, including all meals and activities. A room in the bunkhouse is $120 per night, a duplex room is $125 per night, and the suites are $135 per night, all including meals and activities.

Directions: From Red Bluff, turn east on Highway 36 and drive 107 miles to Susanville. From Susanville, turn east on U.S. 395 and drive 17 miles to Litchfield. From Litchfield, continue north on U.S. 395 for about 30 miles. Look for the signed entrance road (three flagpoles and lighted sign) to Spanish Springs Ranch on the right side of the road.

Contact: Spanish Springs Ranch, P.O. Box 70, Ravendale, CA 96123; 530/234-2150 or 800/272-8282.

Spanish Springs Ranch

14. MCGOVERN'S CHALETS

We include McGovern's Chalets in this book simply because there are so few large cabins and cottages to rent in this area, the southern gateway to Lassen Volcanic National Park. If you're looking for privacy and quiet in a wilderness or rural setting, then these three rentals are probably not suitable for you. But if you're looking for a large cabin or several cabins to house a family or group, with kitchen facilities and bathrooms included, then consider these two-story chalets. All have the basic amenities you need, except for laundry facilities. And the kitchens are a bonus, since dining options are limited around here.

You're within easy driving distance to Lassen Volcanic National Park, Lake Almanor, and Mill Creek. Day trips to these areas promise hiking, fishing, and exploring galore. In the winter, you can cross-country ski, snowshoe, or snowmobile close by.

Luxury rating: 3

Recreation rating: 3

*Lassen Volcanic National Park,
off Highway 36 in Mineral*

Facilities: McGovern's Chalets has three cabins with fully equipped kitchens, three or four bedrooms, living room, dining room, and bathroom. The cabins have decks or patios, and barbecues are provided during the summer, but bring your own charcoal. Woodstoves and firewood are provided. There are no telephones or televisions. The cabins are suitable for children. Leashed pets are allowed. Smoking is permitted.

Bedding: Pillows, blankets, and quilts are provided, but linens and towels are not provided; bring your own or rent linens and towels for an extra fee.

Reservations and rates: Reservations are recommended. The rate is $80 to $150 per night per cabin, or up to $700 per week per cabin for up to 10 persons. Guests ages 12 to 18 are $5 per person per night, and children ages 11 and under are free. Additional persons are $20 per person per night. There is a $50 deposit for pets. Holiday rates are higher. Major credit cards are accepted.

Directions: From Red Bluff, drive 43 miles east on Highway 36 to the town of Mineral and Highway 172. Turn right on Highway 172 and drive one-half block to Mt. Lassen Avenue. Turn right and drive one-half block to Scenic Avenue. Turn right and drive .25 mile to the cabins on the right at 38228, 38234, and 38240 Scenic Avenue.

Contact: McGovern's Chalets, 563 McClay Road, Novato, CA 94947; 530/595-3241, 415/613-8377, or 415/897-8377; website: www.mtlassenchalets.com.

McGovern's Chalets

15. MILL CREEK RESORT

Here's a place on the threshold of Lassen Volcanic National Park and near Lassen National Forest. It sits in the middle of a great outdoor recreation area, with good fishing and hiking nearby. We looked long and hard to find such a place.

It turned out to be Mill Creek Resort, and it is just unknown enough that cabins are usually available. It sits east of Red Bluff at 4,800 feet in elevation, just off remote Highway 172, a little loop

Luxury rating: 3

Recreation rating: 3

Near Lassen Volcanic National Park, off Highway 172 near Mineral

road off the main highway that bypasses Morgan Summit. The reason the resort gets missed by so many is that nobody takes the Highway 172 bypass by accident. In addition, there are no other businesses of any kind on Highway 172. So right off, you have a relatively secret spot.

The resort features nine rustic cabins, all sized at one or two bedrooms complete with a small kitchen and bathroom, at inexpensive rates. The cabins have been around for decades and haven't been refurbished.

A highlight here is nearby Mill Creek, and we mean the stream, not the town. The lodge owners can provide specific directions to the parking area and trailhead on your visit. It's great to take an evening walk along the stream, which babbles and wends its way around rocks and into pools.

Sooner or later, however, you will find yourself making the 15-minute drive north to the entrance of Lassen Volcanic National Park, then exploring for at least a day or two.

Facilities: Mill Creek Resort has nine one- and two-bedroom cabins with bathrooms, kitchens, and propane heat. One cabin has a fireplace. Pets are permitted. A small grocery store and coffee shop are available at the lodge.

Bedding: Linens are provided.

Reservations and rates: Reservations are accepted. Cabin rates are $55 per night for a one-room cabin, $85 per night for a two-room cabin, with no minimum stay required (except for three-day holiday weekends). Major credit cards are accepted.

Directions: From I-5 at Red Bluff, take the Highway 36 exit and drive east on Highway 36 to the town of Mineral. In Mineral, turn right on Highway 172 and drive six miles to the town of Mill Creek. In Mill Creek, look for the sign for Mill Creek Resort on the right side of the road.

Contact: Mill Creek Resort, No. 1, Highway 172, Mill Creek, CA 96061; 530/595-4449; website: www.millcreekresort.net. For a map, ask for Lassen National Forest and send $6 to U.S. Forest Service, Attn: Map Sales, P.O. Box 587, Camino, CA 95709; 530/647-5390, fax 530/647-5389; or visit the website:

16. CHILDS MEADOW RESORT

Do you dream about sitting on a cabin deck overlooking a picturesque meadow with mountains in the background? Well, you can do just that at Childs Meadow Resort (and your view is of Mt. Brokeoff).

Luxury rating: 3

Recreation rating: 4

Lassen Volcanic National Park, off Highway 36 in Mill Creek

This 18-acre resort at 5,000 feet in elevation has a lot to offer. The two-bedroom chalets are spaced closely together and have full kitchens and bathrooms, with outside decks and porches. They are centrally located and are open year-round.

In the summer, there are plenty of recreation opportunities. You can fish (catch-and-release only) or hike along Mill Creek, one mile away. The trailhead for the Spencer Meadow Trail is just east of the resort alongside Highway 36, and it's a 10-mile round-trip to Spencer Meadow and an effervescent spring that is the source of Mill Creek. Horse corrals are available at the resort and there are a number of riding trails in the area.

In the winter, you can cross-country ski or snowshoe right from the resort. Rentals are available, and winter backcountry touring by snowmobile is offered for an additional fee.

Facilities: Childs Meadow Resort has seven two-bedroom chalets, 16 motel rooms, and a campground. Chalets have fully equipped kitchens and bathrooms with shower/tubs. A restaurant, summer laundry facilities, a convenience store, horse corrals, cross-country ski rentals, a bathhouse, a tennis court, a group picnic area, horseshoe pits, a meeting room, and a wedding or reunion area are available. The resort is suitable for children. Leashed pets are allowed. Smoking is permitted in the chalets, but not in the motel rooms.

Bedding: Linens and towels are provided, but if you bring your own you receive a discount.

17. PLUMAS PINES RESORT

Many of the cabin and cottage rentals at Lake Almanor are on the east side of the lake, but Plumas Pines Resort is on the west side. Its one- and two-bedroom cottages with kitchens are popular and often book up a year in advance during the summer season. Set about 40 feet apart, the cabins are almost 800 square feet in size. They have been around for decades, and not much remodeling has taken place. A view of the lake can be seen from most of the cabins, and the lake access is just a short walk across the road.

© SUZ BRAKKEN

Plumas Pines is a full-service resort with lodge rooms, an RV park, and live music on weekends, so don't expect a serene setting with lots of privacy. What you do get, however, is service and convenience. You can come here for a week and probably never have to leave the resort for supplies.

A swimming beach is available, but is only usable when the lake level is not down. All types of boating are permitted, including personal watercraft riding. Besides the myriad of boating and fishing available on the lake, you can hike or bike on the Lake Almanor Recreation Trail, a 9.5-mile paved trail that more or less parallels the shoreline of the lake.

Luxury rating: 3

Recreation rating: 4

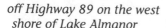

off Highway 89 on the west shore of Lake Almanor

Facilities: Plumas Pines Resort has seven cottages, nine lodging rooms, and an RV park. The cottages have fully equipped kitchens and bathrooms. A barbecue, picnic table, and gas fireplace are provided. Televisions are provided, but telephones are not. Laundry facilities, a waterfront restaurant, a convenience store, a full-service marina, and boat rentals are available. The resort is suitable for children. No pets are allowed. Smoking is permitted.

Bedding: Linens and towels are provided, but there is no daily maid service.

Reservations and rates: Reservations are recommended for up to a year in advance during the summer. Cottages are $85 to $105 per night or $595 to $735 per week. An additional fee of $5 per person per night is charged for more than four persons. There is a two-night minimum on weekends and a three-night minimum on holidays. Major credit cards are accepted. The resort is open from mid-April through October.

Directions: From Red Bluff, take Highway 36 east for 44 miles to the junction with Highway 89. Continue east on Highway 36/89 to Lake Almanor and the next junction with Highway 89 (two miles before reaching Chester). Turn right on Highway 89 and drive five miles to Lake Almanor West Road. Turn left and drive one mile to the resort on the left.

Contact: Plumas Pines Resort, 3000 Almanor Drive West, Canyon Dam, CA 95923; 530/259-4343, fax 530/259-3216.

Plumas Pines Resort

18. KNOTTY PINE RESORT

Most people who stay at Knotty Pine Resort either bring a boat, rent a boat, or do both. The activities are oriented towards boating, sailing, and fishing, and most visitors spend a lot of time on the water. The average water temperature during the summer is between 60°F and 70°F. As with most lake resorts, they book up early during the summer months.

Luxury rating: 3

Recreation rating: 4

Lake Almanor, off Highway 36 near Chester

The resort is located on a peninsula on the east side of the lake. The lakefront log cabins are painted dark brown with red doors; the inside, of course, has knotty pine paneling. They come in one- and two-bedroom sizes and are about 500 square feet. The one bedroom has a queen bed and the two-bedroom has a queen bed and two twin beds. These are traditional cabins but they've been refurbished, so you'll have simple, updated appliances and fixtures. There is also a house available that is about 700 square feet with two bedrooms, dining area, living room, and fireplace insert. The house sleeps six people and has a patio. The resort also has an RV park.

Facilities: Knotty Pine Resort has five cabins and one house with fully equipped kitchen, including microwave. The bathrooms have been refurbished and have a tub/shower. Barbecues, a deck or porch, a picnic table, and boat slip are provided. A recreation room, a full-service marina, bait and tackle, boat rentals, television, table tennis, and board games are available. The resort is suitable for children. Leashed pets are allowed. No smoking is permitted.

Bedding: Linens and towels are provided.

Reservations and rates: Reservations are recommended. The fee is $100 to $110 per night per cabin or $600 to $660 per week. Call the resort for pet fees. There is a one-week minimum from June through August. Major credit cards are accepted. Open May through early October.

Directions: From Red Bluff, take Highway 36 east to Chester and continue for five miles to Highway A-13. Turn right and drive two miles to Peninsula Drive. Turn right and drive approximately two miles to the resort on the left.

Contact: Knotty Pine Resort, 430 Peninsula Drive, Lake Almanor, CA 96137; 530/596-3348, fax 530/596-4404; website: www.knottypine.net.

OTHER CABIN AND COTTAGE RENTALS NEARBY

• Lake Almanor Resort, 2706 Big Springs Road, Lake Almanor, CA 96137; 530/596-3337; website: www.lakealmanor resort.homestead.com.

• Almanor Lakeside Resort, 300 Peninsula Drive, Lake Almanor, CA 96137; 530/596-3959; website: www.lakealmanor resorts.com.

• Almanor Lakefront Village and Almanor Lakeside Resort, 318 Peninsula Drive, Lake Almanor, CA 96137; 530/596-3959; website: www.lakealmanorresorts.com.

• Wilson's Camp Prattville Resort, 2932 Lake Almanor Drive West, Canyon Dam, CA 95923; 530/259-2267; website: www.camp-prattville.com.

• Vagabond Resort, 7371 Highway 147, Lake Almanor, CA 96137; 530/596-3240.

Knotty Pine Resort

19. LITTLE NORWAY RESORT

This resort has been around for decades, and it's established itself as a full-service, friendly establishment. People return to Little Norway Resort year after year, and for that reason you need to make reservations early.

What Little Norway Resort offers are nine one- to four-bedroom cabins surrounded by tall pine trees on the eastern side of Lake Almanor. They can accommodate up to 10 persons per rental and

Luxury rating: 3

Recreation rating: 4

Lake Almanor, off Highway 36 near Chester

they're set up for groups due to their close proximity to one another; in some cases, cabins are spaced only several feet apart. The cabins are small with knotty pine paneling and are modestly decorated; not much updating has occurred over the years. The mobile homes are more contempary than the cabins, with more updated kitchens. The houses are the most spacious and inviting of the rentals. One two-story house has wood paneling, a vaulted ceiling, and an open stairway; it has the classic mountain cabin look and feel. All of the rentals have decks.

The cabins are within a couple hundred feet of the lake and marina, making it easy to access the lake and its activities. You can dock your boat here, and there's easy access for getting on and off the lake, which is set at 4,500 feet in elevation. The resort is situated in a protected cove and it boasts the lake's largest boat fleet; you can rent everything from fishing boats to pontoon boats and from water-ski boats to personal watercrafts. You'll have 52 miles of shoreline to explore at Lake Almanor. This is one of the truly outstanding fishing lakes in Northern California and first-class guides are available for outings.

Facilities: Little Norway Resort has nine cabins, two houses, and two mobile homes. Fully equipped kitchens and full bathrooms with shower are provided. Barbecues, decks, and a boat slip are provided, and some units have woodstoves. A full service marina, bait and tackle, and boat rentals are available. The resort is suitable for children. Leashed pets are allowed. Smoking is permitted.

Bedding: Linens and towels are not provided, but blankets and pillows are provided. There is no daily maid service.

Reservations and rates: Reservations are recommended. The fee is $70 to $135 per night per cabin or $420 to $810 per week. There is a one-week minimum for the smaller cabins during the summer, and a three-night minimum for all cabins during summer holidays. Additional persons are charged $5 per night per person or $30 per week; the additional fee kicks in for the third person for one-bedroom rentals, for the fifth person for a two-bedroom rental, and for the seventh person for a four-bedroom rental. The pet fee is $5 per night or $30 per week. Major credit cards are accepted.

Directions: From Red Bluff, take Highway 36 east to Chester and continue for five miles to Highway A-13. Turn right and drive two miles to Peninsula Drive. Turn right and drive two miles to the resort on the left.

Contact: Little Norway Resort, 432 Peninsula Drive, Lake Almanor, CA 96137; 530/596-3225; website: www.littlenorway.net.

Little Norway Resort

20. LASSEN VIEW RESORT

Some people go cabin camping for one reason: They can do all the things they can't do at home. Dirty clothes on the floor? Who cares! Dirty dishes stacked up in the sink? Perfect place for them! Fishing equipment scattered everywhere? Easier to keep track of! A few empty bottles and cans? Easier to dispose of all at once!

Luxury rating: 3

Recreation rating: 4

Lake Almanor, off Highway 36 near Chester

Well, while not everybody is a slob when they go camping, you certainly have the chance to be one at Lassen View Resort at Lake Almanor. This is a place where you just tend not to worry about anything except the weather and having a good time. And whereas a fair number of families stay here in the summer, it is better known as the number-one fishing and hunting retreat around in the spring and fall, respectively. Guess what? Nobody turns into bigger slobs faster than a group of anglers or hunters when they have the chance.

The cabins are rustic and set in a campground located on the eastern shore of Lake Almanor, a five-minute boat drive from one of the best fishing spots on the lake at Big Springs. This is a classic fish camp; that is, it has everything for the angler, including cabins, a tackle shop, a store, and a small marina with boat ramp and boat rentals. And there are guides and all the advice you can listen to.

Almanor is a very pretty lake, big (13 miles long) and often full, ringed by pines and firs, and set at 4,500 feet near Lassen National Forest. Chester, the small town at the north end of the lake, has supplies and a few restaurants, as well as a small airport. Nearby, there are many other recreation options, including a remote and beautiful section of Lassen Volcanic National Park, Butt Lake, the Feather River, and thousands of acres of national forest.

Facilities: Lassen View Resort has 12 cabins ranging from two to five rooms. Each includes a full kitchen (stove, refrigerator, utensils), bathroom, small deck, and fire ring with grill. A small grocery store, tackle shop, café, and coin-operated washer and dryer are available. A boat launch, dock, swimming area, small marina with boat and motor rentals, gas, and fish-cleaning facility are nearby. Pets are permitted in the cabins as long as they are attended. There is also a campground on the property. Restaurants are located in Chester, about 10 miles away.

Bedding: Linens, pillows, and towels are provided.

Reservations and rates: Reservations are recommended. Cabins range from $75 per night or $450 per week for a one-bedroom to $118 per night or $708 per week for a three-bedroom.

Directions: From I-5 at Red Bluff, turn east on Highway 36 and drive about 75 miles to the junction with Highway 89. Bear north on Highway 89/36 and as you approach the lake, continue straight on Highway 36. Drive through Chester and across the spillway at the north end of the lake. One mile past a lakeside rest stop, turn right (south) on County Road A13 and drive about four miles. The road will cross over the Hamilton Branch, then junction with Highway 147. Turn right and drive about one mile. Look for the large sign on the right side of the road for Lassen View Resort.

Contact: Lassen View Resort, 7457 Highway 147, Lake Almanor, CA 96137; 530/596-3437. For fishing guides, contact Roger Keeling, 530/258-2283 or Mark Jiminez, 530/596-3072.

Lassen View Resort

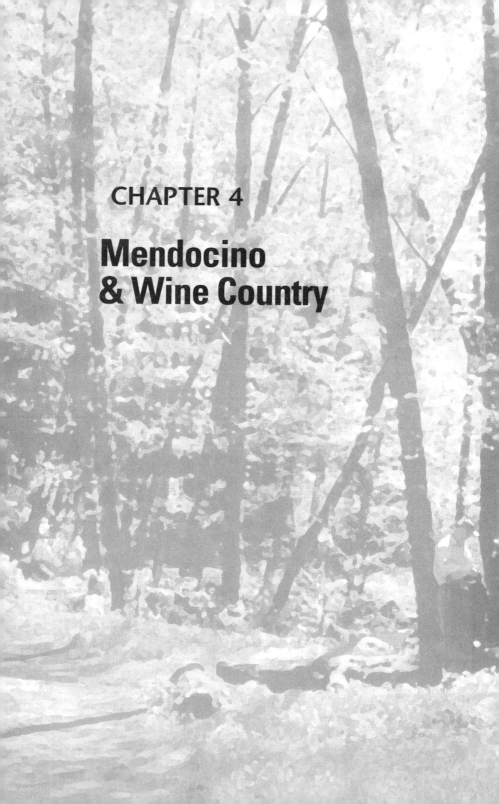

CHAPTER 4

Mendocino
& Wine Country

*F*or many people, this region offers the best possible combination of geography, weather, and outdoor activities around.
The Mendocino coast is dramatic and remote, with several
stellar state parks for hiking, while Sonoma Valley, in the heart
of wine country, produces some of the most popular wines in
the world. Add in the self-indulgent options of mud baths and
hot springs at Calistoga and a dash of mainstream recreation
at Clear Lake, Lake Berryessa, or any other lake, and you have
a capsule summary of why the Mendocino coast and the wine
country have turned into getaway favorites.

For the most part, this area is where people go for romance, fine cuisine, great wine, mineral springs, and anything else that comes to mind spur-of-the-moment. To accommodate this type of high-end vacation, the lodging tends be pricey, especially in the Sonoma and Napa Valleys. You pay for your pleasures here. Auberge du Soleil has freestanding cottages that cost up to $3,000 per night, the most expensive rental in Northern California that we could find. The Heritage House is another romantic getaway where you can reward yourself without being too price conscious.

This region wouldn't be the best of both worlds if there weren't options on the other end of spectrum. Inexpensive cabins, primarily set up for family recreation, are available. Destinations include Clear Lake, Lake Berryessa, and Blue Lakes. If the shoe fits—and for many, it does—you can have a great time fishing, boating, and waterskiing.

The coast features a series of romantic hideaways, and excellent adventuring and hiking. The Fort Bragg area alone has three state parks, all with outstanding recreation, including several easy hikes, many amid redwoods and along pretty streams. Fort Bragg also offers excellent fishing out of Noyo Harbor.

The driving tour of Highway 1 along the coast here is the fantasy of many, and it can live up to that fantasy if you don't mind the twists and turns of the road. Along the way, there are dozens of hidden beaches and untouched coastline where you can stop and explore and maybe play tag with the waves. The prize spots are MacKerricher State Park, Salt Point State Park, and Anchor Bay.

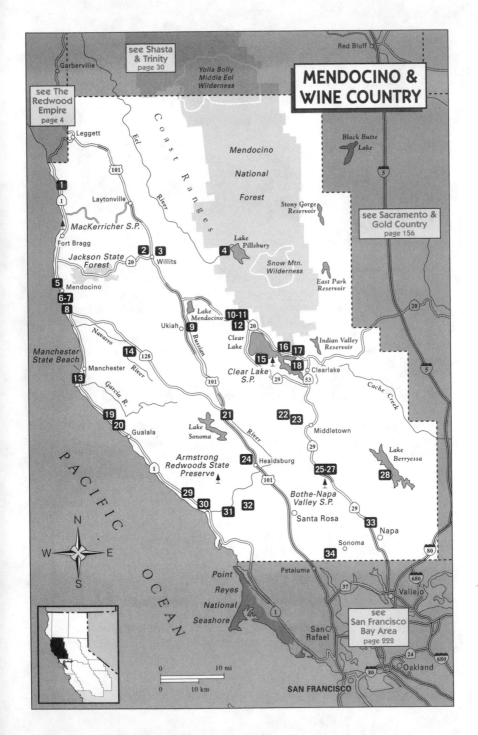

MENDOCINO & WINE COUNTRY

see Shasta
& Trinity
page 30

*Yolla Bolly
Middle Eel
Wilderness*

Red Bluff

Black Butte
Lake

see The
Redwood
Empire
page 4

Garberville

Leggett

Mendocino

National

Forest

Laytonville

MacKerricher S.P.

Fort Bragg

*Jackson State
Forest*

2 **3**

Willits

Stony Gorge
Reservoir

*Lake
Pillsbury*

4

see Sacramento &
Gold Country
page 156

*Snow Mtn.
Wilderness*

*East Park
Reservoir*

5

Mendocino

6-7

8

Navarro

Ukiah

*Lake
Mendocino*

9

10-11

12

*Clear
Lake*

*Indian Valley
Reservoir*

Manchester
State Beach

14

Manchester

13

Garcia R.

Russian

River

*Clear Lake
S.P.*

15

16 **17**

18

Clearlake

Cache Creek

19

20

Gualala

*Lake
Sonoma*

21

River

22 **23**

Middletown

*Lake
Berryessa*

28

*Armstrong
Redwoods State
Preserve*

24

Healdsburg

25-27

*Bothe-Napa
Valley S.P.*

29

30

31 **32**

Santa Rosa

33

Napa

Sonoma

34

P A C I F I C

O C E A N

Petaluma

Vallejo

*Point
Reyes
National
Seashore*

San
Rafael

see
San Francisco
Bay Area
page 222

Oakland

0   10 mi

0   10 km

SAN FRANCISCO

CHAPTER 4
MENDOCINO & WINE COUNTRY

1. HOWARD CREEK RANCH

Imagine this: A beautiful ocean-view cottage with a woodstove fired up when you want it, a hot tub and sauna, a 30-second walk to a long, pristine beach—all on the remote northern Mendocino coast, one of the most divine stretches of ocean frontage anywhere.

Luxury rating: 3

Recreation rating: 4

Mendocino Coast, off Highway 1 near Westport

Although life can't be like this all the time, it can last for as long as you decide to stay at Howard Creek Ranch. There are four cabins among its accommodations, including two with small, private hot tubs on the decks. There are also four rooms available in a renovated barn, and four more in the lodge. A central hot tub and sauna are available; guests usually take turns on an individual couple basis, so privacy is always retained.

Everything near the cabins is cozy, pretty (flowers everywhere), and quiet. The grounds cover 40 acres with a year-round creek. The ranch is a county-designated registered historical site, with a farmhouse built in 1871.

Yet all is not surreal. Those horses, llamas, sheep, cows, cats, and dogs roaming and grazing at the ranch are the real thing. One of the bonuses here is that you can go for a private horseback ride, right down to the beach. What? You say riding a horse makes your butt sore? No problem: You can schedule a professional massage instead.

The property adjoins Westport Union Landing State Beach, about a 30-second walk from the cabins across the road and down to the beach. It's a long, sandy beach, and at low tide you can walk it for three miles. No, yer not dreamin'. From the cabins, the ocean is close enough not only to see, but to hear.

Facilities: Howard Creek Ranch has four cabins, four rooms in a lodge, and four rooms in a renovated barn. Each cabin has a woodstove and bathroom (one has a nice outhouse); three have refrigerators and microwaves. Two cabins have a hot tub on their decks. Full ranch-style breakfast is provided. Barbecues are available. A hot tub and sauna (swimsuits optional) are available, usually on a private basis. Horseback rides to Richochet Ridge are available. A grocery store is available three miles to the south in Westport.

Bedding: Linens and towels are provided.

2. WILLITS KOA

One of the highlights of Willits is the Skunk Train, which makes a classic trip to Fort Bragg on the Pacific Coast. What some do is reserve one of the camping cabins at Willits KOA, then get up the next morning, rested and eager, and take the train ride over to the coast. Some even spend the night at Fort Bragg, then return the next day to Willits. The depot for the Skunk Train is within walking distance of the KOA.

Luxury rating: 2

Recreation rating: 3

off U.S. 101 near Willits

The little cabins at the KOA basically provide a sleeping space and privacy. The rest is like camping: You bring your sleeping bag and pillow and have the use of the facilities on the property. The cabins rate high on the cuteness scale and have become very popular, and for many, it's one of the best bargains of summer when out on a road-touring vacation. This KOA is one of the better ones for youngsters, since it boasts a swimming pool, a fish pond, miniature golf, and a small petting zoo.

Willits itself isn't exactly a vacation destination. It's a small town set at 1,377 feet in the foothills north of the Sonoma Valley amid rolling oak woodlands.

It's called the "Gateway to the Redwoods," but the big redwood groves are about an hour's drive to the north. Worth equal consideration is the drive on Highway 20 over to Fort Bragg, often one of California's most enjoyable driving tours, crossing from foothills to forest to sea.

Other nearby attractions include golf at the Brooktrails Golf Course, wine tasting at seven wineries within close range, and the Black Bart Casino, located about five minutes from the park.

Facilities: Willits KOA has 12 cabins. Each cabin has primitive beds, electric heat and an electrical outlet, a barbecue, a deck, and a swing. A campground is on-site with a restroom with showers, a playground, a swimming pool, hayrides, miniature golf, basketball, volleyball, a fishing pond, and a grocery store. No smoking is permitted. Pets are not allowed in the cabins.

Bedding: Linens are not provided. You must bring a sleeping bag and pillow.

Reservations and rates: Reservations are recommended (call 800/562-8542). The rate is $45 per night for two, $4 for each additional adult, and $3 per night for those ages 7 to 17. Major credit cards are accepted. Open year-round.

Directions: From Willits at the junction of U.S. 101 and Highway 20, turn west on Highway 20 and drive 1.5 miles to the campground.

Contact: Willits KOA, P.O. Box 946, Willits, CA 95490; 707/459-6179, fax 707/459-1489; website: www.koa.com.

Willits KOA

3. EMANDAL FARM

It's not Old MacDonald's Farm, it's Emandal Farm—and it's gone organic. You'll still hear a moo-moo here and an oink-oink there, because cows, pigs, sheep, chickens, ducks, and turkeys live here on 1,000 acres of farmland and wooded open space bordering Mendocino National Forest.

Luxury rating: 2

Recreation rating: 4

off U.S. 101 near Willits

What you get is pretty incredible: a primitive, redwood cabin; family-style meals served in a dining room; access to three miles of Eel River frontage; a five-acre bass lake; and the run of a working farm and its miles of wide open space. And if you want to stay here, your only choices are August and September, since the farm is used for various group camps the remainder of the summer. So here's a quick economics lesson: demand exceeds supply, so if you want a cabin, cross your fingers and call in early January; otherwise you'll probably end up on the waiting list.

This is a lot like camping because the cabins were built in the early 1900s, and not much has changed over the years. Each cabin has cold spring water, electricity, and queen beds and bunk beds. A central bathhouse and restroom are available. Complimentary home-style meals are served three times a day, except for Sunday, when only one meal is prepared. Most of the food, including the meat, is grown organically on the farm. Fresh bread is made almost daily.

So what do you do? You swim in one of several swimming holes, you hike, you read, you lounge in a hammock, you spend time with your family. That's what it's all about. And if you feel like helping out with farm chores, you can pick berries, gather eggs, or dig potatoes. There's always a list of chores; of course, you can do absolutely nothing if you want.

Facilities: Emandal Farm has 17 cabins and three inn rooms. There are no kitchen facilities, but three meals per day Monday through Saturday and a meal on Sunday are provided. A central bathhouse with hot showers and restrooms are available; the inn rooms have private bathrooms. Cold spring water and electricity are provided in the cabins. A small lake with canoes is available. The farm is suitable for children. Pets are not allowed. No smoking is permitted. Some facilities are wheelchair accessible.

Bedding: Linens and blankets are provided but towels are not.

Reservations and rates: Reservations are recommended. The fee is $705 to $868 per week per adult, and $118 to $464 per week for children, depending on age; call for nightly rates. Prices include most meals. Children under the age of two are free. A 10 percent service charge is added to the final bill. There is a two-night minimum on weekends. Major credit cards are accepted. Open August and September only.

Directions: From U.S. 101 in Willits, turn east on East Commercial Street and drive 1.5 miles to a Y intersection. Bear left onto Hearst Willits Road/County Road 306 and drive 1.6 miles to Canyon Road/County Road 308. Drive straight ahead onto Canyon Road, cross a narrow bridge, then continue 4.3 miles to a Y intersection. Turn left on Tomki Road, cross a cement bridge, and continue for 1.6 miles to a T intersection. Turn right on Hearst Willits Road and drive 5.2 miles (crossing the Eel River) to a Y intersection. Bear right at the Emandal sign and drive a short distance (bearing right) to the farm at the end of the road.

Contact: Emandal Farm, 16500 Hearst Post Office Road, Willits, CA 95490; 707/459-5439 or 800/262-9597. *Emandal Farm*

4. LAKE PILLSBURY RESORT

It seems that Lake Pillsbury is growing more popular each year, bit by bit. Not so long ago, this mountain lake had very few visitors. It has always had good weather, plenty of water, lots of trout, and good exploring in the surrounding national forest. Well, with all those attractions, it isn't surprising that more vacationers than ever before are heading here. Covering some 2,000 acres, Pillsbury is by far the largest lake in the Mendocino National Forest.

Lake Pillsbury Resort is set on the southwest shore of the lake in the heart of Mendocino National Forest. It can serve as your headquarters for a vacation involving boating, fishing, waterskiing, or biking. A

Luxury rating: 2

Recreation rating: 4

Lake Pillsbury, off Highway 20 in Mendocino National Forest

boat ramp, small marina, and full facilities make this place a prime attraction in a relatively remote location. This is the only resort on the lake that accepts reservations, and it has some lakefront sites.

If this sounds like a fishing-guy kind of getaway, well, you got it. The cabins are pretty much bulletproof, rustic jobs where you throw out your sleeping bag for the night. There are no showers, but since a campground is on the premises, you have coin-operated showers and other facilities available nearby.

Most of the attention is focused on trout in the early season. That continues into the summer, when higher temperatures drive the trout deep. The hot summer weather also gets the resident populations of bass, bluegill, and green sunfish active in the top 10 feet of water, and makes the lake ideal for swimming, especially right off the Pogie Point Campground.

Lake Pillsbury has a high density of squawfish, which may be one reason the bass grow so big. Bass love to feed on juvenile squawfish. Note that once squawfish reach a foot long, they impact the rest of the fisheries by eating the eggs and fry. There are so many squawfish in Lake Pillsbury, as well as the headwaters of the Eel River, that the Department of Fish and Game is considering many eradication programs for these waters.

Facilities: Lake Pillsbury Resort has eight rustic cabins. Kitchenettes with utensils are provided; private bathrooms are not included. A campground is on the property with coin-operated showers, boat rentals, fuel, a dock, fishing supplies, and a small marina. Pets and smoking are permitted.

Bedding: Linens and towels are not provided; bring your own sleeping bag and towels.

Reservations and rates: Reservations are recommended. The fee is $450 per week for two and $560 per week for a party of four. It is $8 exta per night per additional adult; children under 12 are free. Major credit cards are accepted. Open May through November.

Directions: From Ukiah on U.S. 101, drive north to the junction with Highway 20. Turn right (east) on Highway 20 and drive five miles to East Potter Valley Road (toward Lake Pillsbury). Turn northwest on East Potter Valley Road and drive 5.9 miles to the town of Potter Valley. Continue on East Potter Valley Road to Eel River Road. Turn right and drive 15 miles to Lake Pillsbury and Forest Road 301F. Turn right at Forest Road 301F and drive two miles to the resort.

Contact: Lake Pillsbury Resort, P.O. Box 37, Potter Valley, CA 95469; 707/743-1581, fax 707/743-2666.

Lake Pillsbury Resort

5. AGATE COVE INN

High on a bluff in beautiful Mendocino sit 10 quaint, charming cottages so appealing that they keep appearing on the covers of magazines and directories— posing as the poster cottages of the year. The reason for this is that these cottages at Agate Cove Inn have the right look, with an exquisite oceanfront location, as well as a comfortable, romantic ambience inside. In other words, they have it all.

Luxury rating: 4

Recreation rating: 4

Mendocino Coast, off Highway 1 near Mendocino

All of the cottages are not created equal, nor are they all freestanding; some are in duplex units and two rooms are located in a farmhouse. Most have decks, fireplaces, and large soaking tubs for two, but the big differences are the views; not all have ocean views. For the best views, and we mean dramatic coastline views, rent Obsidian Cottage or Emerald Cottage, located in a duplex unit. You'll pay a little more, but you get more.

Obsidian has an oversized room with double picture windows. The decor is an unusual country mix of floral wallpaper and bedspread with a black-and-white plaid couch and chairs. A white four-poster feather bed dominates the high-ceilinged room and a sitting area with fireplace completes the picture. Emerald has an equally stunning view from the deck and the bed. It also has a multi-angled high ceiling, four-poster king bed, a soaking tub, and a fireplace. It is decorated with a bright, cheerful floral scheme of red, green, and yellow.

The inn is situated on two acres, amid 100-year-old cypress trees, near the edge of the quaint little village of Mendocino. The main farmhouse was built in 1860 and although it has been remodeled, the exterior looks much like it did originally, including the candle-stick-style, white picket fence. Complimentary breakfast is served in the farmhouse kitchen, which offers more breathtaking views of the headlands and sea stacks. For details on the local area, refer to the listing for The Inn at Schoolhouse Creek, below.

Facilities: Agate Cove Inn has 10 cottages with private bathrooms. There are no kitchen facilities but a full breakfast is served. Most cottages have a deck and fireplace. Gift baskets, in-room massages, and wedding and reunion facilities are available. The inn is not suitable for children under the age of 12. Pets are not allowed. No smoking is permitted.

Bedding: Linens and towels are provided.

Reservations and rates: Reservations are recommended. The fee is $159 to $269 per night per cottage, and inn rooms are $119 to $219 per night. A fee of $25 per night per person is charged for more than two persons. Special packages are available. There is a two-night minimum on weekends and from July through September, and a three-night minimum on holidays. Major credit cards are accepted. Open year-round.

Directions: From Mendocino and Highway 1, turn west on Little Lake Road and drive a short distance (.1 mile) to Lansing Street. Turn right and drive .1 mile to the inn on the right (east side) side of the road.

Contact: Agate Cove Inn, 11201 Lansing Street, Mendocino, CA 95460; 707/937-0551 or 800/527-3111; website: www.agatecove.com.

Agate Cove Inn

6. THE INN AT SCHOOLHOUSE CREEK

This is a gorgeous spot where the pace slows and you can spend your mornings and evenings doing nothing but soaking in the surrounding beauty. The grounds are landscaped and pretty, with white-picket fence, flowers, and six pristine cottages (as well as six rooms in a separate lodge unit), often with ocean views. The cottages are cozy, clean, and intimate. They include woodstoves, small kitchens, and full baths. Rose, Heather, and Fuchsia Cottages all have decks with ocean views; Cypress and Willow have ocean views (but no decks); and Hawthorn has a forest-view deck and ocean glimpses.

The Inn at Schoolhouse Creek is located in the town of Little River, three miles south of Mendocino and about 10 miles south of Fort Bragg. The inn is centered around the Ledford House, built in 1862 and nestled on eight acres of spectacular gardens, just east of Highway 1—and across from the ocean. There's a hot tub for four at

Luxury rating: 4

Recreation rating: 4

Mendocino Coast, off Highway 1 in Little River

the top of the meadow with fabulous ocean views; the best time for whale-watching is in the off-season, from Christmas through Memorial Day.

There are many excellent hiking opportunities nearby. Within a 15-minute drive are Van Damme State Park, the Mendocino Headlands, Russian Gulch State Park, Caspar State Beach, and Jug Handle State Reserve. A bit farther south is Navarro River Redwoods, and just north are Fort Bragg, Noyo Harbor, and Jackson Demonstration State Forest. So there are a number of choices for recreation within a very short distance.

There are also excellent driving tours on Highway 1, and for the ambitious, a chance for spectacular scuba diving in shallows, sea kayaking in coves, and coastal fishing for salmon or rockfish. The fastest and easiest way to get a slice of this life is to drive to the town of Mendocino and take the short drive out to the Mendocino Headlands. The views, sunsets, and whale-spout viewing are all spectacular here; there is a short, flat walk along the bluff that provides a continuous lookout at the best of it.

A more secluded hike with an additional payoff is the five-mile round-trip in Russian Gulch State Park to see 36-foot Russian Gulch Falls. This is a divine waterfall, starting in a chute, then staircasing in three steps, finally cascading off a huge boulder into a pool. The entire setting can be stunning, with ferns, giant downed logs, and a forest canopy.

Facilities: The Inn at Schoolhouse Creek has six cottages extremely well-furnished with woodstoves, small kitchens, telephones, televisions, and bathrooms; most have decks and ocean views. There are also six inn-style rooms, most with ocean views. Call for details regarding pet policies.

Bedding: Linens and towels are provided.

Reservations and rates: Reservations are strongly recommended. The fee ranges from $140 to $235 per night for cottages, with discounts for non-weekends and the off-season. Lodge rooms are $130 per night.

Directions: From U.S. 101 at Cloverdale, take the Highway 128 exit, turn left at the stop sign, and drive west on Highway 128 to Highway 1. Turn north (right) on Highway 1 and drive 6.5 miles. Look for the Inn at Schoolhouse Creek on the right (east) side of the road.

Contact: The Inn at Schoolhouse Creek, North Highway One, P.O. Box 1637, Mendocino, CA 95460; 707/937-5525, fax 707/937-2012; website: www.schoolhousecreek.com.

The Inn at Schoolhouse Creek

7. HERITAGE HOUSE

Heritage House is everything it claims to be: a romantic retreat on the rugged coastline with drop-dead gorgeous vistas, good food in an old lodge, and luxurious and often unusual, lodging. The inn has received a ton of publicity over the years, but it is well-deserved. It's difficult to find fault with the place, but if we had to say that there are any negatives, it's that so much lodging has been crammed onto the 37 acres.

Luxury rating: 4

Recreation rating: 4

Mendocino Coast, off Highway 1 in Little River

Lodging ranges from a basic motel-style room to secluded, luxurious accommodations situated on cliffs overlooking a dramatic section of the California coastline. You can also rent a water tower, Ivy 1 Cottage with a piano, or one of the bungalows where the movie *Same Time Next Year*, with Alan Alda and Ellen Burstyn, was filmed years ago. Take your pick, but remember: This is a place where upgrading your accommodations can make a huge difference, resulting in a memorable getaway. We suggest spending the extra money for a luxury cottage.

With a deluxe cottage, you most likely will get a private deck with panoramic ocean view, wet bar, dining table, large bedroom with king-sized bed, sitting area in front of a marble-faced fireplace, large bathroom with whirpool tub for two, and tasteful, traditional decor.

The restaurant is housed in the 1800s-era, ivy-covered farmhouse. Breakfast and dinner are served here, and on weekends, brunch is available.

For details about the Little River area, see the listing for The Inn at Schoolhouse Creek, above.

Facilities: Heritage House has 63 cottages and three inn rooms. There are no kitchen facilities, but a restaurant is available. Amenities vary greatly, and some cottages have a fireplace or woodstove, deck, wet bar, and refrigerator. There are no televisions or telephones. Wedding and retreat facilities are available. Heritage House is not suitable for children. Pets are not allowed. No smoking is permitted inside. Some facilities are wheelchair accessible.

Bedding: Linens and towels are provided.

Reservations and rates: Reservations are recommended. The fee is $120 to $425 per night per cottage. Additional persons are $20 per night per person. There is a two-night minimum on weekends. Major credit cards are accepted. Open year-round, except for late November to mid-December and January to early February.

Directions: From Mendocino, drive south on Highway 1 for approximately four miles to the town of Little River and Heritage House on the right (ocean) side.

Contact: Heritage House, 5200 Highway 1, Little River, CA 95456-9503; 707/937-5885 or 800/235-5885, fax 707/937-0318; website: www.heritagehouseinn.com.

Heritage House

8. ALBION RIVER INN

Luxury rating: 4

Recreation rating: 4

Mendocino Coast, off Highway 1 near Albion

If you like your scenery rugged and breathtaking, your lodging luxurious, and your food divine, then consider Albion River Inn, a 10-acre spread that is several miles south of Mendocino. The 20 New England–style cottages perched high on a bluff overlooking dramatic coastline will make you feel like you're in Maine—although some might say you'll feel like you're in heaven.

Your cottage will likely have an ocean view, a deck, a sitting area with fireplace, plush furnishings, high ceilings, and a big whirlpool tub where you can lounge and enjoy your private view of the ocean. These cottages were designed to please, and they do. They are painted white and ooze romance. In the morning, you'll be treated to a made-to-order breakfast in the inn's restaurant, which has been praised by the food magazine *Bon Appétit*.

The acreage consists of gardens, lawns, and lookout points. The property is so beautiful that it is a popular place for weddings and special events. For details about the local area and recreation opportunities, refer to the listing for The Inn at Schoolhouse Creek, earlier in this chapter.

Facilities: Albion River Inn has 20 cottages with private bathrooms. There are no kitchen facilities but complimentary breakfast, coffee, tea, and wine are provided. A deck, fireplace, and whirlpool tub are provided. A restaurant is available. The inn is not suitable for children. Pets are not allowed. No smoking is permitted. Some facilities are wheelchair accessible.

Bedding: Linens and towels are provided.

Reservations and rates: Reservations are recommended. The double-occupancy rate is $200 to $310 per night per cottage. Additional persons are $20 per night per person. There is a two-night minimum on weekends, and a three-night minimum on holidays. Credit cards are accepted. Open year-round.

9. VICHY SPRINGS RESORT

At Vichy Springs Resort, your body likely will be fizzing, and it won't be from drinking sodas, but from the naturally carbonated mineral baths—the only warm, naturally-occurring ones in North America. The "champagne" baths, the hot soaking pools, the Olympic-size swimming pool, and 700 acres with hiking trails comprise the featured attractions here. As with other hot springs we found, the lodging is considered secondary to the hot springs, and usually is viewed as a convenient place to hang out and sleep while enjoying the resort. You have a choice between cottages and inn rooms, and we strongly recommend a freestanding cottage, which is much more private and quiet.

Luxury rating: 3

Recreation rating: 4

Ukiah, off U.S. 101

This is an historic resort, built in 1854, and such notables as Jack London, Mark Twain, Robert Louis Stevenson, and U.S. Presidents Theodore Roosevelt, Harrison, and Grant soaked their cares away here. The sulfurous, or slightly rotten-egg smelling, water is thought by some to have curative powers for the relief of stomach ailments and circulatory problems, the treatment of topical wounds and poison oak, and the relief of arthritis, gout, and rheumatism. The facilities are open for day use.

The one- and two-bedroom cottages have private bathrooms and are a step up from staying in the inn rooms. They have hardwood floors and redwood, oak, and pine furniture; the bathrooms are tiled with handmade Mexican paver tiles. The cottages feature fully equipped kitchens, and a complimentary buffet breakfast is served. Two of the cottages were built in 1854 and are recognized as the oldest buildings in Mendocino County. As you might guess, these historic cottages are the most requested, largely because London and Twain stayed in them.

In addition to the use of the resort's 700 acres, attractions within a 30-minute drive include scads of wineries and microbreweries, three museums, the Russian River, Lake Mendocino, golf courses, Montgomery Woods State Park, and the Skunk Train.

Facilities: Vichy Springs Resort has eight cottages and 12 inn rooms. The cottages have one or two bedrooms and include a fully equipped kitchen. A pool, hiking trails, massages, and facials are available. The resort is not suitable for children. Pets are not allowed. No smoking is permitted inside buildings. Some facilities are wheelchair accessible.

Bedding: Linens and towels are provided.

Reservations and rates: Reservations are recommended. The double-occupancy rate is $245 per night per cottage, and $110 to $210 per night for inn rooms. Additional persons are $40 per person per night. Breakfast and use of the mineral baths, swimming pool, and hot pools are included. A two-night minimum stay is required for certain periods. Major credit cards are accepted. Open year-round.

Directions: From U.S. 101 in Ukiah, take the Vichy Springs Road/Central Ukiah exit and turn east on Vichy Springs Road. Drive for 1.3 miles and bear right to stay on Vichy Springs Road. Continue 1.7 miles to the resort on the right.

Contact: Vichy Springs Resort, 2605 Vichy Springs Road, Ukiah, CA 95482-3507; 707/462-9515, fax 707/462-9516; website: www.vichysprings.com.

Vichy Springs Resort

10. PINE ACRES BLUE LAKES RESORT

There are a half dozen Blue Lakes in California, but the twin set along Highway 20 north of Clear Lake are often the most overlooked. Vacationers miss them because they are in the shadow of nearby, giant Clear Lake. Yet these lovely lakes offer good fishing for trout, especially in spring and early summer on Upper Blue Lake, and a decent chance the rest of the year. The long, narrow lakes are created from the flows of Cold Creek, which eventually runs into the East Fork Russian River and Lake Mendocino. With a five-mph speed limit in place, quiet boating is the rule. Swimming is good here. No waterskiing is permitted.

Luxury rating: 3

Recreation rating: 4

*Upper Blue Lake, off Highway
20 north of Clear Lake*

Pine Acres Resort is set on Upper Blue Lake, known for its high water quality. The cabins here are a clear step above rustic and a clear step below luxury. For many, it makes a good, comfortable fit. They are well-equipped, maintained daily, and best of all, within short range of the dock. People come here to either fish or swim in the lake.

Upper Blue Lake is stocked in the spring and fall with trout on a bimonthly basis, and at times has the most consistent catch rates in the region. The best trout fishing always happens in the cooler months, however, not in the hot summer, leaving frustrated visitors who show up in July wondering, "Where are all the trout I've heard about?" The answer is that they've either been caught already or they're hiding deep in the thermocline, where the water is cool and oxygenated. When that happens, it is better to switch than to fight. That means fishing instead for bluegill (during the day), largemouth bass (in the mornings and evenings), or catfish (at night). The size of the bass (occasionally over 10 pounds) can be a real stunner here, especially for anglers who think only Clear Lake has fish that big.

Facilities: Pine Acres Resort has five cabins (sleeping four to six persons), six lodge rooms, and a campground. Microwave, dishes, utensils, and television are provided. A clubhouse with kitchen facilities and woodstove is available for groups of up to 100. A sandy beach is on-site. Leashed pets are permitted.

Bedding: Linens and towels are provided.

Reservations and rates: Reservations are recommended. The rate is $65 to $125 for two to four persons, depending on cabin size, with a two-night minimum on weekends and a three-night minimum on holidays. Additional persons are $5 per night for ages 11 and up, $2 per per night for ages 2 to 10, and free for children under age 2. Major credit cards are accepted. Open year-round.

Directions: From Ukiah, drive north on U.S. 101 for five miles to the junction with Highway 20. Turn east on Highway 20 and drive about 13 miles to Irvine Street. Turn right on Irvine Street and drive one block to Blue Lakes Road. Turn right and drive two blocks to the resort.

Contact: Pine Acres Blue Lakes Resort, 5328 Blue Lakes Road, Upper Lake, CA 95485; 707/275-2811, fax 707/275-9549; website: www.bluelakepineacres.com.

Pine Acres Blue Lakes Resort

11. THE NARROWS LODGE RESORT

Not all cabins are created equal. At The Narrows Lodge Resort, the cabins are always in clean and tidy condition. They are well-furnished, too, with bedroom, bathroom, and kitchen. Cabins 7, 8, 9, and 10 all have lake views. The grounds feature a lawn and shade trees, with the pretty waters of Blue Lake nearby. And since a campground is on the property, full facilities are available, including a boat dock. Its location aside, Upper Blue Lake is ideal, and when you put it all together, it can make for a great getaway in foothills of Lake County.

Luxury rating: 3

Recreation rating: 4

Upper Blue Lake, off Highway 20 north of Clear Lake

Upper Blue Lake is very pretty in the spring, when its azure blue waters are contrasted with the surrounding neon green hills. As summer turns the hills gold, the contrast with the water is even more striking. With a five-mph speed limit in place on the lake, tranquility reigns. For some, this lake thus becomes their favorite place.

The lake has trout, bass, crappie, bluegill, and catfish. Trout fishing is good in the spring and fall; bass in the spring and early summer. The weather gets very hot from mid-June through August and the cool, clear waters of the lake provide great relief. It's one of the best swimming holes you could ever want.

Facilities: The Narrows Lodge Resort has 11 cabins of various sizes. They are well-furnished and include private bathrooms. Some have kitchens with utensils. A campground on the property offers modem hookups, a recreation room, boat rentals, a pier, a boat ramp, and a country store with fishing supplies, propane, and ice. Motel-style rooms are also available. Pets with no fleas are permitted, but they must be attended at all times and are not allowed in some cabins. Smoking is not permitted in some cabins.

Bedding: Linens and towels are provided.

Reservations and rates: Reservations are recommended. The rates range from $50 for two people to $118 for up to six per night, and $317 to $708 per week. Major credit cards are accepted. Open year-round.

Directions: From Ukiah, drive north on U.S. 101 for five miles to the junction with Highway 20. Turn east on Highway 20 and drive about 11.5 miles to Blue Lakes Road. Turn right and drive to 5690 Blue Lakes Road.

Contact: The Narrows Lodge Resort, 5690 Blue Lakes Road, Upper Lake, CA 95485; 707/275-2718 or 800/476-2776, fax 707/275-0739.

The Narrows Lodge Resort

12. LE TRIANON RESORT

Le Trianon Resort, set on Lower Blue Lake, is a big RV park that as a bonus provides 14 cabin rentals. This spot is considered a fishing enthusiast's special, with no waterskiing permitted, good trout fishing in spring and early summer—and a chance for giant bass.

Luxury rating: 3

Recreation rating: 4

Lower Blue Lake, off Highway 20 north of Clear Lake

Many anglers do not want anything fancy, but that doesn't always mean their non-fishing companions agree. That is why Le Trianon Resort offers three styles of cabins: studios, family, and deluxe. The studios are fairly primitive, and don't include showers; their one room contains two double beds and a kitchenette. The family cabins are furnished with bathroom, kitchen, and two bedrooms with double beds. The deluxe cabins have the same except for queen-size beds. Because the cabins are part of a large RV camping complex, the available facilities are extensive and not far away. A small store is usually well-stocked, and in addition, a small marina offers a boat ramp and rentals.

And that gets us to the fishing, which is why Lower Blue Lake has become popular. Blue Lakes has quietly become a secret spot for local anglers searching for big bass. When the bite is turned off at Clear Lake (located to the nearby south), or when Clear Lake gets too crowded with skiers or tournament fishermen, these locals head for Blue Lakes. That's because they know a secret.

It is surprising the size of the bass that can be caught in Lower Blue Lake, in some cases over 10 pounds. Crankbaits, such as the Speed Trap, can be very effective when cast parallel to the shoreline. Another trick here is to work a Brush Hog off of any kind of structure. This will give you a fair chance of catching a large bass. There is a five-mph speed limit on the lake; waterskiing and personal watercraft riding are prohibited. Swimming, sailing, windsurfing, kayaking, and canoeing are allowed.

Facilities: Le Trianon Resort has four studio cabins, seven family cabins, and four deluxe cabins. Family and deluxe cabins provide a bathroom with showers, a family room, a fully equipped kitchen, and a porch. Studio cabins do not have showers but do have refrigerators. A large RV park is on the property with a playground, a boat ramp, boat rentals, fishing supplies, coin laundry, a snack bar, and a grocery store. No dogs are permitted in cabins. Smoking is permitted in cabins. No motorcycles are allowed. Those under 21 without parents are not permitted. Night security is provided, with a quiet time enforced from 10 P.M. to 9 A.M.

Bedding: Linens and towels are provided for family and deluxe cabins. They are not provided for studio cabins.

13. MANCHESTER BEACH KOA

This is a privately operated KOA park set beside Highway 1 and near the beautiful Manchester State Beach. Two pluses here are KOA's cute signature log cabins, complete with electric heat, and the new, deluxe camping cottages. They can provide a great sense of privacy, and after a good sleep, visitors are ready to explore the adjacent state park.

Luxury rating: 2

Recreation rating: 4

Mendocino Coast, off Highway 1 near Manchester

The KOA is set just north of Point Arena. It is a cool, quiet camp set in coastal pines, within walking distance of a beautiful driftwood beach. From the bluffs, you can often see the spouts of passing whales.

The camping cabins are small structures where you bring your sleeping bag, pillow, and anything else you need, then use the facilities provided for the RV campground. On the other hand, the camping cottages sleep four and feature a full bathroom and kitchen; you still bring your own sleeping bag, pillow, and towels.

This area offers many attractions, of course. The closest is nearby Manchester State Beach. One of the best ways to explore the park is to take the Alder Creek Trail. The hike here starts adjacent to park headquarters and is routed past Lake Davis to the beach, continuing north along the beach to the mouth of Alder Creek. This is an attractive coastal lagoon, known for many species of birds, including whistling swans. It's also the area where the San Andreas Fault heads off from land into the sea. Some visitors will enjoy the coastal drive up to Fort Bragg. The Skunk Train ride through the redwoods east to Willits is always a highlight. If you time it right, your vacation will be perfect.

Facilities: Manchester Beach KOA has 24 camping cabins and two camping cottages. Each cabin has primitive beds, electric heat, a barbecue, a deck, and a swing. The camping cottages have full bathroom with shower, kitchenette with utensils and dishes, fireplace, and television. The camping cabins do not have kitchen facilities or bathrooms; a campground is on-site with a restroom with showers, modem hookups, a heated pool (seasonal), a hot tub and spa, a recreation room, a playground, a sanitary disposal station, a grocery store, and coin laundry. Some facilities are wheelchair accessible. Pets are permitted in cabins. No smoking is allowed in the cabins.

Bedding: No linens are provided. You must bring a sleeping bag and pillow.

Reservations and rates: Reservations are recommended (call 800/562-4188). Camping cabins are $46 for two per night for one-room cabin and $54 for two per night for two-room cabin; camping cottages are $120 per night for four. Off-season discounts are available. Major credit cards are accepted. Open year-round.

Directions: On U.S. 101 north of Santa Rosa, turn west on River Road and drive 13 miles to Guerneville and Highway 116. Turn west on Highway 116 and drive about 20 miles to Highway 1 at Jenner. Turn north on Highway 1 and drive 55 miles to Point Arena. From Point Arena, continue north about six miles to the park on the left side of the road.

Contact: Manchester Beach KOA, P.O. Box 266, Manchester, CA 95459; 707/882-2375, fax 707/882-3104; website: www.koa.com.

Manchester Beach KOA

14. HIGHLAND RANCH

We really searched to find a large ranch that wasn't near the Sierras, and we found one—overlooking Anderson Valley, an area known more for wine than horses and fishing. The other surprise at Highland Ranch is that the management speaks English, Italian, French, and Spanish. The owner lived in Europe for 24 years and brought back a European clientele with him. This is not a dude ranch, but rather a relaxed, upscale country retreat for people who like horseback riding, hiking, and enjoying good food and drinks with people from all over the world. Put together a group of at least 14 people, and you can have the entire ranch to yourselves.

Luxury rating: 4

Recreation rating: 5

Philo, off Highway 128

You'll have 247 acres of extraordinary redwood groves and open, grassy meadows next to pines and oaks to horseback ride and hike on, as well as the use of a trapshooting range for ages 14 and older. Hendy Woods State Park and several private ranches adjoin Highland Ranch, so the horseback riding and hiking opportunities are enormous, with over 100 miles of trails in the immediate area. If you don't feel like leaving the vicinity of your cabin, you can play tennis, swim in the pool, read a book in a hammock under towering trees, fish in the four-acre bass pond, or make arrangements for a massage.

The staff wants you to enjoy the outdoors, but they also ensure that you aren't roughing it. Although there are many activities to choose from, horseback riding is the emphasis here, and there are daily rides for all levels of riders; English and western saddles are available. Twenty horses live at the ranch, and the owner jokingly refers to them as family. Horseback riding is included in your room fee, but riding lessons, massages, clay pigeon shooting, and baby-sitting are extra.

And when it's chow time, you head over to the dining room for a home-cooked, family-style meal, complete with cocktails and wine and beer from the local wineries and microbreweries. The dining room has the feel of an old-fashioned lodge with a vaulted ceiling, long wooden tables with blue-checkered tablecloths, and deer head mounts hanging from wood-paneled walls. The lodge was built in the 1880s and has received additions and been remodeled over the years.

The one- to three-bedroom cabins have private bathrooms, fireplaces, and decks, and are situated under large redwoods. Most of the cabins are in duplex units, but two of the rentals are freestanding. A typical cabin has wood paneling; vaulted, beamed ceilings; a wood-burning fireplace with large brick hearth; and a decidedly ranch-style look and feel. There are no kitchens, since meals are provided.

Facilities: Highland Ranch has eight cabins with private bathrooms. There are no kitchen facilities, but all meals and drinks are provided. Tennis courts, horseback riding, clay pigeon shooting, mountain bikes, a bass lake, massage, baby-sitting, and conference facilities are available. The ranch is suitable for children. Well-behaved dogs are allowed. Smoking is permitted.

Bedding: Linens and towels are provided.

Reservations and rates: Reservations are recommended. The fee is $285 per night per person and $190 per night for children under 12, and includes all meals and drinks. Infants are free. A 10 percent service charge is added to the final bill. There is a two-night minimum and a three-night minimum on holidays. Major credit cards are accepted. Open year-round.

Directions: From Cloverdale on U.S. 101, turn northwest on Highway 128 and drive about 35 miles to Philo Greenwood Road (marked Hendy Woods State Park and Elk). Turn left on Philo Greenwood Road and drive one mile to the Highland Ranch entrance. Turn left and drive approximately four miles on a paved road to the ranch.

Contact: Highland Ranch, P.O. Box 150, Philo, CA 95466; 707/895-3600, fax 707/895-3702; www.highlandranch.com.
Highland Ranch

15. EDGEWATER RESORT

Soda Bay is one of Clear Lake's prettiest and most intimate spots, and this camp provides excellent access. Edgewater Resort is a large operation featuring eight furnished cabins, two houses, and an adjacent RV park and campground.

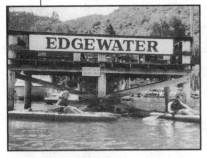

Luxury rating: 3

Recreation rating: 4

Clear Lake, off Highway 29 near Kelseyville

All cabins on the property have two bedrooms, bathrooms, furnished kitchens, and can sleep up to four; the houses can sleep 8 and 12, respectively. The cabins have air-conditioning and cable television. Because a campground is on the property, many bonus amenities are provided. These include a 230-foot fishing pier, rentals of fishing boats or kayaks, and a swimming pool in the summer season. A recreation area is also available. This resort is very popular for groups, such as for reunions, because a clubhouse (with full kitchen, and that can accommodate up to 200 people) with lake views is available.

The recreational highlights of the place are boating, waterskiing, and fishing. Both waterskiing and fishing for bass and bluegill are excellent in Soda Bay, as it is sheltered from north winds; that means quiet water. The shore is tule-lined from Henderson Point all the way around to Dorn Bay—nearly three miles of prime fishing territory.

Maybe Clear Lake should be renamed Fish Lake or Green Lake, because its emerald green waters are full of fish. With high levels of nutrients and algae clouding the water, it is anything but clear—and you can thank nature for creating such a wonderful problem. You see, the lake's substantial nutrients—phytoplankton and algae—as well as a huge minnow population support a high carrying capacity. In simpler terms, a lot of aquatic food equals a lot of fish. Clear Lake produces more big crappie and greater numbers of catfish than any other lake in California, including yellow, blue, and channel catfish. In the 1970s, people said the lake had wall-to-wall crappie. In the 1980s, they talked about the wall-to-wall catfish, and in the 1990s, wall-to-wall bass. Now, in the 21st century, those same folks are saying that Clear Lake could be the first lake in Northern California to produce a 20-pound bass, and maybe even a world record.

Set amid the foothills of Lake County, Clear Lake is quite pretty, covering more than 40,000 surface acres. It is the largest natural freshwater lake within California's borders, and with Highway 20 running aside the eastern shore, it often seems full to the brim. With dozens of resorts and private campgrounds sprinkled along the 100 miles of shoreline, huge numbers of visitors can be accommodated without feeling crowded. Reservations are strongly recommended in the summer.

Facilities: Edgewater Resort has eight cabins that can sleep 4 to 12 people and include kitchens with utensils, bathrooms with showers, air-conditioning, heat, and televisions. A campground is on the property with modem hookups, a game room, a general store, laundry, a swimming pool, horseshoes, volleyball, and Ping-Pong. A swimming beach, boat ramp, fishing pier, boat dock, and watercraft rentals are available nearby. "Good dogs" are permitted in cabins, and a dog run is available at the beach. No smoking is permitted in the cabins.

Bedding: Linens and pillows are provided.

Reservations and rates: Reservations are recommended (call 800/396-6224). The nightly rates are $100 to $150 for up to four persons for the cabins and $200 to $350 for up to 12 persons for the houses. Pets are $5 per night. Discounted winter rates are available. Major credit cards are accepted. Open year-round.

Directions: In Kelseyville on Highway 29, take the Merritt Road exit and drive on Merritt for two miles (it becomes Gaddy Lane) to Soda Bay Road. Turn right on Soda Bay Road and drive three miles to the campground entrance on the left.

Contact: Edgewater Resort, 6420 Soda Bay Road, Kelseyville, CA 95451; 707/279-0208; website: www.edgewaterresort.net.

OTHER CABINS AND COTTAGES NEARBY

• Bell Haven Resort, 3415 White Oak Way, Kelseyville, CA 95451; 707/279-4329 or 877/279-4329; website: www.bellhaven.com.

Edgewater Resort

16. INDIAN BEACH RESORT

You'll be sitting on 300 feet of lake frontage when you rent a cabin at Indian Beach Resort, but if you're like most visitors, you'll be out fishing instead of sitting along the lake's edge. When a resort offers a floating fishing dock with night lighting, you know that fishing is a priority. But if you do decide to sit for a spell, you'll have a view of the nine lakeside cabins set amid oak trees.

The studio to two-bedroom cabins have fully equipped kitchens, bathrooms, and televisions, and some have a deck or porch. Four of the cabins are duplex units, and five of the cabins are freestanding.

Up to 10 persons can be accommodated in the cabins, depending on the rental. Here's the inside scoop on the cabins: The most popular cabins are Cabins 6, 8, and 9 because they're closest to the lake.

Luxury rating: 3

Recreation rating: 4

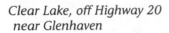

Clear Lake, off Highway 20 near Glenhaven

Cabin 10 is the largest rental, with two bedrooms, two bathrooms, one queen bed, three double beds, and a sofa bed.

Indian Beach Resort is a good setup for a family or group because it also has a swimming beach with its own floating dock, a boat launch, a picnic area with barbecue facilities, a small store, bait and tackle, and even a Ping-Pong table. The facilities are situated in a protected cove, which means that when it gets windy on the lake, the water is calmer here. The resort is located on the eastern edge of the lake in a centralized area that is full of activity, which means more urban conveniences are within a short distance.

Facilities: Indian Beach Resort has nine cabins with fully equipped kitchens and private bathrooms. Televisions are provided, but there are no telephones. A picnic area with barbecues, Ping-Pong, a swimming area, a boat dock and launch ramp, and a small store with bait and tackle are available. The resort is suitable for children. Leashed pets are allowed. Smoking is permitted. One cabin is wheelchair accessible.

Bedding: Linens and towels are provided.

Reservations and rates: Reservations are recommended. The fee is $48 to $125 per night per cabin. Children under the age of two are free. The pet fee is $7 per night per pet. Major credit cards are accepted. Open March through December.

Directions: From U.S. 101 in Ukiah, turn east on Highway 20 and drive about 45 miles to the resort on the right side of the road, at Clear Lake.

Contact: Indian Beach Resort, P.O. Box 648, Glenhaven, CA 95443; 707/998-3760; website: www.ngl.net/indianbeach.

Indian Beach Resort

17. BLUE FISH COVE RESORT

You can have all that Clear Lake has to offer from Blue Fish Cove Resort: a cabin with fully equipped kitchen and deck close to the shoreline, a swimming beach, a lighted fishing pier, boat launch and dock, a hot tub, a small store with bait and tackle, boat

Luxury rating: 3

Recreation rating: 4

*Clear Lake, off Highway 20
near Clearlake Oaks*

rentals, and a game room with pool table and arcade. And what are your outdoor recreation options? You can swim, boat, and fish until you're tired out, then return to your cabin with your day's catch for a barbecue on your deck, maybe followed by a dip in the hot tub or a game of pool.

The cabins come in one- and two-bedroom sizes and can sleep up to five persons, depending on the rental. Three of the cabins are freestanding, and four are duplex style. Not all cabins have a lake view, so if you want one, ask for Cabins 5 or 7. They're clean and cozy and have a breakfast nook. The kitchens have everything you need, including a microwave, toaster, coffeepot with filter, cream and sugar, dishwashing soap, salt and pepper, and towels. All you have to remember to bring is the food. They also provide linens and towels.

For more information about Clear Lake, see the listing for Edgewater Resort, above.

Facilities: Blue Fish Cove Resort has seven cabins with private bathrooms. Most cabins have a fully equipped kitchen, barbecue, cable television, balcony or patio, heater, and evaporative cooler. A lighted fishing pier, a fish-cleaning station, bass boat outlets, boat and personal watercraft rentals, bait and tackle, a hot tub, a pool table, a game room with arcade, a basketball court, horseshoes, and croquet are available. The resort is suitable for children. Leashed pets are allowed. Smoking is permitted. Some facilities are wheelchair accessible.

Bedding: Linens and towels are provided.

Reservations and rates: Reservations are recommended. The double-occupancy rate (except for Cabin 3, which is based on four persons) is $55 to $90 per night per cabin, and $290 to $600 per week; discounts are available for weekly rentals and for renting two or more cabins. Additional persons are $5 per night. The pet fee is $10 per night per pet, and a $100 damage deposit is required. Children under age five are free. Major credit cards are accepted. Open year-round.

Directions: From north of Ukiah on U.S. 101, or at Williams on I-5, turn on Highway 20 and drive to Clearlake Oaks and the resort on the left.

Contact: Blue Fish Cove Resort, 10573 East Highway 20, Clearlake Oaks, CA 95423; 707/998-1769; website: www.bluefishcove.com.

Blue Fish Cove Resort

18. TROMBETTA'S BEACH RESORT

This is a hangout for those who love to fish—the resort is oriented to accommodating their needs. And when anglers are here to catch fish, the lodging is secondary to the other amenities such as boat launch and dock, aluminum boat rentals, fish cleaning room, fishing pier—oh, and did you say cabins? Yes, there also are four cabins

with fully equipped kitchens available. Two of the cabins are freestanding and the other two are in a duplex unit. The duplex units are studio size and the other cabins have two bedrooms each and can sleep up to four people. The cabins include air-conditioning, cable television, barbecue pits, and a patio or porch. A big bonus for families is the heated swimming pool on the premises.

Luxury rating: 3

Recreation rating: 3

Clear Lake, off Highway 20 near Clearlake

The resort is located about one-half block from the lake and a 309-foot pier. The rental cabins are in a setting with six other long-term rental cabins and an RV park. There are no lake views from the resort, and a sea wall lies on this portion of Clear Lake, close to where the lake enters Cache Creek.

For more information about Clear Lake, see the listing for Edgewater Resort, earlier in this chapter.

Facilities: Trombetta's Beach Resort has four cabins with fully equipped kitchens and private bathrooms. Barbecue pits, patio or porch, air-conditioning, and cable television are provided. A heated pool, coin laundry, a fishing pier, a boat launch and boat dock, boat rentals, a fish-cleaning area, and RV hookups are available. The resort is suitable for children. Small leashed pets are allowed. Smoking is permitted.

Bedding: Linens and towels are provided.

Reservations and rates: Reservations are recommended. The fee is $54 to $69 per night per cabin, or $328 to $483 per week. Additional persons are $10 per night per person or $60 per week. Major credit cards are accepted. Open year-round.

Directions: From the town of Lower Lake (near the south end of Clear Lake), drive north on Highway 53 for one mile to old Highway 53. Turn left (west) and drive one mile to the resort on the left.

Contact: Trombetta's Beach Resort, 5865 Old Highway 53, P.O. Box 728, Clearlake, CA 95422; 707/994-2417, fax 707/994-3897.

Trombetta's Beach Resort

19. SERENISEA COTTAGES

Serenisea Cottages is the fantasy-driven spot on the Mendocino Coast, featuring both company owned and privately owned ocean-bluff cottages and homes for rent. For the highest quality, our advice is to reserve one of the privately owned cottages or homes, rather than going for one of the cabins on the property. Many cottages have decks with ocean views and hot tubs, and some have access to nearby sand beaches. There are 25 available, most well-furnished and all designed to provided a memorable vacation. They offer a wide variety of settings and conditions. For instance, five cottages allow pets and 10 allow youngsters under 16. Some are secluded in the forest.

Luxury rating: 3

Recreation rating: 3

Mendocino Coast, off Highway 1 near Gualala

This is a quiet and beautiful stretch of California coast. Touring Highway 1, exploring nearly deserted beaches, and enjoying ocean views make a perfect vacation for many. It's calm and still compared to the intense pace that many experience on a daily basis.

Nearby Gualala Regional Park provides an excellent easy hike, with the headlands-to-beach loop offering coastal views, a lookout of the Gualala River, and many giant cypress trees. Another good side trip is to Salt Point State Park, south of Serenisea, where there is a beautiful cove, kelp forest, and native abalone grounds.

The nearby Gualala River is remote and pretty, and is the best of the smaller coastal rivers in Sonoma and Mendocino Counties. Families and novice rafters find that the Gualala River makes a great place to enjoy an easy float in a canoe or kayak. The river is very scenic, and rafters should be able to see lots of wildlife and a variety of bird species. Swimming is good all along the lower river, which has a few deep swimming holes and even rope swings in a couple of places.

Facilities: Serenisea has three cabins on its property and manages an additional 25 privately owned vacation homes and cottages in the Gualala-Anchor Bay area. Most of these cottages have decks, fireplaces or woodstoves, full kitchens, and televisions. They can sleep between two and eight people per night. Call for details regarding pet policies.

Bedding: Linens and towels are provided.

Reservations and rates: Reservations are required, and there is a two-night minimum stay on weekends. Fees for cottages range from $90 to $170 per night. Vacation homes range from $115 to $205 per night.

Directions: On U.S. 101 north of Santa Rosa, turn west on River Road and drive 13 miles to Guerneville and Highway 116. Turn west on Highway 116 and drive about 20 miles to Highway 1 at Jenner. Turn north (right) on Highway 1 and drive 38 miles to Gualala. Continue on Highway 1 past Gualala for three miles and look for Serenisea on the west (ocean) side of the road.

Contact: Serenisea Cottages, 36100 Highway 1 South, Gualala, CA 95445; 707/884-3836 or 800/331-3836; website: www.serenisea.com.

Serenisea Cottages

20. ST. ORRES

The first time you drive past St. Orres, it's nearly impossible not to give the place a head-craning, full-out gawk. The reason is the unique architecture; it appears as if elaborate, rustic domed structures were lifted from Russia and deposited north of the town of Gualala, then sided with redwood. Maybe it's due to the dramatic ocean scenery on one side of Highway 1, along with the equally dramatic setting at St. Orres on the opposite side of the highway, that makes your brain go into overload. Whatever the reason, this is the kind of place that you don't forget.

Luxury rating: 3

Recreation rating: 3

Mendocino Coast, off Highway 1 near Gualala

There are 13 cottages and cabins dotted around the 12 acres, mostly hidden by the main lodge and the forest. From behind the hotel, a footbridge leads to four cottages and a cabin on the edge of a redwood forest. The most popular rental of this grouping is Treehouse, with a Franklin stove, French doors in the sitting area, a deck, a wet bar, a king-sized bed on an elevated level from the sitting area, and a bathroom with a big soaking tub and shower. This cottage rents for $210 per night. The newly built Black Chanterelle has high ceilings, a sauna, and a large whirlpool tub. Wildflower is a small, rustic cabin that was originally built for logging crews. It has an outside shower with a forest view. Inside, there's a woodburning stove in the sitting area and a sleeping loft with a double bed and skylight. This is the most economical cabin at $110 per night.

In a more secluded area of the property sit eight other cottages, some with ocean views, that share a hot tub, sauna, and sundeck. The largest cottage is Osprey Cove, a two-story home that is suitable for families. It boasts a spacious deck, woodburning stove, master bedroom with king-sized bed, bathroom with sauna, and private hot tub. Ocean views can be seen from this cottage, and a telescope is provided for whale- and bird-watching.

St. Orres also boasts a well-known gourmet restaurant and eight hotel rooms that are reached by climbing a heavy-timbered spiral staircase that circles—get this—a tree trunk. The rooms share three bathrooms. You want friendly, good-natured staff? You get that here.

Ocean and beach access are available across the highway. Two miles south is Gualala Point Park, adjacent to the mouth of the Gualala River. The Headlands Beach Loop is an easy, 1.5 mile hike. For further details on hiking, refer to the guidebook *Foghorn Outdoors: California Hiking.*

Facilities: St. Orres has 13 cottages and cabins and eight hotel rooms. Only one cottage has a kitchen (the others have a refrigerator and coffeemaker), but a complimentary breakfast is provided. Fireplace or woodstove, deck, and whirlpool tubs are available in some of the rentals. Most of the facilities are not suitable for children. Pets are not allowed. No smoking is allowed.

Bedding: Linens and towels are provided.

Reservations and rates: Reservations are recommended. The double-occupancy rate is $110 to $410 per night per cottage or cabin and $80 to $95 per night for hotel rooms. Full breakfast is included. Additional persons are $30 per night per person. There is a two-night minimum on weekends and a three-night minimum on holidays. Major credit cards are accepted. Open year-round.

Directions: On U.S. 101 north of Santa Rosa, turn west on River Road and drive 13 miles to Guerneville and Highway 116. Turn west on Highway 116 and drive about 20 miles to Highway 1 at Jenner. Turn north on Highway 1 and drive 38 miles to Gualala. Continue on Highway 1 past Gualala for two miles to St. Orres on the right.

Contact: St. Orres, 36601 South Highway 1, Gualala, CA 95445; 707/884-3303, fax 707/884-1840; website: www.saintorres.com.

OTHER CABINS AND COTTAGES NEARBY

• The Old Milano Hotel, 38300 Shoreline Highway 1, Gualala, CA 95445; 707/884-3256; website: www.oldmilanoho.com.

St. Orres

21. CLOVERDALE KOA

This KOA campground is set just above the Russian River in Alexander Valley wine country, just south of Cloverdale. Since new owners took over in the mid-1990s, the place has undergone considerable renovation and is now rustic and tidy, with adorable camping cabins. Unlike other KOAs, this one offers one- and two-room camping cabins. With separate rooms, it means mom and dad can have a little well-needed vacation privacy while the kids make all the noise they want in the other room. Another addition is a new 12-person hot tub. It seems the owners add something every year.

Luxury rating: 2

Recreation rating: 3

*Russian River, off U.S. 101
near Cloverdale*

This KOA also provides a fishing pond stocked with largemouth bass, bluegill, catfish, and, when water temperatures are cool enough, trout. The nearby Russian River is an excellent beginner's route in an inflatable kayak or canoe. The water rates Class I, making it easy, fun, and ideal for families. The nearby winery in Asti makes for a popular side trip, too.

Facilities: Cloverdale KOA has 14 cabins in one-room and two-room layouts. Each cabin has primitive beds, electric heat and an electrical outlet, a barbecue, a deck, and a swing. A campground is on-site with showers, modem hookups, a swimming pool, a 12-person spa, a playground, coin laundry, a recreation room, nature trails, a catch-and-release fish pond, nightly entertainment on weekends in the summer, and a grocery store. No smoking or pets are permitted in the cabins.

Bedding: No linens are provided. You must bring a sleeping bag and pillow.

Reservations and rates: Reservations are recommended (call 800/562-4042). Rates for one-room cabins for two are $50 to $60; two-room cabins are $72. Major credit cards are accepted. Open year-round.

Directions: From Cloverdale on U.S. 101, take the Central Cloverdale exit, which puts you on Asti Road. Drive straight on Asti Road to First Street. Turn right (east) and drive a short distance to River Road. Turn right (south) and drive four miles to KOA Road. Turn left and drive to the campground entrance.

In the summer/fall, from south of Cloverdale on U.S. 101, take the Asti exit and drive east a block to Asti Road. Turn right (south) and drive 1.5 miles to Washington School Road. Turn left (east) and drive 1.5 miles to KOA Road. Turn right and drive to the campground entrance. (Note: This route is open May 15 to December 15, when a seasonal bridge is in place.) Both routes are well-signed.

Contact: Cloverdale KOA, P.O. Box 600, 26460 River Road, Cloverdale, CA 95425; 707/894-3337; website: www.koa.com.

Cloverdale KOA

22. BEAVER CREEK

When it comes to unique lodging opportunities in California, this campground and park is definitely on the list. It is one of the few places anywhere where you can rent a tepee or a cabin. This private park has a pond where guests enjoy canoeing and kayaking in summer, a trout creek, and plenty of hiking and bird-watching opportunities. In addition, horseback riding and hot air balloon rides are available nearby.

Luxury rating: 1

Recreation rating: 3

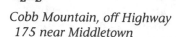

Cobb Mountain, off Highway 175 near Middletown

The two tepees are set next to the pond, and at dawn and dusk, they are a pretty scene, as if locked in time. They provide just enough privacy to appeal to many, and they are booked on most summer weekends. The cabins on the property are just as primitive as the tepees, that is, no indoor water is available and you must bring your sleeping bag and pillow, then use the facilities at the neighboring RV park. The cabins do have porches, and water and electricity are available nearby outside.

This camp is set near Highway 175 between Middletown and Clear Lake, and while there is a parade of vacation traffic on Highway 29, relatively few people take the longer route on Highway 175. Cobb Mountain looms nearby. This is a fun spot for youngsters, with the most popular summer activities being swimming in the pool and kayaking and paddleboating on the pond. A children's playground is a nice bonus. For adults, five golf courses are nearby, two within a five-minute drive.

Note that Beaver Creek was formerly known as Yogi Bear Beaver Creek, one of the more interesting camp names in the state.

Facilities: Beaver Creek has four primitive cabins and two tepees. No bedding, water, or electricity are available inside. An RV park is on the property with drinking water, restrooms, showers, coin laundry, modem hookups, a pool, kayaks and paddleboats, a boating pond, a playground, horseshoes, a recreation hall, and a store. No smoking or pets are permitted in the cabins. Pets are allowed in the tepees.

Bedding: Linens and towels are not provided. Bring your own sleeping bag, pillow, and basic camping gear.

23. PINE GROVE RESORT

"One step up from camping" is the best description for the 16 cabins at Pine Grove Resort. This is a family-oriented resort, with activities designed for children. Coming here is much like taking your family to a large campground or rustic summer camp. Clear Lake is about 20 miles north, but once here, most people are content to hang out on the 33 tree-covered acres, spending their days swimming, playing basketball or volleyball, and using the recreation room. Evenings are usually spent sitting around the campfire, watching the weekly children's talent show, square dancing, or participating in a game.

© EARL THOLLANDER

Luxury rating: 2

Recreation rating: 3

Cobb Mountain, off Highway 29 near Middletown

The one- to three-bedroom cabins were built more than 50 years ago and not much has changed in them over the years. There is a dark-brown paint job on the outside and plywood walls on the inside. They have kitchens and bathrooms, but you must bring your own linens and towels. There are no telephones, televisions, or air-conditioning. Nine of the cabins are set along Kelsey Creek, and the favorite is Grapevine Cabin because it sits up on a hill and is the most private.

The highlights for most families are the two swimming pools and two wading pools; one pool actually is a spring-fed cold pool. The café is open daily for dinner and on weekends for breakfast. The snack bar at the pool area is open daily. The motto here is "Relax and have fun."

Facilities: Pine Grove Resort has 16 housekeeping cabins and a campground for tents, trailers, and RVs. The cabins have fully equipped kitchens, barbecues, and a deck or porch. A café, a small store, two swimming pools, two wading pools, volleyball and basketball courts, horseshoe pits, a children's play area, a recreation room with Ping-Pong, pool table, and video games, and organized activities are available. The resort is suitable for children. Leashed pets are allowed. Smoking is permitted. Some facilities are wheelchair accessible.

Bedding: Linens and towels are not provided, so bring your own.

Reservations and rates: Reservations are recommended. The fee is $100 per night per cabin, or $500 per week. Major credit cards are accepted. Open Memorial Day weekend to Labor Day weekend.

Directions: From Vallejo, drive north on Highway 29 past Calistoga to Middletown and the junction with Highway 175. Turn north on Highway 175 and drive 8.5 miles to Bottle Rock Road. Turn left and drive .5 mile to the resort on the right.

Contact: Pine Grove Resort, 15969 Bottle Park Road, P.O. Box 44, Cobb, CA 95426; 707/928 5222.

Pine Grove Resort

24. BELLE DE JOUR INN

You'll have a romantic white cottage on a hill overlooking rolling hills and vineyards and situated next to an 1870s Italianate farmhouse when you stay at one of the cottages at Belle de Jour Inn. Or,

you can stay in their most popular rental, the 800-square-foot carriage house. Either way, you get a relaxing setting on six acres, in close proximity to wine touring and exploring rural Sonoma County and the Russian River.

Small details that make a difference are what you'll notice here, from the sheets dried in the sun to the fresh flowers and the landscaping. The grounds are beautifully manicured and include footpaths, benches, and even hammocks. It is a peaceful, serene setting made for relaxing. The cottages are adjoined, and each one is decorated with contemporary furniture and accents.

The Caretaker's Suite, once the caretaker's home, has a trellised entry deck,

Luxury rating: 4

Recreation rating: 3

Sonoma foothills, off U.S. 101 in Healdsburg

sitting area with fireplace, a king canopy bed, and a private bath with whirlpool tub for two. It rents for $250 per night. The Carriage House is on the second floor and features a vaulted ceiling, a king bed, sitting areas, a gas fireplace, a stained glass window, and a bathroom with whirlpool tub for two. The color scheme is in warm tones. This suite rents for $300 per night.

Complimentary full breakfast is served in the farmhouse each morning. The Windsor Golf Club is within a 15-minute drive of the inn.

Facilities: Belle de Jour Inn has four cottages and a carriage house, all with private bathrooms. There are no kitchen facilities but a full breakfast is served. Small refrigerator, telephone, fireplace, ceiling fan, and air-conditioning are provided, and some cottages have whirlpool tubs. The inn is not suitable for children. Pets are not allowed. No smoking is permitted.

Bedding: Linens and towels are provided.

Reservations and rates: Reservations are recommended. The fee is $185 to $300 per night per cottage. There is a two-night minimum on weekends, and a three-night minimum on holidays. Major credit cards are accepted. Open year-round.

Directions: From U.S. 101 in Healdsburg, drive north to the Dry Creek Road exit. Take that exit and turn right on Dry Creek Road. Drive 0.5 mile to Healdsburg Avenue. Turn left and drive one mile to the inn entrance road on the right, across the street from Simi Winery. Turn right and drive up the tree-lined driveway to the inn.

Contact: Belle de Jour Inn, 16276 Healdsburg Avenue, Healdsburg, CA 95448; 707/431-9777, fax 707/431-7412; website: www.belledejourinn.com.

Belle de Jour Inn

25. WASHINGTON STREET LODGING

This is the place where souls get recharged, bodies get rejuvenated, and your brain takes a vacation. How? By taking advantage of the town's hot springs, mud baths, towel wraps, massages, and quality dining. In 24 hours, Calistoga finds a way to get inside you and realign your senses.

The cottages at Washington Street Lodging are clean, cozy, pretty inside and out, and believe it or not, you can bring your pet. The first thing you notice when you arrive is that the entire property is loaded with blooming flowers, and that the place is well-kept. The headwaters of the Napa River run right by the cottages. Although the Napa River here is more like a creek, the riparian woodlands provide a nice feel and setting, especially in the early evening. One special feature of Cottages 3 and 4 is the small deck overlooking the creek.

The only downer is for late risers during the spring, fall, and winter. Directly across the stream, behind the cottages, is an elementary schoolyard, and they have recess every morning for 20 minutes starting at 8:15 A.M. The shrieks can be irritating if you are trying to sleep. In summer, it's not a factor, since school is not in session.

Peace is what you come here for, and for the most part, it is peace that you will get. Calistoga has nine hot spring spas, all with mud baths and a variety of treatments that will make your skin glow. The full treatment, which includes a mud bath, hot mineral soak, towel wrap, and massage, will have you surrendering to the final euphoria. Problems? What problems? Taking a mud bath is like sinking into a cauldron of ooze; the hot soak will permeate and loosen every tight muscle in your body; and then the warm towel wrap will have you practically levitating with tingles. Finish it off with a session with a massage therapist, and your mission will be near complete; you will gleam for days. Even the most tightly wound souls will yield and suddenly, in just a few hours, problems will seem unimportant.

Luxury rating: 3

Recreation rating: 4

Napa Valley, off Highway 29 in Calistoga

After reaching this state of harmony, the best way to integrate it into the real world is to visit one of the area's parks for a hike in a natural setting. There are three state parks nearby, two to the south of Calistoga, Bothe-Napa and Bale Grist Mill, and one to the north, Robert Louis Stevenson.

For information about other activities in the area, see the listing for Cottage Grove Inn later in this chapter.

Facilities: Washington Street Lodging has five cottages, each with a small kitchen with microwave and/or stove, and a bathroom with shower. Pets are permitted.

Bedding: Linens and towels are included.

Reservations and rates: Reservations are strongly recommended, both for cottage rentals and for treatments at any of the spas. Cottages are $135 to $150 per night. There is a $15 per pet fee. Full spa treatments are about $100, with some less expensive options.

Directions: From Napa, drive north on Highway 29 for about 30 miles to Calistoga. At the flashing light, turn right on Lincoln Avenue and drive into downtown

Calistoga. Turn left (north) on Washington Street and drive two blocks to 1605 Washington, on the left (west) side of the road. Limited parking is available near the cottages. Parking is available on the east side of Washington Street.

Contact: Washington Street Lodging, 1605 Washington Street, Calistoga, CA 94515; 707/942-6968; website: www.napalinks.com/wsl. For a hot spring resort, try Dr. Wilkinson's Hot Springs, 707/942-4102; there are also several others nearby.

Washington Street Lodging

26. INDIAN SPRINGS

At Indian Springs, you can almost roll out of bed and into a volcanic ash mud bath or Olympic-size mineral pool; that's the big advantage of renting a bungalow here. Almost everyone who stays here visits the full-service, historic spa on the premises or the local wineries—or both.

Luxury rating: 4

Recreation rating: 4

Calistoga, off Highway 29

The resort is situated on 16 acres of volcanic ash and three thermal geysers. Thousand of years before the invention of resorts and spas, the local Native Americans built sweat lodges over the escaping steam, bathed in the warm water, and called this area Oven Place. When the Spaniards arrived in the 17th century, they named the area Agua Caliente. During the 1800s, Sam Brannan, the first California gold rush tycoon, bought the property and built an upscale resort, naming it Calistoga, a combination of California and Saratoga, a lavish East Coast resort. Later, Leland Stanford bought the property and at one time planned to build Stanford University here.

The current bathhouse and pool were built in 1913; the cottages were added in the 1940s, although they have been refurbished recently. Today, Indian Springs is recognized as the oldest continuously operating thermal pool and spa in the state. The temperature of the naturally heated mineral pool fluctuates between 90°F and 102°F, depending on the season. The spa has a full range of services, including 15 different types of massage.

The 18 bungalows are actually duplex units, except for two freestanding cottages with fully equipped kitchens. The duplex rentals have kitchenettes. The remodeling includes whitewashed walls, plank floors, fireplaces, down comforters, and front porches. Each bungalow has a hammock outside. With such nice facilities, it's too bad that the management is not consistently friendly and helpful to their guests and the public.

For details about other activities in the area, see the listing for Cottage Grove Inn, below.

Facilities: Indian Springs has two freestanding bungalows and 18 duplex-style bungalows. All have private bathrooms, front porches, barbecues, televisions, and air-conditioning. The freestanding bungalows have a fully equipped kitchen. A large mineral pool, a full-service spa with mud baths, a tennis court, croquet, bicycle racks, and hammocks are available. The lodging is suitable for children. Pets are not allowed. No smoking is permitted. One cottage is wheelchair accessible.

Bedding: Linens and towels are provided.

Reservations and rates: Reservations are recommended. The fee is $175 to $500 per night per cottage. Additional persons are $15 per night per person. Major credit cards are accepted. Open year-round.

Directions: From Napa, drive north on Highway 29 for about 30 miles to Calistoga. At the flashing light, turn right on Lincoln Avenue and drive approximately one mile to Indian Springs on the right.

Contact: Indian Springs, 1712 Lincoln Avenue, Calistoga, CA 94515; 707/942-4913, fax 707/942-4919; website: www.indianspringscalistoga.com.

Indian Springs

---

27. COTTAGE GROVE INN

Cottage Grove Inn is one of the few high-end lodges in Calistoga with deluxe cottages available. Sixteen of them—with vaulted ceilings, skylights, and hardwood floors—opened in 1996, and they were an instant hit. The location is great for travelers because the cottages are just off the main street, within easy walking distance of restaurants, shopping, the airport, and the spas.

Luxury rating: 4

Recreation rating: 4

Calistoga, off Highway 29

No details were forgotten in the design of these cottages, which include front porches with rocking chairs, large bathrooms with deep whirlpool tubs for two, wet bars, down comforters on king-size beds, and custom-made furniture. Each cottage is decorated individually, and this is one of the few inns that doesn't have a cottage that stands out as being the most desirable or popular.

Rose Floral Cottage has the appearance of a European country sitting room, with its two overstuffed lounge chairs with ottomans, coral hues, and an oil painting that hangs above the fireplace. The Pine Cottage has a huge, fluffy bed that requires a step stool to climb onto. Provence Cottage features a wrought-iron bed.

The cottages are spaced close together, but there are no adjoining walls with neighboring cottages. A private driveway leads to most of the cottages. Although there are no kitchen facilities, an expanded continental breakfast is served in the morning, and in the afternoon a buffet table with Napa Valley wines and a variety of cheeses is available to guests.

Hot-air balloon and glider rides are popular just a few miles north of here. For those of you who have never experienced either of these activities, be aware that they create completely different sensations. Ballooning creates little sensation other than a feeling of floating. It is usually quiet and serene in a balloon, except for the occasional hissing of the gas burner. A glider ride is also quiet and can sometimes feel like floating, but that is where the similarities end. The adrenaline rush you feel the first time the chain is unhooked, disconnecting your glider from the airplane that is towing you, is like nothing else. You suddenly realize that you are airborne in a capsule with wings but no engine, and it darned well better glide. Fortunately, it does glide, as you quickly discover, but you need to remember two things: 1) Bring a plastic bag, and 2) Don't allow the pilot to attempt to break his record for the number of circles completed when catching an uprising thermal draft . . . 19, 20, 21 . . . . Where is that plastic bag?

Facilities: Cottage Grove Inn has 16 cottages with private bathrooms. There are no kitchen facilities but a deluxe continental breakfast and afternoon wine and cheese are provided. A front porch, whirlpool tub for two, fireplace, small refrigerator, television with VCR, and wet bar are provided in each cottage. The inn is not suitable for children. Pets are not allowed. No smoking is permitted. One cottage is wheelchair accessible.

Bedding: Linens and towels are provided.

Reservations and rates: Reservations are recommended. The double occupancy rate is $235 to $295 per night per cottage, plus $50 per night for each additional person. There is a two-night minimum on weekends. Major credit cards are accepted. Open year-round.

Directions: From Napa, drive north on Highway 29 for about 30 miles to Calistoga. At the flashing light, turn right on Lincoln Avenue and drive approximately one mile into downtown Calistoga to the inn on the left.

Contact: Cottage Grove Inn, 1711 Lincoln Avenue, Calistoga, CA 94515; 707/942-8400 or 800/799-2284, fax 707/942-2653; website: www.cottagegrove.com.

OTHER CABINS AND COTTAGES NEARBY

• Mount View Hotel, 1457 Lincoln Avenue, Calistoga, CA 94515; 707/942-6877 or 800/816-6877; website: www.mountviewhotel.com.

Cottage Grove Inn

28. LAKE BERRYESSA MARINE RESORT

Lake Berryessa is the Bay Area's backyard water recreation headquarters, the number-one lake in the greater Bay Area for water sports, loafing, and fishing. This resort is set on the west shore of the main lake, one of several resorts at the lake.

Luxury rating: 3

Recreation rating: 4

Lake Berryessa, off Highway 121

One of the things that sets Lake Berryessa Marine Resort apart from the others is that it offers a series of park model cabins, also called RV cabins, for rent. These are the extremely cute, clean cabins that are built off-site, then trailered in on wheels to their location. Lattice is added around the base of the unit, so it appears permanent, and a deck with a barbecue is added as well. For guests, it means having a cabin by the lakeside without having to spend a fortune. They work great, and though a bit small, the cabins feel more cozy than cramped, especially with the outside deck to provide extra room.

This resort makes a fine headquarters for a vacation at Lake Berryessa. When full, it is a big lake, covering some 21,000 acres with 165 miles of shoreline, complete with secret coves, islands, and an expanse of untouched shore (on the eastern side) where people are off-limits. It is one of California's most popular lakes, and on weekends it is full of happy boaters zooming around, especially pulling kids in tubes or on wake boards. It's also good for waterskiing.

During the week, the lake quiets down significantly, and that is when fishing is best. Trout fishing in the summer is often excellent for people who understand how to troll deep in the thermocline. A lot of the trout range 14 to 17 inches, and what most anglers do is get up before dawn in summer and then troll at either Portuguese Cove or Skiers Cove, which are entrances to the narrows (especially the Rock Slide on the east side of the lakeshore) and the mouth of Markley Cove. The key in the summer is depth, trolling typically 25 to 35 feet deep using lures such as the Rainbow Runners, Triple Teaser (white with a red head), and Humdinger.

Lake Berryessa is loaded with bass in the spring, most ranging from 11 to 14 inches. It is common to catch 20 or 30 bass in a day, casting a variety of lures—plastics are best—along protected shoreline coves. The east shoreline, from the vineyards on into the adjacent cove, is an excellent spot where bass hold from late March through early June. In addition, this lake has dozens and dozens of flooded islands where bass congregate during these times.

Facilities: Lake Berryessa Marine Resort has 11 RV park cabins that sleep up to four, with beds, kitchenettes (no stove), small bathrooms with shower, living rooms, and outdoor decks with barbecue. Bring cooking and eating utensils, charcoal, and a lighter. The resort has coin laundry, complete marina facilities, boat rentals, houseboat rentals, supplies, and groceries. No pets or smoking are allowed in the cabins.

Bedding: Linens and towels are not provided. Bring your sleeping bag, pillow, and towels.

Reservations and rates: Reservations are required and are available by phone and on the resort's website. Rates range $100 to $150 per night, with reduced rates available for weekdays. There is a two-night minimum on summer weekends. There is an $8 fee for additional vehicles and a $10 fee for boat parking and launching. Major credit cards are accepted. Open year-round.

Directions: From Vallejo, drive north on Interstate 80 to the Suisun Valley Road exit. Take Suisun Valley Road and drive north to Highway 121. Turn north on Highway 121 and drive five miles to Highway 128. Turn left on Highway 128, drive five miles to Berryessa-Knoxville Road, turn right, and continue nine miles to 5800 Knoxville Road.

Contact: Lake Berryessa Marine Resort, 5800 Knoxville Road, Napa, CA 94558; 707/966-2161; website: www.lakeberryessa.com. For boat rental reservations, call 707/ 966-4204; houseboat rentals, 707/966-2827.

Lake Berryessa Marine Resort

29. STILLWATER COVE RANCH

Inexpensive lodging with a dramatic oceanside setting on 50 acres is what you get at Stillwater Cove Ranch. You also get direct access to the ocean and Stillwater Cove Regional Park. The ranch is wedged between Salt Point State Park and Fort Ross State Historic Park. For ocean lovers and hikers who like their coastline on the rugged side, this is a perfect location.

Stillwater is a working farm, so you'll share the land with the resident chickens, white pigeons, geese, peacocks, and sheep—even a semi-tame wild pig. The lodging consists of two freestanding cottages, four large inn rooms with kitchenettes, and a bunkhouse with kitchen facilities. These buildings were constructed in the 1930s, and they haven't been updated much.

Luxury rating: 2

Recreation rating: 4

Sonoma Coast, off Highway 1 near Jenner

Teacher's Cottage and Cook's Cottage are the most private lodgings, and are also considered the most romantic. Cook's Cottage is nicknamed the Honeymoon Cottage; you'll have an ocean view from your deck. The cottages do not include kitchens, but hibachis are allowed on the deck and restaurants are nearby. Each cottage has a fireplace and two double beds. The other units have fully equipped kitchens. The Dairy Barn, or bunkhouse, is set up with eight bunk beds, two bathrooms with showers, and a woodburning stove (free wood is provided for the Dairy Barn). You have to bring your own linens and towels. A maximum of 16 persons can be housed in the bunkhouse.

A great hike at the regional park is the Stockoff Creek Loop, which in little more than a mile routes you through a forest with both firs and redwoods, and then along a pretty stream. For details about hiking in the area, refer to the guidebook *Foghorn Outdoors: California Hiking*.

Facilities: Stillwater Cove Ranch has two cottages, four inn rooms, and a bunkhouse. Some cabins have fireplaces. Conference facilities are available. The ranch is suitable for children. Leashed pets are allowed in some cabins. No smoking is permitted.

Bedding: Linens and towels are provided in all facilities except for the bunkhouse.

Reservations and rates: Reservations are recommended. The fee is $45 to $75 per night per rental and $145 per night for the bunkhouse. Additional persons are $10 per night per person. Special rates are available December through March and in July. There is a two-night minimum on weekends, and a three-night minimum on holidays. Children under age three are free. Credit cards are not accepted. Open year-round.

Directions: On U.S. 101 north of Santa Rosa, turn west on River Road and drive 13 miles to Guerneville and Highway 116. Turn west on Highway 116 and drive about 20 miles to Highway 1 at Jenner. Turn north on Highway 1 and drive 16 miles to the ranch on the right.

Contact: Stillwater Cove Ranch, 22555 Highway 1, Jenner, CA; 707/847-3227.

Stillwater Cove Ranch

30. MURPHY'S JENNER INN AND COTTAGES

Jenner Inn is located at the mouth of the Russian River on the Sonoma Coast, one-and-a-half hours from San Francisco, two-and-a-half hours from Sacramento, and only 45 minutes from Santa Rosa. You just get in your car, point it to Sonoma County, and before you know it, you're there—"where the Russian River meets the sea."

When you arrive, you'll find little cottages and homes set on a coastal foothill at the mouth of the Russian River. This is Jenner-by-the-Sea. The main inn is set below a prominent rock outcropping and adjacent cottages and homes are nuzzled into the hillside. Rosebud and Rosewater are waterfront cottages with ocean and estuary views. They also have an adjacent grassy yard that slopes down to the water. This makes for an excellent put-in spot for kayaks or canoes. Riversea Cottage has an exceptional view of the bird refuge on Penny Island and the place where the Russian River meets the sea. Whale Watch Cottage features a great view of the ocean, Tree House is set for a river lookout, and Mill Cottage provides views of a meadow and stream. There are absolutely zero televisions, so you can quickly embrace the natural harmony of the coast.

Luxury rating: 4

Recreation rating: 3

Sonoma Coast, off Highway 1 in Jenner

No matter which way you turn, there are many side trips and adventures available. To the south are Sonoma Coast State Beach (five minutes on Highway 1), Bodega Bay (20 minutes), and Point Reyes National Seashore (one hour). To the north on Highway 1 are Fort Ross (20 minutes) and Salt Point State Park (30 minutes). To the east on Highway 116 are the Russian River, the Russian River wine country (30 minutes), and Armstrong Redwoods State Park (30 minutes).

The closest quality adventure requires just a short drive south on Highway 1 to Shell Beach/Sonoma Coast State Beach. Shell Beach is a beautiful place, and with the trail to Arch Rock and good beach-combing at low tides, you can spend hours here. If you want to hike, just across from the entrance to Shell Beach, on the east side of Highway 1, follow the coastal trailhead for the Pomo-Ohlone Trail. The trail climbs up the foothills, providing beautiful views of the ocean to the west, and eventually gains the ridge for more great views, including those of Goat Rock at the mouth of the Russian River and a sweeping lookout of the coast.

Facilities: Murphy's Jenner Inn and Cottages has four cottages, two homes, and 16 rooms divided into four buildings. Each cottage is unique, but most feature a kitchenette and full bath, with deck, hot tub, and fireplace available. Some cottages and rooms have telephones but none have televisions. A full breakfast is provided. Leashed pets are allowed in some units.

Bedding: Linens and towels are provided.

Reservations and rates: Reservations are recommended. Rates for cottages range from $168 to $268 per night. Rooms range from $88 to $378. A two-night minimum stay is required on weekends.

Directions: On U.S. 101 north of Santa Rosa, turn west on River Road and drive 13 miles to Guerneville and Highway 116. Turn west on Highway 116 and drive about 20 miles to Highway 1 at Jenner. Turn north on Highway 1 and look for Jenner Inn and Cottages on the right side of the road.

Contact: Murphy's Jenner Inn and Cottages, 10400 Coast Highway 1, P.O. Box 69, Jenner, CA 95450; 707/865-2377 or 800/732-2377; website: www.jennerinn.com.

Murphy's Jenner Inn and Cottages

31. HUCKLEBERRY SPRINGS COUNTRY INN AND SPA

After passing through Monte Rio, a little town along the Russian River, we made the assigned right turn at Tyrone Road, though it's so small that we just about missed it. It turned out to be a narrow patch of asphalt that passes a few houses, climbs and turns to gravel, then dirt, and finally narrows even more, passing through a forest of some oaks and redwoods. There was no sign of any resort. "This can't be the right way," we said.

Luxury rating: 3

Recreation rating: 4

Russian River, off Highway 116 near Monte Rio

But it was, it turns out. A moment later, posted on a tree on the right side of the road, we spotted a small sign reading Huckleberry Springs, and in a few minutes, despite all our misgivings, we were pulling into a small parking place next to the lodge headquarters.

It also turns out that this is the most secluded setting for cabin rentals in this region, with four unusual little cabins nestled in the woods in the foothills south of the Russian River. The place is quiet and remote, yet at the same time set close enough for canoeing, hiking, fishing, or just playing in the river. The only downer is that you must drive to take part in the area's outdoor recreation.

The cottages at Huckleberry Springs are like nothing we've seen anywhere. The Cherry Barrel, believe it or not, is literally that—a giant barrel that has been converted into a room, with a pine ceiling and a skylight, along with a bathroom; it's the most unusual cabin imaginable.

Another, Spring Hill, is reached via a five-minute walk up a steep hill. You are rewarded with a small custom-made cottage with a deck and a view of the valley, a bed set high in a loft accessible by a built-in ladder, and a skylight. It is absolutely quiet, and if you're lucky, you might even see shooting stars at night through the skylight.

Facilities: Huckleberry Springs has four cottages, each with a bathroom, television, and VCR. No telephones are provided in the cabins. At the lodge, a telephone, video library, and restaurant-style dining are available. A small swimming pool and spa with gazebo are also available. A private massage cottage is available for spa treatments, including massage, facials, and reflexology for an extra charge. Children must be over the age of 15.

Bedding: Linens and towels are provided.

Reservations and rates: Reservations are required. The rate for cabins ranges from $160 to $185 per night, including a full hot breakfast.

Directions: From Rohnert Park, take Highway 116 northwest. Continue on Highway 116 past Sebastopol and Guerneville. Four miles past Guerneville, at an intersection with a stop sign, go straight (Highway 116 veers to the right) and enter Monte Rio. Turn left on the Bohemian Highway, drive a short distance over the Russian River, then turn right on Main Street. Continue on Main Street through Monte Rio. One mile past the firehouse, turn right on Tyrone Road. Drive .5 mile, then bear right on Old Beedle Road and continue for one mile to Huckleberry Springs.

Contact: Huckleberry Springs Country Inn, P.O. Box 400, Monte Rio, CA 95462; 707/865-2683 or 800/822-2683, fax 707/865-1688; website: www.huckleberrysprings.com.

Huckleberry Springs Country Inn and Spa

32. THE FARMHOUSE INN

Luxury rating: 4

Recreation rating: 3

Russian River, off Highway 116 near Forestville

New owners, eight newly renovated cottages, a restaurant in a Victorian farmhouse, and a new, upscale attitude and ambience are what you'll find at The Farmhouse Inn. The innkeepers have completed a $500,000 renovation of the existing facilities and six acres, and now they're turning their attention to adding eight additional cottages. If you liked the place before, you'll most likely love it now.

The Farmhouse Inn specialty is luxury, with all attention directed towards privacy, quiet, excellent food, and romance. What do you do here? Well, when they sell gift baskets with names like "Sensuous" and "Romance," what do you think you do here? And this certainly is the right place for romance: saunas and double-jetted whirlpool tubs for two, woodburning fireplaces with Italian tile, breakfast delivered to your cottage if you like, feather beds and pillows with handcrafted bedding, oversized furniture, and a four-star restaurant. The setup is so lovely and upscale that it's popular for weddings, and special packages are available.

Cottages 6 and 7 are the largest, with a separate living room, and Cottages 3 and 5 are the smallest, with canopy beds. The favored unit is Cottage 7, which has a raised king bed and customized bedding made from fine European textiles. The suite is decorated in taupe, silver, and black. Good things can come in small packages, and that is the scenario with Cottage 5. It is a dramatic room, decorated in tangerine and ruby, with a wrought-iron canopy bed and white lace duvet cover. Each room is decorated individually and the effect is sophisticated luxury, with a touch of traditional and country decor.

A full gourmet breakfast is served in the conservatory-style dining room or on the outdoor terrace. Or, a deluxe continental breakfast can be delivered to your cottage. The restaurant overlooks a small vineyard and courtyard fountain. Dinner is served Thursday through Sunday, and live, classical guitar music is sometimes played.

Beginning in 2002, three-night, midweek packages are offered that include lodging and activities such as tours of small wineries in Sonoma County and the Russian River Valley, excursions to local culinary businesses, and bicycling, canoeing, and hot air ballooning. The emphasis is on cuisine and adventuring, and up to 16 persons can be accommodated each week.

Facilities: The Farmhouse Inn has eight adjoining cottages. There are no kitchen facilities, but a full gourmet breakfast is provided, and a restaurant is available. Each cottage has a private bathroom, fireplace, sauna, double-jetted whirlpool tub for two, shower, small refrigerator stocked with fine wines and snacks, and television and VCR. A pool, spa, sundeck, movie library, gift baskets, and massage and aromatherapy are available. Wedding and meeting facilities are available. The inn is not suitable for children. Pets are not allowed. Smoking is not permitted. One cottage is wheelchair accessible.

Bedding: Linens and towels are provided.

Reservations and rates: Reservations are recommended. The double-occupancy rate is $145 to $250 per night per cottage. Additional persons are $25 per night. Major credit cards are accepted. Open year-round.

Directions: From U.S. 101 in Santa Rosa, drive on U.S. 101 to the north end of Santa Rosa and the River Road exit. Take that exit and drive west on River Road for 7.1 miles to the inn on the left.

Contact: The Farmhouse Inn, 7871 River Road, Forestville, CA 95436; 707/887-3300 or 800/464-6642, fax, 707/887-3311; website: www.farmhouseinn.com.

The Farmhouse Inn

33. AUBERGE DU SOLEIL

When a resort's motto is "a place without reality checks," you know it's out of the ordinary.

Understated luxury is dominant among the 11 spacious, airy, Mediterranean-style cottages. Private terraces and expansive views overlook the Napa Valley. The facilities are tucked away on a gently sloping hill situated in an olive grove and on 33 acres. Auberge du Soleil translates to Inn of the Sun, and it emanates a quietly cheerful and serene setting.

Luxury rating: 5

Recreation rating: 4

Napa Valley, off Highway 29 in Rutherford

People who lodge here usually fit into one of two categories: very rich or lucky souls who work for companies that are in the black and reward their executives with a business retreat. How do we know that? Well, a freestanding cottage rental goes for $1,500 to $3,000 per night, the highest priced listing in this book, so it's pretty easy to figure out that the average person can't fork over money like that.

The cottages have an abundance of terra cotta tile, adobe-style walls, vaulted ceilings, fireplaces, and oversized, white-painted French doors with shutters. The furnishings are simple yet elegant, with king-size beds with Frette linens, overstuffed chairs, wet bars with small refrigerators stocked with wines and cheeses, and a basket of snacks. The bathrooms are indulgent, with a skylight, a large tub, double sinks, oversized towels, two different types of bathrobes, candles, and fragrant bath salts.

The Napa Valley has a reputation for some of the best food in California, and Auberge du Soleil's restaurant rates near the top. In 1981, when the restaurant opened, its chef at the time, Masataka Kobayashi, was considered by many to be one of the top 10 chefs in the world. After he left, the restaurant seemed to go into a slide, but with a new chef in 2000, Richard Reddington, the restaurant seems poised to make a comeback to its former glory. The restaurant's wine list holds a Wine Spectator's Best of Award.

The extras you get here include 24-hour room service, a top-quality restaurant with bar and private dining rooms, a large swimming pool, tennis courts, a fitness center, a $2 million full-service spa—even a sculpture garden with a collection of large-scale sculptures. If this sounds like your kind of place, here's our suggestion for staying here without completely draining your savings: rent one of the 39 suites or rooms, since they start at $450 per night and you get almost the same amenities as staying in a private cottage. It's still a lot of money, we know, but heck, doesn't that sound better than $3,000 per night? Then again, if you have to ask the price, maybe you're having a reality check in a place that doesn't have reality checks.

Facilities: Auberge du Soleil has 11 cottages and 39 inn rooms and suites. There are no kitchen facilities. Fireplace, telephone, wet bar, and air-conditioning are provided in each unit. Some rentals have televisions. A restaurant and lounge, 24-hour room service, a full-service spa, a hair salon, a boutique, a pool with sundeck, tennis courts and instruction, a gym with hot tub and steam rooms, meeting rooms, picnic areas, and concierge services are available. The facilities are not suitable for children. Pets are not allowed. Smoking is not permitted. Some lodging is wheelchair accessible.

Bedding: Linens and towels are provided.

Reservations and rates: Reservations are recommended. The fee is $1,500 to $3,000 per night per private cottage, and $450 to $1,000 for inn rooms and suites. There is a two-night minimum on weekends, and a three-night minimum on holidays. Major credit cards are accepted. Open year-round.

Directions: From Napa, drive north on Highway 29 to Highway 128 East. Turn east on Highway 128 and drive one mile to a fork in the road. Bear left at the fork and continue on Highway 128 to the Silverado Trail. Turn left on the Silverado Trail and drive a short distance to Rutherford Hill Road. Turn right and drive .25 mile to the resort on the right.

Contact: Auberge du Soleil, 180 Rutherford Hill Road, Rutherford, CA 94573; 707/963-1211 or 800/348-5406, fax 707/963-8764; website: www.auberge dusoleil.com.   *Auberge du Soleil*

34. SONOMA CHALET

You'll think you've stepped into an alpine lodge when you enter Sonoma Chalet, only it's located in the Valley of the Moon, the heart of the Sonoma wine country, and is a five-minute drive from downtown Sonoma. Three storybook cottages are located on the 3.5-acre hillside property, along with a Swiss-style farmhouse with four inn rooms. Set amid towering eucalyptus trees and surrounded by pastures, the cottages are perfect for a quiet getaway; they're close to wine tasting, great cycling routes, shopping, and touring Jack London State Historic Park.

The freestanding cottages and inn rooms are filled with antiques, collectibles, and unique bric-a-brac, and have fireplaces or woodstoves, claw-foot bathtubs, and decks or porches. The inn has a reputation for quirky touches. The most popular rental is Sara's Cottage, which is the most private and is reached by crossing a wooden bridge. Amenities include a good-sized bathroom with clawfoot tub, woodstove, loft, hardwood floors with Oriental rugs, and antiques and collectibles from the 1800s to the 1950s. The size of the cottages ranges from 400 to 600 square feet.

A complimentary breakfast of fresh juice, coffee, fresh fruit, cereal, breads, and pastries is served in the dining room, on a deck overlooking a 200-acre ranch, or it can be delivered to your cottage on request. A garden hot tub and bicycles are available for guests.

Of course, the main attraction of the Sonoma Valley for vacationers is wine tasting. There are a number of wineries in the area, and within three miles, on the east side of Sonoma, are Sebastiani, Ravenswood, Buena Vista, and Gundlach Bundschu. Sonoma Mission Golf Course, an 18-hole course, is located six miles away.

Luxury rating: 4

Recreation rating: 3

Sonoma, off Highway 12

A few miles up Highway 12 is Jack London State Historic Park, where London created his dreams and became one of America's truly great writers and philosophers. It was also here that those dreams were shattered, first by a fire that devoured his ranch home, then by an illness at age 40 from which he never recovered. You can visit London's cottage, winery ruins, barns, and distillery. A one-mile walk on the Lake Trail leads to a small pond that was a favorite recreation area for London and his guests.

Facilities: Sonoma Chalet has three cottages and four inn rooms and suites. The cottages have no kitchens, but a complimentary continental breakfast is served. Private bathrooms and air-conditioning are provided in the cottages. There are no televisions or telephones in the units. A garden hot tub and bicycles are available. The facilities are not suitable for children. Pets are not allowed. No smoking is permitted.

Bedding: Linens and towels are provided.

Reservations and rates: Reservations are recommended. The fee is $185 to $225 for cottages and $110 to $190 for inn rooms. There is a two-night minimum on weekends and a three-night minimum on summer weekends and holidays. Major credit cards are accepted. Open year-round.

Directions: From Sonoma and Highway 12, turn west on West Napa Street and drive five blocks to West Fifth Street. Turn right and drive approximately .75 mile to the end of the road. Continue straight ahead onto a gravel road and drive a short distance to Sonoma Chalet.

Contact: Sonoma Chalet, 18935 Fifth Street West, Sonoma, CA 95476; 707/938-3129; website: www.sonomachalet.com.

Sonoma Chalet

CHAPTER 5

Sacramento
& Gold Country

F rom a distance, this section of the Sacramento Valley looks like flat farmland extending into infinity, with a sprinkling of cities and towns interrupting the view. But a closer look reveals a landscape filled with Northern California's most significant rivers—the Sacramento, Feather, Yuba, American, and Mokelumne. All of these provide water recreation, in both lakes and rivers, as well as serve as the lifeblood for a series of wildlife refuges.

   This is an area for California history buffs, with Malakoff Diggins State Historic Park, Piety Hill Cottages, Sacramento-Metro KOA, and Placerville KOA located in the center of some of the state's most extraordinary history: the gold rush era. In addition, Malakoff Diggins has the lowest cost cabin rentals in the state that we could find—$10 a night. Another great deal is the Lake Oroville Floating Camps, which can sleep 15 and cost only $42 a night.

There are relatively few cabin rentals in the Sacramento Valley and nearby foothills. The ones that are here are either on lakes, such as Camanche, Rollins, Oroville, and Red Bluff, or are getaways in historic towns. These rentals, more than those in any other area of Northern California, represent the most middle range of both pricing and accommodations. But also some of the best deals.

Timing is everything in love and the great outdoors, and so it is in the Central Valley and the nearby foothills. Spring and fall are gorgeous here, along with many summer evenings. But there are always periods of 100-plus temperatures in the summer.

But that's what gives the lakes and rivers such appeal, and in turn, why they are treasured. Take your pick: San Joaquin Delta near Stockton, Lake Oroville in the northern Sierra, Folsom Lake outside Sacramento . . . the list goes on. On a hot day, jumping into a cool lake makes water more valuable than gold, a cold drink on ice worth more than silver. These have become top sites for boating-based recreation and fantastic areas for water sports and fishing.

In the Mother Lode country, three other lakes—Camanche, Amador, and Pardee—are outstanding for fishing. The guidebook Foghorn Outdoors: California Fishing ranks three of this chapter's lakes among the top 10 lakes for fishing in the state—Lake Oroville and Lake Camanche make the list for bass and Lake Amador make it for bluegill and catfish—no small feat considering the 381 other lakes they were up against.

For touring, the state capital and nearby Old Sacramento are favorites. Others prefer reliving the gold mining history of California's past or exploring the foothill country, including Malakoff Diggins State Historic Park.

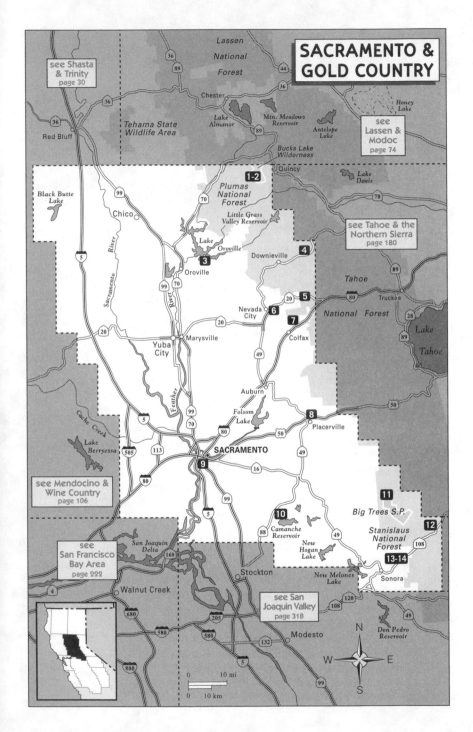

SACRAMENTO & GOLD COUNTRY

see Shasta
& Trinity
page 30

Lassen
National
Forest

see
Lassen &
Modoc
page 74

Honey
Lake

Chester

Red Bluff

Tehama State
Wildlife Area

Lake
Almanor

Mtn. Meadows
Reservoir

Antelope
Lake

Bucks Lake
Wilderness

Quincy

1-2

Plumas
National
Forest

Lake
Davis

Black Butte
Lake

Chico

Little Grass
Valley Reservoir

see Tahoe & the
Northern Sierra
page 180

Lake
Oroville

3

Downieville

4

Oroville

Tahoe

5

Nevada
City

6

7

Truckee

National Forest

Colfax

Marysville

Yuba
City

Lake
Tahoe

Sacramento River

Auburn

Folsom
Lake

8

Placerville

Cache Creek

Lake
Berryessa

Feather

SACRAMENTO

9

see Mendocino &
Wine Country
page 106

11

Big Trees S.P.

10

Camanche
Reservoir

New
Hogan
Lake

Stanislaus
National
Forest

12

see
San Francisco
Bay Area
page 222

San Joaquin
Delta

13-14

Sonora

Stockton

New Melones
Lake

Walnut Creek

see San
Joaquin Valley
page 318

Don Pedro
Reservoir

Modesto

N

W   E

S

0   10 mi

0   10 km

CHAPTER 5
SACRAMENTO & GOLD COUNTRY

1. BUCKS LAKE LODGE

Bucks Lake is one of Northern California's greatest destinations for reclaiming the simple life—taking a cabin by the lake and heading out in a boat each day to try and catch "Walter."

© SUZI BRAKKEN

Luxury rating: 3

Recreation rating: 5

Plumas National Forest, off Highway 89 near Quincy

The lake is set at 5,237 feet in Plumas National Forest, about a 25-minute drive from the town of Quincy, so it feels remote. It is also very pretty, and the cabins, nearby marina, boating, and fishing answer dreams for water enthusiasts.

When you open the door of your Bucks Lake Lodge cabin in the morning, you will notice immediately the smell of pine duff, the clear air, the blue-green water, and the purity of all the nearby streams. The cabins at Bucks Lake Lodge are not luxurious, but they're nice enough, woodsy-looking, and well-suited for families. They can handle couples or groups up to 10.

What makes Bucks Lake a winner for so many is the fishing for rainbow trout in the 11- to 15-inch class by trolling or fishing from shore with bait. There's also the chance for mackinaw trout in the 20-pound range by using deepwater trolling or jigging techniques. Bucks Lake is one of the most consistent producers of trout in California, with the best spot by Rocky Point near where Bucks Creek enters the lake. Another good spot is the old river channel near where Mill Creek enters the lake.

Even though the mackinaw fishery was just established in the 1990s, it is already the source of tremendous anticipation. You never know what you might get when you hook a nice five-pounder, a trophy 20-pounder, or perhaps the next state-record in the 40-pound class. The fishing is best for these giant mackinaw trout just after the lake clears of ice, typically in early May, and stays good until hot weather arrives for summer in July.

Enough 15- to 20-pounders have already been caught to make some believe that a state-record fish may be caught here one day. We call that fish "Walter," just like in the movie *On Golden Pond.*

Facilities: Bucks Lake Lodge has 11 cabins with kitchens sized for groups of 2 to 10. Lodge rooms are also available. A small marina, boat ramp, boat and motor rentals, general store, and restaurant are available nearby. Pets are permitted. Both smoking and nonsmoking cabins and rooms are available.

Bedding: Linens are provided. There is no room service.

Reservations and rates: Reservations are recommended. Rates range from $80 (for two) to $124 (for up to 10) per night. Dogs are $10 per night.

Directions: From Oroville, drive north on Highway 70 to the junction with Highway 89. Turn south on Highway 89/70 and drive 11 miles to Quincy. In Quincy, turn right at Bucks Lake Road and drive 17 miles to Bucks Lake.

Contact: Bucks Lake Lodge, P.O. Box 236, Quincy, CA 95971; 530/283-2262 or 800/481-2825, fax 530/283-5008.

Bucks Lake Lodge

2. BUCKS LAKE MARINA

Vacationers flock here year after year because they know exactly what they'll get: great fishing, beautiful mountain scenery, fresh air, and the same cabin they've stayed in for years. Maybe their grandparents even rented one of these cabins decades ago, since they were built in the 1930s.

© TOM RATH

Luxury rating: 2

Recreation rating: 5

Plumas National Forest, off Highway 89 near Quincy

What visitors find is almost identical to what grandma and grandpa experienced; that is, except for the personal watercrafts. There are one- and two-bedroom cabins with lake views, and they can accommodate two to five persons, depending on the cabin. They have a kitchen, a bathroom, and the basics—no frills added. There are no televisions or telephones, but a pay telephone is available at the marina. Situated about 50 yards above the lake under pine and fir tree cover, the cabins are spaced about 20 feet apart.

Although you'd think that everyone who stays here wants to fish and boat, you might be surprised to find that this is not always true. During the summer, a riding stable is open about a half mile away. And you'll see hunters here in the fall. Bucks Lake Lodge—with a restaurant, store, lounge, and game room—is within walking distance of the cabins here at Bucks Lake Marina.

For more information about Bucks Lake, see the previous listing for Bucks Lake Lodge.

Facilities: Bucks Lake Marina features eight cabins and an RV campground. Each cabin has a fully equipped kitchen and a bathroom with shower. A fire pit and porch are provided. A small store, boat dock, and full-service marina, bait and tackle, and boat and personal watercraft rentals are available.

Bedding: One set of linens and towels is provided. There is no daily maid service; bring extra towels.

Reservations and rates: Reservations are required in the summer. The fee is $65 to $80 per night per cabin, or $430 to $525 per week. A pet fee of $7 per night per pet is charged. There is a one-week minimum during the summer. The cabins are suitable for children. Up to two leashed pets are allowed per cabin. Smoking is permitted. Major credit cards are accepted. Open mid-April through October, weather permitting.

Directions: From Oroville, drive north on Highway 70 to the junction with Highway 89. Turn south on Highway 89/70 and drive 11 miles to Quincy. In Quincy, turn right at Bucks Lake Road and drive 16.5 miles to the lake and the resort on the right.

Contact: Bucks Lake Marina, P.O. Box 559, Quincy, CA 95971; 530/283-4243.

OTHER CABINS AND COTTAGES NEARBY

• Bucks Lakeshore Resort, P.O. Box 338, Meadow Valley, CA 95956; 530/283-6900, fax 530/283-6909; website: www.bucks lake.com.

Bucks Lake Marina

3. LAKE OROVILLE FLOATING CAMPS

It doesn't get any stranger than this, and for many who have tried, it doesn't get any better. We're talking about the double-decker floating camps at Lake Oroville. They're like nothing you've ever seen or experienced.

The floating camps look like giant patio boats. They sleep up to 15 people and include a picnic table, a sink, a food locker, life jackets, a garbage can, a vault toilet, a propane barbecue, and water (not suitable for drinking). For $42 a night, it might be the best family camping deal in the state. There are even floating toilets here—imagine that!

Luxury rating: 1

Recreation rating: 5

Lake Oroville, off Highway 70

What you need is a boat to reach one of these "cabins." Then you can use the vessel as a base camp, swimming platform, even fishing dock, leaving a line out while you enjoy yourself. Shuttle service is not available to these anchored cabins from the boat launch, so BYOB (Bring Your Own Boat).

Lake Oroville is a huge reservoir with a large central body of water and extensive lake arms, in all covering more than 15,000 acres. With warm water and plenty of it, Oroville is an outstanding lake for water sports. And, there is enough room for both water-skiers and anglers.

Did someone say fish? Lake Oroville's got 'em: rainbow trout, brown trout, largemouth bass, catfish, bluegill, crappie, and even a modest salmon population. The bass fishing at Oroville—for numbers of fish in the 15-inch class—often rates among the best anywhere in America. Recent habitat work has given the bass fishing a big help, with 30- and 40-fish days possible in the spring. Try casting plastic worms in the backs of coves where there is floating wood debris.

Facilities: Lake Oroville Floating Camps has 10 floating camps. Picnic tables, food lockers, and fire grills are provided. Vault toilets are available. No drinking water is provided. Leashed pets are permitted.

Bedding: Linens and towels are not provided. Visitors should bring sleeping pads or air beds, along with their sleeping bags.

Reservations and rates: Reservations are accepted for Floating Camps (call 800/444-7275 or visit the website: www.cal-parks.ca.gov). The cost is $42 per night.

Directions: From the Bay Area, drive east on I-80 to Sacramento and the split with Highway 50. Bear north on I-80 and continue a few miles to I-5. Turn north on I-5 and continue a few more miles to the junction with Highway 99/70. Turn north on Highway 99/70 and continue on Highway 70 into Oroville to Highway 162. Turn east on Highway 162 and drive eight miles to Kelly Ridge Road. Turn north (left) and drive 1.5 miles to Arroyo Drive. Turn right and drive to the state park entrance. Once inside the park, head to the boat launch, the closest ramp to the floating cabins.

Contact: Lake Oroville State Recreation Area, 530/538-2200; Lake Oroville Visitor Center, 530/538-2219. Fishing guides: Cash Colby, 530/533-1510; Larry Hemphill, 530/674-0276. *Lake Oroville Floating Camps*

4. SIERRA SHANGRI-LA

The Yuba River is one of the prettiest rivers to flow westward out of the Sierra Nevada. The stretch of river near Downieville is especially gorgeous, flowing from the drops of melting snow from the Sierra crest, with deep pools and miniature waterfalls, often edged by slabs of granite and punctuated with boulders. In the spring, it can be a wild and cold force of water, running blue-white during peak snowmelt. In the summer and fall, it greens up, warms considerably, and takes on a more benign demeanor in its routed canyon course.

Luxury rating: 3

Recreation rating: 4

Yuba River, off Highway 49 near Downieville

From the cabins at Sierra Shangri-La, you can watch the changing faces of this dynamic river. The North Fork Yuba River passes within ear range of the cabins here. Several have views of the river canyon, but from all of them, you will feel the magnetism of moving water.

The reason more people don't know about the Yuba or the secluded cabins near its banks is due to their remoteness. There is no direct way to get here. Even with the best route on Highway 49, you will discover that calling it a "highway" is a mighty stretch. This two-laner is constructed like a narrow pretzel, probably built on an old stagecoach route where grades had to be lengthened by curving the roads in order to give the horse teams a breather.

The secluded Sierra Shangri-La is located on the canyon bottom at 3,100 feet in elevation. The cottages with the best river views are Blue Jay, LaVista, Flycaster, and Jim Crow, while three rooms in the upper level of the lodge also provide great views. By the way, the resort gets its name from the nearby, magnificent Shangri-La wall of river stone.

This stretch of river is good for fly fishing for both rainbow trout and brown trout, and is decent for swimming and rafting out of Goodyear's Bar. The resort has a good swimming hole on the North Fork Yuba within walking distance of the cabins. Another good one is upstream at Union Flat Campground near Quartz Point, six miles east of Downieville on Highway 49.

Facilities: Sierra Shangri-La has eight cabins of various sizes, each with a bathroom, a kitchen, and a woodstove. A lodge with family-style dining is available on the property. Three bed-and-breakfast rooms with river views are also available. No pets are permitted.

Bedding: Linens are provided.

Reservations and rates: Reservations are accepted. Cabin rates are $65 to $160 per night, depending on the size of cabin, season, and length of stay. A minimum stay of a week is required in July and August ($600 per week for a couple). The three bed-and-breakfast rooms at the lodge are rented by the night and start at $65.

Directions: From Auburn, take Highway 49 north to Nevada City and continue (the road jogs left at Nevada City, then narrows) to Downieville. Continue three miles east on Highway 49 and look for the sign for Sierra Shangri-La on the right side of the road.

Contact: Sierra Shangri-La, P.O. Box 285, Downieville, CA 95936; 530/289-3455; website: www.sierrashangrila.com.

Sierra Shangri-La

5. MALAKOFF DIGGINS STATE HISTORIC PARK

A trip here is like a walk through history. Malakoff Diggins State Historic Park is the site of California's largest "hydraulic" mine. Huge cliffs have been carved by mighty streams of water, a gold mining technique involving the washing away of entire mountains to find the precious metal. This practice began in the 1850s and continued for many years. Several major gold mining operations combined hydraulic mining with giant sluice boxes. Hydraulic mining was a scourge to the land, of course, and legal battles between mine owners and downstream farmers eventually ended this method of mining.

Luxury rating: 1

Recreation rating: 3

off Highway 20 near Nevada City

The park also contains a 7,847-foot bedrock tunnel that served as a drain. The visitor center has exhibits on life in the old mining town of North Bloomfield. Tours of the numerous historic sites are available during the summer.

The cabins here are set near a small lake in the park and are the cheapest deal in California at $10 a night. Consequently, as you might expect, the accommodations are primitive. There really isn't much to them except for a couple of bunk beds and a picnic table. There isn't even electricity, so you will need to bring everything, just like on a camping trip. By now you have probably figured out that this isn't where you come if you don't want to rough it.

The drive in from Nevada City is slow and circuitous, with the last mile on dirt, so take your time and enjoy the sights along the way. The park is set at 3,400 feet in elevation.

Facilities: Malakoff Diggins State Historic Park has three primitive cabins along with a state park campground for tents and RVs. No electricity is provided. A picnic table, woodstove, and two double bunk beds that can accommodate up to eight people are provided inside each cabin. A fire pit and picnic table are also provided outside each cabin. Drinking water and flush toilets are available (except mid-November through February) nearby. Pets and smoking are not permitted.

Bedding: Linens and towels are not provided; bring your own sleeping bag and pillow.

Reservations and rates: Reservations are recommended. Call 800/444-PARK (800/444-7275) or visit the website: www.ReserveAmerica.com for Memorial Day through Labor Day. Cabins cost $10 per night, $37 for a group site. Open year-round.

Directions: From Auburn, drive north on Highway 49 to Nevada City and continue 11 miles to the junction of Tyler Foote Crossing Road. Turn right and drive 16 miles (in the process the road changes names: Cruzon Grade, Back Bone Road, Der Bec Road, North Bloomfield Road) to the entrance on the right. The route is well-signed; the last two miles are quite steep and the last mile is dirt.

Contact: Malakoff Diggins State Historic Park, California State Parks, Goldrush District, tel./fax 530/265-2740.   *Malakoff Diggins State Historic Park*

6. PIETY HILL COTTAGES

Situated smack dab in the charming little Victorian town of Nevada City, these cottages combine the best of a bed-and-breakfast inn with a traditional cottage rental. The cottages are nestled in the Sierra foothills, at 2,500 feet in elevation, and set in an updated 1930s auto court.

Luxury rating: 3

Recreation rating: 3

Nevada City, off Highway 49

All of the nine one- to three-room cottages have been nicely refurbished with cheerful, eclectic touches, giving them a homey, comfortable feel. They are spaced closely together around a garden and a tree-shaded grassy courtyard. There are also flower gardens throughout the one-acre property.

White Birch Cottage has a full kitchen and private garden and is the largest rental. Apple Blossom Cottage also has a private garden. Maple Cottage has a woodburning stove (firewood provided). Walnut Cottage is considered the most romantic and features a clawfoot tub. All of the bathrooms are small, but nicely remodeled. What's more, you can have a full, hot breakfast delivered right to your cottage or garden.

Nevada City, a Victorian-theme town of about 3,000, has a historic playhouse (Mark Twain spoke here), antique stores, and small museums. Victorian Christmas festivities are held between Thanksgiving and Christmas, and you must make reservations early for lodging, since this is the most popular event of the year in Nevada City.

The Empire Mine State Park in nearby Grass Valley offers hiking, biking, and equestrian trails. If you're a history buff, you'll want to check out the the park's museum and grounds, which comprise the site of the world's largest-producing gold mine during its heyday.

Within a 40-minute drive of Nevada City, you'll find an abundance of recreational opportunities, including hiking, biking, and fishing in the Tahoe National Forest and Grouse Ridge areas east of Highway 20. Just north of town on Highway 49 is the Yuba River, with good stretches for fishing, kayaking, and rafting, as well as hiking trails. Boating and water sports are available at Scotts Flat Reservoir east of Highway 120, and at Bullards Bar Reservoir and Englebright Lake, west of Highway 20 or north of Highway 49.

Facilities: Piety Hill has nine cottages with kitchenettes; one cottage has a full kitchen. The cottages have full baths, air-conditioning and heat, telephones, televisions, and modem hookups. A gazebo-covered spa is available. A complimentary hot breakfast is provided. The cottages are suitable for children. No pets are allowed. No smoking is permitted.

Bedding: Linens, towels, and daily maid service are provided.

Reservations and rates: Reservations are recommended. The fee is $90 to $165 per night per cabin, and includes a full breakfast and hot and cold beverages. An additional charge of $20 per night per adult and $10 for children ages 3 to 12 is charged for more than two persons. Children under three are free. Rates are slightly higher during November and December. Weekly and corporate rates are available. There is a two-night minimum on weekends. Major credit cards are accepted.

Directions: From Auburn, drive north on Highway 49 to Nevada City. Take the Sacramento Street exit to Sacramento Street. Turn left and drive three blocks to the cottages on the left.

Contact: Piety Hill Cottages, 523 Sacramento Street, Nevada City, CA 95959; 530/265-2245 or 800/443-2245, fax 530/265-6528; website: www.pietyhillcottages.com.

Piety Hill Cottages

7. ROLLINS LAKESIDE INN

Rollins Lake is set in the canyonlands of the Sierra foothills at 2,100 feet in elevation, north of Colfax off I-80. Here at Rollins Lake, right where the foothills meet the forest, a resort with cabins offers the opportunity for a surprising variety of water sports and recreation.

Luxury rating: 3

Recreation rating: 4

Sierra Foothills, off I-80 near Colfax

This area is not only where the valley grasslands rise and give way to conifers, but also where the snow line starts in winter. The result is a reservoir that spans the spectrum from very hot in summer to very cold in winter, with great transition periods in the spring and fall. The summer heat makes excellent conditions for waterskiing, boating, and swimming, and the spring and fall transitions are great for trout and bass fishing. In spring and early summer, when afternoon winds are common out of the west, the lake is also popular for small sailboats and windsurfing.

With its nine well-furnished cabins, Rollins Lakeside Inn is the focal point of the lake. Each of the cabins comes complete with everything you need, including cookware and bed linens, as well as things you don't need, such as cable television. No problem with the latter; just throw a towel over it. The cabins also have air-conditioning.

Rollins Lake has two extensive lake arms that cover 26 miles of shoreline, as well as long stretches of open water near the lower end of the lake. Excellent for waterskiing, these long stretches have water surface temperatures ranging from 75°F to 80°F in the summer. Most anglers choose to fish well up the lake arms, either for bass in the coves during the morning and evening bites in the summer, or for trout near where the feeder streams enter the lake. The latter is where the lake's water is coldest; trout are naturally attracted to the cool water temperatures, oxygenated flows, and the abundant food supply during the hot months.

There are several other lakes in the immediate region, including Englebright, Collins, and Scotts Flat, but only Rollins has cabin rentals.

Facilities: Rollins Lakeside Inn has nine cabins, each with full kitchen, television, and air-conditioning. A solar heated pool, a laundry room, horseshoes, volleyball, and table tennis are available. A boat ramp and marina with boat rentals (aluminum boats with motors, canoes, and paddleboats) are located about a half mile away. Call for details regarding pet policies.

Bedding: Linens and towels are provided.

Reservations and rates: Reservations are accepted. Cabin rates range from $125 for up to four person, to $175 for up to eight persons per night. Weekly rates are $700 to $950. A two-night minimum stay is required, with non-weekend discounts available.

Directions: From Auburn, drive northeast on I-80 for about 20 miles to Colfax and Highway 174. Turn north on Highway 174 (a winding, two-lane road) and drive 3.7 miles (bear left at Giovanni's Restaurant) to Orchard Springs Road. Turn right on Orchard Springs Road and drive about a mile to Rollins Lakeside Inn.

Contact: Rollins Lakeside Inn, P.O. Box 152, Chicago Park, CA 95712; 530/273-0729; website: www.rollinslake.com.

OTHER CABINS AND COTTAGES NEARBY

- Auburn KOA, 3550 KOA Way, Auburn, CA 95602; 530/885-0990.
- Loomis KOA, 3945 Taylor Road, Loomis, CA 95650; 916/652-6737.

Rollins Lakeside Inn

8. PLACERVILLE KOA

Luxury rating: 1

Recreation rating: 3

Shingle Springs, near U.S. 50 in the Sierra foothills

This is a KOA campground, complete with the cute little log cabins KOA calls Kamping Kabins. Accommodations are sparse, so your trip is just like camping, except with privacy, walls, and a bed.

The location of this camp is ideal for many, set near U.S. 50 in the Sierra foothills, the main route up to South Tahoe. Nearby is Apple Hill, where from September to November, local ranches and orchards sell produce and crafts, often with live music. In addition, the Marshall Gold Discovery Site is 10 miles north; gold was discovered there in 1848, setting off the 1849 gold rush.

This is a quiet camp and has a nice family feel. What makes it great for youngsters are the swimming pool and fish pond, both available on-site. White-water rafting and gold panning are popular on the nearby American River.

Renowned artist Thomas Kinkade grew up in nearby Placerville, and his gallery of originals has become a popular side trip for fans of his work. It provides the opportunity to see the largest selection of Kinkade canvases and paper lithographs, including hard-to-find secondary market pieces, as well as a complete selection of Thomas Kinkade plates, library prints, portfolios, cottages, books, calendars, and cards. For information, call 800/398-4266.

Facilities: Placerville KOA has eight one- and two-room cabins equipped with bunk beds and queen beds. Each cabin has electric heat and an electrical outlet. Picnic tables and barbecues are provided. An adjacent campground provides restrooms, drinking water, and flush toilets. Also available are showers, sanitary disposal station, phone, cable TV, modem hookups, recreation room, swimming pool, spa, playground, video arcade, basketball courts, 19-hole miniature golf course, convenience store, snack bar, dog run, petting zoo, fishing pond, bike rentals, pavilion cooking facilities, volleyball court, and horseshoe pits. Some facilities are wheelchair accessible. No smoking or pets are allowed in the cabins.

Bedding: Linens and towels are not provided; bring your own sleeping bag and pillow.

Reservations and rates: Reservations are recommended (call 800/562-4197). Rates are $42 for one-room cabins for up to four people, $50 for two-room cabins for up to six people. There is a $3 per person per night charge for more than two people. Major credit cards are accepted. Open year-round.

Directions: From U.S. 50 west of Placerville, take the Shingle Springs Drive exit (not the Shingle Springs/Ponderosa Road exit). Drive one block to Rock Barn Road. Turn left and drive .5 mile to the campground at the end of the road.

Contact: Placerville KOA, 4655 Rock Barn Road, Shingle Springs, CA 95682; 530/676-2267; website: www.koa.com.

Placerville KOA

9. SACRAMENTO-METRO KOA

When you think of the flat farmland of the Sacramento Valley, you don't think of cabins, and that's why the cabins at the Sacramento-Metro KOA are so popular. Try finding other cabin rentals in the area—there are almost none.

Luxury rating: 1

Recreation rating: 4

West of Sacramento, off I-5 in the Sacramento Valley

This KOA is the choice of vacationers touring California's capital and looking for a layover spot. It's just west of downtown Sacramento near the capitol building, the state railroad museum,

Sutter's Fort, the Sacramento River, and a few miles from Cal Expo, Water World, and the American River. It's also midway between the University of California, Davis, and California State University, Sacramento. You're in the hub of activity here.

The KOA is a busy place year-round and you must have reservations if you want a cabin. There are only a couple of two-room cabins that can accommodate up to six persons; the other cabins have one room and can house up to four persons. Sacramento gets hot in the summer, so a swimming pool and air-conditioning are provided.

Facilities: Sacramento-Metro KOA has 12 cabins and a campground. Bathrooms with flush toilets and showers are available, but they are a short walk from the cabins. Picnic tables, barbecues, porches with swings, heating, and air-conditioning are provided. Modem hookups, playground, swimming pool, coin laundry, recreation room with video games, and groceries are available. The cabins are suitable for children. Leashed pets are permitted in the cabins for no extra fee. No smoking is permitted in the cabins.

Bedding: Beds are provided, but you must bring your own linens and towels.

Reservations and rates: Reservations are recommended. Call 800/562-3403 to reserve. Fees are $41 per night per one-room cabin, and $52 per night per two-room cabin. For more than two persons, an additional fee of $4.50 per person per night is charged, and children under age 18 are free. Major credit cards are accepted. Open year-round.

Directions: From Sacramento, drive west on I-80 about four miles to the West Capitol Avenue exit. Exit and turn left onto West Capitol Avenue, going under the freeway to the first stoplight and the intersection with Lake Road. Turn left onto Lake Road and continue a half block to the camp on the left at 3951 Lake Road.

Contact: Sacramento-Metro KOA, 3951 Lake Road, West Sacramento, CA 95691; 916/371-6771 or 800/562-2747; website: www.koa.com.

Sacramento-Metro KOA

10. CAMANCHE NORTH SHORE

Lots of cool water, hot sun, eager fish, and well-kept housekeeping cabins . . .

Isn't it about time you had some fun?

That's what inspires trips to Camanche Lake, the closest lake to the Bay Area of those in the Central Valley foothills northeast of Stockton. Camanche is a big lake, covering 7,500 acres and 53 miles of shoreline, with enough lake arms, coves, islands, and a canyoned inlet on the Mokelumne River to hide many secrets.

What makes Camanche Lake work for a weekend visit is a gated development called Camanche North Shore. Here you will find a series of rentals in prefab homes that are designed like cottages set in large grassy areas. Because the operation is gated with an entry kiosk, visitors are guaranteed a quiet time from 11 P.M. to 8 A.M.

Luxury rating: 3

Recreation rating: 4

Central Valley Foothills, northeast of Stockton

On a recent trip, we headed out on the lake, cruising across the peaceful emerald waters shortly after dawn. The trout were jumping, leaving beautiful, washtub-sized swirls. Two golden eagles cruised overhead in tandem, and the fresh, white wake behind our boat made working at an office job seem like a sentence at a state prison.

Like most California lakes, Camanche is filled in May, and as the Central Valley turns gold, the high, emerald water is a beautiful contrast to the surrounding bronzed foothills. As summer takes over and the water heats up, there is ample room for waterskiing and personal watercrafts, which are restricted to various areas by speed limits. User conflicts between personal watercraft riders and anglers are kept to a minimum due to the size of the lake and its enforced rules.

The fishing is excellent for bass, and often good for trout and bluegill. Camanche is known as a structure lake, that is, there is a lot of underwater structure where the bass hang out. They can be teased into biting with plastic worms such as Senkos or Brush Hogs. The trout fishing is also very good, with trolling the best along Hat Island and along the old river channel.

Facilities: Camanche North Shore has 12 housekeeping cottages for up to four people, four residential housekeeping cottages for up to 10 people, 20 motel rooms, and a marina with boat rentals, a coffee shop, grassy campsites, and RV sites (hookups only at South Shore). No pets are permitted.

Bedding: Linens and towels are provided.

Reservations and rates: Reservations are recommended, and are often required during summer months. Housekeeping cottages that sleep four cost $98 per night. Residential housekeeping cottages that sleep 10 run $215 per night. Discounts are available by the week, month, and season.

Directions: From Stockton, drive east on Highway 88 to the town of Clements. Just east of Clements, bear left on Highway 88 and drive six miles to Camanche Parkway. Turn right and drive seven miles to the Camanche North Shore entrance gate.

Contact: Camanche North Shore, 2000 Camanche Road, Ione, CA 95640; 209/763-5121. Fishing: The Fisherman's Friend, Lodi, 209/369-0204.

OTHER CABINS AND COTTAGES NEARBY

• Camanche Lake South Shore, P.O. Box 206, Burson, CA 95225; 209/763-5178; website: www.norcalfishing.com.

Camanche North Shore

11. DORRINGTON INN

Folks call this area, "The Big Trees," as in, "I'm heading up to The Big Trees." That's because a large part of what makes this region special is the Calaveras Big Trees, along with the Stanislaus River (where rafting, swimming, and fishing abound). Also popular are trips "up the hill" to Lake Alpine, Bear Valley Ski Area, and all the way to Ebbetts Pass and a great trailhead for the Carson-Iceberg Wilderness.

Luxury rating: 4

Recreation rating: 4

Near Calaveras Big Trees, off Highway 4 near Arnold

Dorrington Inn makes a great headquarters, not only because of its location, but because of its truly intimate cottages. The interiors are knotty pine and decorated in alpine style. With fluffy down comforters and a fireplace, you get the perfect mix of rustic with modern style. A light breakfast is also provided—delicious croissants and muffins, along with fresh fruit, juice, cheese, and fresh-roasted coffee. Complimentary port or sherry is available each evening in the Common Room.

This great little spot is located on Highway 4 in the Sierra Nevada east of Arnold, set at an elevation of 5,000 feet. This is where the legendary Pony Express once rode, and the entire area is filled with history. The primary destination for most visitors is the nearby and easily accessible Calaveras Big Trees and its two trails, North Grove Loop and South Grove Loop. These trees, of course, are known for their tremendous diameters, not height; it can take a few dozen people linking hands to encircle even one.

The only complaint about this area is made by anglers. The Stanislaus River, along Highway 4, supports a puny fishery of a few very small trout. To get anything decent, you need to make the long drive up the hill to Spicer Meadows Reservoir. But the pluses far outshadow that solitary minus. Rafting is excellent on the lower Stanislaus. Hiking is also stellar, with a great, easy hike around Lake Alpine, a superb wilderness trailhead for day hikes up at Ebbetts Pass, and for the ambitious, up at Highland Lakes.

Facilities: Dorrington Inn has cabins available in different configurations, offering a choice of two queen beds (one in a loft), one queen, or one king. A fireplace, small refrigerator, TV, and kitchen are available. A common room with book and film library is also open to guests. Pets are not permitted on the property, and no smoking is allowed indoors.

Bedding: Linens are provided.

12. CABINS AT STRAWBERRY & STRAWBERRY INN

The cabins here are gorgeous, with stream settings and plenty of privacy. Some have decks that overlook the Stanislaus River. All of the cabins are three-bedroom, two-bath units that can accommodate up to eight persons. Each of the bedrooms has a queen bed, plus there is a queen sofa bed in the living room. The cabins feature modern rustic decor with a fireplace, vaulted ceilings, a breakfast bar, and an updated kitchen.

The cabins are a short distance from their sister facility, the Strawberry Inn, which has a newer unit of lodge rooms coupled with its restored 1930s lodge; there is also a restaurant. The lodge rooms are newly redecorated and some have decks overlooking the river. This is a good choice for a single guest or couple, since the cabins are rather large. If you opt for a lodge room, make sure you steer clear of room 7 unless you're deaf; there's a generator outside the room and it ran almost continuously when we were there.

The location of the Cabins at Strawberry & Strawberry Inn is excellent, set aside the South Fork of the Stanislaus River at 5,230 feet, just five miles from the Dodge Ridge Ski Area and 1.5 miles from the Pinecrest Lake turnoff. For

Luxury rating: 4

Recreation rating: 4

Dodge Ridge, off Highway 108 east of Sonora

more details about the area, see the listings for Pinecrest Lake Resort and The Rivers Resort in the Yosemite & Mammoth chapter.

Facilities: Strawberry Inn has eight cabins with fully equipped kitchens. Each cabin has a private bathroom. Fireplace and barbecue are provided, and most cabins have decks. No more than two vehicles are allowed at each cabin. The cabins are suitable for children. One small pet is allowed in some of the cabins. No smoking is permitted. Some facilities are wheelchair accessible.

Bedding: Linens and towels are provided.

Reservations and rates: Reservations are recommended. The fee is $160 per night per cabin off the river and $180 on the river. For pets, a $100 cleaning deposit is required. There is a three-night minimum. Major credit cards are accepted. Open year-round.

Directions: From Sonora, drive east on Highway 108 to the village of Strawberry (just past the turn for Dodge Ridge). Look for Strawberry Inn on the left (a store is on the right).

Contact: Cabins at Strawberry, P.O. Box 109, Strawberry, CA 95375; 209/965-0885 or 888/965-0885; website: www.strawberrycabins.com.

Cabins at Strawberry & Strawberry Inn

13. LAZY Z RESORT CABINS

The "swimming pool" at Lazy Z Resort is one of the most dramatic homemade pools at any resort in California. It looks more like a lake, as if the surrounding stone were carved out of mountain granite, complete with waterfalls that pour forth fresh water. Like a lake, it is not heated, but since air temperatures in the 90s are common during the summer here, the water temperature is perfect. It's even warmer than a real lake would be because this "lake" is eight feet deep. A bonus for pool users are the two adjacent hot tubs. You can hop in and out from pool to hot tub to pool, and in short order start feeling refreshed.

The resort is designed for absolute minimal stress, and you notice it right away in the resort office, which has light classical music playing in the background. The 12 cabins follow that lead,

Luxury rating: 4

Recreation rating: 3

Stanislaus National Forest, off Highway 108 near Twain Harte

all first-class accommodations, supplied with everything that you might need except for food and drinks.

Lazy Z is located just outside of Twain Harte, elevation 3,500 feet, right on the dividing line between oaks and pines in the summer, and rain and snow in the winter. In the summer, this means you are out of the hot foothill country, just high enough in altitude to be in the shade of giant sugar pines. In the winter, it can be snowing like crazy uphill at the Dodge Ridge Ski Area near Pinecrest, but here at Twain Harte it will only be raining. Often you don't have to chain up your tires during winter storms.

The best-known recreation areas nearby are the Stanislaus National Forest and the Stanislaus and Tuolumne Rivers; both bodies of water offer good fishing, swimming, and panning for gold. The best way to explore around here is with a map of Stanislaus National Forest that shows all backcountry roads and access points to the rivers. Within an hour's drive in the mountains, you'll find Beardsley Reservoir, Pinecrest Lake, Lyons Lake, and the Dodge Ridge Ski Area.

But after taking a dunk in the resort's pool, maybe followed by a plunge into the hot tub, few visitors will feel like going anywhere else anytime soon.

Facilities: Lazy Z Resort has 12 cabins of various sizes with bathrooms and fully equipped kitchens. Some cabins have a fireplace, deck, or barbecue. A swimming pool, hot tub, and clubhouse with a game room are on the property. The resort also has a horseshoe pit, table tennis, and walking trails. No pets are permitted.

Bedding: Linens are provided.

Reservations and rates: Reservations are required. Cabin rates on weekends range from $85 to $195 per night, with a two-night minimum stay required. Weekly discounts are available.

Directions: From Manteca on Highway 99, turn east on Highway 120 and drive 17 miles to Oakdale and Highway 108/120. Turn left on Highway 108/120 and drive to Sonora. Continue on Highway 108 for about five miles to Twain Harte. At Twain Harte, turn left at Mono Vista and drive a short distance to Longeway Road (a stop sign). Turn right at Longeway and drive about three miles to where it dead-ends at Middle Camp Road. Turn right on Middle Camp Road and look for the resort on the right side of the road.

Contact: Lazy Z Resort, P.O. Box 1055, Twain Harte, CA 95383; 209/586-1214 or 800/585-1238; website: www.lazyz.com. For a map of Stanislaus National Forest, send $6 to U.S. Forest Service, Attn: Map Sales, P.O. Box 587, Camino, CA 95709; 530/647-5390, fax 530/647-5389; or visit the website: www.r5.fs.fed.us/visitorcenter. Major credit cards are accepted.

Lazy Z Resort Cabins

14. GABLES CEDAR CREEK INN

This is a romantic getaway spot, and for those of you used to the high cost of many of California's resort areas, you'll be surprised at how low the prices are at Gables Cedar Creek Inn.

Luxury rating: 3

Recreation rating: 3

Stanislaus National Forest, off Highway 108 near Twain Harte

For as little as $60 per night, you'll get your own cozy cabin with fireplace, outside deck, antique furnishings, and romantic country decor. And guess what? It's clean, it's surrounded by towering pines and cedars, and it's close to snow skiing, fishing, hiking, golfing, and historic gold rush towns.

Four of the cabins are duplex units, but the other three are freestanding. An expansive lawn area with outdoor furniture is available for all inn guests. Most of the cabins have fully equipped kitchens, except for The Love Nest and The Blue Room, which have kitchenettes. If you're part of a large group, try the two-story Creekside Home, which sleeps seven and includes a master suite with fireplace and sitting area, vaulted ceilings, gas fireplaces, a television, a deck, and plenty of windows allowing the sunlight inside.

By far, the most popular cabin is Hideaway, a secluded log cabin located across the creek and accessible by crossing a stone bridge. It is situated among redwood trees and has a partial view of the golf course. The Loft Room is set next to the creek and has a kitchen and living room with woodburning stove downstairs, and a loft with a double mattress.

Golf lovers will be happy to know that the fourth fairway of the nine-hole Twain Harte Golf Club adjoins the property and guests have been known to start golfing from this point, with permission of course. The town of Twain Harte has a number of restaurants and shops; the innkeepers can direct you. Heading east, the Dodge Ridge Ski Area, with downhill and cross-country skiing and snowboarding, is just a 35-minute drive away. Pinecrest Lake has a variety of water sports and outdoor movies under the stars during the summer. Closer to home, free summer music concerts are held in the Twain Harte city park on Saturday evenings. A few blocks from the inn is Twain Harte Lake, a private recreational lake that's available to inn guests.

Facilities: Gables Cedar Creek Inn has seven cabins and one house. Most of the cabins have fully equipped kitchens. Woodstoves or fireplaces plus telephones and televisions are included. The inn is not suitable for children. Leashed pets are allowed. No smoking is permitted. One rental is wheelchair accessible.

Bedding: Linens and towels are provided, and maid service is available by request.

Reservations and rates: Reservations are recommended. The fee is $70 to $95 per night per cabin, and $125 per night or $900 per week for the house. For more than two people, an extra fee of $9 per night per person is charged. The pet fee is $4 per night per pet. There is a two-night minimum on weekends and a three-night minimum on holidays. Major credit cards are accepted. Open year-round.

Directions: From Sonora, drive east on Highway 108 to Twain Harte and Twain Harte Drive. Turn left on Twain Harte Drive and drive for 1.2 miles to the inn on the left.

Contact: Gables Cedar Creek Inn, P.O. Box 1818, 22560 Twain Harte Drive, Twain Harte, CA 95383; 209/586-3008 or 800/900-4224; website: www.go cedarcreek.com.   *Gables Cedar Creek*

CHAPTER 6

Tahoe &
the Northern Sierra

*M*ount Tallac affords a view across Lake Tahoe like no other: a cobalt blue expanse of water bordered by mountains that span miles of Sierra wildlands. The beauty is stunning. Lake Tahoe is one of the few places on earth where people feel an emotional response just by looking at it. Yosemite Valley, the giant Sequoias, the Grand Canyon, a perfect sunset on the Pacific Ocean . . . these are a few other sights that occasionally can evoke the same response. But Tahoe often seems to strike the deepest chord. It can resonate inside you for weeks, even after a short visit.

"What about all the people?" you ask. It's true that people come here in droves. But we found many spots that we shared only with the chipmunks. You can enjoy these spots, too, if you're willing to read our books, hunt a bit, and most importantly, time your trip to span Monday through Thursday.

This area has the widest range of accommodations: family resorts, romantic lakeside chalets, riverside cottages, dude ranches, fishing cabins, a remote forest hut, and even a lodge (Shore House at Lake Tahoe) where you can book a room, get married, have a wedding reception, and have your honeymoon, all presided over by the lodge owner, who is an ordained minister.

This region also has some of the most popular cabin rentals in California, including Sardine Lake Resort and Angora Lakes Resort, where you begin the reservation process by signing up on a cancellation list and then waiting for 10 years or so for someone to cancel. The reason? These two resorts offer the closest thing to an On Golden Pond setting in California.

Tahoe and the northern Sierra feature hundreds of lakes, including dozens you can drive to. The best for scenic beauty are Echo Lakes, Donner, Fallen Leaf, Sardine, Caples, Loon, Union Valley . . . well, we could go on and on. It is one of the most beautiful regions anywhere on earth.

The north end of the Sierra starts near Bucks Lake, a great lake for trout fishing, and extends to Bear River Canyon (and Caples Lake, Silver Lake, and Bear River Reservoir). In between are the Lakes Basin Recreation Area (containing Gold, Sardine, Packer, and other lakes) in southern Plumas County, the Crystal Basin (featuring Union Valley Reservoir and Loon Lake, among others) in the Sierra foothills west of Tahoe, Lake Davis (with the highest catch rates for trout) near Portola, and the Carson River Canyon and Hope Valley south of Tahoe.

You could spend weeks exploring any of these places, having the time of your life, and still not get to Tahoe's magic. But it is Tahoe where the adventure starts for many, especially in the surrounding Tahoe National Forest and Desolation Wilderness.

One of California's greatest day trips from Tahoe is to Echo Lakes, where you can take a hiker's shuttle boat across the two lakes to the Pacific Crest Trail, then hike a few miles into Desolation Wilderness and Aloha Lakes. Yet with so many wonderful ways to spend a day in this area, this day trip is hardly a blip on the radar scope.

With so many places and so little time, this region offers what can be the ultimate adventureland.

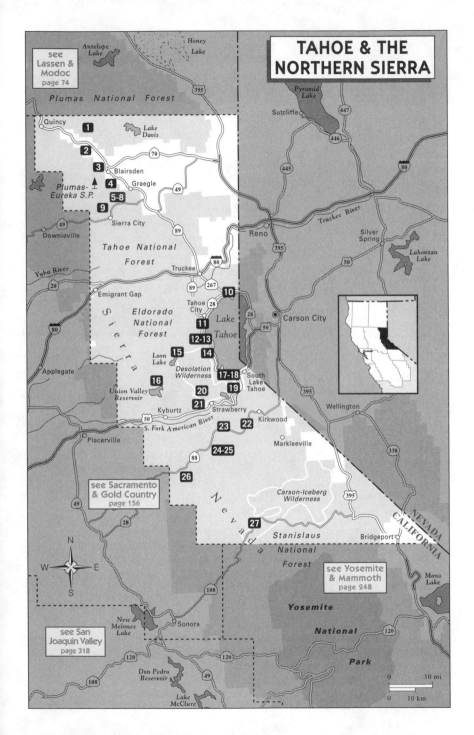

TAHOE & THE NORTHERN SIERRA

see Lassen & Modoc page 74

see Sacramento & Gold Country page 156

see Yosemite & Mammoth page 248

see San Joaquin Valley page 318

CHAPTER 6
TAHOE & THE NORTHERN SIERRA

1. GREENHORN CREEK GUEST RANCH

The folks here don't say "Hi" or "Hello" when you arrive. Instead, it's "Howdy, and welcome to Greenhorn Creek Guest Ranch." This is a genuine western dude ranch. Stay here for a few days and you might start feeling like a cowgirl or cowboy. Stay here for a week and you might not want to return home; not with the scrumptious chuckhouse chow, campfire cookouts, hayrides, trail and pony rides, fishing, western dancing, frog races, amateur mini-rodeo, and Maynard the pet pig to keep you busy.

Luxury rating: 3

Recreation rating: 5

North Plumas, off Highway 89 near Quincy

With more than 600 acres of ranch-land at 4,000 feet in elevation, plus the adjoining Plumas National Forest, you'll have more choices than time to do all the things that make a greenhorn smile. Mom and Dad can leave the younger buckaroos at the kiddie corral, with childcare attendants and a full day of activities, while the older cowpokes explore the ranch by foot or horse, get riding instruction, fish for trout in the pond or one of the surrounding lakes or streams, or swim and sunbathe. It's your choice.

And when it's time to get some shut-eye, you'll have a cozy wood-paneled cabin with western decor and private bathroom to hang your hat. These one- and two-bedroom units are grouped together in rows of four adjoining cabins, with bunk beds for the kids.

The gang at Greenhorn Creek Guest Ranch knows all about making happy trails for their guests.

Facilities: Greenhorn Creek Guest Ranch has 16 cabins and 11 lodge rooms that can accommodate up to six persons per rental. There are no kitchen facilities, but all meals are provided. The cabins have a bathroom with shower and a deck or porch. An outdoor spa, heated pool, lounge, fishing pond, laundry room, recreation room with billiards, exercise room, petting zoo, horseback riding, dancing, volleyball, badminton, Ping-Pong, softball, horseshoes, supervised children's program, and organized activities are available. The ranch is suitable for children. Pets are not allowed. No smoking is permitted.

Bedding: Linens and towels are provided, and there is daily maid service.

Reservations and rates: Reservations are required. For less than one week, the fee is $204 per night per person for ages 16 and over, $131 per night for ages 7 to 15, $72 for ages 3 to 6, and free for under age 3. Weekly rates are $1,000 to $1,113 for ages 16 and over, $650 to $722 for ages 7 to 15, $353 to $392 for ages 3 to 6, and free for under age 3. Friday night stay with no meals or activities is available for $59 for ages 16 and over, and free for ages 15 and younger. Group rates are available for 10 or more persons.

Major credit cards are accepted. Open March through November, weather permitting.

Directions: From Oroville, drive north on Highway 70 to the junction with Highway 89. Turn south on Highway 89/70 and drive 11 miles to Quincy. Continue 11 miles to Greenhorn Ranch Road. Turn left and drive two miles to the ranch on the right.

Contact: Greenhorn Creek Guest Ranch, 2116 Greenhorn Ranch Road, Quincy, CA 95971; 800/334-6939 or 800/334-HOWDY, fax 530/283-4401; website: www.greenhornranch.com.

Greenhorn Creek Guest Ranch

2. LONG VALLEY RESORT

This Plumas County setting provides the ideal location for adventuring, hiking, fishing, and golf. One of the cottages at Long Valley Resort is a convenient launch point, since the place is set along Highway 70/89 in Plumas National Forest country, at elevation 4,300 feet, at the threshold of adventure. There is nearby access to four golf courses in Graegle, as well as a half-dozen drive-to lakes in the Lakes Basin and some 50 lakes in the whole region. The star of the show often ends up being nearby Plumas-Eureka State Park, a very pretty park that is ideal for hiking.

Luxury rating: 3

Recreation rating: 4

Plumas National Forest, off Highway 89 near Quincy

The eight cottages at Long Valley Resort are set about 30 feet apart, yet once inside, are very private. Cottages 6, 7, and 8 have decks with views of a pretty meadow. Often there are deer or horses in the meadow. A creek lined with cottonwoods runs along the edge of the meadow—a stunning setting when the trees turn color in the fall.

Fishing can be excellent at the nearby Middle Fork Feather River. The easiest access to the Middle Fork Feather from Long Valley Resort is to drive a half mile north on Highway 70/89 and turn left on Sloat Road. From there, drive about a mile, turn right, drive over the railroad tracks, continue a short distance to the river, and drive over the river. Here the road turns to dirt and traces along upriver for a spell; this is the fishing access.

Facilities: Long Valley Resort has eight cottages (six two-bedrooms with three beds, one one-bedroom with two beds, and one three-bedroom with three beds). Each has a bathroom and a kitchen with cookware and utensils. A motel with four rooms is also available, often used for overflow lodging. A grocery store/café is available nearby. Pets are permitted with no extra fee.

Bedding: Linens and towels are provided. Daily maid service is included.

Reservations and rates: Reservations are accepted. Rates are $75 per night with a two-night minimum, or $380 per week, with a charge of $6 per day per additional person (more than two). A three-bedroom unit is $85 per night. Off-season discounts are available.

Directions: From Oroville, drive north on Highway 70 to the junction with Highway 89. Turn south on Highway 89/70 and drive 11 miles to Quincy. Continue through Quincy, drive 15 miles, and look for Long Valley Resort on the right side of the road.

Contact: Long Valley Resort, 59532 Highway 70, P.O. Box 30121, Cromberg, CA 96103; 530/836-0754 or 800/887-6653; website: www.longvalleyresort.com.

Long Valley Resort

3. LITTLE BEAR RV PARK

The cabins here are intended to accomplish two things: one, get the tenters off the ground, and two, force the bears to have to knock. The cabins at Little Bear RV Park are primitive, that is, a few beds for sleeping, a table, and that's about it. Your reward: no bugs, no meandering bears, privacy, and hey, you're not on the ground. The cabins are set in a ring around a community fire pit, which provides a camping-style feel to the place.

Luxury rating: 1

Recreation rating: 4

Long Valley, off Highway 70/89 in Blairsden

This privately operated park, at elevation 4,300 feet, is set up primarily for RV campers, and they are what really make the place tick. That, and the opportunity of many nearby recreation attractions. You'll find many outstanding and beautiful golf courses in the nearby vicinity. Most venture out to Plumas-Eureka State Park, only seven miles away. A must-do side trip is the hike up Eureka Peak, elevation 7,447 feet. The panoramic view of the southern Sierra Nevada includes all the peaks of the Gold Lakes Basin, with Mount Elwell (7,818 feet) most prominent to the south, and Plumas National Forest to the north and west, crowned by Blue Nose Mountain (7,290 feet), Stafford Mountain (7,019 feet), and Beartrap Mountain (7,232 feet). To make it requires a three-mile round-trip with a climb of 1,150 feet.

Facilities: Little Bear RV Park has four primitive cabins. Each has a double bed, a bunk bed, and a table; and outside, a chair on the deck, a hammock, a picnic table, and a community fire ring. No electricity is provided. An RV park is on the premises. Drinking water, showers, flush toilets, coin laundry, a grocery store, and ice are available. No smoking is allowed. Pets are not permitted in cabins.

Bedding: Linens and towels are not provided; bring your sleeping bag and pillow.

Reservations and rates: Reservations are accepted. The rate is $28 per night for two, $8 for each additional person, and $3 for children. Open mid-April through October 28th.

Directions: In Truckee, drive north on Highway 89 to Blairsden and the junction with Highway 70. Turn north and drive one mile to Little Bear Road. Turn left on Little Bear Road and drive a short distance to the campground.

Contact: Little Bear RV Park, P.O. Box 103, Blairsden, CA 96103; tel./fax 530/836-2774.

Little Bear RV Park

4. GRAY EAGLE LODGE

For a midrange cabin rental in the Gold Lakes Basin, this is one of the best bets. There are some good cabins with great locations in this area, but none of them provide all of the amenities that you'll find at Gray Eagle Lodge, set in Plumas National Forest at almost 6,000 feet in elevation.

© LAURA READ

Luxury rating: 3

Recreation rating: 4

Graegle, off Highway 70/89

You'll get a private bathroom with shower in your rustic, wood-paneled cabin, and two complimentary meals a day, a big plus for families and vacationers who don't want to fuss with cooking. Gray Eagle Creek flows through the property, and some of the cabins are set along the creek. Alder Cabin is the largest cabin, with two bedrooms and a creekside location. Poplar Cabin and Cedar Cabin also feature creekside settings.

The activity list is long and includes horseback riding and golfing nearby. Swimmers can enjoy one of the local lakes, or the ol' swimming hole at the base of little Gray Eagle Falls, which is situated within 200 feet of the lodge. For hikers and anglers, your options are plentiful. From the lodge, take the Smith Lake trailhead for one mile to reach the lake and its trout inhabitants, where a canoe is available for the first lodge guest to claim it. Continue on this trail for two miles to reach the top of Mt. Elwell at 7,818 feet, with an elevation gain of 2,018 feet over the course of three miles. Other trails leading to pristine mountain lakes can be accessed. For details, refer to the guidebook *Foghorn Outdoors: California Hiking*.

The Gold Lakes Basin is a beautiful area with friendly people, but we found Gray Eagle Lodge to be a little less friendly and less helpful than at the surrounding resorts.

Facilities: Gray Eagle Lodge has 18 one- and two-bedroom cabins. There are no kitchen facilities, but complimentary breakfast and dinner are provided, and box lunches are available for an additional fee. A bathroom with shower and a deck are provided. There are no televisions or telephones in the cabins. A restaurant, lounge, recreation room, and evening campfire are available. The lodge is suitable for children. Leashed pets are allowed, with a two-pet limit per cabin. No smoking is permitted. One cabin is wheelchair accessible.

Bedding: Linens and towels are provided, and there is daily maid service.

Reservations and rates: Reservations are recommended. The fee is $175 to $200 per night for a one-bedroom cabin, and $195 to $215 per night for a two-bedroom cabin. For more than two persons, there is a fee of $60 per night per adult, $45 per night for ages 10 to 16, and $30 per night for ages 2 to 9. The pet fee is $10 per night per pet. There is a three-night minimum, and a five-night minimum when booking a year in advance. Major credit cards are accepted. Open Memorial Day weekend through mid-October, weather permitting.

Directions: From Truckee, drive northwest on Highway 89 toward Graeagle to the Gold Lake Highway (one mile before reaching Graeagle). Turn left on the Gold Lake Highway (Forest Road 24) and drive five miles to the sign for Gray Eagle Lodge. Turn right and drive .3 mile to the lodge.

Contact: Gray Eagle Lodge, P.O. Box 38, Graeagle, CA 96103; 530/836-2511 or 800/635-8778; website: www.grayeaglelodge.com.

Gray Eagle Lodge

5. ELWELL LAKES LODGE

First, let's end the confusion. There is no Elwell Lake. Rather there is nearby Mount Elwell, 7,812 feet in elevation, and the lodge is named for the dozens of lakes in its shadow, including 23 within a three-mile radius of the lodge.

The cabins, both housekeeping cabins and tent cabins, provide a perfect base camp for exploring this area, whether you're hiking, fishing, boating, or windsurfing. Highlights include beautiful Long Lake, located three-quarters of a mile away, where the lodge provides unlimited use of boats and motors for guests, and of course, the Mount Elwell Trail.

This lodge was first built in 1920 and is still owned and operated by the original family. When the lodge opened, almost all of the cabins were tent cabins. Only three tent cabins remain, and these are rented as extra rooms for those renting cabins, such as couples who wish to put the youngsters in a separate room for the night. Another highlight here for families is the recreation building. It features a huge fireplace, a pretty view, and many books and games for those who want to stay at the camp.

Luxury rating: 2

Recreation rating: 5

Lakes Basin, Plumas National Forest, off Highway 89 near Graegle

Although the place retains its rustic qualities, all modern amenities are now provided. The cabins rest amid a pine forest, providing a classic alpine setting. They are wood-sided, often with metal roofs, and most have decks. Each cabin has all of the pots, pans, dishes, and linens you'll need, plus kitchen and bathroom facilities. All you need to bring is your food. The most popular cabin is the Cromwell, a two-person cabin set in the woods on a seasonal creek.

This is one of the best cabin locations in California for hiking to nearby mountain lakes. For newcomers to the lodge, climbing Mount Elwell is like being baptized. It is a three-mile hike one-way to the top, requiring a climb of 1,100 feet. Your reward is a spectacular view of the Lakes Basin, a landscape of granite, pine forest, and scattered lakes, looking like gem after gem.

Note that nearby Gold Lake Lodge (see next listing), located less than a half mile to the north, as well as other lake and cabin settings in the area, provide additional lodging opportunities.

Facilities: Elwell Lakes Lodge has 10 cabins and three tent cabins, each fully equipped with bathroom, kitchenette, and barbecue. Guests have use of a boat on nearby Long Lake and full use of lodge facilities. No pets are permitted.

Bedding: Linens are provided.

Reservations and rates: Reservations are required. Fees vary according to the size of the cabin. A small cabin for two people is $67 per night or $403 per week. A large cabin for up to six people is $121 per night or $725 per week. For additional space, tent cabins are available for $15 per night for one person, with each additional person costing $7 per day. Weekly rates are available. Major credit cards are accepted. Open when the snow clears, usually from June to October.

Directions: From Truckee, turn north on Highway 89 and drive past the town of Clio to the Gold Lake Highway near the southern end of Graegle. Turn left on the Gold Lake Highway (Forest Road 24) and drive up the mountain. Turn right at the signed turnoff for Elwell Lakes Lodge (if you reach Gold Lake, you have gone too far) and drive a short distance to the lodge.

Contact: Elwell Lakes Lodge, P.O. Box 68, Blairsden, CA 96103; 530/836-2347; website: www.members.aol.com/elwelllodge. For a map, ask for Plumas National Forest and send $6 to U.S. Forest Service, Attn: Map Sales, P.O. Box 587, Camino, CA 95709; 530/647-5390, fax 530/647-5389; or visit the website: www.r5.fs.fed.us/visitorcenter.

Elwell Lakes Lodge

6. GOLD LAKE LODGE

The centerpiece of the Lakes Basin Recreation Area is Gold Lake, a beautiful sky-blue lake set in a rock basin in the northern Sierra at a 6,400-foot elevation. It is the largest of the many lakes in the region, and the trout here can get huge. In addition, there are several trailheads around the lake for outstanding hikes to smaller nearby lakes, and a pack station and stable are available near Gold Lake.

Luxury rating: 3

Recreation rating: 5

Lakes Basin, Plumas National Forest, off Highway 89 near Graegle

Perfect, right? There's more. Gold Lake Lodge, located about a half mile north of Gold Lake near the Sierra crest at an even higher 6,620-foot elevation, provides both rustic and standard cabins, and a restaurant serving dinner and breakfast.

The one bugaboo that surprises newcomers all summer long is the wind at Gold Lake. The lake's location near the Sierra crest often causes what is called the venturi effect, especially in the afternoon, when wind is funneled through the mountain gap over the lake, picking up speed as a large mass of air is forced through a relatively small gap in the mountain ridge. Of course, the wind makes for great windsurfing and sailing, at least until it really howls. There is one protected cove that is calm even when the rest of the lake is raging.

The cabins at Gold Lake Lodge are situated largely out of the wind and close to excellent short hiking trails. There are two styles of cabins: The standard cabins have full baths, but the rustic cabins do not, though detached facilities are offered. Although there is no docking or boat launch at nearby Big Bear Lake, in summer the lodge keeps one boat there, which is available only for guests. This pretty lake is a half-mile walk from the lodge and provides good trout fishing, often with higher catch rates than at Gold Lake, though the trout are far smaller.

The trail from Gold Lake Lodge to the north shore of Big Bear Lake (6,485 feet) is one of several excellent short hikes available here. It is slightly downhill, losing about 200 feet, and from Big Bear Lake, it is a short distance to Little Bear Lake, and about a quarter mile to Little Cub Lake. You can then take a half-mile loop that skirts the southern shore of Long Lake (which is quite beautiful), then turns left and passes Silver Lake and Round Lake (at 6,714 feet in elevation) before heading back to the lodge. This great loop hike passes six lakes in all and covers about three miles.

Facilities: Gold Lake Lodge has both rustic and standard cabins. Standard cabins provide a full bath; rustic cabins do not, but have facilities available nearby. No pets are permitted.

Bedding: Linens and housekeeping are provided.

Reservations and rates: Reservations are required. Fees are $95 per night single occupancy for a rustic cabin or $150 per night double occupancy. Rates are $130 per night single occupancy for a standard cabin or $190 per night double occupancy. There is a two-night minimum, with weekly rate discounts.

Directions: From Truckee, turn north on Highway 89 and drive past the town of Clio to the Gold Lake Highway near the southern end of Graegle. Turn left on the Gold Lake Highway (Forest Road 24) and drive up the mountain. About .5 mile past the Lakes Basin Campground, turn right at the signed turnoff for Gold Lake Lodge and drive a short distance to the lodge.

Contact: Gold Lake Lodge, P.O. Box 25, Blairsden, CA 96103; 530/836-2350; website: www.goldlakelodge.com. For a map, ask for Plumas National Forest and send $6 to U.S. Forest Service, Attn: Map Sales, P.O. Box 507, Camino, CA 95709; 530/647-5390, fax 530/647-5389; or visit the website: www.r5.fs.fed.us/visitorcenter. Major credit cards are accepted.

Gold Lake Lodge

7. PACKER LAKE LODGE

What a place: old lakefront log cabins, good trout fishing, low-speed boating, one of the best trails in California for hiking—all set in Tahoe National Forest, where serenity reigns. No, you have not gone to heaven. You have gone to Packer Lake.

Luxury rating: 3

Recreation rating: 5

Lakes Basin, Tahoe National Forest, off Highway 49 near Bassetts

Packer Lake, at a 6,218-foot elevation, is located at the foot of the dramatic Sierra Buttes. The trout fishing is decent here, but there are an additional 15 lakes with fishing within a five-mile radius in the Lakes Basin Recreation Area. Take your pick.

The most dramatic adventure of all, however, is hiking to the awesome and thrilling lookout at the Sierra Buttes. The trailhead is only about a mile away, at the foot of the buttes. From here, you climb 2,369 feet over the course of about five miles. The trail traces the mountain rim to the lookout, topped off by a stairway with 176 steps that literally juts out into open space—an eerie yet unforgettable experience. The view is astounding: hundreds of miles in all directions. It's one of our favorite hikes.

Packer Lake Lodge features 14 cabins, including low-cost log cabins (a bit on the raw side) all the way up to newer cabins with all-electric kitchens, bathrooms, and everything you need except food. A bonus is the small fishing boat that is supplied as part of the package for all cabin guests.

Facilities: Packer Lake has 14 cabins varying in size and amenities. Most have bathrooms and kitchens. A small fishing boat is included in cabin rentals. A small dock, primitive boat ramp, and additional rental boats and canoes are available. A small restaurant is on the property.

Bedding: Linens and towels are provided.

Reservations and rates: Reservations are required. Cabin rates are $66 per day or $430 per week for a one-room sleeping cabin with no kitchen and bath, and $110 to $145 per day or $700 to $945 per week for cabins with a kitchen, depending on cabin size. Open May to mid-October.

Directions: From Truckee, turn north on Highway 89 and drive 20 miles to Sierraville. Turn left on Highway 49 and drive about 10 miles to the Bassetts Store. Turn right (north) on Gold Lake Road and drive one mile. Look for the signed turnoff for Packer Lake/Sardine Lake. Turn left here, drive a short distance, and at the fork, bear right (left goes to Sardine Lake) and drive two miles to Packer Lake.

Contact: Packer Lake Lodge, P.O. Box 237, Sierra City, CA 96125; 530/862-1221. In the off-season (November through April), contact: 2245 Beach Street, Apartment 2, San Francisco, CA 94123; 415/921-5943. *Packer Lake Lodge*

8. SARDINE LAKE RESORT

Staying in a cabin on the shore of Sardine Lake might seem just too good to be true. Unfortunately, it often is. Staying here is the closest thing to an *On Golden Pond* ambience in California. It is one of the prettiest mountain cabin settings anywhere. The lake is small but gorgeous, blue-green and sheltered, with the spiked rim of the Sierra Buttes providing a dramatic backdrop. The cabins are cute and cozy, set near the lake and sheltered in a pine forest. Some have decks with lake views. A small marina is within short walking distance and a first-class restaurant is set along the shore.

Luxury rating: 3

Recreation rating: 5

Lakes Basin, off Highway 49 near Bassetts

How could this be too good to be true? Because it is just about impossible to get a reservation and actually spend a week at a cabin here. These cabins are always reserved far in advance. The only way to arrange a stay is to sign up on a waiting list, then hope for a cancellation. Some people who have fallen in love with the place admit to a wait of up to 10 years before getting a chance to relive *On Golden Pond*. The owners requested we leave the place out of the book because they didn't want to continue disappointing people who have to be turned away. Sorry. This place is just too good to not at least get on the waiting list.

The scenic beauty of the area is stunning. Though the lake is small, it is pristine—almost divine—set at 6,000 feet. The contrast between the calm blue-green waters and the towering granite mountain backdrop, with an army of conifers at its base, can inspire a feeling of greatness in all who see it. There is no substitute for natural beauty and there is no substitute for Sardine Lake.

On the lake, a five-mph speed limit is in effect, perfect for little boats, especially canoes. Rentals are available at the marina. The lake provides good catch rates for rainbow trout, especially trolling near the inlet along the back wall. The hiking is exceptional, with a great jaunt up to Upper Sardine Lake, where a small waterfall can be discovered on the stream that connects Upper Sardine Lake to Lower Sardine Lake. The hiking trail to the top of the Sierra Buttes cannot be accessed directly from Sardine Lake. The trailhead is located at a access point near Packer Lake.

If you take one look at this place—the mountain beauty, the little cabins, the fishing, boating, and hiking—you will want to stay here, too. Good luck in your quest.

Facilities: Sardine Lake Cabins has a series of small lakeside cabins with kitchenette and bathroom. A marina with boat rentals and a restaurant (reservations required) are available. A primitive, narrow dirt boat ramp is accessible only to small boats on trailers. No smoking is allowed. Pets are not permitted.

Bedding: Linens are provided.

Reservations and rates: Reservations are recommended. However, all cabins are always reserved in advance. You instead sign up on a waiting list and hope for a cancellation. The fees are $600 to $900 per week. Open when snow clears, usually June to October.

9. YUBA RIVER INN

A mixture of the old and the new is what you'll get here. The cabins range from 1930s-era to newly built, some with kitchen, some with woodburning stove, some with hot tub, and some allowing smoking. Take your pick, but you better choose quickly if you want a cabin with a kitchen, because those go fast. Could the fact that there's no restaurant within walking distance have anything to do with this?

Luxury rating: 2

Recreation rating: 4

 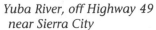

Yuba River, off Highway 49 near Sierra City

Each cabin can accommodate up to six persons, depending on the unit. The cabins without kitchens have a small refrigerator, and the fully equipped kitchens include a microwave. The Wild Plum Cabin is the most deluxe lodging, with two bedrooms, a woodburning stove, and a whirlpool tub. The cabins are surrounded by pines, cedars, and firs at an elevation of 4,100 feet.

The inn is located on 20 acres with one-third mile of North Fork Yuba River frontage; you can fish for rainbow, brown, and brook trout. The Pacific Crest Trail is one-half mile east of the inn, with easy access. Well-known and popular mountain biking trails along the Yuba River are a few miles downstream, as are white-water rafting and kayaking.

This is a beautiful and relatively quiet area of California, and there's no quick and easy way to get here. Once you reach the foothills, the scenery is often outstanding and you might want to poke around some of the gold rush–era towns as you work your way to the Yuba River Inn.

Facilities: Yuba River Inn has 10 log cabins with bathroom and shower. Kitchen facilities are provided in some of the cabins. One cabin has a woodburning stove and whirlpool tub. A pool is available in July and August. The cabins are suitable for children. Leashed pets are allowed, with a two-pet limit per cabin. Smoking is permitted in some of the cabins.

Bedding: Linens and towels are provided; there is no daily maid service.

Reservations and rates: Reservations are required during the summer for cabins with kitchens. The fee is $45 to $50 per night for two persons for a cabin without a kitchen, and $65 to $130 per night for four to six persons for a cabin with a kitchen. A pet fee of $10 per pet per night is charged. Credit cards are not accepted. Open year-round.

Directions: From Auburn, take Highway 49 north to Nevada City and continue (the road jogs left at Nevada City, then narrows) past Downieville to Sierra City. Continue on Highway 49 for .5 mile to the inn on the right.

Contact: Yuba River Inn, P.O. Box 236, Sierra City, CA 96125; 530/862-1122.

Yuba River Inn

10. SHORE HOUSE AT LAKE TAHOE

When they say they're "full service" at the Shore House at Lake Tahoe, they mean it. That's because the innkeeper is an ordained minister and he also performs weddings at the complex. He'll make your room reservation, put on his robe, and marry you, and then he and his wife will organize your reception if you want. The rest is up to you.

But you don't have to get married to stay here. It's a quiet, romantic, lakefront hideaway for couples wanting a break from their hectic routines. What you'll find are two freestanding and seven adjoining cottages with gas fireplaces, decks, feather beds, and down comforters. From your deck or balcony, you'll look out over the lawn and pier to the beautiful tourmaline waters of Lake Tahoe and the surrounding mountains.

Each cottage is unique and decorated individually; among them are Opa's Room, The Pine Room, The Moon Room, The Terrace Room, and The Studio. The Lakeview Room has floor-to-ceiling sliding glass doors with great views, and the rainbow trout and mackinaw painted on the shower walls appear to be swimming around you. The Tree House is on the second story and situated between two large ponderosa pines and sports a Native American decor. The Honeymoon Cottage is a separate cabin near the lakefront with a queen-size log bed, two-person whirlpool tub in the bedroom, knotty-pine walls, vaulted ceilings, and breathtaking views.

Luxury rating: 4

Recreation rating: 4

North Shore of Lake Tahoe, off Highway 28 at Tahoe Vista

Facilities: Shore House at Lake Tahoe has nine cottages for up to two persons. There are no kitchen facilities, but a full breakfast and homemade cookies are provided. A small refrigerator, deck, and gas log fireplace are provided. Telephones and televisions are not available in the cottages. An outdoor hot tub, pier, lawn area with chaise lounges, and wedding facilities are available. The facilities are not suitable for children. Pets are not allowed. No smoking is permitted.

Bedding: Linens and towels are provided.

Reservations and rates: Reservations are recommended. The fee is $160 to $285 per night per cottage. There is a two-night minimum most of the year. Major credit cards are accepted.

Directions: From Truckee, drive south on Highway 167 to Highway 28/North Lake Boulevard. Turn right (south) and drive .75 mile to the cottages on the left (lakeside).

Contact: Shore House at Lake Tahoe, P.O. Box 499, 7170 North Lake Boulevard, Tahoe Vista, CA 96148; 530/546-7270 or 800/207-5160; website: www.tahoeinn.com. *Shore House at Lake Tahoe*

11. THE COTTAGE INN AT LAKE TAHOE

Lake Tahoe takes the prize as the number one romantic getaway for residents of California and Nevada. We're smitten by the place ourselves, and even got hitched in a little chapel overlooking the lake as snowflakes fell softly from the sky. No, it wasn't near the Cottage Inn, but this facility is typical of the type of romantic accommodations that are so popular at Lake Tahoe.

You'll think you've stepped into a fairy tale when you arrive at The Cottage Inn at Lake Tahoe. The 15 gingerbread-type cottages were built in 1938 and are a holdover of the "old Tahoe"–style lodging, although they have been renovated with modern amenities. Each theme cottage has its own stone fireplace and knotty-pine paneling, and your fee includes a hearty breakfast, homemade cookies, and coffee.

Luxury rating: 3

Recreation rating: 5

West Shore of Lake Tahoe, off Highway 89 near Tahoe City

Among the cottage offerings are Stagecoach Stop, Game Room, Rustic Retreat, Enchanted Cottage, Skier's Chalet, and Hunter's Hideout. The Old Fishin' Hole Cottage is recommended for fishermen and liars, the Tahoe Teepee Cottage has Native American decor and a lake view, and Romantic Hideaway features a natural-rock hot tub with waterfall. Whatever your mood, you should find a room to your liking.

There's probably no other place in California that has the variety of year-round activities that you'll find at Lake Tahoe. Within minutes, you can be boating, fishing, swimming, hiking, cycling, snowskiing, golfing, or even gambling. The summer is the busiest season at Lake Tahoe, but winter is also busy once the ski season begins. We have found June and September to be the best times for visiting; the masses of people are gone and the weather is gorgeous.

Facilities: The Cottage Inn has 15 cabins that can accommodate up to four persons. Only one cottage has kitchen facilities. All units have a fireplace. Breakfast, cookies, and coffee are provided. A private beach is available. The cottages are not suitable for children under age 12. Pets are not allowed. No smoking is permitted.

Bedding: Linens and towels are provided.

Reservations and rates: Reservations are recommended. The double-occupancy rate is $149 per night for a one-bedroom cottage, $175 to $200 per night for a cottage suite, and $235 to $245 per night for a deluxe suite. Additional persons are $20 per night per person. There is a two-night minimum on weekends and a three-night minimum on holidays. Major credit cards are accepted. Open year-round.

Directions: From Truckee, drive south on Highway 89 through Tahoe City. Continue south on Highway 89 for two miles to the inn on the left (lakeside).

Contact: The Cottage Inn at Lake Tahoe, 1690 West Lake Boulevard, P.O. Box 66, Tahoe City, CA 96145; 530/581-4073 or 800/581-4073; website: www.the cottageinn.com.

The Cottage Inn at Lake Tahoe

12. TAHOMA MEADOWS BED AND BREAKFAST

The little red engine that could would fit right in among the little red cottages at Tahoma Meadows Bed and Breakfast. The cottages are all cute, quaint, and old-fashioned. Even when they compare the place to bigger, more modern resorts, some visitors prefer the comfort and feel of yesteryear that abounds here.

Luxury rating: 3

Recreation rating: 4

West Shore of Lake Tahoe, off Highway 89 in Tahoma

In addition to the bed-and-breakfast inn, there are three freestanding cottages with fully equipped kitchens. The Angler is a two-room cottage with fly-fishing decor and a claw-foot tub/shower, queen bed, and queen-size futon in the sitting room. The Boat House has a cream-colored interior, claw-foot tub/shower, queen bed, and trundle bed in the sitting room. There are two bedrooms in the Tree House, which has a fireplace, queen bed, two twin beds, and a futon in the living room; the cottage is cheerful and bright. Breakfast is not provided with a cottage rental.

The innkeeper is an avid fly fisher and is happy to give you current conditions and advice. This is a great place for cycling, since the trail from Tahoe City runs past the facilities. Rafting the Truckee

River is popular in spring and summer, and many vacationers feel that their trip to West Shore isn't complete unless they've stopped to look at the giant trout at Fanny Bridge in Tahoe City.

Facilities: Tahoma Meadows Bed and Breakfast has three cottages that can accommodate up to six persons. There are also 10 inn rooms. Fully equipped kitchens are provided in the cottages.

Bedding: Linens and towels are provided.

Reservations and rates: Reservations are recommended. The fee is $145 to $255 per night per cottage for up to four persons; additional persons are $10 per night per person. Complimentary breakfast is not included with the cottages. The inn rooms are $95 to $179 per night and include breakfast. There is a two-night minimum during the summer season and a three-night minimum during the Christmas holiday. Major credit cards are accepted. Open year-round.

Directions: From Truckee, drive south on Highway 89 through Tahoe City. Continue south on Highway 89 for eight miles to the inn on the right, next to the big red-and-white barn.

Contact: Tahoma Meadows Bed and Breakfast, 6821 West Lake Boulevard, P.O. Box 82, Homewood, CA 96141; 530/525-1553 or 800/862-8881; website: www.tahomameadows.com.

Tahoma Meadows Bed and Breakfast

13. TAHOMA LODGE

Luxury rating: 3

Recreation rating: 5

 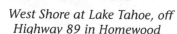

West Shore at Lake Tahoe, off Highway 89 in Homewood

Tahoma Lodge is a good choice for a family or group vacation: you have access to a beach and pier, you have a pool, hot tub, basketball court, and play area, you have a choice of cabin sizes up to four bedrooms, and you have your pooch with you. Everybody's happy, right?

The location is a plus since it's halfway between North Shore and South Shore, yet far enough away from Tahoe City to avoid the crowds and congestion that build up in those three areas. And in winter, you're a five-minute drive from Homewood ski and snowboard resort. When most people think of the old Tahoe, they think of the Homewood area.

And so it is with Tahoma Lodge, a not-so-fancy place with rustic cabins in a wooded setting. The accommodations are 1950s-style with a few updates; the decor is knotty pine, linoleum floors, metal roofs, and dark interiors. All of the cabins have a deck with barbecue and picnic table, television, telephone, and some have a fireplace or woodstove. For a large group, we suggest the Redwood unit, which has four bedrooms, sleeps nine, and includes a washer and dryer and a dishwasher.

The West Shore is wonderful for cycling and hiking. A bike trail meanders for miles along the highway and lake from Tahoe City to Homewood. For hiking, the views along the Rubicon Trail in D.L. Bliss State Park are hard to surpass. You'll climb above Lake Tahoe for wide-open vistas of the lake and surrounding mountains and the clear, blue-green water and rocky shoreline below. Sit down on a rock for a snack or picnic lunch and you'll soon discover that this must be the chipmunk capital of California. Unbelievable how cute and quick the little ones are to steal your heart—and lunch.

Facilities: Tahoma Lodge has 10 cabins with fully equipped kitchens. Barbecues are provided, and most units have a deck or porch and fireplace or woodstove. A heated pool (summer only) and basketball court are available. The cabins are suitable for children. Leashed pets are allowed with permission. No smoking is permitted.

Bedding: Linens and towels are provided.

Reservations and rates: Reservations are recommended. The fee is $105 to $235 per night per cabin, and $355 per night for the four-bedroom cabin. Major credit cards are accepted. Open year-round.

Directions: From Truckee, drive south on Highway 89 through Tahoe City. Continue south on Highway 89 for approximately eight miles to the lodge.

Contact: Tahoma Lodge, 7018 West Lake Boulevard, P.O. Box 72, Tahoma, CA 96142; 530/525-7721 or 866/819-2226; website: www.tahomalodge.com.

Tahoma Lodge

14. MEEKS BAY RESORT AND MARINA

Meeks Bay Resort has developed into its own micro-universe at Lake Tahoe—it has a little bit of everything. At the heart of the resort are eight cabins, 12 condo-style units, a campground, and the awesome Kehlet Mansion. Most of the cabins have lake views, and the mansion actually has a deck that extends over the water.

As you likely guessed, the cabins can be on the pricey side, and with a one-week minimum stay during the peak season (early July to early September), the pretty two-story jobs will set you back

Luxury rating: 3

Recreation rating: 5

West Shore of Lake Tahoe, off Highway 89 near Tahoma

better than a grand. The cheapest you can get still costs $650.

But what the heck, life ain't a dress rehearsal, right? You're better off spending it on yourself and your family than at the casinos, and here you get vacation grounds set on the threshold of outstanding boating, swimming, biking, and hiking. While the resort does not rent boats, it does have a concrete boat ramp that provides powerboats with access to nearby Emerald Bay to the south, the prettiest spot on the prettiest lake in California. There is also a great beach and a roped-off swimming area within short walking distance of the cabins.

A trailhead for access to Eldorado National Forest and the Desolation Wilderness (a wilderness permit is required for overnight use) is located virtually across the highway from the resort. The famed West Shore Bicycle Path is nearby to the north.

Facilities: Meeks Bay Resort and Marina has eight cabins in a variety of sizes, each with a bath and kitchen with cookware and utensils. There are also 12 condo-style units, the Washoe House which sleeps 10, and Kehlet House which sleeps 12. A small general store, campground, beach, roped-off swimming area, boat ramp, and marina with boat rentals are available. No pets are permitted.

Bedding: Linens and towels are provided.

Reservations and rates: Reservations are recommended. Cabins rent for between $189 and $787 per night, depending on the size of cabin, with a two-night minimum. Weekly rates range from $1,260 to $5,250. A one-week minimum occupancy is required from the July 4th weekend through Labor Day.

Directions: From Truckee, take the Highway 89 exit and drive to Tahoe City. Continue south on Highway 89 for 10 miles to Meeks Bay Resort at 7901 West Highway 89 (on the lake side of the road).

Contact: Meeks Bay Resort and Marina, P.O. Box 787, Tahoma, CA 96142; 530/525-6946 or 877/326-3357; website: www.meeksbayresort.com. Bike rentals are available at The Back Country, 530/581-5861, and Olympic Bike Shop, 530/581-2500, both in Tahoe City. Fishing charters are available in Tahoe Vista through Mac-A-Tac Charters, 530/546-2500.

Meeks Bay Resort and Marina

15. LOON LAKE CHALET

Loon Lake Chalet is set at the west end of Loon Lake, a gorgeous lake at 6,378 feet in elevation. It is located deep in a national forest, about 10 miles north of Robbs Hut (see listing below). This chalet once served as a year-round forest service outpost, and is still ideal as a winter base camp for cross-country skiing (with one warning about snow on the access road, and we'll get to that), and a great launch point for a summer vacation.

Luxury rating: 1

Recreation rating: 5

*Loon Lake, off U.S. 50
in Crystal Basin*

Fishing, boating, and camping are popular at Loon Lake. The lake covers 600 acres and reaches a depth of 130 feet at its deepest point. It provides good trout fishing and an occasional huge brown trout. It is surrounded by Eldorado National Forest, and there is an excellent trailhead for a hike leading to a series of lakes to the east: Winifred, Spider, and Buck Island Lakes, and on into Desolation Wilderness, up the Rockbound Valley.

The chalet is rustic, but at least electricity, a heating system, and a small kitchen are provided. Barbecues are available for use on the outside deck. If you don't mind the rustic setting, these facilities take care of the needs of many. Obviously, this is slightly one step higher than camping. You will need to bring sleeping bags and all of your cooking utensils.

What more could ya ask for? Bathrooms? Wind-free weather? Well, there is no real bathroom, but there are vault toilets that are attached to the building. And the lake can get windy, especially on early-summer afternoons, so if you go out in a small boat, do it early, from dawn to midmorning. But that's not much of a problem—go hiking or explore the other lakes in the area in the afternoon.

Be aware that the nearest phone is an outdoor pay phone available at the Crystal Basin Information Station on Ice House Road; cell phones work reliably at one location: the second dam. In the winter, the access road is not plowed on weekends, so you could get snowed in here.

Facilities: Loon Lake Chalet is a forest service recreation cabin for up to 20 people that provides a warming room, sleeping areas with pads, picnic tables, small kitchen, gas fireplace, electrical and gas heating, attached building with vault toilets, and deck with barbecue. A boat ramp is available nearby. Smoking is not allowed. Pets are not permitted.

Bedding: Linens and towels are not provided. Be sure to bring your sleeping bag and pillow.

Reservations and rates: Reservations are required (call 877/444-6777 or visit the website: www.ReserveAmerica.com). The rate is $65 per night. There is a $200 security deposit. You must pick up your permit and a key at the Eldorado National Forest Information Center (see directions). The key must be returned when your visit is complete.

Contact: Loon Lake Chalet, Eldorado National Forest, Information Center, 3070 Camino Heights Drive, Camino, CA 95709; 530/644-6048. Eldorado National Forest, Pacific Ranger District, 530/644-2349.

Directions to Information Center: From Sacramento, drive east on U.S. 50 to Placerville. Continue 5.5 miles east to Camino Heights Drive. Turn right and look for the center at the first building on the right.

Directions to Loon Lake Chalet: From Placerville, drive east on U.S. 50 to Riverton and the junction with Ice House Road/Soda Springs-Riverton Road on the left. Turn left and drive 34 miles to a fork at the foot of Loon Lake. Turn left and drive about two miles (just past the powerhouse) to the chalet.

Loon Lake Chalet

16. ROBBS HUT

Robbs Hut is the bunkhouse for a lookout station that was constructed in 1934, set atop Robbs Peak at 6,686 feet in elevation. The views are extraordinary, of course, especially looking east at the west flank of Crystal Range into Desolation Wilderness. It also overlooks Union Valley Reservoir, set just three miles to the south, one of the prettiest lakes in the entire Sierra. Other lakes in the vicinity that can make side trips include to Gerle Creek Reservoir, Loon Lake, and Ice House Reservoir.

Luxury rating: 1

Recreation rating: 5

Near Union Valley Reservoir, off U.S. 50 in Crystal Basin

This is a primitive setting, basically Advanced Camping 1A, except that a propane cooking stove and sleeping surfaces are available. The bonuses are the location—a quiet, gorgeous area—and the fantastic recreation available nearby. Compared to other lookouts, this one is far more private, since you can lock the gate on the short access road, and also because the sleeping quarters are not at a glass-encased lookout, but at an adjacent hut.

The Crystal Basin Recreation Area is among the most popular backcountry destinations for campers from the Sacramento area. A prominent granite Sierra ridge, which looks like crystal when covered with frozen snow, is the source of its name. One highlight of the region is nearby Union Valley Reservoir, a giant lake that covers nearly 3,000 acres.

Union Valley is set at an elevation of 4,900 feet, near Ice House Reservoir to the south and Loon Lake farther to the north. The lake is shaped kind of like a horseshoe, with several feeder streams located up each of the arms. It can provide excellent fishing for rainbow trout and kokanee salmon and an occasional giant-sized mackinaw trout.

In summer, mountain biking is excellent in the vicinity of the hut, and in winter, skilled cross-country skiers will find a brilliant setting. Note that in winter, the access roads are not plowed on weekends.

Facilities: Robbs Hut has a bunkhouse that can sleep six. It includes a gas fireplace, two-burner propane cooking stove, three sleeping platforms, mattresses, six wool blankets, ax, shovel, and bucket. No water or electricity are available. An outdoor barbecue, fire ring, picnic table, and an outdoor toilet are available nearby. A boat ramp is available five miles away at Union Valley Reservoir. No smoking is allowed. Pets are not permitted.

Bedding: No linens are provided. Bring your own sleeping bag and pillow.

Reservations and rates: Reservations are required (call 877/444-6777 or visit the website: www.ReserveAmerica.com). The rate is $45 per night. You must pick up your permit and combination for the lock at the Eldorado National Forest Information Center (see directions).

Directions to Information Center: From Sacramento, drive east on U.S. 50 to Placerville. Continue 5.5 miles east to Camino Heights Drive. Turn right and look for the center at the first building on the right.

Directions to Robbs Hut: From Placerville, drive east on U.S. 50 to Riverton and the junction with Ice House Road/Soda Springs-Riverton Road on the left. Turn left and drive 23 miles to Robbs Peak Turnoff. Turn left and drive 2.7 miles to a gate. Unlock the gate and continue .3 mile to the hut.

Contact: Loon Lake Chalet, Eldorado National Forest, Information Center, 3070 Camino Heights Drive, Camino, CA 95709; 530/ 644-6048. Eldorado National Forest, Pacific Ranger District, 530/644-2349.

Robbs Hut

17. RICHARDSON'S RESORT

The cabins at Richardson's Resort are set amid a thin pine forest, creating an airy feel. The cabins are also within walking distance of Lake Tahoe. The camp-like setting can make it feel as if you are far away from the masses. Yet in truth you are only minutes away from many attractions. These include a great paved bicycle trail, mountain bik-

Luxury rating: 3

Recreation rating: 5

South Lake Tahoe, off Highway 89 near South Lake Tahoe

ing in a national forest, skiing at Heavenly in the winter, and gambling at the casinos year-round.

Set on the southwest shore of Lake Tahoe, Richardson's Resort is a perfect location for all kinds of outdoor recreation. Add some 37 cabins, many with great lake views, and you have a recipe for one fantastic vacation. The cabins are rustic, complete with knotty-pine ceilings, and most have woodstoves. The resort is completely self-contained, so you don't have to drive anywhere once you get here.

A great three-mile bike route runs right through the resort, then loops around the lake for another three miles, almost all of it perfectly flat for easy biking. Depending on your level of fitness and ambition, you can extend mountain bike trips for miles and miles into the adjoining Eldorado National Forest.

In the winter, the same routes make for some of the best cross-country skiing available anywhere, crowned by awesome lake views. The experience is absolutely wondrous at night under a full moon.

Top it off with a dinner at South Shore's only lakeside restaurant, Beacon Bar & Grill (530/541-0630), and a night in your cabin, and you've got the entire package. No extra pushing needed.

Facilities: Richardson's Resort has 37 cabins (18 are open year-round), each with a bathroom, kitchen, and woodstove with gas heater. A boat ramp, boat rentals, and marina are within walking distance. Bike rentals are also available. A grocery store is on the property, and there's a lakefront restaurant offering lunch and dinner. In the winter, sleigh rides and cross-country skiing take place at the resort. No pets are allowed.

Bedding: Linens and towels are provided, with maid service available for an extra charge.

Reservations and rates: Reservations are required. In the summer, cabin fees range from $565 to $1,535 per week. Discount rates are provided in the winter, along with a reduced two-night minimum stay on weekends. A special ski package is offered in the winter and includes lift tickets, lodging, light breakfast, skier gift package, and discount coupons for dinner.

Directions: From Sacramento, take Highway 50 to South Lake Tahoe. At the junction of Highway 50 and Highway 89, turn north on Highway 89 and drive 2.5 miles to the resort on the right side of the road.

Contact: Richardson's Resort, P.O. Box 9028, South Lake Tahoe, CA 96158; 530/541-1801 or 800/544-1801; website: www.camprichardson.com.

Richardson's Resort

18. ZEPHYR COVE RESORT

A heavenly force casts a spell over many visitors at Lake Tahoe. Your heart opens to Lake Tahoe because of its immense scope and cobalt-blue waters set in high mountains. Add cabins with views of the lake, a mile of sandy beach, a one-minute walk to a marina with boat rentals, paddleboats, and headquarters for the Tahoe cruise ship M.S. *Dixie II,* and you can figure out why Zephyr Cove Resort has become one of the most popular spots in South Tahoe.

Luxury rating: 3

Recreation rating: 5

South Tahoe, Nevada, off Highway 50 near Stateline

If you rent a cabin at Zephyr Cove, you can park your car and hide the key for as long as you stay. Zephyr Cove Resort is located on the Nevada side of South Shore, just over four miles from Stateline. It offers 28 cabins of different sizes, most with a bath and kitchenette, but all are within a minute's stroll of the lakeshore and beach. Some of the cabins have lake frontage, and of course, some are closer to the water than others.

The resort has a mile of beach frontage. Got that? A mile of beach frontage! At Tahoe? At Tahoe! This is where sand is about as valuable as gold. Like we said, it takes only about a minute to walk from the cabins to the beach. Now remember: What did we tell you to do with your car keys?

The adjacent marina provides a huge variety of water sports activities, including the lake's famous tour on the giant paddleboat M.S. *Dixie II.* At the marina, also within a very short walking distance, you can rent paddleboats or boats with motors, or arrange a fishing trip.

One of the best fishing spots for big mackinaw trout is at the southern end of the lake, just offshore of the casinos at a place called "the Nub." Even though the lake bottom is about 750 feet deep in this area, the Nub rises up like a giant dome to 160 feet deep, with its 50-yard crown covered with weeds and grass. This is where the big mackinaw hide out, and right at dawn, if you troll a minnow or J-Plug over the top of the grass, you have the chance of catching some huge trout. Refer to the guidebook *Foghorn Outdoors: California Fishing* for more details.

Facilities: Zephyr Cove Resort has 28 cabins of different sizes, each with a bath and most with a kitchenette. Five lodge rooms are also available. A small general store, restaurant, bar, and a marina with boat rentals, paddleboat, and Lake Tahoe tours on the M.S. *Dixie II* are available. There's a campground with both RV and tent sites. Pets are permitted.

Bedding: Linens and towels are provided.

Reservations and rates: Reservations are often required. Fees range from $95 to $315 per night for cabins, depending on the number of people and size of the cabin. Rooms at the lodge range from $80 to $100 per night, with discounts available in the off-season.

Directions: From Sacramento, take Highway 50 east and continue for 100 miles to Stateline. Continue on Highway 50 past Stateline for four miles and look for the sign for Zephyr Cove Lodge on the left side of the street. Turn left (before the traffic signal) and park at an area just off the highway. Walk a short distance on a sidewalk to the resort office for check-in.

Contact: Zephyr Cove Resort, P.O. Box 830, Zephyr Cove, NV 89448; 775/588-6644; website: www.tahoedixie2.com.

Zephyr Cove Resort

19. LAZY S LODGE

Luxury rating: 2

Recreation rating: 4

South Shore of Lake Tahoe, off Highway 89

You could stay here for weeks and not run out of different activities for each day—and each night. Most of them will require a short drive, walk, or bike ride. But isn't that lucky for you when you're in such a beautiful mountain setting next to one of the world's most beautiful lakes?

The accommodations are plain and simple here: 1950s-era with some updating in the 1960s and 1970s. The two-room cottages have fully equipped kitchens and some have fireplaces. The studio rooms have a wet bar, microwave, and refrigerator. The rectangular-shaped pool is big enough for lap swimming, and there's also a hot tub and large lawn area with tables and barbecue. Tall trees surround the lodge.

You're five miles from Heavenly Valley ski resort, and at least four other major ski resorts are within an hour's drive—perfect for a winter vacation. And in the summer, boy oh boy, do you have choices. You're just down the road from the south shore of Lake Tahoe, which has plenty of fine beaches, miles and miles of biking and walking paths, fishing and boat cruises, golfing, horseback riding, and some excellent hiking trails. Did we forget anything? Oh, yes, if you're so inclined and feel lucky, there are gambling casinos and plenty of nightlife in town.

You could do all of this, or then again, you could be lazy and do nothing but sit in a chaise lounge next to the pool at the Lazy S Lodge.

Facilities: Lazy S Lodge has 20 cottages and studio rooms. The cottages have fully equipped kitchens and the studios have a microwave, refrigerator, and wet bar. A heated pool, hot tub, picnic tables, and barbecues are available. The lodge is suitable for children. Pets are not allowed. Smoking is not permitted.

Bedding: Linens and towels are provided.

Reservations and rates: Reservations are recommended. The fee is $99 to $124 per night per cottage and $59 to $84 per night per inn room. During holidays, add $20 to the room or cottage rate. Rollaway cribs are $5 per night. Ski packages are available. Major credit cards are accepted. Open year-round.

Directions: In South Lake Tahoe at the junction of Highway 89 and U.S. 50, turn north on Highway 89 and drive one mile to the resort on the right.

Contact: Lazy S Lodge, 609 Emerald Bay Road, South Lake Tahoe, CA 96150; 530/541-0230 or 800/862-8881; website: www.lazyslodge.com.

Lazy S Lodge

20. ANGORA LAKES RESORT

Luxury rating: 2

Recreation rating: 5

Upper Angora Lake, South Tahoe, off Highway 89 near Fallen Leaf Lake

For many people, a vacation at Angora Lakes is perfection. Unfortunately, perfection has its price. About the only way to reserve a spot here is to call in January for the coming summer and get on the list.

It can take a long time on the waiting list to finally get a chance to stay at a cabin here. There are just eight of them, relatively primitive at that, but they are remote and situated on a pristine lake surrounded by Eldorado National Forest, so remote that a shuttle ride is provided for cabin guests.

The resort is absolutely beautiful. The water often seems to be almost as blue as Lake Tahoe, circled by both beach and boulders, and backed by forest. The boulders are perfect for making flying leaps into the lake for swimming if you can stand the cold water. Little rowboats are available for cruising around, the trout fishing is decent, although the fish are often small, and the hiking in the area is excellent.

But trying to get a reservation will turn even the most die-hard Tahoe lover into a prisoner of hope. First off, there is a carryover list of guests who stay here for a week each year; that locks up most of the cabins for the summer. What is left is snatched up by those on a waiting list compiled over the winter, or when there is a rare cancellation. Your best bet is to make contact with the staff at Angora Lakes Resort in January, ask for a waiting list form, fill it out, send it in, and start hoping.

Rarely do you come across a place so worth the wait. Angora Lakes is one of those places.

Facilities: Angora Lakes Resort has eight cabins of varying design and size. Each has a kitchen, electricity, hot shower, and chemical toilet. No pets are permitted. No smoking is allowed. Rowboats are available for rent.

Bedding: No linens, towels, or laundry facilities are provided.

Reservations and rates: Reservations are required, and signing up on a cancellation list is available. Cabin rates range from $800 to $950 per week, depending on the size of the cabin.

Directions: From Sacramento, take Highway 50 east to the Highway 50/89 split in South Lake Tahoe. Turn north on Highway 89 to Fallen Leaf Lake Road. Turn left on Fallen Leaf Lake Road and drive up the hill for two miles. When the road forks, bear left for .25 mile to Forest Service Road 12N14. Bear right and drive 2.3 miles (past the Angora Fire Lookout) to the end of the road and a parking lot. A .5-mile shuttle ride to the cabins is available for guests and their gear; otherwise you must make the short hike uphill.

Contact: Angora Lakes Resort, P.O. Box 8897, South Lake Tahoe, CA 96158; 530/541-2092 (summer) or 805/545-9332 (winter). For a map, ask for Lake Tahoe Basin Management Unit and send $6 to U.S. Forest Service, Attn: Map Sales, P.O. Box 587, Camino, CA 95709; 530/647-5390, fax 530/647-5389; or visit the website: www.r5.fs.fed.us/visitorcenter. Major credit cards are accepted.

Angora Lakes Resort

21. ECHO LAKE CHALET

Echo Lakes is an exquisite place—a high, blue, beautiful alpine lake set in granite and surrounded by forest. Here you will find 10 old cabins in only fair shape but with decks, great views, and such a beautiful setting that you may feel as if you have been deposited in heaven.

Luxury rating: 3

Recreation rating: 5

Echo Lake, South Tahoe, off Highway 50 near Echo Summit

It is set at an elevation of 7,500 feet in a canyon near the Desolation Wilderness, not far from Echo Summit off Highway 50. The lake is shaped like an hourglass, with the lower portion best for waterskiing. Boats are run in a clockwise direction around the lake. The upper portion is quiet, sprinkled with a few little islands, and is the choice for fishing and low-speed boating, like paddling in a canoe during an awesome evening sunset. The one problem at the lake is the wind in the early summer; it can absolutely howl out of the west in the afternoon.

A great adventure is to take the hiker's shuttle boat to the head of Upper Echo Lake. From there it is a fantastic hike on the Pacific Crest Trail into Desolation Wilderness, with rock-sprinkled Aloha Lake the primary destination. This is a relatively easy day hike, seven miles round-trip. There are several other lakes along the way, as well as long-distance views to the east of Echo Lakes, and once over the pass, heading north, to the east of the back side of Mt. Tallac and to the west of Desolation's bare granite slopes.

For a short walk with a great view from the chalet, walk across the dam, and from there, you will find a short hike that climbs up to the right. It ends with a great view of South Lake Tahoe, from the valley on out to the lake.

Fishing is also good at Echo Lakes, with most anglers trolling to catch rainbow trout. The best bite is at dawn, when the lake is glassed out, and when the pools from rising trout can look like raindrops. It is one of the most beautiful places on earth.

Facilities: Echo Lake Chalet has nine cabins with bathrooms. All but one have kitchenettes, cookware, and utensils. A boat ramp, dock, and rental boats are nearby, as well as a small store. Small, quiet, clean pets are permitted and must be attended at all times.

Bedding: Linens and towels are provided.

Reservations and rates: Reservations are required. Cabin rates range from $90 per night for two to $138 per night for four, and from $540 per week to $828 per week. Open Memorial Day weekend to mid-September depending on snow conditions.

22. SORENSEN'S RESORT

It might seem like a pipe dream to imagine a place in the high Sierra where log cabins are set amid pines and firs, with a pretty stream within walking distance, and several lakes nearby for first-rate fishing.

Luxury rating: 4

Recreation rating: 4

Toiyabe National Forest, off Highway 88 in Hope Valley

In Hope Valley, this pipe dream is a reality at a place called Sorensen's Resort—although it is really more of a cabin village than a resort. Here you can make your base camp, using one of the cabins as your retreat, then spend as much time as you wish exploring the area by hiking or fishing at great recreation destinations such as the West Fork Carson River, Caples Lake, or the Pacific Crest Trail, among many.

Hope Valley is located along Highway 88, the winding two-laner that rises out of the Central Valley at Stockton. This is the little highway that passes Lower Bear River Reservoir, Silver Lake, and Caples Lake before finally rising over Carson Pass and being routed down into Hope Valley. Here at 7,000 feet is Sorensen's, and once you set up shop in one of its cabins, you probably won't feel like going home for a long time.

There are 33 cabins, including 10 gorgeous log cabins. All but three have kitchens, but none have telephones or televisions to disrupt your stay. The walls are thick, and it is usually quiet, so you don't lose the sense of mountain solitude. A small but outstanding restaurant is located at lodge headquarters, and in the summer an outside deck is available for dining.

Because of the high elevation, there is often snow here from late November or early December through May. This appeals to skiers in the winter, and Kirkwood Ski Area is located about 15 miles to the west off Highway 88.

You don't have to go far for a pretty walk or fishing. Just across the road from Sorensen's is a meadow and the West Fork Carson River, which provides an easy hike and also fair fishing for rainbow trout. There are also several quality lakes in the area. The best for fishing is Caples Lake, located 12 miles to the west, and Blue Lakes, located off Blue Lakes Road 12 miles to the east. Other nearby lakes include Woods Lake, Red Lake, Kirkwood Lake, Burnside Lake, and Tamarack Lake.

Our favorite hike here starts at Carson Pass, elevation 8,540 feet, at the trailhead for the Pacific Crest Trail. Heading north, the trail is routed up over a mountain rim for about two miles, with a great view below of Caples Lake. After topping the rim, the Upper Truckee River Canyon comes into view to the north along with the headwaters for the Truckee River, and if you look to the far north, you can make out giant Lake Tahoe, an unforgettable scene.

Facilities: Sorensen's Resort has 33 cabins of various sizes, including 10 log cabins. All but three have kitchens. All provide electricity, but there are no electronic devices in the rooms; cabins do not have telephones or televisions. Pets are permitted in selected units. No smoking is permitted, and there is a $500 fine for violations.

Bedding: Linens and towels are provided.

Reservations and rates: Reservations are recommended. Cabin fees range from $115 to $140 for two-person cabins and $130 to $225 for four-person cabins. Log cabin fees range from $215 to $275 per night. Discounts are available for off-season and midweek stays. A two-night minimum is required on weekends.

Directions: From Sacramento, drive east on U.S. 50 for about 90 miles to the U.S. 50 junction with Highway 89. Turn right (south) on Highway 89 and drive over Luther Pass to Highway 88. Turn left (east) on Highway 88 and drive one mile to Sorensen's Resort on the right side of the road.

From Stockton, drive east on Highway 88 for about 110 miles, passing through Jackson and Kirkwood and over Carson Pass. When you reach the Highway 88 and Highway 89 junction, continue straight on Highway 88 for one mile to Sorensen's Resort.

Contact: Sorensen's Resort, 14255 Highway 88, Hope Valley, CA 96120; 530/694-2203 or 800/423-9949; website: www.sorensensresort.com.

Sorensen's Resort

23. CAPLES LAKE RESORT

Some people complain that they have "No place to go, nothing to do." Then we ask them, "Have you been to Caples Lake?" They usually respond with a look that resembles a deer staring into headlights. With its blue-green waters surrounded by forest at 7,800 feet with a backdrop of high wilderness peaks, Caples Lake is not only pretty, but the cabin rentals and huge array of outdoor recreation possibilities can make any vacation seem far too short. The cabins are open year-round, offering boat and bike rentals and horseback riding in the summer and snowshoes in the winter. Kirkwood Ski Area is only a few miles away.

Luxury rating: 3

Recreation rating: 5

Eldorado National Forest, off Highway 88 near Kirkwood

Caples Lake Resort overlooks pretty Caples Lake, set in the high alpine country near Carson Pass. There is a beautiful view of the lake and mountains from the second floor of the lodge. The cabins have furnished kitchens, modern bathrooms, wall heaters, and bedding, and in winter, the fireplaces add a great touch. Note that Cabins 2, 3, and 5 are closest to the lake. Lodge rooms are also available and have been remodeled with private bathrooms across the hall. Two bonuses here are a dry sauna heated by a woodstove (a real plus in cold weather) and an on-site restaurant. A small marina provides boat rentals: 12- and 14-foot aluminum motorboats for fishing, as well as canoes and paddleboats.

Of the half-dozen lakes in the immediate area, Caples provides not only the most consistent trout fishing, but typically the biggest fish as well. There are several trails from the resort for biking or horseback riding. There are also several wilderness trailheads (no bikes allowed) in the nearby region. The best two short hikes are from Woods Lake to Round Top Lake and from Carson Pass to Winnemucca Lake, both about four miles round-trip.

Facilities: Caples Lake Resort has seven cabins that vary in size. Each has been remodeled to provide a private bathroom. Full kitchens with cookware, utensils, and gas stoves are provided, and a boat dock, ramp, small marina, and small store are available nearby. There are also six guest rooms in the lodge. You can rent boats, bikes, and horses, and in the winter, snowshoes. No pets are allowed. No smoking is allowed.

Bedding: Linens and towels are provided.

Reservations and rates: Reservations are recommended. Cottage rates vary from $90 to $175 per night, depending on the size of the cabin, number of people, day of the week, and season.

24. KIT CARSON LODGE

The cabins at Silver Lake look so perfect that upon first sight, you might think they are private retreats for a few lucky rich folks. Guess again. They are private retreats all right, but for anybody who wants to rent them.

© NAOMI BRAZIER GILGERT

Luxury rating: 3

Recreation rating: 5

Eldorado National Forest, off Highway 88 near Silver Lake

There are a lot of Silver Lakes in California and all of them are beautiful, but this one might just be the most special. This Silver Lake is set at 7,200 feet on the western slopes of the Sierra Nevada along Highway 88; it's pretty and blue, surrounded by granite and national forest, and well-stocked with trout. It is one of several lakes in the immediate region, along with Caples Lake, Woods Lake, Red Lake, and Kirkwood Lake, all located within a few miles. With relatively short drives, you can also reach Frog Lake, Blue Lakes, Burnside Lake, and Lost Lakes to the east.

And like we said, the cabins look perfect, sprinkled about the forest along the lake's northern shore. Although they are well-equipped, it is critical that you remember to bring your own towels and dish soap because they are not provided. Several cabins have lake frontage, including Beaver, Eastern Brook, Black Bear, and Wolf, and most of the others have lake views. The view from Eastern Brook cabin, for instance, is very beautiful, with little islands in the foreground and a sky painted that magic deep blue you see only in the high country. Silver Lake laps at the shore a short distance from your front porch.

Since this is the high country, expect extraordinary amounts of snow and ice in rough winters. In typical years, Silver and the nearby lakes will start melting off their ice between May and early June, with enough snowmelt in the adjacent forest for the lakes to become accessible by Memorial Day weekend.

Kit Carson Lodge provides boat rentals, but this country is suited for visitors to bring their own car-top boat, such as a canoe. With a canoe you can lake-hop for days, hitting them all—fishing, paddling, and playing.

This is also an excellent area for hiking, with several great trails available, including the short wilderness hike to Winnemucca Lake.

Facilities: Kit Carson Lodge has 19 cabins in a variety of sizes and accommodations. Bathroom, full kitchen with utensils, fireplace, gas stove, and deck are included in each cabin. Boat rentals, a boat dock, a small beach, and a swimming area are available. A store, a post office, and a coin laundry are nearby. No pets are permitted. No smoking is allowed.

Bedding: Linens are provided but towels, dish soap, and toiletries are not provided.

Reservations and rates: Reservations are recommended and required for discounted rates. Rates range from $730 per week to $1,420 per week during summer. Prior to June 22 and after September 3, nightly rentals are available and rates range from $140 per night to $215 per night, with discounts for midweek stays.

Directions: From Jackson, drive east on Highway 88 for 50 miles to Silver Lake. Turn at the signed entrance road for Kit Carson Lodge.

Contact: Kit Carson Lodge, Kit Carson, CA 95644; 209/258-8500 (summer), 530/676-1370 (winter—November 1 to May 31); website: www.kitcarson lodge.com.

Kit Carson Lodge

25. KAY'S SILVER LAKE RESORT

You want a pretty Sierra mountain lake offering fishing, hiking, and boating, and a rustic mountain cabin to go along with it? Then stop here. You'll find a traditional mountain getaway next to Silver Lake, a classic granite cirque just below the Sierra ridge at 7,200 feet.

The cabins come in three sizes: studio, one-bedroom, and two-bedroom. All have fully equipped kitchens, private bathrooms, and decks. The studio cabins also have a living room with double bed. With a one-bedroom cabin, add a bedroom and daybed. The two-bedroom cabins include a dining area, large living area with two daybeds, and another bedroom. A big plus is the gas heating in these cabins, since the temperatures can fluctuate greatly at this elevation.

Luxury rating: 3

Recreation rating: 4

Eldorado National Forest, off Highway 88 near Kirkwood

Winter weather sometimes requires guests to walk in up to 200 yards uphill to the cabins; a trail is not maintained. If you have to hunker down during a storm, you'll be relieved to know that the resort has a store with basic supplies. The Kirkwood Ski Area is a 10-minute drive east on Highway 88; downhill and cross-country skiing are available, as is snowmobiling.

During warmer weather at Silver Lake, you can rent 13-foot aluminum boats with 7.5 horsepower motors; a boat launch is available. The fishing is good; refer to the guidebook *Foghorn Outdoors: California Fishing* for more information. A great hike starts at the trailhead on the east side of the lake; it's a two-mile tromp to little Hidden Lake, one of several nice hikes in the area.

Facilities: Kay's Silver Lake Resort has nine cabins with fully equipped kitchens and private bathrooms. Fire pits, gas heating, and decks are provided. A small store, bait and tackle, boat rentals, and boat launch are available. The resort is suitable for children. Pets are not allowed. Smoking is permitted.

Bedding: One set of linens and towels is provided; there is a $1.50 fee for each extra set. There is no daily maid service.

Reservations and rates: Reservations are recommended. The fee is $65 to $130 per night per cabin and $380 to $760 per week. Cash discounts are available. There is a two-night minimum most of the year, and a four-night minimum on holidays. Major credit cards are accepted. Open year-round.

Directions: From Jackson, drive east on Highway 88 for 52 miles to the resort on both sides of the road.

Contact: Kay's Silver Lake Resort, 48400 Kay's Road, Pioneer, CA 95666; 209/258-8598.

Kay's Silver Lake Resort

26. BEAR RIVER LAKE RESORT

As you venture into the mountains on Highway 88, heading east "up the hill," Bear River Reservoir is the first of three quality mountain lakes you will come to (Silver Lake and Caples Lake are the other two). For many, there is no need to drive further. This place has most everything you could want.

With a lower elevation—5,900 feet—Bear River Reservoir has an advantage over Silver and Caples Lakes. The ice here melts off sooner, and correspondingly, the spring trout stocks and fishing get going earlier, too. Yet the lake is high enough on the Sierra slopes to often get a ton of snow, creating outstanding winter recreation, including 75 miles of snowmobile trails and many snow-play areas.

Luxury rating: 4

Recreation rating: 4

Bear River Reservoir, off Highway 88 in Eldorado National Forest

Bear River Lake Resort is a complete vacation service lodge that makes a superb headquarters for a vacation getaway. The cabins are not true luxury, but provide everything: a kitchen with all the goodies, private bedroom with fresh linens, and full bathroom. The cabins are located above the west shore of the lake.

The reservoir covers 725 acres and is set in a canyon on the edge of the national forest. It was put on the map because of its fishing, often excellent for rainbow, brown, and brook trout. The cobalt-blue lake gets a double-barreled dose of trout, receiving plants from both the Department of Fish and Game and the private resort here, which adds bonus trophy fish. You get the picture: lots of fish. Almost every week, someone catches a trout in the 5- to 10-pound class.

Facilities: Bear River Lake Resort has eight deluxe cabins that sleep four. Each includes a bedroom, additional fold-out bed in the living room, full bathroom, full kitchen, and cooking utensils. A playground, volleyball, beach area, and a game room are available for children. A boat ramp, a grocery store, boat rentals, a restaurant, and a cocktail lounge are available nearby. In winter, snowmobile service is available. No smoking is permitted. Pets are not allowed.

Bedding: Linens and towels are provided.

Reservations and rates: Reservations are recommended. Double-occupancy rates range from $93 per single night to $450 per week. There is a $5 charge per night for additional persons and a $100 damage deposit. Major credit cards are accepted. Open year-round (call for access conditions in winter).

Directions: From Stockton, drive east on Highway 88 for about 80 miles to the lake entrance on the right side of the road. Turn right and drive 2.5 miles to a junction (if you pass the dam, you have gone .25 mile too far). Turn left and drive .5 mile to the entrance on the right side of the road.

Contact: Bear River Lake Resort, 40800 Highway 88, Pioneer, CA 95666; 209/295-4868, fax 209/295-4585; website: www.bearriverlake.com.

Bear River Lake Resort

27. LAKE ALPINE LODGE AND CABINS

One of the Sierra Nevada's great summer jewels is Lake Alpine and its cabins, campsites, and lodge, as well as the hiking, fishing, and many other nearby adventures. Though hardly a secret, it still gets missed by many simply because it is located on Highway 4, near Bear Valley/Mount Reba, rather than on either the I-80 or U.S. 50 corridor to Reno and Tahoe.

Luxury rating: 3

Recreation rating: 5

Stanislaus National Forest, off Highway 4, near Bear Valley

The lake is set at 7,320 feet and covers 180 surface acres, high enough in the mountains to capture the best of the Sierra, small enough to keep the setting quiet and intimate, and big enough for low-speed boating and for the trout to grow.

All the cabins at Lake Alpine Lodge and Cabins have lake views and are within walking distance of the lake. It's not quite like finding your own Golden Pond, because the cabins are set on a sloping hillside on the opposite side of the highway from the lake, but that is actually a bonus, since the distance provides privacy and quiet from the activity at the lake.

Hiking in the area is outstanding. Most visitors will take two hours and hike completely around the lake, a flat four-mile trip, which was recently widened, ending conflicts among low-speed hikers, shoreline anglers, and high-speed cyclists. But better trails are available. One is the 1.3-mile climb to Osborne Ridge (the trailhead is located just east of Silver Tip Campground), where you get a gorgeous view of the lake and into the Carson-Iceberg Wilderness. If you like views, this one is a must. Another must is the 1.5-mile tromp to Duck Luck (trailhead at Silver Valley Campground), a tiny, picturesque setting with some old pioneer cabins along the route. The ambitious can extend the hike into the adjacent Carson-Iceberg Wilderness to Rock Lake, a pristine lake with clear, blue water set in granite; it's an eight-mile round-trip hike.

Alpine Lake is an ideal lake for a small boat; there's a good boat ramp, and a 10-mph speed limit keeps the lake quiet. In other words, there are no Jet Skis or similar personal watercrafts, no water-skiers, and no big, fast boats. Just folks putting around, trolling, and sometimes paddling canoes or oaring small inflatable rafts.

Facilities: Lake Alpine Lodge and Cabins has six bedroom cabins and three studio cabins. All cabins have at least two beds. Most include a bathroom with shower, refrigerator, cookware, barbecue, and decks. Tent cabins with fewer amenities are also available. A nearby lodge provides a small store, bar, and restaurant. Pets are permitted.

Bedding: Linens are provided.

Reservations and rates: Reservations are recommended. Cabin rentals are priced from $95 to $120 per night for two people, $10 for each additional person.

Directions: From Stockton, turn east on Highway 4 and drive into the Sierra Nevada. Continue east past Arnold about 25 miles to Lake Alpine (on the right) and Lake Alpine Lodge (on the left).

Contact: Lake Alpine Lodge and Cabins, P.O. Box 5300, Bear Valley, CA 95223; 209/753-6358; website: www.lakealpinelodge.com.

Lake Alpine Lodge and Cabins

CHAPTER 7

San Francisco Bay Area

*I*t's ironic that many people who have chosen to live in the Bay Area are often the ones who complain the most about it. We've even heard some say, "Some day I'm going to get out of here and start having a good time."

We wish we could take anyone who has ever had these thoughts on a little trip in our airplane and circle the Bay Area at 3,000 feet. What you see is that despite strips of roadways and pockets of cities where people are jammed together, most of the region is wild, unsettled, and beautiful. There is no metropolitan area in the world that offers better and more diverse recreation and open space so close to so many.

The Bay Area has 150 significant parks (including 12 with redwoods), 7,500 miles of hiking and biking trails, 45 lakes, 25 waterfalls, 100 miles of coast, mountains with incredible lookouts, bays with islands, and in all, 1.2 million acres of greenbelt with hundreds of acres being added each year with land bought by money earmarked from property taxes. The land has no limit. Enjoy it.

Along with the unique recreation possiblities here comes unique lodging. We discovered rustic cabins at Mt. Tamalpais and others nearby on an ocean bluff . . . the opportunity to stay overnight on a yacht in San Francisco's Fisherman's Wharf and Oakland's Jack London Square . . . romantic cabins in the North Bay foothills and Point Reyes National Seashore . . . tent cabins at Big Basin Redwoods, the region's number-one hiking park . . . and park model cabins in the San Joaquin Delta within walking distance to private docks and boating.

Note that proximity to a metropolitan area means two things: the demand is higher and the price is higher. So plan ahead and don't expect the midweek or off-season deals that are common in more rural areas.

There are many world-class landmarks to see while staying in the Bay Area. In San Francisco alone, there are the Golden Gate Bridge, Fisherman's Wharf, Alcatraz, Ghiradelli Square, Chinatown, Pacific Bell ballpark, the Crissy Field waterfront, cable cars, South Beach, Fort Point, the Cliff House and Ocean Beach, and Fort Funston.

In fact, instead of going far away for a vacation, residents might consider what so many do from all over the world: Stay and discover the treasures in your own backyard.

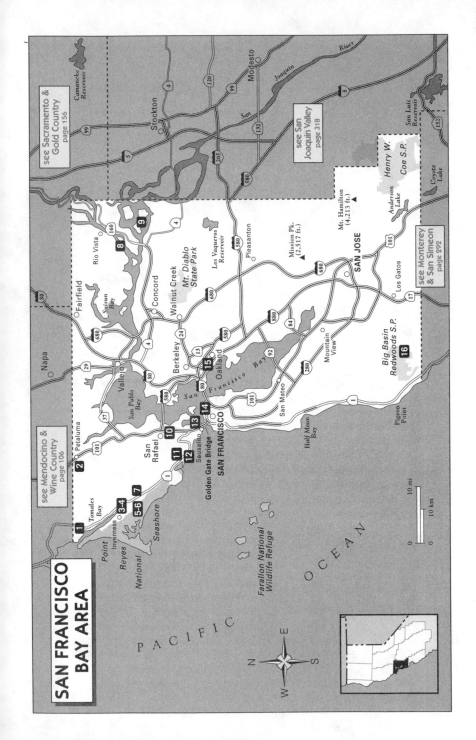

SAN FRANCISCO BAY AREA

see Sacramento & Gold Country page 156

see San Joaquin Valley page 318

see Monterey & San Simeon page 292

see Mendocino & Wine Country page 106

Camanche Reservoir

Modesto

River

San Joaquin

Stockton

San

Rio Vista

Fairfield

Napa

Suisun Bay

Concord

Walnut Creek

Mt. Diablo State Park

Los Vaqueros Reservoir

Pleasanton

San Luis Reservoir

Coyote Lake

Anderson Lake

Henry W. Coe S.P.

Mission Pk. (2,517 ft.)

Mt. Hamilton (4,213 ft.)

SAN JOSE

Los Gatos

Berkeley

Oakland

Mountain View

San Mateo

San Francisco Bay

Vallejo

San Pablo Bay

San Rafael

Sausalito

SAN FRANCISCO

Golden Gate Bridge

Petaluma

Tomales Bay

Inverness

Point Reyes National Seashore

Half Moon Bay

Pigeon Point

Big Basin Redwoods S.P.

Farallon National Wildlife Refuge

PACIFIC OCEAN

10 mi

10 km

N E S W

222 Northern California Cabins & Cottages

CHAPTER 7
SAN FRANCISCO BAY AREA

1. DILLON BEACH RESORT

It doesn't take long to become enchanted with Dillon Beach, the oceanside community set at the mouth of Tomales Bay. The cottages here provide sweeping ocean views, access to excellent beach walks, clamming (in season), beachcombing, and boat rentals just a mile away. If you can arrange to stay at Dillon Beach Resort during the week, do so; although this area is a popular Bay Area spot for weekend getaways, during the week the place attracts relatively few people. The cottages are furnished with everything but food and drink. That means you can relax in comfort, that is, unless you're out adventuring.

Luxury rating: 3

Recreation rating: 4

Dillon Beach, off Highway 1 near Tomales

Weather is always a wild card, with fog common in the summer. But no matter how rough the ocean is, Tomales is often surprisingly calm, sheltered from west winds by Inverness Ridge at Point Reyes National Seashore. That makes Tomales Bay great for sea kayaks and small boats.

Other great features include some of the best clamming beds on the Bay Area coast. It requires a short boat ride to reach the best areas. Boat rentals and detailed where-to-go information is available nearby at Lawsons' Landing (707/878-2443). The best times are always during the minus low tides that arrive about every two weeks from late fall through winter to early spring.

Facilities: Dillon Beach Resort has three cottages; a linked business, Dillon Beach Property Management, has 25 vacation homes. All are completely furnished, including kitchens with cookware and utensils. A grocery and tackle store is available. Pets are not permitted.

Bedding: Linens and towels are provided.

Reservations and rates: Reservations are recommended. The rate is $330 per night for up to six persons. A two-night minimum stay is required on weekends.

Directions: In Petaluma on U.S. 101, take the East Washington Boulevard exit and drive west (it turns into Bodega Avenue) for 10 miles. Turn left at Tomales Road (if you reach the town of Two Rock, you've gone a mile too far) and drive six miles to the town of Tomales at Highway 1. At the stop sign, turn right on Highway 1 and drive .25 mile to Dillon Beach Road. Turn left on Dillon Beach Road and drive four miles to Dillon Beach Resort.

Contact: For cottage rentals, Dillon Beach Resort, P.O. Box 97, Dillon Beach, CA 94929; 707/878-2094. For vacation home rentals, write Dillon Beach Property Management, P.O. Box 151, Dillon Beach, CA 94929; 707/878-2204; website: www.DillonBeach.com.

Dillon Beach Resort

2. SAN FRANCISCO NORTH/ PETALUMA KOA

This KOA is set on the outskirts of the Bay Area, 34 miles north of San Francisco. The property is a 60-acre farm setting, so it provides a rural feel despite the relative proximity of one of the America's most active urban areas. Though San Francisco is a big draw, heading to the nearby wineries in the Napa-Sonoma valley can be more appealing. Or, drive west on the country roads to Bodega Bay and the Point Reyes National Seashore, the Russian River corridor, or the redwoods (Armstrong Redwoods State Reserve is located just north of Guerneville). In addition, there are 12 golf courses in the vicinity and a driving range within walking distance of the KOA. To the south is Six Flags Marine World near Vallejo, and Sears Point International Raceway. Another fun option is to take a horse-drawn carriage through historic downtown Petaluma and its Victorian neighborhoods; for information, contact Elegant Carriage Co./Storybook Carriages at 707/823-7833.

Luxury rating: 2

Recreation rating: 4

Sonoma Valley, off U.S. 101 near Petaluma

But while you're out sight-seeing, don't forget that you have your own little cabin waiting for you, back at the ranch. The campground is less than a mile from U.S. 101, and has an entry gate, which guarantees privacy. There are 34 of KOA's Kamping Kabins, which have become one of the hottest inventions KOA has ever devised. The cabins are set adjacent to an excellent RV park, as with all KOAs.

Facilities: San Francisco North/Petaluma KOA has 34 cabins in both one- and two-room configurations. Each cabin has primitive beds, electric heat, electrical outlet, barbecue, deck, and swing. Restrooms, showers, coin laundry, a small store, a large heated pool, hot spa, a petting farm, summer recreation program, and live entertainment are available. A recreation hall, shuffleboard, horseshoes, volleyball, badminton, basketball, children's play area, and game arcade are also available. Leashed pets are not allowed in the cabins. Smoking is not allowed in the cabins.

Bedding: No linens are provided. You must bring a sleeping bag and pillow.

Reservations and rates: Reservations are recommended (call 800/562-1233). The fee is $49 to $65 per night. Major credit cards are accepted. Open year-round.

Directions: From Petaluma on U.S. 101, take the Penngrove exit and drive west for .25 mile on Petaluma Boulevard to Stony Point Road. Turn right (north) on Stony Point Road and drive to Rainsville Road. Turn left (west) on Rainsville Road to the campground.

Contact: San Francisco North/Petaluma KOA, 20 Rainsville Road, Petaluma, CA 94952; 707/763-1492; website: www.koa.com.

San Francisco North/Petaluma KOA

3. DANCING COYOTE BEACH

A romantic getaway about an hour from San Francisco? Private deck and beach access? Fireplace? And it costs as little as $100 per night? No way!

Yes, you better believe it. It's Dancing Coyote Beach in Inverness, close to Point Reyes, where four adjoining cottages are situated about 50 feet from the beach with bay views. These are older units that have been renovated with a modern, open look on the inside.

Luxury rating: 3

Recreation rating: 3

Point Reyes, off Highway 1 in Inverness

Three of the two-story cottages are identical and have cathedral ceilings, private deck, bedroom, living area, kitchen, fireplace, and skylights. The Sky Cottage has the same amenities, plus a sleeping loft with fireplace and picture window the width of the loft, with a view of the bay. There's also an enclosed, private shower on the deck that is popular with guests. You'll find your refrigerator stocked with food items to cook yourself a full breakfast each day, and several restaurants are nearby.

Guests have access to a private, sandy beach. Inverness is a sleepy little village with an ideal location for exploring Tomales Bay and Point Reyes National Seashore. This area is good for hiking, biking, bird watching, whale watching, beachcombing, or reading and relaxing.

Facilities: Dancing Coyote Beach has four adjoining cottages with fully equipped kitchens and private bathrooms. Decks, fireplaces, and food items to prepare a full breakfast are provided. Barbecues are available near the beach; they are not allowed on the decks. The cottages are not suitable for children. Leashed pets are allowed with prior permission. No smoking is permitted.

Bedding: Linens and towels are provided.

Reservations and rates: Reservations are recommended. The fee is $100 to $175 per night per cottage, and $15 per person per night for more than two persons. There is a two-night minimum on weekends. Weekly rates are available. Credit cards are not accepted.

Directions: From U.S. 101 in Marin, take the San Anselmo/Sir Francis Drake Boulevard exit and drive west for about 20 miles to Highway 1 at Olema. Turn right (north) on Highway 1 and drive 2.3 miles to Sir Francis Drake Boulevard. Turn left and drive 3.5 miles to Inverness. Continue driving for about 100 yards to the cottages on the right at 12794 Sir Francis Drake Boulevard.

Contact: Dancing Coyote Beach, P.O. Box 98, Inverness, CA 94937; 415/669-7200.

Dancing Coyote Beach

4. MANKA'S INVERNESS LODGE

Call it rustic and elegant. Call it quirky and cozy. Call it upscale and inviting. Most people just call it Manka's Inverness Lodge.

Luxury rating: 4

Recreation rating: 3

Point Reyes, off Highway 1 in Inverness

The former hunting and fishing lodge has been transformed into one of the most unique and romantic lodging facilities in the Bay Area. The owners say they have a simple formula: great beds, blazing fires in the lobby and in the cabins, deep reading chairs, a long wine list and a short menu, indulgent baths, quiet nights, and windows with a view of either the water or the woods. And guess what? It works.

Manka's offers two cabins, eight lodge rooms, and a suite on-site, as well as three cabins off-site. These are not ordinary cabins and rooms, though. Depending on your rental, your furnishings could include a buffalo or bear rug, antiques, unpeeled cypress or four-poster log bed, white linen curtains, plaid bedding, or stuffed animals.

The Boathouse is a restored boathouse that was built in 1911. It stands over Tomales Bay, with large decks, two bathrooms, a living room, and a two-room den. Perched over the Boathouse is the Boatman's Quarters with fantastic views, a fireplace, and a deck with outdoor shower. Both are located two blocks from the lodge.

There's also the Chicken Ranch, a renovated rose- and vine-trellised cottage from the mid-1800s, officially recognized as the oldest home in western Marin County. Originally, this building was a hunting cabin; then it became part of a chicken ranch in the late 1800s. You'll feel like you've entered a time machine when you stay here. This cottage is located one mile from the lodge.

The most popular cabin, by far, is the Fishing Cabin; it can take months to garner a reservation for this one. The owners refer to this cabin as "rustic luxury," and we agree. You'll sleep in a king-size bed with a bear rug at your feet, sit in an overstuffed down and feather couch or hickory chairs in front of the ocean-rock fireplace, shower or take a hot tub on your private deck, and admire the old fishing memorabilia.

One last bit: Manka's has a superb restaurant (open for dinner only Thursday to Monday and open daily for breakfast for lodge guests only), with an assortment of unusual game entrées and an extensive wine list.

Facilities: Manka's Inverness Lodge has two cabins, eight lodge rooms, and a suite on-site, and three cabins off-site. Full bathrooms and fully equipped kitchens are provided in the cabins, but not in the lodge rooms. A fireplace, oversized tub or claw-foot tub, deck, and hot tub are provided in some of the rentals. There are no telephones or televisions in the rooms, but stereo/CD systems are provided. A restaurant is available. The lodge is not suitable for children. Leashed pets are allowed. No smoking is permitted.

Bedding: Linens and towels are provided.

Reservations and rates: Reservations are required. The fee is $365 to $465 per night per cabin, $185 to $285 per night for lodge rooms, and $315 per night for the suite. The pet fee is $50 per night per pet. There is a two-night minimum on weekends. Major credit cards are accepted.

Directions: From U.S. 101 in Marin, take the San Anselmo/Sir Francis Drake Boulevard exit and drive west for about 20 miles to Highway 1 at Olema. Turn right (north) on Highway 1 and drive for two miles to Sir Francis Drake Boulevard. Turn left and drive four miles to Inverness. Continue one block to Argyle Way. Turn left and drive 150 feet to the lodge on your right.

Contact: Manka's Inverness Lodge, P.O. Box 1110, Inverness, CA 94937; 415/669-1034 or 800/58-LODGE; website: www.mankas.com.

Manka's Inverness Lodge

5. HOLLY TREE INN

So you want to be close to Point Reyes National Seashore, but you don't want to camp and you don't want a motel room? At the Holly Tree Inn, you can have your own cottage with kitchen and hot tub, and you're only one mile from the Bear Valley Visitors Center at Point Reyes.

Luxury rating: 4

Recreation rating: 4

Point Reyes, off Highway 1 in Inverness

This is a bed-and-breakfast inn with four rooms in the main house, a charming cottage on-site, and two additional cottages nearby. The private and cheerful Cottage in the Woods is located on the grounds; it's a two-room retreat featuring a king-size bed, vaulted ceiling, pine floors, woodburning stove, hot tub, and an old-fashioned bathtub. A complimentary breakfast is also included.

Sea Star Cottage is located a few miles down Sir Francis Drake Boulevard at the end of a—er, dock. Yup, the cottage is situated at the end of a 75-foot dock, resting on stilts over the edge of Tomales Bay, complete with water and mountain views, including of Mount Tamalpais to the south. The little house contains a living room, kitchen, solarium with hot tub, queen-size four-poster bed draped in white linen, fresh flower arrangements, and complimentary breakfast.

A 20-minute drive from the inn is Vision Cottage, a two-bedroom cabin good for families and groups. Set beneath an old growth forest of Bishop pines, the cottage features two decks and floor-to-ceiling windows in the living room that provide a forest view. Other amenities include a fully equipped kitchen and a refrigerator stocked nightly with a fully prepared breakfast for you to heat up in the morning. You'll also have use of a gas log fireplace, hot tub, queen-size beds, down comforters, and handmade quilts. From the front door, you can walk down the path straight to Shell Beach at Tomales Bay, 1.3 miles downhill.

Facilities: Holly Tree Inn has one on-site cottage, two off-site cottages, and four inn rooms. Fully equipped kitchens are provided in the off-site cottages, and a complimentary full breakfast is prepared and placed in the cottage refrigerators the night before. The on-site cottage does not have a full kitchen, but breakfast is brought to the front door. A private bathroom with shower is included in all units. Fireplace, hot tub, and patio are available in some of the rentals. Although the inn can accommodate children, the facilities are more suitable for adults. Pets are not allowed. No smoking is permitted.

Bedding: Linens and towels are provided.

Reservations and rates: Reservations are recommended. The fee is $190 to $285 per night per cottage, and $130 to $180 for inn rooms. For more than two persons in a cottage, $30 per person per night for ages 12 and over and $15 per person per night for children under age 12 is charged. There is a two-night minimum on weekends. Major credit cards are accepted.

Directions: From U.S. 101 in Marin, take the San Anselmo/Sir Francis Drake Boulevard exit and drive west for about 20 miles to Highway 1 at Olema. Turn right (north) on Highway 1 and drive .2 mile to Bear Valley Road. Turn left on Bear Valley Road and drive approximately two miles to Silverhills Road. Turn left and drive a short distance to the inn at 3 Silverhills Road.

Contact: Holly Tree Inn, P.O. Box 642, Point Reyes Station, CA 94956; 415/663-1554, fax 415/663-8566; website: www.hollytreeinn.com.

Holly Tree Inn

6. GRAY'S RETREAT AND JASMINE COTTAGE

This place has such a secret location that the innkeeper refuses to give detailed directions until you've made reservations. Karen Gray says that privacy is the key element at the three lodging options here—Gray's Retreat, Jasmine Cottage, and a barn loft—situated on five acres and located two miles from the entrance station to Point Reyes National Seashore.

Gray's Retreat is a country home with a fully equipped kitchen that sleeps up to six persons comfortably but can also accommodate

Luxury rating: 3

Recreation rating: 3

Point Reyes, off Highway 1 in Inverness

larger groups. The home is ideal for a family, and pets are allowed. Nine-foot-high French doors and windows frame the view of Point Reyes to the west and Elephant Mountain to the east. A fireplace, barbecue, two patios, small library of Point Reyes writings, telephone, and television with VCR are provided. A high chair, jogger stroller, and childrens' books and games are available.

Jasmine Cottage has a romantic, intimate feel and can house up to four persons. You'll be surrounded by bouquets of flowers, candles on the table, a library, and a double hammock outside. Although there is a fully equipped kitchen, complimentary continental breakfast is delivered to the cottage. A fireplace, shared garden hot tub, laundry room, porch, and outdoor furniture are provided, but there are no telephones or televisions.

The barn loft has the best views on the compound, and guests enjoy the spectacular sunsets from this vantage point. Amenities include a sleeping loft with skylight, a tiny kitchen, complimentary continental breakfast, tea, and coffee, and a shared garden patio with hot tub. Wander around outside and you'll probably be greeted by the neighboring donkeys. The loft can sleep four people when the sofa bed is used.

For details about Point Reyes National Seashore, see the listing for Point Reyes Seashore Lodge, below.

Facilities: Gray's Retreat and Jasmine Cottage has a house, a cottage, and a barn loft; each comes with a fully equipped kitchen and private bathroom. The facilities are suitable for children. Well-behaved pets are allowed. No smoking is permitted.

Bedding: Linens and towels are provided.

Reservations and rates: Reservations are required. The double-occupancy rate is $145 per night for the barn loft, $220 per night for Jasmine Cottage, and $245 per night for Gray's Retreat. The seventh night is free, and additional persons are $15 per night per person. Children under age two are free. The pet fee is $25 per stay per pet. There is a two-night minimum on weekends and a three-night minimum on holidays. Major credit cards are accepted.

Directions: Call for directions; the innkeeper insists on privacy for guests.

Contact: Gray's Retreat and Jasmine Cottage, P.O. Box 56, Point Reyes Station, CA 94956; 415/663-1166; website: www.jasminecottage.com.

Gray's Retreat and Jasmine Cottage

7. POINT REYES SEASHORE LODGE

This lodge is well known to Point Reyes National Seashore visitors because they travel right past the inn on their way to the park entrance. But what is somewhat secret is that there are two cottages available. These private hideaways can sleep four to six persons and have kitchens and spas. The two-acre property is filled with gardens, a lawn, curving pathways, and serene sitting areas. No, you won't be roughing it here.

Luxury rating: 4

Recreation rating: 4

Point Reyes, off Highway 1 in Olema

Creekside Cottage is located on Olema Creek and has a garden patio, bedroom, sofa sleeper, and television with VCR. Casa Olema is a historic building with living room, dining area, loft bedroom, television with VCR, large spa, and sleeping room for six. The decor is traditional and upscale. A restaurant is available if you don't feel like cooking.

Point Reyes Seashore Lodge is only 35 miles north of San Francisco, but it seems like you're a thousand miles from the hubbub of a city. You're midway between Tomales Bay and Stinson Beach, and the Bear Valley Visitor's Center at Point Reyes is only a few miles away. Some activities at the park you shouldn't miss are viewing the tule elk at Pierce Point, visiting the old lighthouse, and hiking or biking, on the lookout all the while for the unusual white deer. For swimming or beachcombing, check out Heart's Desire Beach.

Facilities: Point Reyes Seashore Lodge has two cottages and 21 inn rooms. fully equipped kitchens and private bathrooms are provided in the cottages. A restaurant, recreation room with pool table, and reception and conference facilities are available. The inn is suitable for children. Pets are not allowed. No smoking is permitted. One lodge room is wheelchair accessible.

Bedding: Linens and towels are provided.

Reservations and rates: Reservations are recommended. The fee is $325 per night per cottage, and $135 to $230 per night for inn rooms. Additional persons are $25 per person per night, and $5 per night for children under age 12. Major credit cards are accepted.

8. SNUG HARBOR RESORT, LLC

If you want a romantic vacation getaway, go for the one-bedroom Snuggle Inn. If you've got a big family or group, or just need some space, go for Snuggle Inn Number 1. But do plan ahead . . . these units book quickly for the summer.

Now, you ask, what the heck is a Snuggle Inn?

A Snuggle Inn is a park model cabin set on prime waterfront land. Park model cabins have been built off-site and then transported to the resort; they are small, cozy, clean, and comfortable. Snug Harbor also offers a large three-bedroom, two-bath home located on a peninsula. The units are designed for those who want to have the feel of camping with the comforts of home. The place has a diverse clientele because it is so well suited for a family outing, a romantic getaway, or a boating or fishing adventure.

Luxury rating: 4

Recreation rating: 5

Ryer Island, the Delta, off Highway 12 near Rio Vista

Snug Harbor is unique in many ways, and it starts with the trip here. Most visitors will need to take one of the cabled ferry rides to reach Ryer Island. So from the start, you are off the beaten path. Yet it's a nice place, with clean cabins, full-service marina, and an excellent location to explore the boating paradise of the Delta. The waterfront sites with docks give Snug Harbor the feel of a Louisiana bayou. Snug Harbor is an excellent location for fishing and water sports, especially waterskiing. Anglers will find good prospects for striped bass, largemouth bass, and catfish.

Facilities: Snug Harbor, LLC has five cabins in varying sizes and a three-bedroom house. All have furnished kitchens and bathrooms. Restrooms, hot showers, an RV dump station, a convenience store, a swimming beach, a children's play area, a boat launch, paddleboats, propane gas, and a full-service marina are available. Some facilities are wheelchair accessible. There are also waterfront sites for RVs or tents. No pets or smoking are allowed in the Snuggle Inns.

Bedding: Towels and sheet sets are not included, but can be rented for $5.

Reservations and rates: Reservations are recommended and a deposit is required. Rates range from $98 per night for a cabin for two to $240 per night for a cabin for 12. Extra charges apply if a cleanup is required. Other fees include $10 for boat launch and $10 for day-use visitors. Major credit cards are accepted. Open year-round.

Directions: From San Francisco, take I-80 to Fairfield and Highway 12. Turn east on Highway 12 and drive to Rio Vista and Front Street. Turn left on Front Street and drive under the bridge to River Road. Turn right on River Road and drive two miles to the Real McCoy Ferry (signed Ryer Island). Take the ferry across the Sacramento River to Ryer Island and Levee Road. Turn right and drive 3.5 miles on Levee Road to Snug Harbor on the right.

Contact: Snug Harbor Resort, LLC, 916/775-1455; website: www.snugharbor.net.

Snug Harbor Resort, LLC

9. LUNDBORG LANDING

This park is set on Bethel Island in the heart of the San Joaquin Delta. There's a program in place that calls for 39 waterfront park model cabins to be installed. This will be the only place on Bethel Island to rent a place overnight, and the design is nice, with each cabin providing a carport and deck; a swimming pool will also be available.

Luxury rating: 3

Recreation rating: 4

Sacramento River Delta, off Highway 4 on Bethel Island

A park model cabin is a great little unit that comes preassembled on wheels—hence the name RV park model cabin. Once installed, however, it becomes a permanent-style residence. They are small but very nice, new, and clean. They typically come with cedar siding, beds, and a kitchen with appliances; some come with a holographic fireplace. It's the darndest thing you've ever seen—an image of a fire, and it actually puts out heat! Many people buy these RV cabins, then lease them back to the resort to be used as rentals.

The location makes a stay at Lundborg Landing an outstanding destination for boating, waterskiing, and bass fishing. The boat ramp here provides immediate access to an excellent area especially for waterskiing, and it turns into a playland on hot summer days.

In the fall and winter, the area often provides good striper fishing at nearby Frank's Tract, False River, and San Joaquin River. The fishing for largemouth bass at Frank's Tract is rated among the best in North America, casting "frogs" and "rats"—lures that resemble them—on the mossy weed pads. It's some of the most exciting fishing imaginable to see a big bass blast through the weeds to hit the floating lure.

Fishing for catfish in surrounding slough areas is also good year-round. The Delta Sportsman Shop at Bethel Island has reliable fishing information. Live web camera pictures of Frank's Tract are available on the Lundborg Landing website.

Facilities: Lundborg Landing is in the process of installing 39 park model cabins that come complete with a kitchenette, bathroom, furniture, and beds. The resort also has 76 RV sites with full hookups. Restrooms, a laundry room, showers, an RV dump station, propane gas, a playground, a boat ramp, and a full restaurant and bar are available. Some facilities are wheelchair accessible.

Bedding: Visitors may be required to bring their own bedding and pillows; call ahead for the latest requirement.

Reservations and rates: Reservations and a deposit are required. The fee is $95 per night per cabin, $300 for Friday through Sunday.

Directions: From Antioch, turn east on Highway 4 and drive to Oakley and Cypress Road. Turn left on Cypress Road, drive over the Bethel Island Bridge, and continue .5 mile to Gateway Road. Turn right on Gateway Road, drive two miles, then turn left into the park at the large sign and tugboat.

Contact: Lundborg Landing, P.O. Box 220, Bethel Island, CA 94511; 925/684-9351; website: www.lundborglanding.com.

Lundborg Landing

10. GERSTLE PARK INN

Tucked into a hill in the heart of San Rafael is an inn with cottages that will take you back in time to the 1880s, then return you to the present. Gerstle Park Inn is a two-acre estate with a Craftsman-style home and former carriage house, barn, and cottage that have all been renovated with modern amenities, yet still retain the charm of yesteryear. The property contains a fruit orchard, and large trees are dotted around the buildings. The inn caters to vacationers as well as business travelers.

Luxury rating: 4

Recreation rating: 3

San Francisco Bay,
off U.S. 101 in San Rafael

The former carriage house contains two suites, Sunrise and Sunset, located about 50 yards from the inn. Both suites have a fully equipped kitchen, a living room, and a bedroom. The units share a garden patio with chaise lounges. Sunrise is decorated in shades of soft green, black, and white and features a pair of French doors that open from the living room. Sunset's decor is colored in earth-tones and blue, with French doors that lead to a deck overlooking the garden.

Garden Cottage is a former barn, but you'd never guess that now. It houses a living room, bedroom, and galley kitchen with old-style marble countertop. The color scheme features dark and medium blues, and there are Adirondack chairs outside the cottage that face the garden.

By far the most popular cottage is two-story Orchard, which is the most secluded lodging on the property. Downstairs, you'll find a living room with queen sofa bed, a galley kitchen, and a breakfast nook. Upstairs is a bedroom with queen-size bed, vaulted ceiling and deck, and a bathroom with tub/shower and skylight. The decor is country French with a color scheme of cream, rose, and light blue.

Eight suites are located inside the inn, where a full complimentary breakfast is served each morning and wine is provided later in the day. The innkeeper has managed to combine old-fashioned comfort with modern sophistication, using a combination of antiques and upscale, traditional decorating. Gerstle Park is in the same neighborhood as the inn and offers trails, redwood trees, and a tennis court. You're only a short walk to downtown San Rafael, although once inside the grounds, you'll feel like you're miles away.

Facilities: Gerstle Park Inn has two cottages, two suites in a carriage house, and eight inn rooms. The cottages and carriage house suites have fully equipped kitchens and private bathrooms. Telephone, television with VCR, and modem hookups are provided. Complimentary full breakfast and beverages are provided. A video library is available. Although the inn can accommodate children, it is more suitable for adults. Pets are not allowed. No smoking is permitted.

Bedding: Linens and towels are provided.

Reservations and rates: Reservations are recommended. The double-occupancy rates are $189 to $275 per night for the cottages, and $179 to $240 per night for the inn rooms. Additional persons are $25 per night per person. A two-night minimum stay is required, and a three-night minimum on holidays. Major credit cards are accepted.

11. WEST POINT INN

The primitive wood cabins at West Point Inn provide one of the Bay Area's lesser-known and yet most spectacular hideaways. The lodge is located high on the south face of Mt. Tamalpais (a.k.a. Mt. Tam) in Marin. Hikers and bikers who frequent the trails know West Point Inn as the place to get lemonade on Sunday. But the refreshing drink isn't the best thing going for the inn—it is the series of woodsy, rustic cabins and inn rooms (all without electricity) that are available for lodging. The experience is a lot like camping—just throw out your sleeping bag.

Luxury rating: 1

Recreation rating: 5

Mt. Tamalpais, off Highway 1 near Mill Valley

The inn's location near the 2,571-foot summit of Mt. Tam makes for breathtaking views and sunsets, and the nearby trail system is among the best in the Bay Area for hiking and biking. The inn is set on the dirt railroad grade running up Mt. Tam. In fact, most find it for the first time as a rest stop while exploring the nearby trails and fire roads on foot or bicycle. West Point Inn is a historic structure, constructed in 1904 to serve customers of the Mt. Tamalpais and Muir Woods Railroad. Except for occasional repairs and paint, the inn has not changed much in the past century; it's still without electricity, though a commercial gas-powered kitchen is provided for groups who rent the entire inn.

If you want to check the place out before deciding to book a trip, drive up to the Pantoll parking area and trailhead at Mt. Tamalpais State Park. From here, it's a two-mile hike to the inn. Note that it is also accessible out of Rock Springs Trailhead and that mountain bikers must take fire roads to reach the inn. If there's a trick, it's to get your reservation in early. Reservations are accepted 90 days in advance, and the openings go fast.

Although temperatures are not usually cold, we have heard complaints that it can feel cold. The reason it feels cold is because a marine layer off the ocean can pour moist, dense air across the lower slopes of the mountain. So bring a few warm layers and a good sleeping bag, of course.

That same weather phenomenon creates some of the most magical views in the Bay Area. When a layer of fog encroaches the coast, the summit of Mt. Tam often pokes through the top of the fog layer like an island. From the summit, looking out to the west, the fog appears as a pearlescent sea that extends forever. Yet at the same time, looking east, the bay can look something like the Mediterranean Sea, cobalt blue, sprinkled with islands. Every sunset from this vantage point is memorable.

The hiking and biking here is outstanding. You'll find several great trailheads, including:

East Peak: 330-foot climb to the Mt. Tam summit.

Pantoll: 4-mile round-trip into Steep Ravine (stream canyon), and 8-mile round-trip out Matt Davis/Coastal Trail (coastal views).

Rock Springs: 2-mile round-trip to O'Rourke's Bench and Barth's Retreat (coastal views).

Laura Dell: 2.5-mile round-trip to Cataract Falls (series of cascades in wooded canyon).

Muir Woods: 3-mile round-trip on Main Trail and Hillside (giant redwoods, creek, and forest slope).

Facilities: West Point Inn has five cabins and seven inn rooms. Beds, a large full kitchen, and outside chemical toilets are available. No electricity is provided and no smoking or candles are permitted. Bring a sleeping bag, flashlight, and food. No pets are permitted.

Bedding: No linens are provided. Bring a sleeping bag.

Reservations and rates: Reservations are required for weekends, available up to 90 days in advance. The fee is $30 per night, $15 for those under 18 years of age, and $600 for groups reserving the entire inn. Payment is required in advance. No refunds or changes are allowed. West Point Inn is open for lodging Tuesday night through Saturday night. A parking permit is required at Pantoll or Rock Springs at Mt. Tamalpais State Park.

Directions: From U.S. 101 in Marin, take the Stinson Beach/Highway 1 exit. Drive west for one mile to the stoplight at the T intersection with Highway 1/Shoreline Highway. Turn left and drive 2.5 miles uphill to Panoramic Highway. Bear right and continue up the hill for 5.5 miles to Pantoll. Turn left at the Pantoll parking area and ranger station. Hike about two miles to West Point Inn (cyclists must take the old Railroad Grade).

Contact: West Point Inn, 1000 Panoramic Highway, Mill Valley, CA 94941; 415/646-0702; Mount Tamalpais State Park, 801 Panoramic Highway, Mill Valley, CA 94941; 415/388-2070; California State Parks, Marin District, 415/893-1580.

West Point Inn

12. STEEP RAVINE CABINS

This is one of the best cabin deals in California—$15 a night for a rustic cabin set on an ocean bluff overlooking the Pacific Ocean.

Luxury rating: 1

Recreation rating: 4

Mount Tamalpais State Park, off Highway 1 near Stinson Beach

First, you must schedule your stay as far ahead as possible—reservations are available seven months in advance. For a weekend in August, for instance, you can book your trip in January. Do that and you get a cabin. Do anything else and you stand a chance of missing out.

Steep Ravine Cabins are located at Rocky Point on the Marin coast, close enough to hear the waves. These are primitive cabins, but at least firewood for the stove is available. You must bring everything else: sleeping bag, pillow, lantern, flashlight, food, and anything else to keep you satisfied. Officially, they are called environmental campsites; when you call for reservations, ask for Mount Tamalpais State Park Environmental Campsites at Steep Ravine. A gate on the access road, located on the ocean side of Highway 1, keeps the camp secluded and relatively hidden from many people.

There are passing ships, fishing boats, and lots of marine birds, especially in the summer when pelicans and murres are abundant here. On clear days, the sunsets can be breathtaking. In the winter, you might even spot passing whales, noticeable by their spouts, which look like little puffs of smoke.

There are two beach walks from the cabins. The closest is down to the cove just north of Rocky Point and to Redrock Beach. The walk is short, with the trail routed right out of the camp. The other trail is on the south side of Rocky Point and reaches a tiny but secluded beach. To get there, you walk back up the access road, turn right, then look for the trail on the right down to the cove.

The trailhead for the gorgeous Steep Ravine Trail is across the highway from the gated access road, with a small jog to the right.

Facilities: Steep Ravine has 10 cabins, each with a woodstove, picnic table, and flat wood surface for sleeping. There are also six walk-in campsites. Piped water and firewood are available.

Bedding: Linens and towels are not provided. Bring your own sleeping bag and pillow.

Reservations and rates: Reservations are required (call 800/444-7275 or visit the website: www.ReserveAmerica.com). The cabin fee is $15 per night; walk-in campsites are $7 per night.

13. CASA MADRONA

Not sure what type of lodging you want? At Casa Madrona in downtown Sausalito you have a choice: cottage, casita, or hotel room. You also get to choose from a wide selection of theme decorations, amenities, and prices—all with San Francisco Bay views. And there's even a full-service European day spa on the premises.

Luxury rating: 4

Recreation rating: 3

San Francisco Bay, off U.S. 101 in Sausalito

Imagine a beautiful hillside retreat with fireplace and kitchen, watching the yachts sail by from your deck . . a peaceful, terraced setting just steps away from a 100-year-old Victorian mansion housing all the hotel services you might want. At Casa Madrona, this dream can come true.

The Painter's Cottage, which sleeps four, has a Norman Rockwell theme and includes an easel, paints, and brushes. The Calico Cabin has yellow gingham bedding, pine furniture, a porch, a window seat, and a woodburning stove. In La Tonnelle Cottage, you'll find a tiled tub for two, woodburning stove, rattan furniture, and a garden patio.

The hotel's philosophy is to give guests a "small oasis of tranquility" next to a hectic urban setting. Is this concept popular? Here's a clue: At press time, the hotel had purchased the neighboring property and was building a new day spa as well as more lodging.

Facilities: Casa Madrona has eight cottages, 17 casitas, and 10 hotel rooms. All include private bathroom. A deck or porch is provided, and some rentals have a fireplace or woodstove. Some of the cottages have fully equipped kitchens. Complimentary breakfast and an evening wine and cheese social hour are provided. A restaurant, hot tub, full-service European day spa, catamaran cruises, and conference and reception facilities are available. The cottages are suitable for children; the hotel is not. Pets are not allowed. No smoking is permitted. Some facilities are wheelchair accessible.

Bedding: Linens and towels are provided, and there is maid service twice a day.

Reservations and rates: Reservations are recommended. The double-occupancy rate is $195 to $525 per night per rental on weekdays, and $230 to $625 per night on weekends. For additional persons, $25 per night per person is charged. Children under age 18 are free. A two-night, midweek romantic getaway package is available. There is a three-night minimum on weekends during the summer, and a two-night minimum on weekends during the rest of the year. Major credit cards are accepted.

Directions: From San Francisco, drive north on Highway 101 across the Golden Gate Bridge. After crossing the bridge, exit on Alexander Avenue (first exit after the bridge crossing). Bear right on Alexander Avenue (it becomes Bridgeway Road) and drive two miles to Sausalito. Continue a short distance to the hotel on the left.

Contact: Casa Madrona, 801 Bridgeway, Sausalito, CA 94965; 415/332-0502 or 800/567-9524; www.casamadrona.com.

Casa Madrona

14. DOCKSIDE BOAT AND BED— SAN FRANCISCO

If you are captivated by the extraordinary, Dockside Boat and Bed can provide it for you and a friend. This accommodation is a floating cottage, that is, a luxury-furnished yacht moored at Fisherman's Wharf in San Francisco—one of the most unique lodging opportunities. And it's becoming so popular that the owners offer a similar deal at Jack London Square (see listing below). Here you can hide out like Howard Hughes and Lana Turner and make believe you just won the lottery and are planning to cruise around the world in your new boat.

Luxury rating: 4

Recreation rating: 5

Pier 39 at Fisherman's Wharf, off U.S. 101 in San Francisco

Your choices are *Big Bopper, Bodacious, Fog City, Athena,* and *Physical Attraction,*

and they are all moored at San Francisco's Pier 39. You get a complimentary continental breakfast, *San Francisco Chronicle* newspaper—
perhaps with a column by a certain outdoors writer—and flowers
delivered to your yacht.

Fog City is the most economical yacht at $165 per night for two per-
sons. It's a 36-foot Hunter Legend sailboat with two staterooms, a microwave, a sink, an icebox, a coffeemaker, a television with VCR, and
teak interior trim. If that gives you a few ideas, well, dream a little.

Athena is a midrange-priced motor yacht located just 10 feet from
the breakwater. This 51-foot boat has three staterooms, two bathrooms, an entertainment center, a refrigerator, and a microwave.
There's a dining area for four persons and an upper sundeck with
deck furniture and bay views. This yacht rents for $325 per night for
two persons, and for an additional $65, it includes a two-hour
cruise—that's right, cruising among the world-class landmarks of the
bay: the Golden Gate Bridge, Alcatraz, Treasure Island, the water-
fronts of San Francisco, Sausalito, Tiburon, and the San
Francisco–Oakland Bay Bridge.

Once aboard, most people just want to hide out. But adjacent Pier
39 has more than 100 shops, nine restaurants, and a colony of sea
lions, and has become one of the top tourist attractions in San Francisco. The cable car landing is within walking distance.

Facilities: Dockside Boat and Bed has five yachts with private bathrooms. Some
yachts have full galleys, staterooms, microwaves, refrigerators, wet bar, and
dining area. Charters, catered dinners, limousine service, and on-board massages are available, and the yachts are also available for business meetings.
Continental breakfast is provided. The facilities are not suitable for children. Pets
are not allowed. Smoking is not permitted.

Bedding: Linens and towels are provided.

Reservations and rates: Reservations are required. The fee is $165 to $340 per
night per boat for up to two people. Additional persons are $25 to $100 per
night per person. There is a two-night minimum on holidays. Major credit
cards are accepted.

Directions: From westbound I-80 in San Francisco, take the Embarcadero/Harri-
son Street exit on the left-hand side of the road. Turn right on Harrison Street
and drive five blocks to Embarcadero Street. Turn left on Embarcadero and
drive past the piers on the right to Bay Street. Continue on Embarcadero
Street for two blocks to the Pier 39 garage on the left.

Contact: Dockside Boat and Bed, Pier 39, C Dock, San Francisco, CA 94133;
415/392-5526 or 800/436-2574; website: www.boatandbed.com.

Dockside Boat and Bed—San Francisco

15. DOCKSIDE BOAT AND BED— OAKLAND

Oakland has never looked so good. And Jack London Square has never had this kind of a deal. The idea of spending a night on a luxury yacht doesn't cross most people's minds every day—if at all. But there's a place where dreams like this come true, and believe it or not, you don't have to go to heaven to get it. Now you can take your pick of seven yachts, the most unusual lodging opportunity imaginable. The boats range from a 35-foot, center cockpit sailboat to a lavish 65-foot motor yacht. The boats are docked at Jack London Square in Oakland, and you never leave your boat slip unless you pay an additional charter fee. Complimentary continental breakfast and fresh flowers are provided.

Luxury rating: 4

Recreation rating: 4

*Jack London Square,
off I-880 in Oakland*

Gali is a 36-foot Sabre aft cockpit sailboat with a master stateroom, bathroom with shower, and a second double berth in the aft area. The decor is hunter green with inlaid floors, wood interiors, television with VCR, and a teak dining table. The galley has a microwave, refrigerator, sink, and coffeemaker. It rents for $140 to $175 per night for two persons.

At the upper end is *Capriccio*, a custom-built, 65-foot motor yacht with upper and lower sundecks and deck chairs, and two staterooms with private bathrooms. The decor is more contemporary, with Berber carpet, bleached-wood interiors, and white leather couch. Inside, you'll find a refrigerator, beverage center, two microwaves, an ice maker, a coffeemaker, a television, and a VCR. And that's not all. Topside is a spacious wheelhouse with seating for eight and views of the San Francisco skyline. All this luxury comes at a steep price—$400 per night for two persons.

What a deal. For many it would be difficult to conjure a more unique place to spend a wedding night, honeymoon, or anniversary. But what Dockside Boat and Bed has discovered is that people don't always need to wait for a special occasion or a special time. Just the right place, with the right person.

Jack London Square has 15 restaurants, plenty of shopping, a nine-screen theater complex, and a Sunday farmer's market.

16. BIG BASIN REDWOODS STATE PARK

This beautiful state park in the Santa Cruz Mountains, Big Basin Redwoods, has tent cabins available for rent, which means that you can just pick up and go without elaborate planning. The cabins are set on a loop road near Huckleberry Camp, well spaced in a towering redwood forest.

Luxury rating: 1

Recreation rating: 5

Big Basin, off Highway 9 near Boulder Creek

Made out of wood and canvas, the tent cabins measure 12 by 14 feet and feature two full-size beds, a table, and a wood-stove. If you visit during cold weather, it is vital to bring a stack of firewood with you to keep warm. Duraflames, Presto Logs, and other artificial logs are not permitted; bundles of firewood (five or six small logs) are sold at $7.50 a whack at the park's General Store, but they provide warmth for only a few hours. Most visitors bring a sleeping bag, lantern, cooking gear, cooler, and firewood.

Big Basin, of course, is best known for its giant redwoods near park headquarters, Berry Creek Falls (a 70-foot waterfall), and excellent hiking trails. There are 90 miles of hiking routes across a largely un-touched landscape, highlighted by the 4.7-mile trip (one-way) to Berry Creek Falls, a beautiful silver cascade falling under a redwood canopy. This rivals Point Reyes National Seashore as the Bay Area's best hiking parkland.

The forest is very quiet out here and sound really carries, so a quiet time at the campground is enforced between 10 P.M. and 8 A.M.

Facilities: Big Basin Redwoods State Park has 35 tent cabins. Two full-size beds with mattress pads, a table, bench, and woodstove are provided. A picnic table, food locker, and fire pit with grill are located outside each cabin. There are two restrooms nearby, one with a coin-operated shower and another with a coin-operated washer and dryer. A stocked camper store is located at park head-quarters. Lanterns can be rented for $6 per night and small bundles of firewood are available for $7.50 each at the Big Basin Store. Restaurants are available in Boulder Creek.

Bedding: Linens are not provided. Bring your sleeping bag or rent bedding for $10 per stay.

Reservations and rates: Reservations for cabins are required (call the tent cabin host at 800/874-8368). The fee is $49 per night.

Directions: From Santa Cruz, turn north on Highway 9 and drive approximately 12 miles to Boulder Creek. At Boulder Creek, turn left on Highway 236 and drive about 10 miles to the entrance sign for Big Basin Redwoods State Park. Continue for 1.5 miles, turn right at the sign for Huckleberry Campground, drive .25 mile, and then turn right again at the access road for campsites 6 to 41. The camp host is at site 7 in a small trailer.

Contact: Urban Parks, 21600 Big Basin Way, No. 4., Boulder Creek, CA 95006. To contact Big Basin Redwoods State Park, phone 831/338-8860.

Big Basin Redwoods State Park

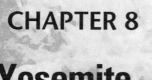

CHAPTER 8

Yosemite
& Mammoth

*S*ome of nature's most perfect artwork has been created in Yosemite and the adjoining eastern Sierra near Mammoth Lakes, as well as some of the most profound natural phenomena imaginable.

Yosemite Valley is the world's greatest showpiece. It is also among the most highly visited and well-known destinations on earth. Many of the cabins and cottages listed in this section are set within close driving proximity of Yosemite National Park. In fact, it may surprise many to learn that several rental cabins are available inside the park. When it comes to cabin rentals in this region, the variety is extraordinary. The price range also varies tremendously.

Anything in Yosemite, or in its sphere of influence, is going to be in high demand almost year-round, and the same is true near Mammoth Mountain. At Yosemite, the zenith is Ahwahnee Cabins, where upscale lodging is coupled with the perfect location—the center of the most beautiful place on earth.

Many family recreation opportunities exist at lake-based settings, including at Lake Alpine, Pinecrest Lake on the western slopes of the Sierra, and at June Lake, Silver Lake, Lake Mary, Twin Lakes, Convict Lake, and Rock Creek Lake on the eastern Sierra. We noticed that the prices are very reasonable in the vicinity of Highway 4 and Calaveras Big Trees, and Highway 108 and Pinecrest. That's what happens when you're competing with Yosemite.

A highlight of the Mammoth and June Lake areas is the historic setting for lodging. The high-end toppers are Double Eagle Resort at June Lake and Tamarack Lodge Resort, which is old-style but luxurious, complete with a gourmet restaurant.

The entire region is sprinkled north to south with ski resorts and snow-play areas, and that makes most of the cabin and cottage rentals a year-round opportunity. In fact, demand can be higher in winter. One of the most unusual winter offerings is at Rock Creek Lodge, where to reach your cabin, you are transported two miles by snowmobile. Another anomaly is at Tioga Lodge, where incredible demand to stay at the Soiled Dove cottage may be due to its bordello theme. According to the lodge owner, wives have argued with other wives over who gets to stay here, while their chagrined husbands look on sheepishly.

Of course, every visit to this area must start with a tour of Yosemite Valley. It is framed by El Capitan, the Goliath of

Yosemite, on one side and the three-spired Cathedral Rocks on the other. As you enter the valley, Bridalveil Falls comes to view, a perfect free fall over the south canyon rim, then across a meadow. To your left you'll see the two-tiered Yosemite Falls, and finally, Half Dome, the single most awesome piece of rock in the world.

The irony is that this is all most people ever see of the region, even though it represents but a fraction of the fantastic land of wonder, adventure, and unparalleled natural beauty. Though 24,000 people jam into five square miles of Yosemite Valley each summer day, the park is actually 90 percent wilderness. Other landmark areas you can reach by car include the Wawona Grove of Giant Sequoias, Tenaya Lake, Tuolumne Meadows, and Hetch Hetchy.

But that's still only scratching the surface. For those who hike, another world will open up: Yosemite has 318 lakes, dozens of pristine streams, the Grand Canyon of the Tuolumne River, Matterhorn Peak, Benson Lake (with the largest white sand beach in the Sierra), and dozens of spectacular waterfalls.

If you explore beyond the park boundaries, the adventures just keep getting better. Over Tioga Pass, outside the park and just off Highway 120, are Tioga Lake, Ellery Lake, and Saddlebag Lake (10,087 feet), the latter of which is the highest lake in California accessible by car. To the east is Mono Lake and its weird tufa spires, which create a stark moonscape.

The nearby June Lake Loop and Mammoth Lakes area is a launch point to another orbit. Both have small lakes with on-site cabin rentals, excellent fishing, and great hiking for all levels. In addition, just east of Mammoth Lakes airport is a series of hot springs, including a famous spot on Hot Creek, something of a legend in these parts. A bonus in this region is Hunewill Guest Ranch, a 140-year-old cattle ranch—not just a dude ranch, but a working operation with everything kept historically accurate.

More hiking (and fishing) opportunities abound at Devils Postpile National Monument, where you can hike to Rainbow Falls. At nearby Agnew Meadows, you'll find a trail that hugs the pristine San Joaquin River up to Thousand Island Lake and leads to the beautiful view from Banner and Ritter Peaks in the Ansel Adams Wilderness.

If you didn't already know, many of California's best lakes for trout fishing are in the Yosemite and Mammoth area. They include Bridgeport Reservoir, Twin Lakes, June Lake, Convict Lake, and Crowley Lake in the eastern Sierra, and Beardsley and Spicer Meadows in the western Sierra.

This region has it all: beauty, variety, and a chance at the hike or fish of a lifetime. There is nothing else like it on earth.

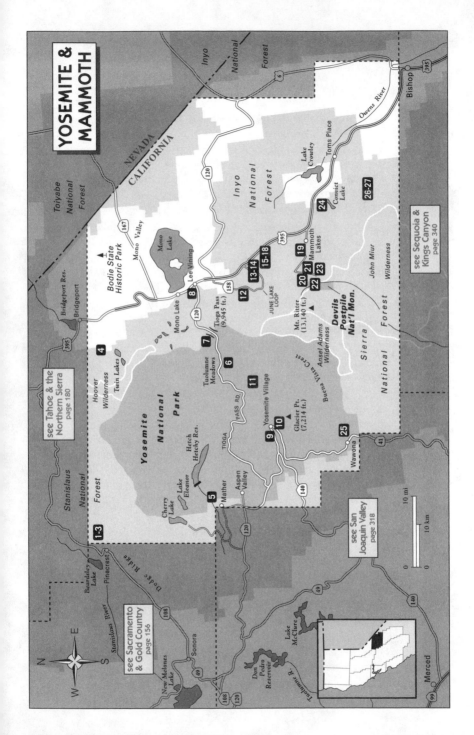

CHAPTER 8
YOSEMITE & MAMMOTH

1. THE RIVERS RESORT

The Rivers Resort gets a thumbs up, and this is why: prime location near the Dodge Ridge Ski Area, close proximity to local lakes and rivers, nearby hiking and horseback riding, and a setting right on the South Fork of the Stanislaus River at approximately 5,400 feet in elevation.

These are 1960s-style cottages with full kitchens, walls and ceilings of knotty pine, rock-and-brick fireplaces, and redwood decks. The furniture is modest and simple with wagon-wheel designs popular in the decor. The cabins receive some level of upgrade virtually every year, so some cabins may be slightly more updated than others.

Luxury rating: 3

Recreation rating: 4

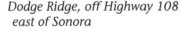

Dodge Ridge, off Highway 108 east of Sonora

All of the cabins have river views, except Cabin 1, which overlooks the pool. Cabin 2 has a river view from the deck only. By far, the most popular rental is Cabin 3 because it's closest to the river, commanding a great view, but it books up quickly in the summer.

One- to four-bedroom cottages are available, and all are two stories and free-standing, which means you don't share a common wall. They are referred to as condominiums because they are privately owned and rented to the public by the resort's manager. A big plus is the large, heated swimming pool with sundeck and changing rooms that is available in the summer. Another plus is access to the Stanislaus River from the property; within a few steps of your cottage, you can go trout fishing.

Five miles from your cottage is the Dodge Ridge Ski Area, which recently underwent a $3.5 million expansion that included opening new runs. Downhill and cross-country skiing and snowboarding are available. Snowmobiling is another option in the local area. Plenty of hiking is accessible in the Stanislaus National Forest and Emigrant Wilderness. Swimming and boating are popular at Pinecrest Lake (one mile from the resort) and Beardsley Reservoir; waterskiing and personal watercraft riding are permitted at Beardsley Lake. You can also ride horses at nearby Kennedy Meadows or Aspen Meadows, or tour the state fish hatchery at Moccasin.

Facilities: The Rivers Resort has 10 condominium cottages with fully equipped kitchens and private bathrooms. Fireplace, deck or porch, television, and barbecue are provided. There are no telephones. A heated swimming pool, sundeck, and changing facilities are available. The resort is suitable for children. Leashed pets are permitted in some of the cottages. Smoking is permitted in some units. One cottage is wheelchair accessible.

Bedding: One set of linens and towels is provided, but there is no daily maid service.

Reservations and rates: Reservations are recommended. The fee is $95 to $195 per night per cottage, and $500 to $900 per week. Additional persons are $5 per night per person. Linens and towels can be rented for $1 per set of two. Major credit cards are accepted. Open year-round.

Directions: From Sonora, drive east on Highway 108 for approximately 31 miles (near Dodge Ridge turnoff) to the resort on the right.

Contact: The Rivers Resort, P.O. Box 81, Strawberry, CA 95375; 209/965-3278 or 800/514-6777; website: www.gorrr.com.

The Rivers Resort

2. PINECREST LAKE RESORT

No secrets here. The word is out about Pinecrest Lake as a first-class family destination for easy camping, light boating, fishing, swimming, hiking, biking, and watching outdoor movies under the stars during the summer. Pinecrest Lake is set at 5,621 feet, covers 300 acres, and is the centerpiece of a fully developed family vacation resort.

Luxury rating: 3

Recreation rating: 4

Stanislaus National Forest, off Highway 108 east of Sonora

The surrounding area is beautiful, best known for its big sugar pines and cedars, with exceptional hiking and biking trails. The water is clear and cold, but by mid-summer it is good for swimming on a hot summer day. A bonus is a small but excellent marina that rents all types of boats. Some families will rent a pontoon boat so they can enjoy a picnic or barbecue on the water, then use the boat as a swimming or fishing platform. Small sailboats, paddle-boats, and rowboats (outboard motors extra, of course) are also available for rent. The lake gets regular stocks of rainbow trout, which join a small resident population of brown trout.

At the center of all the activity is Pinecrest Lake Resort. One of its main attractions is its relative proximity to the Bay Area, far closer than most mountain destinations in Northern California. The resort provides a variety of cabins, townhouses with fireplaces, and deluxe hotel rooms. Another big plus is that this is a year-round resort, an ideal location for skiers, with Dodge Ridge Ski Area nearby and special midweek ski packages available at a discount.

The number-one adventure for families is to hike at least a portion of the Pinecrest National Recreation Trail, usually parlaying it with a picnic. It's an easy, pleasant hike around the scenic shore of Pinecrest Lake that is suitable for the entire family. Pack along your binoculars and bird book because the bird watching is quite good. Picnic spots abound, especially near the inlet located at the east end of the lake.

Bicycles are allowed along the paved bike path that goes through the Pinecrest Picnic Area along the shoreline. The same path is also wheelchair accessible. Where the pavement ends and the trail begins, bicycles are not allowed. Add an extra two miles to the journey with an easy and peaceful hike to Catfish Lake, which in reality is a set of shallow ponds surrounded by old-growth forest.

Facilities: Pinecrest Lake Resort offers cabins in different configurations, accommodating four, six, or eight people. All come with wall-to-wall carpet, television, and fully equipped kitchen. Townhouse-style cabins also include a fireplace and shower-tub combination. No pets are allowed, and no smoking is permitted at any indoor resort facility.

Bedding: Linens, blankets, pillows, and towels are provided.

Reservations and rates: Reservations are recommended. Cabin rentals are priced according to season and size, as low as $120 per night Sunday through Thursday in spring and fall for a two-bedroom cabin that sleeps four, and as high as $1,300 per week in summer for a three-bedroom townhouse that sleeps eight. A one-week minimum is required in July and August. Motel rooms are also available.

Directions: From Manteca at Highway 99, drive east on Highway 120 to Oakdale and Highway 108/120. Turn east on Highway 108/120 and drive to Sonora. Continue northeast on Highway 108 for 30 miles toward Sonora Pass to the Pinecrest turnoff. Turn right onto the Pinecrest Lake Road.

Contact: Pinecrest Lake Resort, P.O. Box 1216, Pinecrest, CA 95364; 209/965-3411; website: www.pinecrestlakeresort.com.

Pinecrest Lake Resort

3. PINECREST CHALET

You want to get up close and personal with Dodge Ridge Ski Area? Well, this is the closest lodging you'll find, only 3.5 miles from the ski resort. Pinecrest Chalet is only one-half mile from Pinecrest Lake. Summer or winter, you have plenty of recreational choices.

You'll also have plenty of choices for lodging, because Pinecrest Chalet has various cabins, townhouses, and an RV park situated on seven acres with the North Fork Tuolumne River running through the property. These may look like rustic cabins on the outside, but on the inside they are modern, with plaster board walls and contemporary decor.

Luxury rating: 3

Recreation rating: 5

Dodge Ridge, off Highway 108 east of Sonora

The popular mini-chalets are one-room cabins with fully equipped kitchens, fireplaces, and cathedral-style, knotty pine ceilings; some chalets have hot tubs. The larger townhouses and deluxe cabins have two to four bedrooms, fully equipped kitchen, and living room with woodburning fireplace. For budget lodging, try a one-room economy cabin—these sleep two to four persons and have a bathroom and limited kitchen facilities.

Pinecrest Chalet is situated in the Stanislaus National Forest among large sugar pines, the conifers with the gigantic pine cones. Guests have use of a large pool, basketball court, play area, and volleyball court. The setting is ideal for families and groups. Fishing, boating, horseback riding, and hiking are close by. A few people have caught brown trout in the Tuolumne River, which runs by the resort, but the fishing is marginal here. Winter recreation includes downhill and cross-country skiing, snowboarding, ice-skating, snowmobiling, snowshoeing, and sledding. For details about the area, see the listings for Pinecrest Lake Resort and The Rivers Resort, above.

Facilities: Pinecrest Chalet has 16 cabins and seven townhouses. An RV park is on the premises. Some rentals have full kitchens, and all units have a small refrigerator, coffeemaker, and microwave. Barbecue and television are provided, but there are no telephones. A pool, laundry facilities, a basketball court, volleyball, horseshoes, and a children's play area are available. The facilities are suitable for children. Pets are not allowed. Smoking is not permitted. Some facilities are wheelchair accessible.

Bedding: Linens and towels are provided.

Reservations and rates: Reservations are recommended. The fee is $95 to $295 per night and $910 to $1,918 per week with full kitchens; $55 to $85 per night and $358 to $552 per week for studios without full kitchens. Additional persons are $5 per night per person. A rollaway bed may be rented for $20 per night. There is a two-night minimum on weekends and a three-night minimum on holidays. Major credit cards are accepted. Open year-round.

Directions: From Manteca at Highway 99, drive east on Highway 120 to Oakdale and Highway 108/120. Turn east on Highway 108/120 and drive to Sonora. Continue east on Highway 108 to the Pinecrest exit and Pinecrest Lake Road. Bear right and drive .2 mile to Dodge Ridge Road. Turn right and drive .8 mile to the chalets on the right.

Contact: Pinecrest Chalet, 500 Dodge Ridge, P.O. Box 1279, Pinecrest, CA 95364; 209/965-3276, fax 209/965-3849; website: www.pinecrestchalet.com.

Pinecrest Chalet

4. HUNEWILL GUEST RANCH

It's not the Ponderosa, but it sure feels like it.

That sensation will surface for anybody who remembers the old *Bonanza* show once you set your boots on Hunewill Guest Ranch, a 4,500-acre cattle ranch that was established 140 years ago. This is the real thing, a genuine cattle ranch, where life is simple and informal, and guests usually help out with cattle chores. That means you'll be horseback riding—a lot. Is your butt ready for this?

Luxury rating: 3

Recreation rating: 4

off U.S. 395 near Bridgeport

The ranch caters to families, groups, and anglers. Most vacationers stay for a week. Visitors have the option of trail rides six days a week; riders are split into groups of beginning, intermediate, and advanced, and families often divide into different groups for the day. Since riders must be at least six years of age, childcare is available for the younger members of a family.

If you are concerned about oversleeping your scheduled morning wake-up, don't worry. Your cabin is located next to the horse pasture, and the thundering noise of the horses galloping in each morning will awaken you. But you'll want to watch this spectacular event, because it gets your juices racing and reminds you of why you came here in the first place.

You're surrounded by about 1,200 cows, 120 horses, sheep, llamas, pigs, and authentic cowboys and cowgirls, as six generations of the Hunewill family have been raised on and worked on the ranch; they know every facet of ranch life and cattle work. On a typical day, you'll be riding through open meadows and across streams at 6,500 feet in elevation, surrounded by snowy peaks and mountains, including Yosemite National Park to the west. You may even stop at one of the ol' swimming holes for a quick dip. More advanced riders have the option of working alongside one of the Hunewills, learning the ropes of doctoring cattle, tracking a cow and not getting lost, roping, and understanding "cow logic."

Hiking and catch-and-release fishing are available for those who don't want to go riding; a four-acre, spring fed fly-fishing pond stocked with two- to five-pound rainbow trout was established several years ago, and float tubes and rafts are allowed. An extra fee is charged for pond fishing. Excellent fishing is also available in the nearby East Walker River and in streams and lakes in Toiyabe National Forest; refer to the guidebook *Foghorn Outdoors: California Fishing*, available at bookstores, for details.

The dinner bell calls you to dinner at the original 1860s-era Victorian ranch house, where you'll eat home-style meals in a large dining room. There are also creekside cookouts, campfire sing-alongs, square dancing, talent night, roping practice, and an occasional hayride.

Cabins are simple duplex-style units with two rooms, two bathrooms, a porch, and a connecting door between rooms in case you want to join two units. Aspen, Bristlecone, Cedar, and Juniper are the newer cabins and are a little more expensive than the older cabins.

In addition to the general activities at the ranch, if you have intermediate to advanced riding skills you can sign on for special trail rides and the annual fall cattle drive. These trips are for more adventurous riders and sometimes involve camping out and riding up to 60 miles from the ranch to the herd's wintering grounds in Nevada. Check with the ranch for details.

Facilities: Hunewill Guest Ranch has 25 cabins with no kitchen facilities, but all meals are provided. Each cabin has a private bathroom. A fly-fishing pond, coin-operated laundry, horseshoes, table tennis, volleyball, organized activities, childcare, private riding lessons, aerobics, personal training, and massage are available. One room is wheelchair accessible. Pets are not allowed. No smoking is permitted.

Bedding: Linens and towels are provided.

Reservations and rates: Reservations are recommended. The fee is $909 to $1,018 per week per person for ages 13 and older, $681 to $724 for children ages 10 to 12, $455 to $483 for children ages 3 to 9, and $200 for children ages 2 and under. Daily rates are available on a space-available basis. Reduced rates are possible for non-riding guests and visitors bringing their own horse; special trail ride packages are available. Open late April through October.

Directions: From Bridgeport on U.S. 395, turn southwest on Twin Lakes Road and drive five miles to the ranch on the left.

Contact: Hunewill Guest Ranch, P.O. Box 368, Bridgeport, CA 93517 (summer) and 200 Hunewill Lane, Wellington, NV 89444 (winter); 760/932-7710 (summer) or 775/465-2201 (winter), fax 775/465-2056; website: www.hunewillranch.com.

Hunewill Guest Ranch

5. EVERGREEN LODGE

Hetch Hetchy is the Yosemite you hear little about, and that is why the cabins at Evergreen Lodge remain a relatively well-kept secret. Hetch Hetchy is a giant lake set in the dammed Tuolumne River canyon in the remote northwest sector of Yosemite National Park. Evergreen Lodge is located just a mile outside the park entrance and eight miles from the lake and the site of an excellent trailhead for hiking and horseback riding. The cabins are quite old but comfortable and come complete with porches.

Evergreen Lodge is located at an elevation of 4,600 feet and is surrounded by Stanislaus National Forest. What makes Evergreen special is the short hop to Hetch Hetchy and the great hikes to Wapama Falls and Tueala Falls. A bonus is that lodge guests are provided free access to Camp Mather and its swimming pool; horse rentals are also available there.

Every year thousands of people at overloaded Yosemite end up stuck without a spot, spending the night in their cars. Many would pay a million dollars for one of these cabins, but they just don't know they exist.

Luxury rating: 3

Recreation rating: 5

Hetch Hetchy, Yosemite National Park, off Highway 120 near Mather

Facilities: Evergreen Lodge has 19 one- and two-room cabins with bathrooms, heat, and television. There are no kitchens in the cabins, but a lodge restaurant is nearby. A swimming pool and horseback riding outfitter are located one mile away at Camp Mather, with free access provided to lodge guests. No pets are permitted.

Bedding: Bed linens are provided with daily maid service.

Reservations and rates: Reservations are recommended. Cabin rates on weekends range from $69 for two to $105 for four, with no minimum stay. Weekly and seasonal discounts are available. The season runs from late April through October.

Directions: From Manteca at Highway 99, drive east on Highway 120 to Oakdale and Highway 108/120. Turn east on Highway 108/120 and drive 25 miles to the turnoff for Highway 49/120 and Chinese Camp. Turn right on Highway 49/120 and drive 12 miles to Moccasin and Highway 120. Turn left on Highway 120 and drive about five miles to Groveland and continue for 28 miles (six miles past Harden Flat) to Evergreen Road. Turn left and drive seven miles and look for Evergreen Lodge on the left side of the road.

Contact: Evergreen Lodge, 33160 Evergreen Road, Groveland, CA 95321; 209/379-2606 or 800/935-6343; website: www.evergreenlodge.com.

Evergreen Lodge

6. TUOLUMNE MEADOWS LODGE

Tuolumne Meadows, set at 8,600 feet on the brink of the Yosemite wilderness, is one of the best jumping-off points for an adventure of any place in North America, especially for hikes that are easy and extraordinarily beautiful.

 © YOSEMITE PARK & CURRY CO.

Luxury rating: 1

Recreation rating: 5

Tioga Pass, off Highway 120 in Yosemite

Your base for this adventure is Tuolumne Meadows Lodge, where there are 69 canvas tent cabins that sleep up to four. This is a vast improvement compared to the Curry Village combat camping scenario in Yosemite Valley (see Yosemite Valley Tent Cabins later in this chapter). This is the high country, and everything is different compared to the valley scene. The air is thin and light, the smell of pine duff is in the air, and the magic of the next day's adventures looms when you put your head down on your pillow to sleep for the night.

Well, that is, if you have a pillow. Many folks just bring their sleeping bags, though bedding is available for a few bucks. This is a fairly primitive setting, with all facilities available nearby in a campground setting. But a great bonus here is that the lodge provides a central dining tent with extremely sumptuous breakfasts and dinners that can satiate even the most prodigious appetites.

With your body well-fueled and acclimated to the altitude, you will be ready for some of the greatest day hikes in America. Starting from Tuolumne Meadows, an excellent option for your first trip is to take the Pacific Crest Trail out to the north. The trail begins with gentle walking as it follows the Tuolumne River towards the Grand Canyon of the Tuolumne River. It stays easy to Glen Aulin, where you get a great view of several small waterfalls and 100-foot Tuolumne Falls, pouring through a granite slot, then cascading into a foaming crater, full of blue-white bubbles.

The ambitious can continue down into the Grand Canyon of the Tuolumne, dropping more than 1,000 feet in the process to see Waterwheel Falls and several other beautiful waterfalls. This trip is eight miles one-way from Tuolumne Meadows, and the climb out of the canyon late in the day can make it a genuine butt-kicker.

Another option from Tuolumne Meadows is to hike south on the John Muir Trail, up Lyell Fork toward Donohue Pass. For the first four miles, you walk along the John Muir Trail, where it seems nearly flat, with the pretzel-like Lyell Fork running nearby. The fishing for small brook trout is often excellent at Lyell Fork, but often best after hiking in at least three miles.

A sensational hike is the climb up Lembert Dome (9,450 feet) for spectacular views. The trailhead is located up the road toward Tioga Pass, on the left. From here it is a steady climb of about 1.5 miles, with the views of wilderness peaks and Tuolumne Meadows just incredible. It's Rambob's favorite spot. You know ol' Rambob, right? (OK, he's Tom's brother.)

Of course, you could choose instead to be waiting in the long pizza line, crowded with all the other flatlanders, down there in the valley.

Facilities: Tuolumne Meadows Lodge has 69 canvas tent cabins that sleep up to four. A woodstove for heat and candles for lighting are provided; there is no electricity. Restroom facilities and showers are available nearby. Breakfast and dinner is available in a central dining tent. Smoking is permitted. No pets are allowed.

Bedding: Linens with a daily maid service are available with an extra cost.

Reservations and rates: Reservations are required. The rate is $53 per night for one person with an additional charge of $8.25 per adult and $4 per child. Major credit cards are accepted. There is a $20 park entrance fee, which is good for a week. Open June through September.

Directions: From Mariposa in the Central Valley, drive east on Highway 140 to the El Portal entrance station for Yosemite National Park. Continue east on Highway 140 to the Highway 120/140 junction. Turn left on Highway 120 and drive eight miles to a fork and bear right on Highway 120 east. Continue east on Highway 120 for 54 miles to Tuolumne Meadows Lodge on the right. Note: An alternate route is available from Highway 120 out of Manteca/Chinese Camp.

From the eastern Sierra, take U.S. 395 to the junction with Highway 120 (just south of Lee Vining). Turn west on Highway 120 and drive to the Tioga Pass entrance station. Continue about 10 miles to Tuolumne Meadows Lodge on the left.

Contact: Yosemite Concession Service, 5410 East Home Avenue, Fresno, CA 93727; 559/252-4848; website: www.nps.gov/yose/home.htm (click on Lodging). For information about Yosemite, call 209/372-0200. For an excellent hiking map of the area, contact Tom Harrison Cartography at 415/456-7940.

Tuolomne Meadows Lodge

7. TIOGA PASS RESORT

How would you like to enjoy all the elements of Yosemite's high-country wilderness, avoid the hassles of an overcrowded park, and have a cozy cabin each night? That combination is exactly what makes Tioga Pass Resort a winner.

Luxury rating: 4

Recreation rating: 5

Tioga Pass, off Highway 120 near Yosemite

This is the high country—elevation 9,600 feet. It's a land of wilderness, granite peaks, mountain slopes sprinkled with lodgepole pine, and pristine lakes. Tioga Pass Resort is located just two miles from the eastern entrance station of Yosemite National Park, and also within close range of Tioga and Ellery Lakes. The surrounding landscape has all the recreational qualities of Yosemite, yet is actually part of Inyo National Forest, with several nearby lakes for car-top boating, much better fishing than in the park, and excellent hiking. And if you want to make the quick getaway into Yosemite, a five-minute drive puts you inside park borders, and another 15 minutes gets you to Tuolumne Meadows.

When you first arrive, you will discover the cabins set on a hillside behind the general store, in a variety of sizes to accommodate couples, families, or small groups. A creek runs nearby. Because this entire area is set high near the Sierra crest, it is subject to cold nights and afternoon winds. No problem, though. After all, you have a cabin to stay in, right? Right.

Within a mile or two are Ellery Lake to the east and Tioga Lake to the west, both beautiful alpine lakes that run pure, cold, and pristine, and are stocked with trout. Just four miles away, via a bumpy Forest Service road, is Saddlebag Lake. At 10,087 feet, it is the highest lake in California accessible by car, providing more alpine beauty, an excellent trailhead, and good boating and fishing. And then there is Yosemite, with outstanding hiking out of Tuolumne Meadows either up Lyell Fork, to Cathedral Lake, down to Glen Aulin along the Tuolumne River, or up Lembert Dome.

Note: In the winter, the roads to the resort are not plowed. Access is still available from Yosemite's eastern entrance, but you'll have to ski in.

Facilities: Tioga Pass Resort provides 10 cabins in one- and two-bedroom configurations, plus four motel units. Each cabin includes a kitchen with utensils, cookware, a stove, and a refrigerator. An electric heater is provided. Central kitchen and bath facilities are provided in the winter. A small store and restaurant are on-site. Pets are not allowed.

Bedding: Linens are provided in the summer.

Reservations and rates: Reservations are required, and there's a weeklong minimum stay in the cabins. A two-day minimum stay is required in the motel-style units. Cabin prices range from $840 to $1,015 per week, depending on the size of the cabin. Motel units rent from $80 to $90 per day.

Directions: From Mariposa in the Central Valley, drive east on Highway 140 to the El Portal entrance station for Yosemite National Park. Continue east on Highway 140 to the Highway 120/140 junction. Turn left on Highway 120 and drive eight miles to a fork and bear right on Highway 120 east. Continue east on Highway 120 and drive 65 miles to the Tioga Pass entrance station. Continue two miles and turn left at Tioga Pass Resort. Note: An alternate route is available from Highway 120 out of Manteca/Chinese Camp.

From the eastern Sierra, take U.S. 395 to the junction with Highway 120 (just south of Lee Vining). Turn west on Highway 120 and drive 12 miles up the grade toward Yosemite National Park. After passing the Saddlebag Lake turnoff, drive about .25 mile and turn right at Tioga Pass Resort.

Contact: Tioga Pass Resort, P.O. Box 7, Lee Vining, CA 93541 (summer), or P.O. Box 307, Lee Vining, CA 93541 (winter); 209/372-4471; website: www.tiogapassresort.com. For an excellent hiking map of the area, contact Tom Harrison Cartography at 415/456-7940.

Tioga Pass Resort

8. TIOGA LODGE

Near the shores of Mono Lake sits a historic resort that was nearly comatose before it was given new life a few years ago. It would have been easy for the owners to raze the structures at Tioga Lodge and start fresh, what with the boarded up, decaying buildings that had become an eyesore. But the owners had a vision to restore the place to its former glory days—a time when Mark Twain and Ansel Adams visited and President Theodore Roosevelt's wife planted a pine tree there. Today, the restoration is well underway and some new buildings have been added, blending the old West look with the new.

Located in the Mono Basin National Scenic Area, the lodge consists of 13 cottages, a restaurant, a saloon, a gift shop, and a gazebo. The 23-acre property overlooks Mono Lake and the little islands Negit and Paoha, and includes a half mile of Mono Lake frontage. The lodge is on one side of U.S. 395 and the remainder of the property is across the road, toward the lake. Since the property is situated on this major highway, expect some traffic sights and sounds. Still, the grounds are lovely, with walkways, a white-painted bridge, outdoor swing, and a creek meandering through the property. The restaurant and gift shop were transported to the Tioga Lodge site in the 19th century from the town of Bodie, now a historical ghost town.

Luxury rating: 2

Recreation rating: 4

Mono Lake, off U.S. 395 near Lee Vining

The 13 cottages consist of two free-standing cottages, a duplex unit, an A-frame building housing five lodge rooms, and another building with four rooms. The cottages are more like inn rooms than cottages, with no kitchen facilities. The rooms are decorated in themes that reflect the history of the lodge and the area. The Mountain Man Room is designed in honor of the explorer Joseph Walker and sports a handmade aspen log bed and an elk head and long rifle mounted on the wall. The Poet's Room is where Mark Twain and Ansel Adams supposedly stayed when they visited, and it is carpeted and contains a dark metal bed and a writing credenza with chair.

Other rooms include Old California, Paiute, Mono Lake, Wilderness, Bodie, Soiled Dove, Nelly Bly, and Log Cabin Mine. The favorite? It's the wildly popular and ultra-feminine Soiled Dove, a tribute to the lodge's one-time bordello heritage. And guess what? It's women, not men, who request this room by a wide margin. At press time, the owner, a former contractor, was making arrangements to build another brothel theme room to keep up with demand.

The restaurant features an outdoor rock patio overlooking Mono Lake. When the restaurant originally opened in 1918, the attire was formal—the waiters dressed in tuxedos, and the tables were decorated with silver candelabras and lace linens. Well, you can leave your tuxedo and formal clothes at home because the attire is casual now. The restaurant is open only for dinner, but breakfast is served on weekends. The saloon serves wine and beer and has the ambience of a cellar, with old stone walls, sand floor, old Western movie posters, and a rustic wood ceiling.

The Mono Lake Tufa State Reserve is the highlight of this area, where you can visit Mono Lake and its strange and remarkable Tufa Towers. Resembling a moonscape, this is truly one of the most extraordinary landscapes in California. It is best seen on a one-mile loop trail or by canoe. Mono Lake is vast, covering 60 square miles, and is estimated to be more than 700,000 years old, making it one of the oldest lakes in North America. About 80 percent of California's gull population nests here.

For hikers, the fall color in Lundy Canyon is spectacular. Refer to the guidebook *Foghorn Outdoors: California Hiking*, for details.

9. AHWAHNEE CABINS

This is the kind of place where you can fall in love for keeps. Hey, it happened to us.

© CHAMBERS LORENZ/KASPAROVITCH PHOTOGRAPHY

Luxury rating: 5

Recreation rating: 5

Yosemite Valley, off Highway 120 in Yosemite

Yosemite Valley is the spectacle of all spectacles. Few places in this country provide more breathtaking scenery than Yosemite, with its dramatic canyon walls, rimmed by El Capitan, Cathedral Rocks, and many other glacial-carved monuments—anchored by Half Dome. This 360-degree-panorama sparkles with the most spectacular waterfalls in the world.

It doesn't get any better than this. And your stay doesn't get any better than at the Ahwahnee. This is Yosemite-style luxury, with gorgeous lodging rooms and cottages set within walking distance of the base of Yosemite Falls. Everything is drop-dead beautiful, from the Native American–style blankets and surrounding interior decor to the most inviting hiking trails in the world just past your front door.

In addition, the setting of the restaurant at the Ahwahnee is also world-class, the kind of place where you just have to sit there for a while to take it all in—the scenery and the food. The Sunday buffet, for instance, is something of a gorge; when you get done, you often feel like somebody could drill three holes in you and use you for a bowling ball.

What we suggest is to get up at dawn, while everybody else is in dreamland, and walk around Yosemite Valley when there is scarcely another human out and about. Across a pristine meadow is Yosemite Falls, charged full with foaming, spraying water, silver-tasseled in reflected light. At 2,425 feet long, it is the tallest waterfall in the world. Across the valley is Bridalveil Falls, 620 feet high and perhaps just as beautiful.

You might take the shuttle to Happy Isles and the trailhead for the Mist Trail. Up you go, first to Vernal Falls, a wide, free-flowing cascade of silver, 317 feet high, then with a steep, stair-step tromp upstream, you reach Nevada Falls, tumbling 594 feet at the foot of Liberty Dome.

For an easy bonus, we suggest the Mirror Lake Trail, which skirts the base of Half Dome and extends out to the entrance of Tenaya Canyon. In the afternoon, this trail gets inundated with people. At dawn, when all is quiet—and not a single soul is out but you—it's like walking in the beginning of time.

Facilities: Ahwahnee Cabins has 24 cottages, four luxurious parlor rooms, and 99 luxury hotel rooms. Bathroom, small refrigerator, television, and telephone are provided. A small patio is available outside. Some units have a fireplace or woodstove. A restaurant with dress code (no jeans, shorts, or tennis shoes; men must wear coats; T-shirts are permitted for men and women) is available. No smoking is allowed. Pets are not permitted. Open year-round.

Bedding: Linens and towels are provided.

Reservations and rates: Reservations are required. The rate is $366 per night (single or double occupancy) and $20 for each additional person. Children under 12 are free if they stay in the same room. Discounted rates are available in the off-season. Major credit cards are accepted. Open year-round. There is a $20 park entrance fee, which is good for a week.

Directions: From Mariposa, drive east on Highway 140 to the El Portal entrance station for Yosemite National Park. Continue east on Highway 140 to the Highway 120/140 junction. Continue east and drive seven miles into Yosemite Valley (the Little Chapel will be on the right and Yosemite Falls on the left) to a stop sign. Turn left on Sentinel at the Stone Bridge (crossing the Merced River) and continue a short distance to another stop sign. Turn right and drive a short distance to Village Drive. Turn left and continue to Ahwahnee Road. Turn right and drive a short way to Ahwahnee Hotel. The route is well-signed.

Contact: Yosemite Concession Service, 5410 East Home Avenue, Fresno, CA 93727; 559/252-4848; website: www.yosemitepark.com (click on Lodging). For Yosemite National Park information, call 209/372-0200.

Ahwahnee Cabins

10. YOSEMITE VALLEY TENT CABINS

The Yosemite Valley Tent Cabins at Curry Village embody the definition of combat camping. It's as if you hide out in your army bunker (tent cabin) all night, trying to fortify yourself as best you can; then come morning, you get your courage up and head out amid the crowds—typically 24,000 people in five square miles every summer day.

It's astounding that the park service concessionaire put 427 tent cabins in here by design. The walls are thin and you can hear other people nearby, and not just in your own tent, of course, but in other tents. There are stories of one guy snoring so badly, with so many people kept awake by it, that a battalion of combat campers invaded his tent cabin, ready to kick him out to his own personal bivouac.

The irony is that for many, the tent cabins somehow do the job. They provide a place to bed down for the night in the most magical place in the world, Yosemite Valley. In turn, when you wake up in the morning, you have no need to drive anywhere. You are already there. You just hike out (the Mist Falls Trailhead at Happy Isles is nearby), rent a bike, or ride the shuttle bus to your choice of a dozen world-class destinations. The shuttle to Glacier Point, for instance, provides a series of eye-popping views, crowned by the chance to hike the Pohono Trail on the southern rim of Yosemite Valley.

Luxury rating: 1

Recreation rating: 5

Curry Village, off Highway 120 in Yosemite

Facilities: Curry Village has 427 tent cabins, 102 cabins, and 19 lodge rooms. Cabins are furnished with two beds; some have private bathrooms. Tent cabins sleep one to five people. Drinking water, restrooms, and coin showers are available nearby. A few heated tent cabins are available in fall and winter. No electricity, kitchens, televisions, nor phones are provided. Coin laundry and a restaurant are available in the area. In summer, ranger programs are available each night in a nearby amphitheater and Curry Village Pavilion serves buffet-style breakfasts and dinners. A gift shop, ice-skating in winter, bicycle rentals, and guided rafting trips are available in the area. Smoking policy varies according to lodging and season. No pets are allowed.

Bedding: Linens and towels are provided.

Reservations and rates: Reservations are required (call 559/242-4848). Cabin rates vary according to season and accommodations. In summer, tent cabins are $54 per night, cabins without bathrooms are $77 per night, cabins with bathrooms are $92 per night, and lodge rooms are $112 per night. Some units are available year-round. Major credit cards are accepted. There is a $20 park entrance fee, which is good for a week.

Directions: From Mariposa, drive east on Highway 140 to the El Portal entrance station for Yosemite National Park. Continue east on Highway 140 to the Highway 120/140 junction. Continue east and drive seven miles into Yosemite Valley (the Little Chapel will be on the right and Yosemite Falls on the left) to a stop sign. Continue straight to a stop signed for Curry Village. Turn right and drive a short distance to the Curry Village parking lot.

Contact: Yosemite Concession Service, 5410 East Home Avenue, Fresno, CA 93727; 559/252-4848; website: www.yosemitepark.com (click on Lodging). For Yosemite National Park information, call 209/372-0200.

Yosemite Valley Tent Cabins

11. YOSEMITE HIGH SIERRA CAMPS

Here you get all the qualities of a prime wilderness experience: the dramatic beauty, the quiet, the views, and the pristine lakes, streams, and meadows of Yosemite. Yet, you get it all without the pounding physical punishment of backpacking, meal prep, or cleanup.

What makes it work are a series of five hike-to (or horseback ride–to) camps set in the wilderness, where you are provided with meals, a bed in a tent cabin, and hot showers. These trips are so popular that a lottery is held every winter for the daily quota of positions available at each of the five camps. Yet there is often considerable availability for the tent cabins into summer because of cancellations.

The five High Sierra camps are spaced roughly 6 to 10 miles apart, so you can create a weeklong loop trip in the wilderness. Many also simply hike in to one of the camps, then stay there for a few days, using the location as a launch point for stellar wilderness day trips without having to carry any gear, just a canteen and trail snacks.

Here are the camp profiles at a glance:

Glen Aulin, at 7,800 feet, is located at the head of the Grand Canyon of the Tuolumne River, an easy, near-level 5.7-mile hike on the Pacific Crest Trail heading north out of Tuolumne Meadows. Featured side trips include seeing nearby Tuolumne Falls, Waterwheel Falls, and exploring the remote Cold Creek Canyon.

May Lake, at 9,700 feet, is a very pretty alpine lake set at the foot of spectacular Mount Hoffman (10,850 feet), with forest and meadow backing the southern end of the lake. Reaching it requires only a

Luxury rating: 1

Recreation rating: 5

Yosemite National Park,
off Highway 120
near Tuolumne Meadows

1.2-mile hike, crossing up and down a short rise. A highlight is climbing around the slopes of Hoffman for great views.

Sunrise, at 9,400 feet, is reached by an easy 5.3-mile hike from Tioga Road or a 7.8-mile hike from Tuolumne Meadows. The camp is set adjacent to the John Muir Trail and a pristine alpine meadow that absolutely glows at sunrise, hence the name. A side trip to Cathedral Lake is a must.

Merced Lake, at 7,150 feet, is a shocker for newcomers. It is pristine, gorgeous, and big (for the alpine zone), situated in remote wilderness midway between Vogelsang Pass and the cut-off trail to Half Dome. A great side trip is hiking up the hill for beautiful views of the backside of Half Dome, and visiting Emeric Lake (and other lakes).

Vogelsang, at 10,300 feet, is reached by a seven-mile tromp from Tuolumne Meadows, including a 1,700-foot climb (with switchbacks) out of Lyell Fork over Vogelsang Pass. The setting is somewhat stark, made up of granite, meadows, ice, and a few pines. Several nearby pristine lakes make this a fantastic base camp for day tripping.

Facilities: Yosemite National Park has five High Sierra camps with canvas tent cabins, steel frame beds with mattresses, and restroom facilities with hot showers. Exception: there are no showers at Vogelsang. Pets are not permitted. Smoking is not allowed.

Bedding: Pillows, woolen blankets, and comforters are provided; guests provide their own sheets, sleeping bags, and towels (also available for purchase).

Reservations and rates: Reservations are required. The fee is $100 per day and includes breakfast and dinner served in main dining tent. Box lunches are available for an additional $8 per day.

Directions: From Mariposa, drive east on Highway 140 to the El Portal entrance station for Yosemite National Park. Continue east on Highway 140 to the Highway 120/140 junction. Turn left on Highway 120 and drive eight miles to a fork and bear right on Highway 120 east. Continue east on Highway 120 and drive to the appointed trailhead for the selected High Sierra camp. Note: An alternate route is available from Highway 120 out of Manteca/Chinese Camp.

Contact: High Sierra Desk, 559/253-5674. At the end of the message, leave your name, phone number, and preference for camp location and date; applications for each winter's lottery for the following summer are available October 15 to November 30. For information on saddle trips to camps, contact Yosemite Stables, 209/372-8348. To learn more about the camps via the Internet, visit www.nps.gov/yose/home.htm (click on High Sierra Camps).

Yosemite High Sierra Camps

12. SILVER LAKE RESORT CABINS

No television. No telephone. Cozy cabin. Pretty high-mountain lake. Little general store. Boats. Trout. Hiking trails. Stream nearby. Skiing in the winter. This is the recipe for a vacation at Silver Lake.

Luxury rating: 3

Recreation rating: 5

Silver Lake, off U.S. 395 on the June Lake Loop

For most visitors, it is everything they've ever wanted. Silver Lake is less developed than June Lake—the principal lake in the June Lake Loop—but it is just as pretty, set at 7,600 feet with 10,909-foot Carson Peak looming in the background. It is one of four drive-to lakes on the loop, just west of U.S. 395 in the eastern Sierra.

A large but exposed campground and RV park is located directly north of Silver Lake, but nearby, off the northwest shore, is Silver Lake Resort and its 16 cabins, each different from the next. The cabins come in all sizes and prices. You can get fresh bed linens when needed, and fresh towels are provided daily. Each cabin also has a propane wall heater. The operation is not so much a resort as it is a camp.

Silver Lake gets its name from the way the sun and afternoon winds send reflected silver flashes off its surface—a pretty scene, especially when the lake's deep blue-green colors are contrasted with the stark, ashen granite of the high mountain walls backing the Sierra Nevada.

Most people come here for the trout, and there are usually plenty, particularly near the dam, boat ramp, and in Reverse Creek near the campground. Boat and motor rentals are available through the resort. If you decide to boat here, the best advice is to set your alarm and be on the lake early. The trout not only bite best here after first light (a high sun and clear water can make them spooky at midday), but the lake is at its calmest between dawn and 9 A.M.

A great wilderness trailhead (Rush Creek Trailhead) is located behind the adjacent RV park, with a trail that is routed 2.1 miles to Agnew Lake with a steady climb of about 1,200 feet on the way. The trail is literally cut into the granite slope, and with nothing blocking your view to the east, you get great vistas of Silver Lake. After topping the rim, you're treated to a divine look at Agnew Lake, set in granite. The trail skirts the north shore of the lake and in another mile rises to the shore of Gem Lake, which can be astonishing in its natural beauty.

Facilities: Silver Lake Resort has 16 cabins, each furnished with a stove and refrigerator and all kitchen utensils. The cabins have propane heat but no telephones or televisions. No pets are permitted.

Bedding: Towels are provided daily, and fresh linens are provided when needed, depending on the length of your stay.

Reservations and rates: Reservations are required, with a deposit of 50 percent of the total fee. Prices are $69 per night for a small cabin for two people, $80 to $124 per night for a cabin for four people. The Creek House costs $185 per night and the Road House $195; both of these can handle up to eight people.

Directions: From Lee Vining, drive south on U.S. 395 and turn right at the first Highway 158/June Lake Loop turnoff. Drive west on Highway 158 past Grant Lake at Silver Lake. Just as you arrive at Silver Lake, turn right at the small store adjacent to the RV campground and park.

Contact: Silver Lake Resort, Route 3, Box 17, June Lake, CA 93529; 760/648-7525; website: www.silverlakeresort.net.

Silver Lake Resort

13. LAKE FRONT CABINS

At Lake Front Cabins, you may be near the lake's edge, but don't expect a lake view; a row of trees on Forest Service land blocks the view. But it doesn't really matter—the accommodations are comfortable and updated, the owners are friendly and helpful, and the price is right.

Since the eight cabins surround a yard, the setup is ideal for groups who wish to rent the whole place. The cabins were originally built in the 1950s as a fishing getaway, appealing primarily to men on fishing vacations. Since the cabins have been nicely redecorated, they now appeal to couples and families as well. The cabins feature forest green carpet and maroon-and-green bedspreads, along with the original knotty pine interior and eight-foot ceilings. The decor gives the cabins a homey, country look. Televisions, thermostat heat, and electric blankets are provided.

Luxury rating: 2

Recreation rating: 4

June Lake, off U.S. 395 on the June Lake Loop

The cabins are situated only 400 feet from June Lake and 500 feet from the marina, an easy walk. There are studios and one- and two-bedroom cabins with full kitchens and bathrooms. These can accommodate up to six persons. Some of the cabins have adjoining walls. There are also a fire pit and patio area next to the lawn, making a good setup for reunions and families with small children.

You're two blocks from the village of June Lake and its restaurants, stores, and shops. And if you rent a boat for a day while you're staying at one of the cabins, you'll get a discount. For more information about June Lake, refer to the listing later in this chapter for The Four Seasons.

Facilities: Lake Front Cabins has eight cabins with fully equipped kitchens and bathrooms, barbecues, patios, and televisions. A fish cleaning station is available. The cabins are suitable for children. Pets are not allowed. Smoking is not permitted.

Bedding: Linens, towels, and electric blankets are provided.

Reservations and rates: Reservations are recommended. The fee is $90 per night per studio, $100 per night per one-bedroom, and $120 per night per two-bedroom, based on occupancies of two, two, and four respectively. Additional persons are $7 per night per person. Rates are slightly higher during holidays. There is at least a two-night minimum during the summer and on holidays. Major credit cards are accepted. Open the end of April through October, and during the Christmas holidays.

Directions: From Lee Vining, drive south on U.S. 395 (passing Highway 158 North) for 20 miles (six miles past Highway 158 North) to June Lake Junction (a sign is posted for June Lake Village) and Highway 158 South. Turn right (west) on Highway 158 South and drive 2.5 miles to June Lake Village and Knoll Road. Turn right and drive two blocks to Brenner Street. Turn right and drive 100 feet to the cabins on the right at 32 Brenner Street.

Contact: Lake Front Cabins, P.O. Box 696, June Lake, CA 93529-0696; 760/648-7527, fax 760/648-7810; website: www.lake-front-cabins.com.

Lake Front Cabins

14. THE HAVEN

If you want to spend time in the gorgeous June Lake area but you're on a tight budget, The Haven should meet your needs. Here you're treated to lodging with a full kitchen, a private bathroom, and maybe a fireplace, and you're only one-half block from the marina and one block from the village. The cottages have adjoining walls and are surprisingly updated. All this is yours for as little as 50 bucks a night.

Luxury rating: 2

Recreation rating: 4

June Lake, off U.S. 395 on the June Lake Loop

The Haven offers cottages from studios to two-bedrooms with a living room that can sleep up to four persons. The cottages have light-colored walls, a few antiques, and cheerful, country decor. Some of the rentals are two-story and have fireplaces or woodstoves, but you must bring your own firewood. The cottages are set around a patio and indoor spa, and you'll get a lake view from the deck.

For details about the June Lake area, see the listing for The Four Seasons later in this chapter.

15. JUNE LAKE PINES COTTAGES

In the old days, nobody spent the winter at June Lake. That was back in the 1920s, before the town of June Lake was established as a summer fishing village and great winter ski area. Eighty years later, it's still known for its outstanding fishing in summer, but also for its winter sports, hiking, cycling, and horseback riding. The old, white-and-royal-blue-trimmed cottages at June Lake Pines Cottages are a reminder of June Lake's beginnings and its transformation into a thriving resort town.

Luxury rating: 2

Recreation rating: 5

June Lake, off U.S. 395 on the June Lake Loop

The one- to three-bedroom cottages are located in the heart of June Lake, across from the general store, and they can accommodate up to six persons. They're old, they're cute, they're wedged in between commercial businesses, and they are close to just about everything in June Lake. All of the cottages have a full kitchen, a private bathroom, and a television; some even have a fireplace. Inside, the decor is 1950s style with knotty pine walls and a few updates. The cottages are clean and functional, and the owners, Harley and Betty Wilmot, are knowledgeable and helpful.

For information about the June Lake area, refer to the listing for The Four Seasons below.

Facilities: June Lake Pines Cottages has 12 cottages with fully equipped kitchens and bathrooms. Barbecues and television are provided, and some units have a fireplace. Laundry facilities and ski packages are available. The facilities are suitable for children. Leashed pets are allowed during the summer only. Smoking is permitted in some of the cottages.

Bedding: Linens and towels are provided, and there is limited daily maid service.

Reservations and rates: Reservations are recommended. For two people, the rate is $70 to $110 per night during the summer, and $55 to $85 per night during the winter. Holiday rates are slightly higher. Discounts are offered for stays of five nights or more. An additional fee of $8 per night per person is charged. Pets are $5 per night per pet. Ski packages are available. Major credit cards are accepted. Open year-round.

Directions: From Lee Vining, drive south on U.S. 395 (passing Highway 158 North) for 20 miles (six miles past Highway 158 North) to June Lake Junction (a sign is posted for June Lake Village) and Highway 158 South. Turn right (west) on Highway 158 South and drive 2.5 miles to June Lake Village and the cottages on the left, across the street from the general store.

Contact: June Lake Pines Cottages, P.O. Box 97, June Lake, CA 93529; 800/481-3637

June Lake Pines Cottages

16. THE FOUR SEASONS

When a lot of people envision a cabin in the mountains, they see an A-frame, one of those high-peaked, steeply sloped cabins with a large downstairs and a loft for sleeping.

Luxury rating: 3

Recreation rating: 5

*off Highway 158
in June Lake Village*

That is exactly what makes the Four Seasons so appealing to vacationers, along with a location near June Lake that's ideal for fishing, boating, hiking, and in the winter, snow skiing. What you get here is a chance to stay in an A-frame mountain chalet, complete with a wood-stove and a view of the nearby high Sierra, and the chance to take part in your favorite outdoor sports.

Where? These cabins are located less than a mile from the June Lake Ski Area, less than a mile from Reverse Creek, and only a few miles from Silver Lake to the west, and Gull and June Lakes to the east. In other words, it is situated in the middle of some of the best year-round recreation opportunities in the June Lake Loop.

The cabins are all electric, which means you get complete kitchen facilities, television (hey, you can always unplug the thing), and electric blankets. They are designed to sleep up to seven people, with rates adjusted according to group size and season, of course. Prime time in this area is mid-December through early March for skiing, July and August for fishing, boating, and hiking, and mid-September to mid-October for viewing the fall colors.

With the ski area less than a mile away, winter is when the cabins are most heavily booked and when reservations are most likely to be required. June Mountain is a small hill compared to nearby Mammoth to the south, but it is plenty big enough for most beginner and intermediate skiers, with six lifts, one tram, and 2,500 vertical feet of skiing.

Of the lakes, June Lake is the prettiest, but it has the most commercial development; Gull Lake is the smallest, but often has the best fishing; and Silver Lake is pretty and has good fishing, but is susceptible to west winds, common in the early summer.

Facilities: The Four Seasons has all-electric A-frame chalets with full kitchens, living rooms with woodstove and television, beds with electric blankets, and bathrooms with tub/shower combinations. The cabins are designed to handle up to seven people. No pets are permitted.

Reservations and rates: Reservations are recommended in summer and often required in winter. Rates range from $89 per day for two people up to $189 per day for seven people. A minimum stay of two nights is required, longer during holiday weekends. The resort is open from the last Saturday in April through October, then closes until mid-December, when it reopens for the Christmas holidays, closing again after the New Year.

Directions: From Lee Vining, drive south on U.S. 395 (passing Highway 158 North) for 20 miles (six miles past Highway 158 North) to June Lake Junction (a sign is posted for June Lake Village) and Highway 158 South. Turn right (west) on Highway 158 South and drive two miles to June Lake. Continue for two miles past June Lake Village (one mile past the ski park), and turn left at the signed driveway for the Four Seasons.

Contact: The Four Seasons, Star Route 3, Box 8-B, June Lake, CA 93529; 760/648-7476; website: www.junelake.com/lodging.

The Four Seasons

17. DOUBLE EAGLE RESORT AND SPA

You want it all? You get it all at Double Eagle Resort and Spa, but you better have a credit card with a high limit ready to hand over.

It's difficult to decide the best features of the place: the superb recreational opportunities nearby or the luxurious amenities at the resort. In any case, you won't be hearing complaints from your partner or your family that they're bored.

First, let's talk about the resort. There are 13 upscale two-bedroom cabins with all the bells and whistles, including living room with fireplace or woodstove, an outside patio with barbecue, a full kitchen with microwave, a ski locker, a telephone, and a television with VCR. Walk outside your cabin and you'll find a pool; a hot tub; a full-service spa; a state-of-the-art fitness center with yoga, meditation, and tai chi classes; catch-and-release fishing ponds, fishing guides, and a fly-fishing school for women; organized activities and day trips, including ski and snowboard trips; and a restaurant. Take your pick.

Luxury rating: 4

Recreation rating: 5

June Lake, off U.S. 395 on the June Lake Loop

The spa features 10 different types of massage, aromatherapy, hydrotherapy, body therapies, facials and skin care, manicures, pedicures, waxing, hair stylists, and make-up lessons. And get this: some of the private treatment rooms have fireplaces. What happened to a good, old-fashioned, sweaty hike in the mountains, followed by an invigorating hot shower?

For winter sports, the ski lodge at June Mountain is only two miles from the resort. The much larger Mammoth Mountain complex is a 20-minute drive south where you can downhill or cross-country ski. Ice-skating is available, and there are hundreds of miles of groomed trails for snowmobiling.

In the summer, four lakes with excellent fishing are within eight miles; refer to the guidebook *Foghorn Outdoors: California Fishing* for details. Other nearby recreation opportunities include superb hiking, horseback riding, and cycling.

Facilities: Double Eagle Resort and Spa has 13 two-bedroom cabins with fully equipped kitchens and bathrooms. Barbecue, deck, fireplace or wood stove, ski locker, television with VCR, and telephone are provided. A pool, a hot tub, a full-service spa, fishing ponds, fly-fishing guides, a fly-fishing school for women, ski and snowboard packages, a restaurant, a fitness center, and organized activities are available. The resort is suitable for children. Leashed pets are allowed in some of the cabins. No smoking is permitted.

Bedding: Linens and towels are provided, and there is daily maid service.

Reservations and rates: Reservations are recommended. The fee is $213 to $257 per night per cabin during the summer, and $228 to $271 per night during the winter. Family discount packages are available. There is a three-night minimum on holidays. Major credit cards are accepted.

Directions: From Lee Vining, drive south on U.S. 395 (passing Highway 158 North) for 20 miles (six miles past Highway 158 North) to June Lake Junction (a sign is posted for June Lake Village) and Highway 158 South. Turn right (west) on Highway 158 South and drive two miles to June Lake. Continue for five miles to the resort on the right.

Contact: Double Eagle Resort and Spa, 5587 Boulder Road/Highway 158, Route 3, Box 14C, June Lake, CA 93529; 760/648-7004, fax 760/648-7017; website: www.double-eagle-resort.com. ***Double Eagle Resort and Spa***

18. BIG ROCK RESORT

If you must have June Lake water frontage and a lake view to go along with it, then Big Rock Resort is your ticket. Situated about five miles from the town of June Lake and right next to the actual lake are eight cabins with kitchens and decks. A marina with boat rentals and paddleboats is available, and guests receive complimentary launching and docking.

Luxury rating: 3

Recreation rating: 5

*June Lake, off U.S. 395
on the June Lake Loop*

We think this is one heck of a deal for the price: you get a nice, comfy cabin, great location, and direct access to beautiful June Lake. The price won't knock your boots off either since fees run just $85 to $130 per night during the summer. And Fido can go on vacation with you, since dogs are allowed. The cabins range from one to three bedrooms; the two-bedroom cabins are duplexes. The one-bedroom cabin is about 20 feet from the lake, and the three-bedroom cabin is a runner-up for closest distance to the water. The duplexes are spaced farther back, about 150 feet from the lake.

In the winter, you're 1.5 miles from June Mountain Ski Area, with 2,500 vertical feet of skiing. Cross-country skiing is possible from your doorstep, and snowmobiling is offered in the June Lake Loop. You're in close proximity to Mono Lake, the ghost town of Bodie, Yosemite National Park, Devils Postpile National Monument, and Rainbow Falls. For details about fishing and hiking in the June Lake area, refer to the guidebooks *Foghorn Outdoors: California Hiking* and *Foghorn Outdoors: California Fishing*.

Facilities: Big Rock Resort has eight cabins; all have a fully equipped kitchen, barbecue, deck, and television. Some units have a fireplace. A boat slip is provided. A full-service marina, bait and tackle shop, and boat rentals are available. The resort is suitable for children. Leashed pets are allowed from late April through October. No smoking is permitted.

Bedding: Linens and towels are provided.

Reservations and rates: Reservations are recommended. For two people, the rate is $85 to $130 per night per cabin during the summer, and $80 to $160 per night during the winter. Prices are slightly higher during holidays and on winter weekends. During the winter, the sixth night is free. For additional persons, $10 per night per person is charged. Pets are $5 per night per pet. Major credit cards are accepted. Open year-round.

Directions: From Lee Vining, drive south on U.S. 395 (passing Highway 158 North) for 20 miles (six miles past Highway 158 North) to June Lake Junction (a sign is posted for June Lake Village) and Highway 158 South. Turn right (west) on Highway 158 South and drive approximately 2.5 miles to the resort on the right at the west end of the lake, next to the fire station.

Contact: Big Rock Resort, P.O. Box 126, June Lake, CA 93529; 760/648-7717 or 800/769-9831, fax 760/648-1067; website: www.mammothweb.com /lodging/bigrock.

OTHER CABINS AND COTTAGES NEARBY

- Gull Lake Lodge, P.O. Box 25, June Lake, CA 93529; 760/648-7516 or 800/631-9081; website: www.gulllakelodge.com.
- Reverse Creek Lodge, Route 3, Box 2, June Lake, CA 93529; 760 /648-7535 or 800/762-6440; website: www.reversecreek-lodge.com.
- Fern Creek Lodge, 4628 Highway 158, June Lake, CA 93529; 760/648-7722 or 800/621-9146; website: www.ferncreek-lodge.com.
- Boulder Lodge, P.O. Box 68, 2282 Highway 158, June Lake, CA 93529; 760/648-7533 or 800/458-6355, fax 760/648-7330; website: www.boulderlodge.com.
- June Lake Motel and Cabins, P.O. Box 98, 2716 Boulder Drive, June Lake, CA 93529; 760/648-7547 or 800/648-6835; website: www.junelakemotel.com.
- Still Meadow Cabins, P.O. Box 694, June Lake, CA 93529; 760/648-7794 or 800/648-2211.
- Whispering Pines, Route 3, Box 14B, June Lake, CA 93529; 760/648-7762 or 800/648-7762; website: visitwhispering-pines.com.

Big Rock Resort

19. EDELWEISS LODGE

Many people love the natural beauty and recreational activities of the Mammoth Lakes area, but they hate the crowds, the high prices, and the motel/hotel complexes. Here's our solution to enjoying the area in a reasonably priced cabin close to town, but out of the main traffic flow: Edelweiss Lodge.

Luxury rating: 3

Recreation rating: 4

Mammoth Lakes, off U.S. 395

Located on a wooded acre a couple of miles from town are eight cabins within walking distance of Mammoth Creek. Most of these cabins have been here for decades, and they're in much the same condition as they were years ago. You'll find knotty pine interiors, fireplaces, and high ceilings with carved beams. They all have fully equipped kitchens, televisions, and telephones, and barbecues are available in the summer.

Most of the clientele are repeat customers who've been staying here for years because of the clean, comfortable accommodations in an ideal location surrounded by towering Jeffrey pines. The cabins are popular with families and couples who like to hike and fish in the summer and ski during the winter. You can even bring your dogs, with advance permission. July and August are by far the busiest months at the lodge; you need to make reservations months in advance if you want to stay here during peak period. The lodge is low-key, and they do very little advertising; they don't need to.

For details about the area, refer to the listing for Crystal Crag Lodge later in this chapter. For hiking and fishing options, check out the guidebooks *Foghorn Outdoors: California Hiking* and *Foghorn Outdoors: California Fishing*. The ski lifts are a five-minute drive from the lodge, and the ski shuttle is close by.

Facilities: Edelweiss Lodge has four cabins and four suites; all feature a fully equipped kitchen, bathroom, fireplace, telephone, and television. Barbecues are available during the summer. A hot tub is available. The cabins are suitable for children. Leashed dogs at least two years of age are allowed in some of the cabins with prior permission; cats are not allowed. No smoking is permitted.

Bedding: Linens and towels are provided (every other day), and daily maid service is available for an additional fee with prior notice.

Reservations and rates: Reservations are recommended. The double occupancy rate is $100 to $190 per night per cabin during the summer, and $120 to $210 per night during the winter. An additional charge of $10 per night per person is charged. The pet fee is $25 per stay per pet. Ski packages are available. There is a two-night minimum, and a three- to five-day minimum on selected holidays. Major credit cards are accepted. Open year-round.

Directions: From Lee Vining on U.S. 395, drive south for 25 miles to Mammoth Junction and Highway 203. Turn west and drive approximately two miles to Old Mammoth Road. Turn left and drive two miles to the lodge on the right at 1872 Old Mammoth Road.

Contact: Edelweiss Lodge, P.O. Box 658, Mammoth Lakes, CA 93546; 760/934-2445 or 877/233-3593; website: www.mammothweb.com/lodging/edelweiss.

Edelweiss Lodge

20. WILDYRIE RESORT

Your own spot on one of the many beautiful lakes in the Mammoth Lakes area is the highlight here, with 11 cabins situated next to Lake Mamie, one of the quieter lakes. The cabins are old—so old they may as well be called historic—but they're clean and comfortable.

What we like best about these cabins are the spacious front decks, with some commanding a lake view. The cabins are set on a hillside, spaced two to three deep. Cabins 3, 5, 6, and 7 are closest to the water, and Cabin 9 is set farther away from the others. The cabins range in size from one bedroom to four bedrooms. If you have a large family or group, Cabin 1—four bedrooms and three bathrooms—can sleep 10 people. The cabins represent different time periods from old with antique furnishings to new with more modern decor. All have fully equipped kitchens and private bathrooms. There are no televisions or radios, and no daily maid service.

Luxury rating: 2

Recreation rating: 4

*Lake Mamie, off U.S. 395
at Mammoth Lakes*

Lake Mamie is small and narrow with clear water, and is easily fished by boat or bank. The Department of Fish and Game stocks it with rainbow trout throughout the summer. For details, see the book *Foghorn Outdoors: California Fishing.* Rowboat rentals, bait and tackle, and a launch ramp are available at the resort; no motors are allowed on the lake. For details about activities in the area, see the listing for Crystal Crag Lodge later in this chapter.

Facilities: Wildyrie Resort has 11 cabins; each has a fully equipped kitchen and private bathroom. Lodge rooms are also available. Continental breakfast is provided. A boat dock, boat rentals, bait and tackle, and guest lounge are available. The resort is suitable for children. Pets are not allowed. No smoking is permitted.

Bedding: Linens and towels are provided, but there is no daily maid service.

Reservations and rates: Reservations are required for a minimum visit of one week. The fee is $672 to $1,533 per week per cabin. Credit cards are not accepted. Open early June through early October.

Directions: Follow U.S. 395 to Mammoth Junction and Highway 203/Minaret Summit Road. Turn west on Highway 203 and drive four miles to Lake Mary Road. Continue straight through the intersection to Lake Mary Road and drive 2.3 miles to Twin Lakes Loop Road. Turn right and drive past Twin Lakes and Lake Mary to Lake Mamie and the resort on the left.

Contact: Wildyrie Lodge, P.O. Box 109, Mammoth Lakes, CA 93546; 760/934-2444.

OTHER CABINS AND COTTAGES NEARBY
• Mammoth Mountain Chalets, P.O. Box 513, Mammoth Lakes, CA 93546; 760/934-8518 or 800/327-3681, fax 760/934-5117

Wildyrie Resort

21. TAMARACK LODGE RESORT

Every so often, you find a gem like Tamarack Lodge Resort: a historic mountain operation in a gorgeous setting that has been lovingly cared for to retain the old-style charm, yet providing upscale, modern amenities. Many of these lodges began as ski resorts, and so it is with Tamarack.

Luxury rating: 3

Recreation rating: 5

*Twin Lakes, off U.S. 395
at Mammoth Lakes*

Situated in tree cover along the shoreline of Twin Lakes are 26 cabins and 12 lodge rooms. Ranging in size from studio to three bedrooms, the cabins have a kitchen, private bathroom, and gas wall heater. The amenities vary greatly from cabin to cabin; some have a fireplace. Although not all cabins have lake views, they are no more than 100 to 300 feet from the lake, depending on the cabin.

Cabin 14 is the newest lodging and opened in 2001. The management says this cabin is representative of the direction the resort is headed with its construction. The outside looks like your basic modern cabin with dark brown paint, large deck with Adirondack chairs, and a lake view. The inside of the two-bedroom, two-bath rental is more rustic and customized, in keeping with the traditional design of the early days of the lodge. You'll find white pine floors; wood walls; vaulted, beamed ceilings; large stone fireplaces; and Native American and western decor with area rugs and period furniture and decorations.

Tamarack is a well-known cross-country ski area offering 45 kilometers of groomed trails, ski skating lanes, snowshoeing, and rentals and instruction. You can ski or snowshoe from your cabin door in winter. The shuttle for Mammoth Mountain is close by, and at Mammoth, three miles away, you'll find plenty of downhill skiing terrain.

In summer, you're steps away from Twin Lakes, where you can boat, swim, and fish; the lake is stocked with rainbow trout. Twin Lakes are a pair of small lakes on little Mammoth Creek at an elevation of 8,700 feet. The lakes and waterfall are absolutely beautiful, set amid Sierra granite and ringed by stands of old pines. Your hiking options are almost limitless. For dining, the lodge's lakeside restaurant is known for its excellent gourmet, California-French cuisine and extensive wine list.

Facilities: Tamarack Lodge Resort has 26 cabins with fully equipped kitchens and bathrooms, as well as 12 lodge rooms. Some cabins have a porch and a fireplace or woodstove. A restaurant is available. The resort is suitable for children. Pets are not allowed. No smoking is permitted.

Bedding: Linens and towels are provided and can be exchanged at the front desk, but there is no daily maid service.

Reservations and rates: Reservations are recommended. The fee is $120 to $325 per night per cabin, and $80 to $150 per night for lodge rooms. Rates are higher during the Christmas holiday. Packages including breakfast and skiing are available. There is a two-night minimum on weekends, four- or five-night minimum on holidays, and a five-night minimum during the summer.

Directions: From Lee Vining on U.S. 395, drive south for 25 miles to Mammoth Junction and Highway 203/Minaret Summit Road. Turn west on Highway 203 and drive four miles to Lake Mary Road. Continue straight through the intersection and drive 2.3 miles to Twin Lakes Loop Road. Turn right and drive .4 mile to the resort on the left.

Contact: Tamarack Lodge Resort, P.O. Box 69, Mammoth Lakes, CA 93546; 760/934-2442 or 800/237-6879, fax 760/934-2281; website: www.tamarack lodge.com.

Tamarack Lodge Resort

22. WOODS LODGE

It's picture postcard–perfect here—the kind of place you've seen in a movie and wish you knew the location. Well, this is one of those spots, but unfortunately, it's not a secret. In summer, it can seem like you and a thousand other people are competing elbow-to-elbow for your share of paradise in this area of Mammoth Lakes.

Luxury rating: 3

Recreation rating: 5

*Lake George, off Highway 203
near Mammoth Lakes*

But take heart: the big advantage you have at Woods Lodge is your location at the end of the road. That's right, it means you can carve out your own niche next to beautiful Lake George, without the general public infringing on your turf.

From the resort, at 9,200 feet in elevation, you're overlooking unparalleled beauty that's only found in the Sierra high country—an exquisite alpine lake surrounded by trees and rocky terrain jutting up behind the forest. The cabins are interspersed over a hillside, with meandering rows spaced three deep from the lake. Cabins 15, 16, and 23 are closest to the lake—and to the road and boat launch.

The one- to three-bedroom cabins range from new to old and rustic; furnishings are traditional, with some antiques. They all have fully equipped kitchens and private bathrooms. Families love it here because it's so easy to make yourself at home and wander down to the lake each day for boating, fishing, or swimming. You can bring your own boat or rent a rowboat or motorboat; lake access is simple from the boat launch at the lodge.

Lake Mary is less than a mile away, and Twin Lakes is nearby. Riding stables are in close proximity, and you're in an excellent area for hiking; you can hike a short distance from your cabin door to various trailheads. For details, refer to the guidebook *Foghorn Outdoors: California Hiking.*

Facilities: Woods Lodge has 25 cabins with fully equipped kitchens and private bathrooms. A deck and a fireplace or woodstove are provided in some of the cabins. Boat launch, boat rentals, bait and tackle, and a snack shop are available. The lodge is suitable for children. Leashed pets are allowed in some cabins. No smoking is permitted.

Bedding: Linens and towels are provided.

Reservations and rates: Reservations are made for one week or longer stays only. The fee is $78 to $236 per night per cabin, or $504 to $1,512 per week. Additional persons are $8 per night per person. The pet fee is $8 per night per pet. Credit cards are not accepted. Open late May to mid-October.

Directions: Drive on U.S. 395 to Mammoth Junction and Highway 203/Minaret Summit Road. Turn west on Highway 203 and drive four miles to Lake Mary Road. Continue straight through the intersection and drive four miles to Lake Mary Loop Drive. Turn left and drive one-third of a mile to Lake George Road. Turn right and drive a short distance to the lodge at the end of the road.

Contact: Woods Lodge, P.O. Box 108, Mammoth Lakes, CA 93546; 760/934-2261.

Woods Lodge

23. CRYSTAL CRAG LODGE

The natural beauty of Lake Mary is astonishing. It's a deep, blue pool set in Sierra granite, with Crystal Crag, an awesome granite spire, in the background. Located high in the eastern Sierra at 8,900 feet, it is the largest lake in the Mammoth Lakes region. Crystal Crag Lodge makes a great vacation setting, with 21 cabins with kitchens and bathrooms set just upslope from the lake, a boat ramp and boat rentals available, decent fishing, excellent hiking trails, and many other adventures possible in the region.

And get this: This is one of the last cabin rentals in the eastern Sierra that stills accepts pets (with a fee, of course).

Newcomers to this area always want to see "Mammoth Lake." Guess what? There is no such place. The town is called Mammoth Lakes, but there is no Mammoth Lake. Instead, there are Lake Mary,

Lake George, Lake Mamie, and Twin Lakes. All are within a 10-minute drive of each other.

Luxury rating: 3

Recreation rating: 5

Lake Mary, off Highway 203 near Mammoth Lakes

Another nearby destination that makes for a great day trip is Devils Postpile National Monument and its two-hour round-trip hike to beautiful Rainbow Falls. To get there, take the Minaret Summit Road over Mammoth Pass. The trailhead is at the monument, past the Mammoth Ski Area. (Noncampers arriving between 7:30 A.M. and 5:30 P.M. are required to take a shuttle bus from the Mammoth Mountain Ski Area to Devils Postpile National Monument and other nearby recreation options, including Reds Meadows, the San Joaquin River, and trailheads for the Ansel Adams Wilderness; to avoid taking the shuttle and paying the $5 to $9 shuttle fee, get there before 7:30 A.M. or after 5:30 P.M.)

A great short walk starts at the back of Coldwater Camp, located just south of Lake Mary, and is routed up to Emerald Lake, about a mile away. A longer, more strenuous hike is accessed from the same trailhead. It runs south along Mammoth Creek up to Arrowhead Lake, and then in turn up to Skeleton Lake, Barney Lake, and finally, up to Big Duck Lake. Duck Lake is even bigger than Lake Mary, always a surprise at first sight, and is just a mile from the Pacific Crest Trail.

Fishing can also be excellent. Lake Mary receives more trout stocks than any other lake in the Mammoth region, and that includes special batches of trophy-sized fish arranged by the lodge.

Note: Because this lake is located at an elevation of 8,900 feet, snow can prevent the opening of Crystal Crag Lodge until late May or early June. After a heavy winter, there can be snow near the lake into July. Make sure you call ahead if you're planning a trip to Crystal Crag Lodge in late spring or early summer.

Facilities: Crystal Crag Lodge has 21 cabins with kitchens and bathrooms. There is also a small marina with 10 aluminum boats (with or without motors) available for rent by the day or week. Coin laundry is available. Leashed dogs are permitted. A small grocery store, horseback riding facilities, and a Forest Service campground are nearby.

Reservations and rates: Cabin reservations are recommended. Fees range from $75 per night for one person in a studio cabin to $143 per night for up to five people in a two-bedroom cabin to $232 per night for a four-bedroom cabin that sleeps eight. Pets cost an additional $8 per night.

24. CONVICT LAKE RESORT

Convict Lake, in the high southeastern Sierra, is one of the most beautiful drive-to settings in North America. The lake is deep and blue-green, set below tall, sheer mountain walls and granite peaks, the kind of mountain beauty that you never forget. At the head of the lake, a small forest grows along the feeder creek, and beyond you can see a canyon that leads up to the bordering John Muir Wilderness. The air is fresh and quiet. This is the high country, 7,583 feet, and it is pristine and stunning.

Luxury rating: 3

Recreation rating: 5

Inyo National Forest, off U.S. 395 near Mammoth Lakes

Here you will find a series of rustic cabins that you can make your headquarters for a mountain vacation. The cabins have names such as Loch Leven, Golden, and Steelhead, and vary in the number of people they can accommodate. Most are small, with just a kitchen, bathroom, and living space. However, there are also giant, deluxe, vacation homes recently constructed that can sleep up to 32. It is an ideal destination for hiking, fishing, boating, horseback riding, and exploring the nearby hot springs at Hot Creek. A small store, marina, and dinner restaurant are located at Convict Lake, so you get the best of both worlds: the beauty of the high Sierra wilderness, as well as full accommodations and facilities.

The lake is small enough, about a mile long and a half-mile wide, to keep the setting intimate, yet deep enough to provide excellent fishing. Some giant brown trout are mounted in the Convict Lake store, testimonials to what is possible.

The hiking can also be spectacular. From a signed trailhead off the access road, one route follows Convict Lake's north shore, providing very pretty views. It rises in long, graded switchbacks above the lake and is routed back through the Convict Creek canyon, still climbing, but with a steady grade. Hiking up to the creek and back is a great morning trip; horseback rides are also offered here.

Nearby Hot Creek has a great section where cold stream water is mixed with very hot springwater. It's about three miles off U.S. 395, east on the road just north of the airport. Floating in the hot spring is a remarkable sensation—it is possible to feel very hot water at your chest and shoulders, cold water at your thighs, and warm water at your feet; move a step in the stream and the mix changes completely. Maps of several hot springs are available at the Convict Lake Store.

Facilities: Convict Lake Resort has 25 cabins with kitchens and bathrooms. There is also a small marina offering 32 boats with six-horsepower motors, a pontoon boat with an eight-person capacity, and a launch ramp; horseback riding rentals; a four-star restaurant; a general store; a fish-cleaning facility; and pay phones. Pets are permitted with an additional fee. Open year-round.

Bedding: Linens, pillows, and blankets are provided.

Reservations and rates: Cabin reservations are strongly recommended. Fees range from $83 for two Sunday through Thursday and $99 Friday through Saturday to $650 per night for a six-bedroom vacation house that can sleep 32. The pet fee is $10 per stay.

Directions: From Lee Vining, drive south on U.S. 395 (past the Mammoth Lakes turnoff) to Convict Lake Road, located adjacent to the Mammoth Lakes Airport. Turn right (west) and drive two miles to the Convict Lake Store on the right.

Contact: Convict Lake Resort, Route 1, Box 204, Mammoth Lakes, CA 93546; 800/992-2260; website: www.convictlake.com. For reservations at The Restaurant At Convict Lake, call 760/934 3803. *Convict Lake Resort*

25. THE REDWOODS

The biggest surprises at Yosemite National Park are not Half Dome, El Capitan, Yosemite Falls, Bridalveil Falls, or the spectacular, glaciated beauty of the valley. You already knew about them, right? Of course.

The biggest surprises at Yosemite are the 125 cabins and mountain vacation homes available for rent near Wawona at the southern border of the park. For people who have never ventured to the park's southern reaches, it can be a shock to discover there is an entire little township set within park borders, complete with a grocery store.

The town is a short distance from the trailhead for the hike to Chilnualna Falls, the prettiest waterfall in Yosemite's southern region, as well as Mariposa Grove, the ancient forest of giant sequoias.

Badger Pass Ski Area is 17 miles away, and it is about a 45-minute drive to either Glacier Point or Yosemite Valley. If you have never been here, you will likely be astounded to discover there is also a golf course nearby—that's right, a golf course in Yosemite National Park.

Luxury rating: 3

Recreation rating: 4

Yosemite National Park, off Highway 41 in Wawona

The settlement of dwellings is called The Redwoods, and it is composed of vacation cabins, cottages, and homes that vary from a one-bedroom rustic cabin to a six-bedroom mountain home. They are all privately owned but are listed with The Redwoods for vacation rentals. Since the owners occasionally use them, they are furnished with whatever they would need for their own vacations, and that includes darn near everything.

The most popular nearby hike is the traditional venture to Mariposa Grove, located just east of the southern park entrance. A better romp for the ambitious is the hike out to Chilnualna Falls, with the trailhead at road's end at the Redwoods in North Wawona. It's a strenuous eight-mile round-trip, climbing 2,000 feet to the base of the falls at 6,000 feet. To reach the trailhead from Wawona, turn east on Chilnualna Falls Road and drive 1.7 miles to the road's end and park in the lot on the right side of the road; walk back to the road and look for the hiking trail at the edge of the pavement.

Facilities: The Redwoods has 125 privately owned cabins and mountain homes for rent. Each is completely furnished, including cookware and utensils. A small grocery store is located nearby. Pet policies vary by unit.

Bedding: Bring your own linens and towels or participate in the bed linen exchange program at the main office.

Reservations and rates: Reservations are required. Cabin and home rentals range from $141 per night for a one-bedroom cabin for two to $553 per night for a six-bedroom mountain home for 12. Winter discounts are available, and different promotions are available each season. A $20 entrance fee to Yosemite National Park is charged for each vehicle; the pass is good for one week.

Directions: From Highway 99 at Merced, turn east on Highway 140 and drive to Mariposa. In Mariposa, turn south on Highway 49 and drive 30 miles to Highway 41 at Oakhurst. Turn left on Highway 41 and drive into the southern entrance station for Yosemite National Park. Continue on Highway 41 to Wawona. Turn east on Chilnualna Road and drive 1.3 miles to the Redwoods. (You will receive specific directions to your cabin at the main office when your reservation is confirmed.)

Contact: The Redwoods, P.O. Box 2085, Wawona Station, Yosemite, CA 95389; 209/375-6666; website: www.redwoodsinyosemite.com. For an excellent hiking map of the area, contact Tom Harrison Cartography at 415/456-7940. A free map/brochure of Yosemite National Park is provided at park entrance stations as part of the entrance fee.

The Redwoods

26. ROCK CREEK LODGE

A winter wonderland is what you'll find most of the year at Rock Creek Lodge, one of the best lodging options in this book for accessing the outdoors experience, rustic style. Located in Inyo National Forest, the lodge was built in the 1920s as one of the first ski resorts in the country. There's still plenty of cross-country skiing and snowshoeing in winter, and you'll get a taste of the way it used to be, which is also the way it still is here.

Luxury rating: 2

Recreation rating: 5

Rock Creek, off U.S. 395 near Tom's Place

There are 13 cabins nestled in a glacial canyon at 9,373 feet in elevation at the edge of the John Muir Wilderness. All of the cabins have full kitchens, and some have private bathrooms; a central bathroom is also provided. These are rustic cabins and there's nothing fancy about them, and it's important to know what is and isn't provided because the amenities change from summer to winter. For instance, complimentary breakfast and dinner are provided in the dining room during the winter, but not in the summer. Two primitive ski-to huts are also available. In the winter, snowmobiles drive you two miles from your vehicle to the lodge, since the road isn't plowed. Get the idea? You're in true backcountry.

If you like snow sports, then you'll be in winter heaven, because there are 15 kilometers of groomed trails. The possibilities include cross-country skiing, snowshoeing, hut skiing, ski touring, and track skiing; rentals and lessons are available. For the adventurous, two ski-to huts (Mosquito Flat and Tamarack) can be accessed by skiing or snowshoeing two to three miles from the lodge. These are tent cabins with primitive cooking facilities and pit toilets, and you must haul all your own bedding, food, and equipment, much like backpacking.

But let's not forget summertime, which is equally rewarding for outdoor enthusiasts, with outstanding hiking and fishing. Hilton Lake, Tamarack Lake, Ruby Lakes, and the Little Lakes Valley are within walking distance. Ruby Lake was named for its gem-like qualities, and the Little Lakes Valley features excellent fishing for brook trout and occasional big brown trout. Many of the higher-elevation lakes nearby have golden trout.

Facilities: Rock Creek Lodge has 13 cabins with fully equipped kitchens (summer only) and woodstoves. There are two winter ski-to huts. Breakfast and dinner, plus electric heaters, are provided in the winter only. Eight of the cabins have private bathrooms; a central bathroom is available. A sauna, a restaurant, a general store, bait and tackle, and cross-country ski and snowshoe rentals are available. The cabins are suitable for children. Leashed pets are allowed.

Bedding: Linens and towels are provided during the summer only; only pillows and pillow cases are provided during the winter, so be sure to bring your own sheets and blankets.

Reservations and rates: Reservations are recommended. The double occupancy rate is $75 to $140 per night per cabin during the summer, and $90 to $115 per night per cabin during the winter. Additional persons are $10 to $15 per night per person. Children ages 6 to 12 are half price, and children under age five are free. The pet fee is $15 per night per pet. The Mosquito Flat ski-to hut is $27 per night per person; contact the Sierra Mountain Center, 760/873-8526, about the Tamarack ski-to hut. The winter snowmobile shuttle to and from the lodge is free. Major credit cards are accepted. Open year-round.

Directions: From the junction of U.S. 395 and Highway 203 (the Mammoth Lakes turnoff), drive 15 miles south on U.S. 395 to Tom's Place. Turn right (south) on Rock Creek Road and drive eight miles to the lodge on the left.

Contact: Rock Creek Lodge, Route 1, Box 12, Mammoth Lakes, CA 93546; 760/935-4170, fax 760/935-4172; website: www.rockcreeklodge.com.

Rock Creek Lodge

27. ROCK CREEK LAKES RESORT

The owners at Rock Creek Lakes Resort ask that no sissies need apply. In other words, no whiners, please. This is the kind of place for down-to-earth people who can live without a telephone, television, pool, spa, and the like.

What you have here are one- to three-bedroom cabins set in a secluded lodgepole pine forest, located about a quarter mile behind the resort. Two new cabins were added in 2001. Each cabin has a full kitchen, private bathroom, living room, and gas heater. In addition, the resort's café has some of the best homemade pie you'll ever taste. What Rock Creek Lakes Resort lacks in amenities, it makes up for in setting; at nearly 10,000 feet in elevation, this is one of the best locations imaginable for exploring the eastern Sierra. And it's *the* place for adventure lovers looking for a break from the urban routine.

The resort is set in a dramatic canyon with towering granite peaks, just across the road from Rock Creek Lake, a natural beauty with a five-mph speed limit and great fishing; refer to the book *Foghorn Outdoors: California Fishing* for details. Take your pick of hiking trails that lead into the John Muir Wilderness; more than 50 lakes are within a two-hour hike of Rock Creek Canyon. If you don't want to walk, rent a horse at the Rock Creek Pack Station, one-half mile from the resort. Mountain biking is also popular in this area, and Lower Rock Creek and Sand Canyon have two of the most difficult and desirable trails around; we advise you to avoid them unless you're an experienced rider.

Luxury rating: 2

Recreation rating: 5

Inyo National Forest, off U.S. 395 at Rock Creek Lake

In addition to pies, the café serves excellent chili, burgers, and soups, but remember that it's not open for dinner; it closes at 6 P.M., but you can order a late lunch and call it dinner if you like. "Pies and skies" are what the resort is most noted for, and cyclists have been known to ride 50 miles round-trip just to get a piece of pie. Those crazy mountain bikers.

Facilities: Rock Creek Lakes Resort has 11 cabins with fully equipped kitchens, bathrooms with showers, barbecues, decks or porches, and thermostat heating. Do not bring electrical appliances; the resort generates its own electricity. A café, a general store, and fishing supplies are available. Cabins do not have televisions or telephones. The resort is suitable for children. Pets are not allowed. Smoking is permitted in some of the cabins. One cabin is wheelchair accessible.

Bedding: Linens and towels are provided.

Reservations and rates: Reservations are recommended. The fee is $90 per night or $617 per week for a one-bedroom, $130 to $155 per night or $819 to $990 for a two-bedroom, and $240 per night or $1,512 per week for the two-story cabin. A four-night minimum is required in July and August. Major credit cards are accepted. Open mid-May to mid-October, weather permitting.

Directions: From the junction of U.S. 395 and Highway 203 (the Mammoth Lakes turnoff), drive 15 miles south on U.S. 395 to Tom's Place. Turn right (south) on Rock Creek Road and drive nine miles to the resort on the right.

Contact: Rock Creek Lakes Resort, P.O. Box 727, Bishop, CA 93515; 760/935-4311, fax 760/935-9101; website: www.rockcreeklake.com. For Rock Creek Pack Station, call 760/935-4493 (summer only).

Rock Creek Lakes Resort

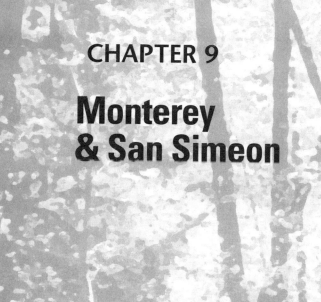

CHAPTER 9

Monterey
& San Simeon

The scenic charm seems to extend to infinity from the seaside towns of Santa Cruz, Monterey, Big Sur, and San Simeon. The primary treasure is the coast, which is rock-strewn and sprinkled with inshore kelp beds, where occasionally you can find sea otters playing Pop Goes the Weasel. The sea here is a color like no other, often more of a tourmaline than a straight green or blue.

From Carmel to Lucia alone, touring the Big Sur on Highway 1 is one of the most captivating drives anywhere. The inland strip along Highway 1 provides access to state parks, redwoods, coastal streams, Los Padres National Forest, and the Ventana Wilderness. As you explore farther south on the Pacific Coast Highway, you will discover a largely untouched coast. Here also are San Simeon, Hearst Castle, Morro Bay, inland canyons, and three of the most fish-filled lakes anywhere: Lake San Antonio, Lake Nacimiento, and Santa Margarita Lake.

Most vacations to this region include several must-do trips, often starting in Monterey with a visit to Fisherman's Wharf and its domesticated sea lions, and then to the nearby Monterey Bay Aquarium. In addition, Carmel-by-the-Sea is well-known for its shops, selling everything from small vacation mementos to high-class art worth thousands of dollars.

From there, most head south to Big Sur to take in a few brush strokes of nature's canvas, easily realizing why this area is beloved around the world. At first glance, however, it's impossible not to want the whole painting. That is where the cabin and cottage rentals come in. They provide both the ideal getaway and a launch point for adventure.

At Big Sur, the cabin accommodations are what many expect: small hideaways in the big redwoods. Most are in a variety of settings, some near Big Sur River, others set in the forest. But amid these is one place like no other place on earth: Post Ranch Inn. It actually has a deluxe tree house that costs $835 a night!

Other good opportunities are available in Carmel and in the Monterey area. Most of these are midrange to high-end, and most are reserved well in advance. In the foothills, a series of big lakes sets the scene for cabin-style lodgings, which are ideal for families.

During the summer, only the fog on the coast and the intense heat just 10 miles inland keep this region from attaining perfection.

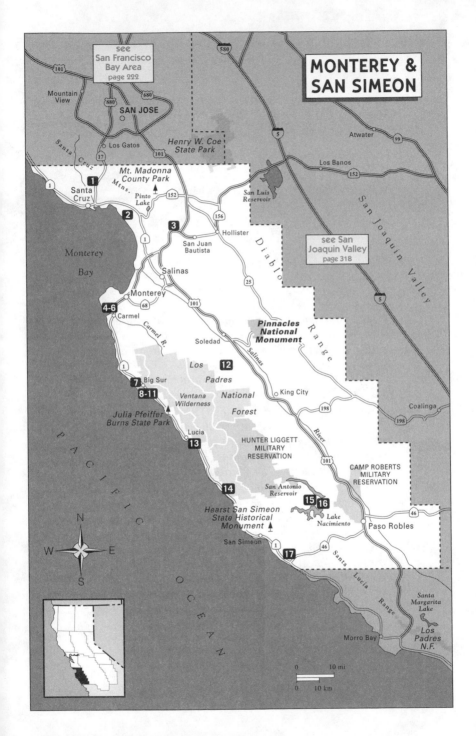

MONTEREY & SAN SIMEON

see
San Francisco
Bay Area
page 222

Mountain
View

SAN JOSE

Los Gatos

Santa Cruz Mtns.

Henry W. Coe
State Park

Atwater

Los Banos

Santa Cruz

Mt. Madonna
County Park

Pinto Lake

San Luis
Reservoir

San Joaquin Valley

Hollister

San Juan
Bautista

see San
Joaquin Valley
page 318

Monterey
Bay

Salinas

Monterey

Carmel

Diablo Range

Pinnacles
National
Monument

Soledad

Los

Padres

Ventana
Wilderness

National

Forest

Big Sur

Julia Pfeiffer
Burns State Park

Lucia

King City

Coalinga

HUNTER LIGGETT
MILITARY
RESERVATION

San Antonio
Reservoir

Hearst San Simeon
State Historical
Monument

CAMP ROBERTS
MILITARY
RESERVATION

Lake
Nacimiento

Paso Robles

San Simeon

PACIFIC OCEAN

Santa Lucia Range

Santa
Margarita
Lake

Los
Padres
N.F.

Morro Bay

N
W E
S

0   10 mi
0   10 km

CHAPTER 9
MONTEREY & SAN SIMEON

1. COTILLION GARDENS RV PARK

Cotillion Gardens RV Park is set among the redwoods in the Santa Cruz Mountains, next to the San Lorenzo River. Two of the cabins here are located along the river—by far the best location at the park—and come with fireplaces. The others are set near the forest, adjacent to an RV park with 80 sites.

Luxury rating: 2

Recreation rating: 4

Santa Cruz Mountains, off Highway 9 near Felton

The accommodations are fairly spartan, that is, you bring your own bedding or sleeping bag, along with towels, dishes, and utensils. Most cabins don't have a private bathroom, so come prepared to share one with your neighbors. One of the cabins is very primitive and we classify it as simply a sleeping unit. . . . No, we didn't spend our wedding night here.

But a great highlight of a stay here is the beauty of the redwoods and the many possible side trips. Since you're near the edge of the Santa Cruz Mountain redwoods, you have easy access to Henry Cowell Redwoods State Park and the San Lorenzo River. Monterey Bay is only about a 10-minute drive from the park. Other side trips include a steam train ride along the San Lorenzo River, offered by Roaring Camp Train Rides in Felton, and visiting Loch Lomond Reservoir near Ben Lomond for hiking, boat rentals, or fishing.

Facilities: Cotillion Gardens RV Park has five camping cabins with varying accommodations. Two have fireplaces and kitchens with a microwave; all have televisions. No kitchen utensils or plates are provided. Some units have a private bathroom. Communal showers, a recreation room, a swimming pool, and a small store are available on the property. Some facilities are wheelchair accessible. Leashed pets are permitted.

Bedding: No linens are provided.

Reservations and rates: Reservations are recommended. Cabin fees are $75 to $95 per night. Major credit cards are accepted. Open year-round.

Directions: From Los Gatos, drive west on Highway 17 for 20 miles toward Santa Cruz to the Mount Hermon Road exit/Scotts Valley (second exit in Scotts Valley). Take the Mount Hermon Road exit to the stoplight. Turn right on Mount Hermon Road and drive 3.5 miles to Felton and Graham Hill Road. Turn right on Graham Hill Road and drive 50 feet to Highway 9. Turn left on Highway 9 and drive 1.5 miles to the park.

Contact: Cotillion Gardens RV Park, 300 Old Big Trees, Felton, CA 95018; 831/335-7669.

Cotillion Gardens RV Park

2. SANTA CRUZ-MONTEREY KOA

This KOA provides security, kitsch, and nearby recreation. That's what makes it work.

Luxury rating: 2

Recreation rating: 4

Manresa State Beach, off Highway 1 near Aptos

When you first drive up, you will see an entrance kiosk and sometimes even a security officer. After entering and passing a swimming pool on the right, you see an adorable double-tiered line of cabins on a hillside to the left. Along the way, you also see a line of bicycles available for rent—this location is ideal for a short ride to nearby Manresa State Beach and maybe a walk or a game of tag with the waves. Then you will notice that to keep the dust down, there is a lot of asphalt leading to the 50 cabins and 230 tent and RV sites across 30 acres of campground.

The security is a nice touch. Although it may never be needed—because the campground is set in a friendly area—the presence of someone looking out for you is usually enough to keep things friendly. The cute factor is high here, too, with those irresistible KOA log cabins lined up neatly, each with a bunk bed and a queen bed (bring your sleeping bag), electric heat if needed, and a swing out front. A few two-room models are available here as well.

But the best feature of this place is its proximity to Manresa State Beach. It's only a short bike ride to this beautiful state park, set along the shore of Monterey Bay, with good beachcombing and hiking. The ocean is often quite calm here. Fishing is poor to fair for perch, with better prospects on boats leaving out of Santa Cruz or Monterey. Sunsets can be spectacular.

Facilities: The Santa Cruz-Monterey KOA has 50 cabins and 230 sites for tents or RVs, plus a convenience store and 24-hour security gate. Bicycle rentals, a pool, a hot tub, a game room, horseshoes, volleyball, basketball, and miniature golf are available. No pets are allowed in the cabins.

Reservations and rates: Cabin reservations are recommended year-round. A one-room cabin for two is $66 per night, a two-room cabin is $75, and an additional fee of $3 per child and $6 for each additional adult is charged.

Directions: From Santa Cruz, drive south on Highway 1 for 12 miles to the San Andreas Road exit. Take that exit, turn west on San Andreas Road, drive 3.5 miles, and look for the well-signed entrance on the left side of the road at 1186 San Andreas Road.

Contact: Santa Cruz-Monterey KOA, 1186 San Andreas Road, Watsonville, CA 95076; 831/722-0551 or 831/722-2377; website: www.koa.com.

Santa Cruz-Monterey KOA

3. McALPINE LAKE AND PARK

McAlpine Lake has been put on the map by its new trophy trout program, where every time you throw your line in the water, there's a chance of catching a 10-pound rainbow trout or better.

Luxury rating: 1

Recreation rating: 4

McAlpine Lake, off Highway 129 near San Juan Bautista

That's why the camping cabins here are designed for fishing enthusiasts. They look like miniature log cabins, cute and comfortable, and are pretty much bulletproof. You should think of your stay here as a camping trip: Bring everything you need, including sleeping bags. You share the same facilities as the campers at the park. The only difference is the privacy and security of solid walls and a roof over your head.

McAlpine Lake is no little kid's pond like you occasionally see at parks, but rather a 40-foot-deep lake. That's deep enough to provide sufficient oxygen and a food chain to support a good fishery. The highlights are trophy-size rainbow trout and catfish, and enough stocks to keep catch rates high. The success of the fishing program has ranked stories in outdoor recreation newspapers. That makes this one of the best fishing opportunities in the area. The best trout fishing is in late winter and spring here, with catfish taking over the top spot once the hot weather arrives for keeps.

Other highlights of the park include its proximity to Mission San Juan Bautista and the relatively short drive to the Monterey-Carmel area.

Facilities: McAlpine Lake and Park has a campground and camping cabins with picnic tables and fire grills. Flush toilets, showers, a RV dump station, a recreation room, a swimming pool, coin laundry, propane gas, and groceries are on-site. Some facilities are wheelchair accessible. Leashed pets are permitted.

Bedding: Linens and towels are not provided. Bring your sleeping bag and pillow.

Reservations and rates: Reservations are recommended. The rate is $43 per night for cabin rentals, $5 for each additional adult, and $5 per night for each extra vehicle. Major credit cards are accepted.

Directions: From U.S. 101, take the Highway 129 exit west and drive 100 feet. Turn left onto Searle Road (frontage road) and drive to the stop sign. Turn left again on Anzar Road and drive under the freeway to the park at 900 Anzar Road.

Contact: McAlpine Lake and Park, 900 Anzar Road, San Juan Bautista, CA 95045; 831/623-4263; website: www.mcalpinelakeandpark.aol.com.

McAlpine Lake and Park

4. LA PLAYA HOTEL COTTAGES

You can't go wrong with these five storybook cottages, featuring either a kitchen or wet bar, right in the heart of Carmel. Not only are they centrally located, but they are tucked away about one block from the hotel, toward the ocean. It's quieter and more private at the cottages than at the hotel, but if you suddenly feel like mixing with people, you can wander over to the hotel and use its facilities, including the heated pool surrounded by gardens.

To reach the cottages, you follow a meandering path past flowers and foliage. Each cottage has one to three bedrooms, a television, a radio, a terrace, and a garden patio. Don't want to cook, but you don't feel like going to a restaurant? Easy. Just order the hotel's room service; your meal will soon be delivered to your quaint cottage. These upscale units have that trademark Carmel charm, from the tasteful, informally coordinated furniture, woodburning fireplace, and cheerfully painted walls to the upstairs sleeping area and deck with white Adirondack chairs.

Luxury rating: 5

Recreation rating: 3

Monterey Coast, off Highway 1 in Carmel

The overall effect is inviting and serene, and it's obvious that these cottages were designed to please the most discriminating guests.

Facilities: La Playa has five cottages with fully equipped kitchens or wet bars, televisions, and garden patios. Most of the cottages have a fireplace, and most have more than one bathroom. Up to eight persons can be accommodated, depending on the cottage. Room service is available, and there is a restaurant, lounge, and heated pool at the hotel. The hotel has 75 rooms. The cottages are suitable for children, but the hotel is more adult-oriented. Pets are not allowed. No smoking is allowed.

Bedding: Linens and towels are provided.

Reservations and rates: Reservations are recommended. The fee is $295 to $595 per night for cottages, and $155 to $295 per night for hotel rooms. Additional persons are $20 per night. There is a two-night minimum on weekends and three-night minimum on holidays. Major credit cards are accepted.

Directions: From San Jose, drive south on U.S. 101 for 40 miles to the junction with Highway 156. Turn west on Highway 156 and drive five miles to Highway 1. Turn south on Highway 1 and drive 15 miles to Carmel and Ocean Avenue. Turn right on Ocean Avenue and drive .5 mile to Camino Real. Turn left and drive two blocks to the hotel on the corner of Camino Real and 8th Avenue.

Contact: La Playa Hotel Cottages, P.O. Box 900, Carmel-by-the-Sea, CA 93921; 831/624-6476 or 800/582-8900, fax 831/624-7966; website: www.laplayacarmel.com.

La Playa Hotel Cottages

5. MISSION RANCH

© ROBERT BROWN

Luxury rating: 4

Recreation rating: 3

Monterey Coast, off Highway 1 in Carmel

The Ranch is one of the few historic tracts of land in Carmel, 22 acres to be exact, that hasn't been turned into a shopping center or condo complex. Not that the developers haven't tried. Clint Eastwood bought the property in 1986, rescuing this special place from a proposed condominium development. Since then, the Ranch has been painstakingly renovated, with the goal of retaining its 150-year-old history while providing modern amenities.

During the 1800s and early 1900s, the property was a 160-acre dairy ranch. Next it became an officers' club during World War II, with a well-known reputation for dance bands and a popular bar scene. Then the local school district and the state bought the property.

Nowadays, the renovated buildings reflect different architectural periods of the ranch's history, including the farmhouse built in the 1850s. The Bunkhouse is the oldest building on the Ranch and sleeps up to four people. It's surrounded by large eucalyptus and cypress trees and has newly planted gardens. Other unique lodgings here include the Honeymoon Cottage and the Hay Loft.

The views from Mission Ranch are breathtaking and are sure to make your day. Looking to the south, you'll see undisturbed, pristine meadows, adjacent to wetlands and Carmel River Beach. Look farther and you'll see Point Lobos across the bay. Some of the cottages have ocean views, and the restaurant and piano bar—both on-site—feature panoramic views.

It's hard to believe you're only one block from Carmel Mission, one-half mile from shopping centers, and 2.5 miles from Point Lobos State Reserve.

Facilities: Mission Ranch has 31 varying lodging units, including a hayloft, a farm-house, a bunkhouse, a triplex, and a cottage; all have bathrooms. Some rooms have ocean views. There are no kitchen facilities, but a complimentary continental breakfast is provided. Bed sizes vary from queen to king, and some cottages have a twin sofabed. Fireplace and hot tub are available in some rooms. A restaurant, a piano bar, six championship tennis courts, and a fitness facility are available. The ranch is not suitable for children. Pets are not allowed. Smoking is not permitted. Some facilities are wheelchair accessible.

Bedding: Linens and towels are provided.

Reservations and rates: Reservations are recommended. The rates range from $95 to $275 per night per lodging unit. Additional persons are charged $15 per person per night. There is a two-night minimum stay on weekends. Major credit cards are accepted.

Directions: From San Jose, drive south on U.S. 101 for 40 miles to the junction with Highway 156. Turn west on Highway 156 and drive five miles to Highway 1. Turn south on Highway 1 and drive 15 miles to Carmel and Rio Road. Turn right on Rio Road and drive approximately .25 mile (passing Carmel Mission) to Lasuen Drive. Turn left and drive .5 mile to the ranch.

Contact: Mission Ranch, 3637B Dolores Street, Carmel, CA 93923; 831/624-6436 or 800/538-8221, fax 831/626-4163.

Mission Ranch

6. CARMEL RIVER INN

This is a popular place for dogs as well as people. You see, dogs are welcome here, and their owners and families seem to like the inn, too.

You can tell you're in Carmel because of the beautifully quaint cottages, painted red with white shutters and sporting Kelly green roofs. Yes, it's bright and cheerful here at these 24 cottages set among towering cypress trees. The Carmel River Inn backs up to—what else?—the

Carmel River. Although the inn is close to the highway, the trees and the river seem to buffer the traffic noise.

The cottages include lodgepole pine–crafted beds, pastel painted walls, and a furnished patio outside. Cottages vary in size from intimate to family size, and can accommodate up to six persons comfortably. Bed sizes also vary, from double to king.

Luxury rating: 3

Recreation rating: 3

Carmel River, off Highway 1 in Carmel

The grounds are landscaped and there is a large heated pool big enough for lap swimming if it's not crowded. There's also plenty of decking for sunbathing.

The motto here is "great location, great rates," and we have to agree with them. It's definitely not a wilderness experience here, but if you're looking for a cute cottage in close proximity to a popular getaway town, you've found it. You may not be able to watch deer and squirrels from your yard, but surely the neighbor's golden retriever will let you pet her.

Facilities: Carmel River Inn has 24 cottages and 10 motel rooms varying in size and amenities. All rentals include a bathroom with shower. fully equipped kitchen, deck, and woodburning fireplace are provided in some of the cottages. A heated pool is on-site. The inn is suitable for children. Leashed pets are allowed. No smoking is permitted. Some facilities are wheelchair accessible.

Bedding: Linens and towels are provided.

Reservations and rates: Reservations are recommended. The fee is $149 to $219 per night per cottage and $134 to $139 per night for motel rooms. Additional persons are $20 per night. The pet fee is $25 per pet per night. There is a two-night minimum on weekends and three-night minimum on holidays. Major credit cards are accepted.

Directions: From San Jose, drive south on U.S. 101 for 40 miles to the junction with Highway 156. Turn west on Highway 156 and drive five miles to Highway 1. Turn south on Highway 1 and drive 15 miles to Carmel and Oliver Road. Turn right on Oliver Road and drive a short distance to the inn on the right.

Contact: Carmel River Inn, Highway 1 at the Bridge, P.O. Box 221609, Carmel, CA 93922; 831/624-1575 or 800/882-8142, fax 831/624-0290; website: www.carmelriverinn.com.

OTHER CABINS AND COTTAGES NEARBY

• Centrella Inn, 612 Central Avenue, Pacific Grove, CA 93950; 831/371-3372 or 800/233-3372; website: www.centrellainn.com.

Carmel River Inn

7. RIPPLEWOOD RESORT

Everybody has a favorite chair. You know, the kind that makes you feel just right, no matter what mood you're in, what you are going through, or how long you have been away from it. Ripplewood Resort in Big Sur has entire cabins like this. In fact, they have 17 of them. Each one is different enough so that after surveying the place, you have a good chance of finding one that suits you perfectly. Just like your favorite chair.

Cabin 2 is the most secluded. Cabin 6 has a postcard view of the Big Sur River. Cabins 1, 14, and 15 have stone fireplaces. On the low end is a cabin that looks like a small motel room, Cabin 17. On the high end is a multiple-room chalet with a redwood-beamed ceiling and stone fireplace, Cabin 15. Get the idea? Right. Take a look, survey a few, and you'll find one that's right for you.

Luxury rating: 3

Recreation rating: 4

off Highway 1 near Big Sur

A real bonus here is the small grocery store and the fact that most of the cabins have kitchens. That means if you don't feel like going to a restaurant or just want to spare the expense, you can make a quick shopping trip and create a meal yourself without having to drive too far. There are very few cabin settings where this is possible.

Ripplewood is set along Highway 1 in the heart of Big Sur, an ideal location for a mini-vacation. The cabins are surrounded by redwoods, several of them along the Big Sur River. There is excellent hiking in the area, best of all in Andrew Molera State Beach, Point Sur State Historic Park, Julia Pfeiffer Burns State Park, Los Padres National Forest, and Ventana Wilderness.

What you will remember about Ripplewood is the coziness and character of the cabins.

Facilities: Ripplewood Resort has 17 cabins of various sizes and settings that can accommodate up to five people, depending on the unit. All have bathrooms and decks, most have kitchens, and some have river views. The kitchens are not fully stocked, but kitchen kits are available for $10. There is also a café that serves breakfast and lunch, a small grocery store, a library, and a gas station. Children are suitable here, but groups are discouraged. Each person must have a bed; no sleeping bags in lieu of beds. No pets are allowed. No smoking is permitted. Major credit cards are accepted.

Bedding: Linens and towels are provided.

Reservations and rates: Reservations are required and should be made six months in advance. The fee is $55 to $93 per night for two people. Additional persons are $5 per person per night. Children under age five are free. On weekends, there is a two-night minimum stay.

Directions: From Carmel, drive 25 miles south on Highway 1. Look for Ripplewood Resort on the east side of the road. Ripplewood's small gas station and store are directional landmarks.

Contact: Ripplewood Resort, Highway 1, Big Sur, CA 93920; 831/667-2242; website: www.ripplewoodresort.com.

Ripplewood Resort

8. BIG SUR CAMPGROUND AND CABINS

This camp is like a miniature park, set in the redwoods near the Big Sur River. The cabins range from primitive tent cabins to fully-furnished minihomes, that is, two-bedroom cabins with fireplace, kitchen, and beds. You share the park with a campground and you have use of its facilities, too.

Luxury rating: 3

Recreation rating: 4

Monterey Coast, off Highway 1 at Big Sur

Big Sur is drop-dead gorgeous and a popular getaway, of course. These cabins provide a blessed sense of privacy. By staying in the redwoods, you have the opportunity to hike on great trails and explore nearby Pfeiffer Big Sur State Park. This is one of California's most beautiful state parks, with woods and water, forest hideaways, and coastal lookouts. It is the top adventure destination for visitors staying at this park. The must-do trip for all visitors here is the easy romp to see Pfeiffer Falls, a pretty 60-foot cascade; though a bit wispy and narrow, it still captures the attention of most. After all, it takes less than an hour to make the trip, so the payoff is definitely worth the effort.

Nearby Los Padres National Forest and Ventana Wilderness in the mountains to the east provide access to remote hiking trails with ridge-top vistas. Cruising Highway 1 south to Lucia and back offers endless views of breathtaking coastal scenery.

Facilities: Big Sur Campground and Cabins has 13 cabins with varying levels of size and accommodation. Most have fireplaces and furnished kitchens. Four tent cabins are designed mainly as sleeping units, with few private amenities. There is also an 80-site campground on the property with restrooms, drinking water, flush toilets, showers, a RV dump station, a playground, a small store, and a laundry room. Some facilities are wheelchair accessible. Pets are permitted in tent cabins only; no smoking or pets in the other cabins.

Bedding: Linens and towels are provided in some cabins; bring sleeping bag and pillow if staying in a tent cabin.

Reservations and rates: Reservations are recommended. Tent cabins for two people cost $50, one-bedroom cabins for two cost $145, two-bedroom cabins run $155, and each additional person is $13. Major credit cards are accepted. Open year-round.

Directions: From Carmel, drive 27 miles south on Highway 1 to the campground on the right side of the road.

Contact: Big Sur Campground and Cabins, Highway 1, Big Sur, CA 93920; 831/667-2322.

Big Sur Campground and Cabins

9. BIG SUR LODGE

You're in the heart of Big Sur here, and if you're looking for exceptional hiking among the redwoods and along the ocean, then look no further. While these cottages aren't exceptional, Pfeiffer Big Sur State Park itself is. That doesn't mean we don't recommend the lodge; it's just that the accommodations are the predictable condo-type, and the spectacular scenery is out on the trail, not at your doorstep.

Luxury rating: 3

Recreation rating: 5

Monterey Coast, Pfeiffer Big Sur State Park off Highway 1

Since the park is so popular, especially during the summer months, and the lodge is located inside the park, you'll probably be aware of the constant flow of people through the park. But that's easy to remedy. First, try visiting during the week and off-season—it's just as beautiful. Next, avoid the most popular trails during prime time, which is midmorning to midafternoon.

A must-see is 60-foot Pfeiffer Falls, an easy 1.5-mile round-trip hike through old redwoods and along Pfeiffer Redwood Creek. Wildlife is abundant in this park; be on the lookout for condors soaring overhead and taking rests in the redwood trees. Whale watching is best in January and March. And for music lovers, the Big Sur Jazz Fest is held in early May.

Your room price includes admission to the park, as well as nearby Point Lobos State Reserve, Andrew Molera State Park, Julia Pfeiffer Burns State Park, and Limekiln State Park.

Facilities: Big Sur Lodge has 61 cottages total, with two to six cottages per building. Each unit has a full bathroom and a deck or balcony. Fully equipped kitchens and a fireplace or woodstove are provided in some of the cottages. All beds are queen size. There are no in-room telephones, televisions, radios, or alarm clocks. A heated swimming pool, a restaurant, a grocery store, and a gift shop are on the premises. The facilities are suitable for children. Pets are not allowed. No smoking is permitted.

Bedding: Linens and towels are provided.

Reservations and rates: Reservations are recommended. The fee is $139 to $199 per night per cottage. A two-night minimum is required on weekends, and a two- to three-night minimum is required on holidays. Major credit cards are accepted.

Directions: From Carmel, drive south on Highway 1 for 26 miles to the Pfeiffer Big Sur State Park entrance. Turn left and continue to the lodge.

Contact: Big Sur Lodge, 47225 Highway 1, Big Sur, CA 93920; 831/667-3100 or 800/424-4787; website: www.bigsurlodge.com.

Big Sur Lodge

10. RIVERSIDE CAMPGROUND AND CABINS

When it comes to rating the quality of a cabin- or cottage-based vacation, there are really two main factors: one, is there a comfortable bed to sleep in? and two, is there a bathroom with a shower?

Luxury rating: 3

Recreation rating: 4

Big Sur River, off Highway 1 in Big Sur

The answer to both is yes at Riverside Campground and Cabins. On the Big Sur coast, there can be a fine line between nice and rustic, and rustic and camping. The privately operated Riverside Campground and Cabins is one of the nice places—one of the better opportunities designed for folks cruising Highway 1 touring the Big Sur area.

This camp is set amid redwoods near the Big Sur River. It's a great headquarters for hiking adventures and exploring the Big Sur coast.

Side trips include hiking out to remote beaches at Andrew Molera State Park; rangers can often advise the best places to spot sea otters playing on the edge of kelp beds. There are also great hikes in redwood forests and to waterfalls at Julia Pfeiffer Burns State Park.

Of course, there are several fine restaurants to visit for a dining adventure. Those on a budget can try Nepenthe (831/667-2345); those who can light cigars with $100 bills can visit the Ventana Inn (831/667-4242).

Facilities: Riverside Campground and Cabins has seven cabins. Five of the seven have bathrooms. No smoking or pets are allowed. A 46-site campground is located on the property. Open year-round.

Bedding: Linens and towels are provided.

Reservations and rates: Reservations are recommended. The rate is $60 to $110 per night for two persons, with $3 additional per person per night and $6 per night for each extra vehicle. Major credit cards are accepted. Open year-round.

Directions: From Carmel, drive 25 miles south on Highway 1 to the campground on the right.

Contact: Riverside Campground and Cabins, P.O. Box 3, Big Sur, CA 93920; tel./fax 831/667-2414.

Riverside Campground and Cabins

11. POST RANCH INN

It seems like there should be a sign when you enter Big Sur that reads, "Spectacular scenery, spectacular prices." That's certainly the case at the Post Ranch Inn, where you get an exceptional setting and accommodations with a big price tag to go along with it. Although the inn is beyond the financial realm of most of us, if you want to know how the other half lives when they go on an outdoors-oriented vacation, then read on.

© BATISTA MOON/ PATRICK TREGENZA

Luxury rating: 5

Recreation rating: 4

Monterey coast, off Highway 1 in Big Sur

What do you get on these 96 acres? Well, a lot. For starters, the cabins are spacious, contemporary, and perched about 1,200 feet above the ocean. Want an ocean view from your bed and bath? Then rent an Ocean House, a freestanding structure with curved roofs covered with wildflowers and grass, floor-to-ceiling windows, and a two-sided fireplace.

Feel like playing Tarzan and Jane? Try a Tree House, a triangular-shaped house on stilts, nine feet off the ground. Don't worry, a stairway leads to the door. The bed is in the center of the room, and you have the tranquil views of the forest and mountain.

In addition, there are the circular Coast Houses and Mountain Houses, designed to replicate redwood trees. The Coast Houses have ocean views from the bed and tub and include terraces. The Mountain Houses provide views of the mountains. If you feel like soaring, try a Butterfly House, shaped like a butterfly, of course, with its wings extended.

This is a spa- and hiking-oriented resort, and the selection of services for these activities is extensive. The spa can provide everything from facials, herbal wraps, and massages to private yoga and meditation—available for an extra fee. Hiking guides can personalize private walks according to your ability and interest level. Whether it's a shorter hike to a secret spot or meadow, or a more challenging up-and-down hike to the beach for a picnic lunch, they can make it happen. Of course, you're also free to hike on your own.

When you're done with the day's activities, you can dine at the inn's gourmet restaurant, known for its four-course dinners. All the collective amenities make the Post Ranch Inn the second most expensive listing in this book.

Facilities: Post Ranch Inn has 30 cabins; each has a private bathroom with slate spa tub, a deck, a fireplace, a king bed, a wet bar, and a small refrigerator. There are no kitchen facilities. All cabins have ocean or mountain views. A restaurant, a pool, and full spa treatments are available. There are no televisions in the cabins, but a video-viewing room is available. The facility is not suitable for children. Pets are not allowed. No smoking is permitted. Some facilities are wheelchair accessible.

Bedding: Linens, towels, and robes are provided.

Reservations and rates: Reservations are required. The fee is $455 to $835 per night per cabin, including gourmet continental buffet breakfast and a glass of wine upon arrival. For more than two persons, an additional $100 per night per person is charged. A two-night minimum is required on weekends and a three- or four-night minimum is required on holidays. Major credit cards are accepted.

Directions: From Carmel, drive south on Highway 1 for 30 miles to the inn on the right (west) side of the road.

Contact: Post Ranch Inn, P.O. Box 219, Big Sur, CA 93920; 831/667-2200 or 800/527-2200, fax 831/667-2512; website: www.postranchinn.com.

OTHER CABINS AND COTTAGES NEARBY

• Deetjen's Big Sur Inn, Highway 1, Big Sur, CA 93920; 831/667-2377.

• Ventana Inn, Highway 1, Big Sur, CA 93920; 831/667-2331 or 800/628-6500; website: www.ventanainn.com.

Post Ranch Inn

12. PARAISO HOT SPRINGS

At Paraiso Hot Springs, you can soak your troubles and stress away; people have been doing so for more than a hundred years. Not much has changed over the years, except for the addition of some mobile homes and a yurt. In addition to these rentals, you can stay in a cabin or cottage.

Luxury rating: 3

Recreation rating: 3

Soledad foothills, off U.S. 101 near Soledad

Lodging ranges from spartan to comfy. Understand that if you rent a hillside cabin, you're not getting much more than a bed, a small refrigerator, a hot plate, a sink with cold running water, and a shared bathhouse a short walk away.

For more deluxe accommodations, try the yurt or a mobile home, where you get a fully equipped kitchen and private bathroom, and in some cases a living room and dining room. The yurt is set away from the other rentals and is more private and more expensive. Most people come here for the hot springs, though, and not so much for the rentals; visitors view the lodging as a convenient place to stay, more than as a destination in itself.

No matter which unit you stay in, you get full use of the facilities: two outdoor mineral pools, a large swimming pool, and a smaller warm pool. The temperature of the large pool is usually in the high 90s to low 100s. There is also an enclosed hot tub and an old bathhouse. The bathhouse consists of two original tile tubs that date back to the 1800s. The water temperature within this old structure ranges from 75°F to 102°F.

And although many visitors are content to spend a day or two relaxing at the hot springs, those who venture out usually don't pass up wine tasting at Paraiso Springs Winery, five miles away. For a day trip, Pinnacles National Monument is about 20 miles east, where you can hike, visit Bear Gulch Caves, or rock-climb. Although Bear Gulch Caves have been closed to the public since 1998 to complete studies of Townsend long-eared bats—a threatened species—it probably will reopen in the spring of 2002. For current status, contact Pinnacles National Monument at 831/389-4485 or visit the website: www.nps.gov/pinn.

Facilities: Paraiso Hot Springs has 10 cabins, eight cottages, six mobile homes, one yurt, and a campground. fully equipped kitchens and bathrooms are provided in the cottages and yurt. Bathrooms are provided in the mobile homes, and some have a fully equipped kitchen; others have a small refrigerator and a hot plate. A kitchenette is provided in the cabins, but there is no private bathroom;

a central bathhouse is available. Two outdoor mineral pools, an enclosed hot bath, an old bathhouse, a snack bar, a game room, a reading library, a basketball court, and a picnic area are available. The lodging is suitable for children. No pets are allowed. Smoking is permitted in some of the rentals.

Bedding: Linens and towels are provided.

Reservations and rates: Reservations are recommended. The cabin fee is $80 per night per person, and $40 per person per night for more than two persons. Mobile homes are $125 to $130 per night for up to two persons, and $60 per person per night for more than two. Cottages are $160 to $185 per night for two persons, and $50 to $60 per night per person for additional guests. Yurts are $150 per night for two and $450 per night for up to eight; additional persons are $66 per person per night. Major credit cards and local checks are accepted; out-of-town checks are not accepted.

Directions: From Salinas, drive south on Highway 101 for 24 miles to the Arroyo Seco Road exit. Turn right (west) and drive one mile to a three-way stop. Drive straight on Paraiso Springs Road for four miles to a T intersection. Bear left (it still is Paraiso Springs Road) and drive four miles to Paraiso Hot Springs.

Contact: Paraiso Hot Springs, Soledad, CA 93960; 831/678-2882, fax 831/678-0834.

Paraiso Hot Springs

13. LUCIA LODGE

For those of you who've been here before, don't expect the same accommodations on your next visit. There's a new owner and he's remodeling the place faster than we can write this book. At press time, most of the cabins already had been refurbished, and the direction the lodge is headed is more upscale and romantic.

Luxury rating: 4

Recreation rating: 3

Los Padres National Forest, off Highway 1 near Lucia

Cabins 1 through 6 are the lowest-priced at $175 per night double occupancy; these have a queen bed. Cabins 7 through 9 have more amenities and ocean views, and are priced at $225. The deluxe cabin is number 10, also known as the honeymoon suite, and it has the best view. It rents for $250 per night. All of the cabins are only a few feet apart from each other.

The restaurant is known for its excellent food and even more excellent views and sitting decks. The setting is awesome, with the lodge situated on a 500-foot cliff. Don't even think about walking to the beach from here—there is no beach. There's nothing but jagged rocks and cliffs from the lodge to the rugged surf below.

Sand Dollar State Beach is about eight miles south, and the entrance fee is $5 per day per vehicle. That's where most people go if they're looking for a beach. For hiking and sightseeing, head to Limekiln State Park, 1.5 miles north of the lodge on the east side of the highway. The highlight is Limekiln Falls, a one-mile round-trip hike that starts off easy, then switches to boulder-hopping across a stream. You can also check out the limekilns, which date from the 1800s. A $3 per vehicle day-use fee is charged. A trail map is available for a fee at the entrance station.

Facilities: Lucia Lodge has 10 cabins with full bathrooms. Two to four persons can be accommodated, depending on the cabin. There are no kitchen facilities, and some of the cabins have gas fireplaces. Complimentary continental breakfast is provided. A restaurant, communal barbecue, and horseshoe pits are on-site. The facilities are suitable for children. Pets are not allowed. No smoking is permitted.

Bedding: Down comforters, linens, and towels are provided.

Reservations and rates: Reservations are recommended. The fee is $175 to $250 per night per cabin during the summer season, and approximately $25 less per cabin during the off-season. Major credit cards are accepted. An Adventure Pass is required for each vehicle when parking in the national forest area; fees are $5 per day or $30 for an annual pass.

Directions: From Carmel, drive south on Highway 1 for 48 miles to the lodge on the right (west) side of the road.

Contact: Lucia Lodge, 62400 Highway 1, Big Sur, CA 93920; 831/667-2391 or 866/424-4787.

Lucia Lodge

14. GORDA SPRINGS RESORT

If you're looking for a little coastal hamlet, without the congestion of Carmel or cold weather of California's north coast, try the small town of Gorda and the cottages at Gorda Springs Resort. The 10-acre resort has been around for decades, and the owners have retained the charm of the original buildings and grounds, while upgrading the accommodations with more modern decor and amenities.

Luxury rating: 4

Recreation rating: 3

Ventana Wilderness, off Highway 1 in Gorda

The ocean-view cottages range in size from studios to two-bedrooms and can accommodate four to six persons. There's also the Rock House with two bedrooms, a full kitchen, a living room, and a fireplace. The house has one queen bed, one double bed, and a sofabed in the living room. The cottages and house sit on a hill above Highway 1.

This is a beautiful area of the central coast, and the resort can accommodate weddings, receptions, and groups. They have well-maintained gardens throughout the property that include a garden gazebo and deck for special events.

The Whale Watcher Cafe (831/927-1590) is a treat in itself and is open for breakfast, lunch, and dinner. Located on the property, it has casual dining indoors or on the heated garden patios, where you can watch out for whales as you eat. The café is known for outstanding gourmet meals and some of the best whale-watching around. They also have live music events throughout the year.

There's no ocean access from the resort; the closest beaches are Willow Creek Beach, one mile north, and Sand Dollar State Beach, four miles north. There is a $5 per vehicle per day fee at the state beach. The beach just below Gorda is a designated sanctuary for elephant seals.

Facilities: Gorda Springs Resort has six ocean-view cottages with bathrooms and refrigerators, and a house with two bedrooms, living room, fireplace, and full kitchen. There are also four inn rooms. Some cottages have a spa, a private patio, and a fireplace. There are no televisions or phones in the cottages or inn rooms. Laundry facilities, a restaurant, a gas station, a petting zoo, an antique and gift shop, and a grocery store with deli are available on-site. The cottages are suitable for children. Pets are not allowed. No smoking is permitted. Some facilities are wheelchair accessible.

Bedding: Linens and towels are provided.

Reservations and rates: Reservations are recommended. The fee is $175 to $375 per night for a studio cottage, $225 to $475 per night for a two-bedroom cottage, and $250 to $500 per night for the house. Inn rooms are $175 to $350 per night. Major credit cards are accepted. An Adventure Pass is required for each vehicle when parking in the national forest area; fees are $5 per day or $30 for an annual pass.

Directions: From Carmel, drive south on Highway 1 for 65 miles to the town of Gorda. The cottages are on the left (east) side of the road. Check in at the Pacific Market, next to the cottages.

Contact: Gorda Springs Resort, Town of Gorda Springs, Highway 1, The South Coast, Big Sur, CA 93920; 805/927-3918 or 805/927-4600, fax 805/927-4588; website: www.bigsurgordasprings.com. For a map of Los Padres National Forest, send $6 to U.S. Forest Service, Attn: Map Sales, P.O. Box 587, Camino, CA 95709; 530/647-5390; or visit the website: www.r5.fs.fed.us/visitorcenter.

Gorda Springs Resort

15. LAKE SAN ANTONIO RESORTS

This is a fantastic year-round destination for water lovers who like good weather and lots of activities. Lake San Antonio Resorts offers mobile homes close to the water, perfect for the variety of activities that a family or group might want in the course of a day. The rentals can accommodate up to 10 people, depending on the unit, and most of the homes have lake views.

Luxury rating: 3

Recreation rating: 5

Lake San Antonio, off U.S. 101 near Paso Robles

Want to fish? Good idea. This is one of the top lakes in the state for bass fishing, best in spring and early summer. It is also good for striped bass, catfish, crappie, sunfish, and bluegill.

Want to swim? Hey, it's a warm-water lake with average temperatures in the 70s during the summer. Want to boat or water-ski? The resort and the lake offer rentals, and with 60 miles of shoreline, there is plenty of room to accommodate the different water enthusiasts. In fact, Lake San Antonio is considered one of the top waterskiing lakes in California.

This lake also provides the best wintering habitat in the region for bald eagles, and eagle-watching tours are available. Closer to home (or your rental that is) you'll find that the resort is part of a park with a playground, a volleyball court, and a grassy area right next to the mobile homes.

All in all, for a lake vacation, this setup is hard to beat.

Facilities: Lake San Antonio Resorts has 19 mobile homes, 17 on the south shore and 2 on the north shore. Each mobile home has a fully equipped kitchen, including dishwasher and microwave, full bathroom, deck with awnings, barbecue; one marina slip is provided. Some mobile homes have air-conditioning and daily maid service. A pool, a recreation room, a restaurant, a general store, a pay telephone, a full-service marina, and boat rentals are available. There are no telephones or televisions in the rentals. The facilities are suitable for children. Pets are not allowed. Smoking is allowed in some of the units.

Bedding: Linens and towels are provided.

Reservations and rates: Reservations are recommended. The fee is $130 to $150 per night or $800 per week for four persons; $140 to $165 per night or $975 per week for six persons; $150 to $170 per night or $1,025 per week for eight persons; and $170 to $225 per night or $1,275 per week for 10 persons. For additional persons, $30 per person per night is charged. There is a two-night minimum on weekends. Major credit cards are accepted.

Directions: To reach the north shore, on U.S. 101 (just north of King City), take the Jolon Road/G-14 exit. Turn south on Jolon Road and drive 27 miles to Pleyto

Road (curvy road). Turn right and drive three miles to the north shore entrance of the lake. Note: When arriving from the south or east on U.S. 101 near Paso Robles, it is faster to take G-18/Jolon Road exit.

To reach the south shore from the north, on U.S. 101 (just north of King City), take the Jolon Road/G-14 exit. Turn south on Jolon Road and drive 20 miles to Lockwood and Interlake Road (G-14). Turn right and drive 13 miles to San Antonio Lake Road. Turn left and drive three miles to the south shore entrance of the lake. From the south, on U.S. 101 at Paso Robles, take the 24th Street exit (G-14 West) and drive 14 miles to Lake Nacimiento Drive. Turn right and drive across Lake Nacimiento Dam to Interlake Road. Turn left and drive seven miles to Lake San Antonio Road. Turn right and drive three miles to the south shore entrance.

Contact: Lake San Antonio Resorts, Star Route Box 2620, Bradley, CA 93426; 805/472-2313 or 800/310-2313.

Lake San Antonio Resorts

16. LAKE NACIMIENTO RESORT

Lodging with lake views and great boating, water sports, and fishing make Lake Nacimiento Resort one of the top recreation lake destinations in California. It is an outstanding operation that can serve as headquarters for a fun trip centered around a big lake and its 70° summer water temperatures. The lake features 165 miles of shoreline with an incredible number of arms. There are often loads of high-speed boats ripping around on hot summer weekends. Several five-mph zones are enforced for safety, with a boat patrol on duty. That said, some of the best waterskiing in California can be had here.

Luxury rating: 3

Recreation rating: 4

Lake Nacimiento, off U.S. 101 near Paso Robles

The fishing for white bass can be incredible; it's possible to catch dozens by vertical jigging a Horizon jig. Nacimiento hosts 25 fishing tournaments per year. Not only is bass fishing good, but there are also opportunities for trout (in cool months) and bluegill and catfish (in warm months).

The cabin-like lodge units are the most popular, with most designed as duplexes. Some have views of the lake. It's the kind of place where people show up with their boat, dock it for a weekend, and use the lodge units for a private retreat. Accommodations are also available for groups up to 14. The resort has a great restaurant with a lake view. Youngsters would be lucky to have their parents bring them to Lake Nacimiento.

Facilities: Lake Nacimiento Resort has 19 lodge units, eight travel trailers, and two mobile homes. A boat ramp, boat docks, boat rentals, stables, a playground, a swimming pool, a restaurant, a recreation room, laundry facilities, a grocery store, and fishing licenses are available nearby. Swimming beaches, basketball and volleyball courts, and horseshoe pits are also on-site. Pets are not permitted, and smoking is not allowed indoors.

Reservations and rates: Reservations are accepted. Rates for cabin-like lodges are $200 for four people, $275 for 5 to 10 people, and $385 for up to 14. Travel trailers cost $95 per night and mobile homes cost $275 for 8 to 10 people. Discounts are available for midweek stays. Major credit cards are accepted. Open year-round.

Directions: From U.S. 101 in Paso Robles, take the 24th Street/Lake Nacimiento exit. Turn west on 24th Street (becomes Lake Nacimiento Road/G-14) and drive for nine miles. Bear right on Lake Nacimiento road for seven miles to the resort entrance on the left. If you cross the Lake Nacimiento dam, you've gone too far.

Contact: Lake Nacimiento Resort, 10625 Nacimiento Lake Drive, Bradley, CA 93426; 805/238-3256 or 800/323-3839; website: www.nacimientoresort.com.

Lake Nacimiento Resort

17. CAMBRIA PINES LODGE

They call them one-room cabins, but we call them rooms. They are rustic and have wood paneling, and you can bring your pooch. But don't expect to cook here—there are no kitchen facilities.

Luxury rating: 3

Recreation rating: 3

San Simeon, off Highway 1 in Cambria

Don't worry about going hungry, though, because a complimentary breakfast is provided and the lodge has a restaurant. You'll share a wall with the cabin next door, but the place is quiet and comfortable. You'll have a bathroom with a shower; some cabins have tubs and showers.

The lodge is situated on 25 acres of Monterey pine forest and gardens. The setting is ideal for weddings and special events, and they have a garden gazebo for this purpose. But you don't have to attend a wedding ceremony to explore and enjoy the grounds or watch the deer, squirrels, and racoons wander.

The property overlooks the east village of Cambria, a town of about 6,000 located approximately two miles from the ocean. The older section of town has a quaint village atmosphere.

For exploring, San Simeon State Beach and Hearst Castle are just five and six miles north on Highway 1. One of California's best inshore fisheries is available right here at San Simeon Bay. You'll find a wide variety of rockfish, with big bonuses of halibut in the spring and early summer and lingcod in the fall. Fishing charters are available from Virg's Landing. A newly rebuilt pier opened in 2001.

Facilities: Cambria Pines Lodge has 125 lodging units ranging from duplex cabins to inn rooms and townhouse-style suites. They all have full bathrooms. A small refrigerator and microwave are provided in the suites. Fireplaces and televisions are available in some units. A complimentary buffet breakfast is provided. A heated indoor pool, a spa, a sauna, an exercise room, volleyball courts, conference facilities, a restaurant, and a lounge with nightly entertainment are available. The lodge is suitable for children. Pets are allowed in some cabins. No smoking is permitted. Some facilities are wheelchair accessible.

Bedding: Linens and towels are provided.

Reservations and rates: Reservations are recommended. The fee is $79 to $139 per night for garden cabins, $90 to $150 per night for fireside cabins, $90 to $190 per night for lodge rooms, and $110 to $329 per night for lodge suites. The fee for children ages 10 and above is $10 per night and includes breakfast. Children under age 10 are free. Pets are $25 per night per pet. There is a two-night minimum on weekends, and reservations should be made six months in advance for summer weekends. Major credit cards are accepted.

Directions: From Monterey, drive south on Highway 1 for about 95 miles to the town of Cambria and Burton Drive. Turn left on Burton Drive and drive .25 mile to the lodge on the left.

Contact: Cambria Pines Lodge, 2905 Burton Drive, Cambria, CA 93428; 805/927-4200 or 800/445-6868, fax 805/927-4016; website: www.cambriapineslodge.com. For fishing information, contact Virg's Landing, 805/772-1222.

OTHER CABINS AND COTTAGES NEARBY

• Santa Margarita KOA, 4765 Santa Margarita Lake Road, Santa Margarita, CA 93453; 805/438-5618; website: www.koacamp grounds.com.

Cambria Pines Lodge

CHAPTER 10

San Joaquin Valley

This section of the San Joaquin Valley is noted for its searing weather all summer long. But that is also when the lakes in the foothills become the Garden of Eden for boating and water sports enthusiasts. The region also offers many settings in the Sierra foothills, which can serve as launch points for short drives into the alpine beauty of Yosemite, Sequoia, and Kings Canyon National Parks.

Almost all of the cabin and cottage rentals in this region are family-oriented. The majority of them are on access roads to Yosemite. A bonus is that most have lower prices than their counterparts in the park, and like we said, are more hospitable to children. In a 10-mile radius of Groveland, we found a huge range of lodgings: cabins, cottages, historic inns, yurts, and tepees. One place that stands out, The Homestead (luxury rating 4), even provides lodging for your horse.

For those not heading to Yosemite, area lakes are the primary recreation attraction, with the refreshing, clean water revered as a tonic against the valley heat all summer long. When viewed from the air, the closeness of these lakes to the Sierra Nevada mountain range is surprising to many. Their proximity to the high country results in cool, high-quality water—the product of snowmelt sent down river canyons on the western slope. Some of these lakes are among the best around for waterskiing and powerboat recreation, including Lake Don Pedro east of Modesto, Bass Lake near Oakhurst, Lake McClure near Merced, Pine Flat Reservoir east of Fresno, and Lake Kaweah near Visalia.

In addition, Lake Don Pedro, Pine Flat Reservoir, and Lake Kaweah are among the best fishing lakes in the entire Central Valley; some anglers rate Don Pedro as the number-one all-around fishing lake in the state. The nearby Sierra rivers that feed these lakes (and others) also offer the opportunity to fly-fish for trout. In particular, the Kaweah and Kings Rivers boast many miles of ideal pocket water for fly fishers. While the trout on these streams are only occasionally large, the catch rates are often high and the rock-strewn beauty of the river canyons is exceptional.

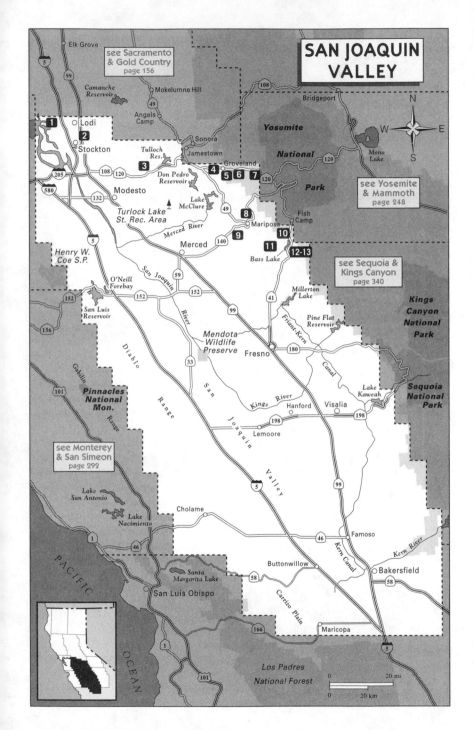

CHAPTER 10
SAN JOAQUIN VALLEY

1. TOWER PARK MARINA AND RESORT

Cabins and cottages are difficult to find in the Delta, but the invention of the park model cabin is starting a new trend here, and with it, new opportunities for vacationers. Park models are actually classified by the state of California as RVs, believe it or not, though they look nothing like RVs. The reason for this classification is that the models are built off-site, supplied with an axle and wheels, and then trailered into the park. Once in position, the wheels are removed, brick or lattice is added around the base, and decks are constructed to give them a more spacious feel.

Luxury rating: 3

Recreation rating: 4

*San Joaquin Delta, off I-5
near Lodi*

Simply add a vacation destination nearby, and you're in business. For years, Tower Park Marina and Resort has provided exactly that as a launch point into the back San Joaquin Delta. With the addition of park models at Tower Park (three were installed in 2001 and more are on the way), this getaway can be transformed into something special. The cabins at Tower Park are the deluxe models, which means they include an operating kitchen; many of the park models at other locations offer only a barbecue outside on the deck. The cabins are completely furnished with just about everything you need except for your food, your toothbrush, and a view of the water.

The resort is set on Little Potato Slough near the Mokelumne River. This huge resort is ideal for boat-in campers who desire a full-facility marina. In the summer, this is a popular waterskiing area. Some summer weekends are like a continuous party. For people who love hot weather, cool water, and water sports, this place fits the bill.

Facilities: Tower Park Marina and Resort has three park model cabins with more scheduled to arrive. Cabins are completely furnished, including kitchen and outside deck with barbecue. The resort also has a pavilion, boat rentals, overnight boat slips, a double boat launch, a playground, a restaurant, coin laundry, a gift shop, a grocery store, and propane gas. Some facilities are wheelchair accessible. Smoking and pets are permitted in the cabins.

Bedding: Linens and pillows are provided.

Reservations and rates: Reservations are recommended. There is a $150 deposit plus $60 per night or $295 per week. Major credit cards are accepted. Open year-round.

Directions: From Stockton, head north on I-5 for 14 miles to the Lodi/Highway 12 exit. Turn west on Highway 12 and drive about five miles to Tower Park Way. Turn left (before the first bridge) and drive a short distance to the park.

Contact: Tower Park Marina and Resort, 14900 West Highway 12, Lodi, CA 95242; 209/369-1041, fax 209/943-5656; website: www.westrec.com.

Tower Park Marina and Resort

2. STOCKTON-LODI KOA

Getting stuck in Lodi is not so horrible; some of the nicest, friendliest people imaginable live here. And it's amazing how many people intentionally plant themselves, or try to plant themselves, in one these KOA Kamping Kabins. Since there are only two cabins, reservations are a necessity.

Luxury rating: 2

Recreation rating: 3

*Lodi, near I-5 in
San Joaquin Valley*

These one-room cabins sleep up to four persons, and as with all KOA Kabins, they provide the beds, but you must bring your own bedding and towels. Bathrooms with showers are a short walk away.

It's well-known that vacationers often use this KOA as a layover on trips up and down Highway 99 or I-5, or when traveling east and west from the coast to the mountains. What is not as well-known is that Lodi is a thriving wine-producing region, and you can sample vino to your heart's content.

The San Joaquin Delta is 15 miles west from your cabin doorstep and provides boating and fishing galore. The best access is off Highway 12 to Rio Vista and Isleton. Some travelers like to explore the back roads and tiny towns throughout this region, but always remember to carry a map with you because, speaking from experience, it's easy to get lost around here, both on water and land.

Facilities: Stockton-Lodi KOA has two cabins and a campground for tents or RVs. Picnic tables, barbecues, front porch with swing, heating, and air-conditioning are provided. Restrooms, showers, a grocery store, coin laundry, modem hookups, a recreation room, a swimming pool, and a playground are available. The cabins are suitable for children. Pets are not allowed in the cabins. No smoking is permitted in the cabins.

Bedding: Linens and towels are not provided; bring your own sleeping bag and pillow.

3. LAKE TULLOCH RV CAMP AND MARINA

Just about everybody has a yearning to find their own Golden Pond. The vision starts with a cabin on a lake, with a boat waiting just outside your private dock.

Luxury rating: 2

Recreation rating: 4

Lake Tulloch, off Highway 120 near Jamestown

Well, there's a place where visions like this are real, and Lake Tulloch is that place. Of the 10 shoreline cabins here, five have their own personal docks. The other five have sandy beaches from which you can land a boat virtually at the foot of the cabin. The owners calls the accommodations "buck cabins," which means no showers or kitchens are provided. But they do have refrigerators and microwaves, and in addition, a full RV and tent campground is available on the property, and as a guest, you have use of all the facilities there. While Golden Pond it's not, it still has that magic combination: cabins, docks, and boats.

Lake Tulloch is set at an elevation of 500 feet and is adjacent to the Table Mountain range, with views and mature oaks throughout. It is a favorite destination for people who love the Central Valley's reservoir. It's a big lake, shaped like a giant X with extended lake arms adding up to 55 miles of shoreline. Unlike so many reservoirs in the foothill country, this one is nearly always full of water. In addition, it is one of the rare places where anglers and water-skiers live in harmony. That is due to the many coves and one six-mile-long arm with an enforced five-mph speed limit. Because much of the lake is protected from wind, the water surface is often calm, and in turn, can offer some of the best waterskiing in California. Not only is fishing often good for bass and catfish, but a secret at Tulloch is that prospects are also good for crawdads, using bacon or chicken necks for bait.

Facilities: Lake Tulloch RV Camp & Marina has 10 lakeside cabins that sleep up to eight. A dinette, microwave, refrigerator, and electricity are provided inside. There is no kitchen or shower. Just outside, a porch, picnic table, barbecue, and either a private dock or boat landing are available. The nearby resort and campground has showers, a laundry room, a store, RV dump station, propane gas, a playground, a restaurant, volleyball, horseshoes, tetherball, table tennis, a marina, boat rentals, boat launch, and a boat ramp. Some facilities are wheelchair accessible, including three of the cabins. Pets and smoking are permitted in the cabins.

Bedding: Beds with mattresses are provided, but not linens or towels.

Reservations and rates: Reservations are recommended (call 800/894-2267). Cabins rent for $85 per night or $450 per week; a $100 deposit is required. Launch fee is $3. Credit cards are accepted. Open year-round.

Directions: From Manteca, drive east on Highway 120 (it becomes Highway 108) to Oakdale. Continue east for 13 miles to Tulloch Road on the left. Turn left and drive 4.6 miles to the campground entrance and gatehouse at the south shore of Lake Tulloch.

Contact: Lake Tulloch RV Camp and Marina, 14448 Tulloch Dam Road, Jamestown, CA 95327; 209/881-0107; website: www.laketullochcampground.com.

Lake Tulloch RV Camp and Marina

4. THE GROVELAND MOTEL AND INDIAN VILLAGE

The Groveland Motel and Indian Village's claim to fame is that it has the widest variety of accommodations along the Highway 120 route to Yosemite. You can take your pick from tepees, cabins, mobile homes, campsites, or a Victorian home. Staying here is a lot like staying in a large campground or RV park, and children love it, especially if they are able to talk the adults into renting one of the tepees, which seem to have a magical effect on the little ones.

Luxury rating: 2

Recreation rating: 3

Groveland, off Highway 120 west of Yosemite

The canvas tepees come in single or double size and are arranged either village style around a central bonfire or set apart in a private tepee camp. And you thought there was only one type of tepee! Inside the tepees you'll find concrete floors, electric lights, and queen and double beds. All linens are provided and a central bathhouse with restrooms and showers is available. The facilities include a picnic table, outside light, fire ring, and water. In other words, sleeping in a tepee isn't much different than camping, except there's no tent to set up.

The cabins accommodate two to six persons and have private bathrooms, air-conditioning, and cable television, and some have either a patio or porch. The Victorian home features three bedrooms with two queen beds and one double bed, a fully equipped kitchen, a bathroom with clawfoot tub and shower, a covered porch, and period furnishings. The mobile homes range from one to four bedrooms and most have fully equipped kitchens. Some, but not all, mobiles have a porch, deck, and living room. The mobile homes—the largest of which is 1,600 square feet—can accommodate six to twenty persons.

Within one block of The Groveland Motel and Indian Village are restaurants, a grocery store, a deli, a gas station, a community park, and a children's playground. The town of Groveland is the last full-service community before entering Yosemite National Park, so pack up on supplies if you need them. The Pine Mountain Lake airport is a 10-minute drive from the motel, and shuttle transportation is available by arrangement.

Note that this is not a hideaway with perfect quiet. Its location adjacent to Highway 120 means there is highway noise round the clock.

Facilities: The Groveland Motel and Indian Village has 10 cabins, 14 tepees, 12 mobile homes, a Victorian house, and campsites. A central bathhouse and restrooms are available, and small barbecues are available by request. The facilities are suitable for children. One leashed pet per rental is allowed. Smoking is permitted. Some of the facilities are wheelchair accessible.

Bedding: Linens and towels are provided.

Reservations and rates: Reservations are recommended. The fee is $32 to $39 per night per tepee, $69 to $89 per night per cabin, $89 to $199 per night for a mobile home, and $149 per night for the Victorian home. Group rates are available. Major credit cards are accepted. Open year-round.

Directions: From Manteca, drive east on Highway 120 (it becomes Highway 108) for 30 miles to the Highway 120/Yosemite exit. Bear right on Highway 120 and drive about 15 miles to Groveland. The motel is on the right, across from the Ferreti Road intersection.

Contact: The Groveland Motel and Indian Village, 18933 Highway 120, P.O. Box 175, Groveland, CA 95321; 209/962-7865 or 888/849-3529, fax 209/962-0664; website: www.grovelandmotel.com.

The Groveland Motel and Indian Village

5. INN AT SUGAR PINE RANCH

This is not your ordinary bed-and-breakfast. It's set on 60 acres of oak, cedar, and pine forest and consists of freestanding cottages away from the main house. Yes, you *can* have privacy and quiet and still be fairly close to the Big Oak Flat entrance station of Yosemite National Park. This is a quiet, restful place at 3,250 feet in elevation, designed for meditating, exploring trails on the vast property, swimming in the large pool, and lounging around the gazebo.

The five freestanding cottages are located about 300 feet from the main house and are spaced about 20 feet apart. Originally built in the late 1940s, they were renovated in 1996 and feature nine-foot ceilings and country decor. Three of the cottages have whirlpool tubs and some have fireplaces. There are no kitchen facilities, but a big breakfast is served in the main house dining room, as well as afternoon tea.

Luxury rating: 3

Recreation rating: 3

Groveland, off Highway 120 west of Yosemite

The two-story main house, built in 1860, is a charming farmhouse evocative of yesteryear. Three inn rooms are located here. Another four rooms are available in the Uptown Cottage, a short walk from the main house.

When you decide to venture out, you're only 22 miles from Yosemite National Park and 10 miles from fishing in the South Fork Tuolumne River. For hiking, just walk across the road to Stanislaus National Forest, where you'll find several trails.

Facilities: Inn at Sugar Pine Ranch has five cottages and seven inn rooms, all with private bathrooms. There are no kitchen facilities, but complimentary full breakfast and afternoon tea are provided. Some cottages have fireplaces and whirlpool tubs. A pool is available. There are no televisions or telephones in the rooms. Children under the age of six are not allowed. Pets are not allowed. Smoking is not permitted.

Bedding: Linens and towels are provided.

Reservations and rates: Reservations are recommended. The fees range from $110 to $150 per night per cottage. Additional persons are $25 per night per person. There is a two-night minimum on weekends. Major credit cards are accepted. Open year-round.

Directions: From Manteca, drive east on Highway 120 (it becomes Highway 108) for 30 miles to the Highway 120/Yosemite exit. Bear right on Highway 120 and drive about 19 miles to the inn on the left.

Contact: Inn at Sugar Pine Ranch, 21250 Highway 120, Groveland, CA 95321; tel./fax 209/962-7823; website: www.bizware.com/sugarpine.

Inn at Sugar Pine Ranch

6. YOSEMITE LAKES

Think big, think family-oriented, think variety of lodging options and on-site activities, and you'll be thinking of Yosemite Lakes. It's set on a 400-acre preserve at 3,400 feet in elevation, with the South Fork of the Tuolumne River running through it. Yosemite Lakes is an affiliate of Thousand Trails, a camping conglomerate with facilities around the country. At this particular location, you can choose between yurts, cabins, camping trailers, houses, a hostel, or a campground.

Although Yosemite Lakes is a membership-based facility, rentals are available to the general public for a slightly higher price than members pay. This is an unusual deal, since Thousand Trails facilities normally are completely off-limits to the general public; an exception was made in this case because the resort is so close to Yosemite National Park—five miles from the west entrance station.

Luxury rating: 2

Recreation rating: 4

*off Highway 120
near Groveland*

All 10 cabins are small (one room) and rustic, with minimal provisions and no private bathroom or kitchen facilities. The camping trailers sleep four to six persons and come in various sizes up to 35 feet in length. This is just like RV camping, only you rent one of their RVs instead of bringing your own. Fire rings and a central bathhouse and restrooms are provided for those staying in a cabin or cottage. Linens and towels can be rented.

The cottages are a big step up from the cabins, featuring two bedrooms, fully equipped kitchens including microwave and dishwasher, private bathrooms, satellite televisions, and telephones, and sleeping six persons. The cottages are grouped together in their own area of the preserve, so these rentals would be suitable for a large group. Some people will find this hard to believe, but some of the most deluxe accommodations here are the yurts, with floors, windows, a gas fireplace, air-conditioning, a fully equipped kitchen with microwave, a bathroom, a television, and a deck or porch with barbecue. Linens and towels are provided.

Thousand Trails is much like a resort, with a huge variety of recreational options and organized activities. It's definitely not a romantic getaway, but rather a family-oriented preserve. This is the kind of place where several generations of a family can come and spend time together, each participating in the activities that suit them, then meeting up for meals or at the end of a day. The restaurant is open for dinner on Friday and Saturday and for breakfast on Saturday and Sunday; you're on your own for meals during the rest of the week. There is 24-hour security.

The South Fork of the Tuolumne River is stocked weekly with rainbow trout. Fishing and swimming in this river are allowed. If hiking interests you, trails are available throughout the 400 acres. For details on activities in the local area, see the next listing for Yosemite Gatehouse Lodge.

Facilities: Yosemite Lakes has 10 bunkhouse cabins, 10 yurts, 6 garden cottages, 13 trailers, a campground, and a hostel. Some lodgings have a deck or porch, fireplace, air-conditioning, and television. A convenience store, weekend restaurant, TV room, recreation lodge, playground, basketball and volleyball courts, horseshoe pits, table tennis, shuffleboard, miniature golf, and laundry facilities are available. Equipment for rent includes kayaks, paddleboats, inner tubes, and bicycles. A fish-cleaning station and 24-hour security are provided. The facilities are suitable for children. Leashed pets are allowed in some facilities. Smoking is permitted in some accommodations. Some facilities are wheelchair accessible.

Bedding: Linens and towels are provided for the cottages, yurts, and trailers.

Reservations and rates: Reservations are recommended. Per night, the fee is $39 to $49 for cabins, $79 to $89 for cottages, $49 to $59 for trailers, $79 to $144 for yurts, and $39 to $59 for the hostel. Linens and towels can be rented for $5 per stay for two persons. The pet fee is $5 per pet per stay. Open year-round.

Directions: From Groveland, drive east on Highway 120 for 18 miles to the entrance road for Yosemite Lakes. Turn right and drive a short distance to the facilities.

Contact: Yosemite Lakes, 31191 Hardin Flat Road, Groveland, CA 95321; 209/962-0121 or 800/533-1001; website: www.thousandtrails.com.

Yosemite Lakes

7. YOSEMITE GATEHOUSE LODGE

Location and affordability are the buzzwords at Yosemite Gatehouse Lodge, which is just one mile from the Big Oak Flat entrance to Yosemite National Park. Four older cabins in duplex units are situated up the hill behind the lodge, nestled among ponderosa and sugar pines, cedars, redwoods, and a few oak trees. The lodge also has two motel suites and a room, one of which is a freestanding unit located between the lodge and the cabins.

The dark-brown cabins here are cozy, almost 400 square feet in size. Built in the 1940s, they've been updated over the years to include everything you need to set up camp for a few days: fully equipped kitchen, private bathroom, bedroom, linens and towels, back porch—all in your own little spot in the forest. There's not much difference between the cabins, but our recommendation is Cabin 3 because it was updated most recently and has the best mattresses. A small store at the lodge supplies convenience-store fare.

Luxury rating: 2

Recreation rating: 3

off Highway 120
near Groveland

Many who stay here are vacationers stopping by on their way to Yosemite National Park. Although practically everyone knows about the benefits of heading east to Yosemite, not as well-known are the attractions you'll find by heading west on Highway 120 towards Groveland. Rainbow Pools, on the North Fork of the Tuolumne River in Stanislaus National Forest, is less than 10 miles west and is a popular swimming area, with a waterfall and series of pools created by the river. There are rock cliffs used for jumping into the water, as well as granite-chute slides that deposit visitors into the main swimming hole. White-water rafting is also available near here.

Facilities: Yosemite Gatehouse Lodge has four cabins, two motel suites, and a motel room. The cabins have fully equipped kitchens, private bathrooms with showers, and porches; there is no daily maid service. The motel suites and room have a small refrigerator and microwave. Televisions and wall heating are provided in all facilities. A small store is available. The facilities are suitable for children. Pets are not allowed. Smoking is not permitted indoors.

Bedding: Linens and towels are provided.

Reservations and rates: Reservations are recommended. The fee is $106 to $126 per night per cabin and $86 to $130 per night for motel suites and rooms. Additional persons are $10 per night per person. Major credit cards are accepted. It is open May through November.

Directions: From Groveland, drive east on Highway 120 for 27 miles to the lodge on the right, one mile before the Yosemite National Park entrance station.

Contact: Yosemite Gatehouse Lodge, 34001 Highway 120, Groveland, CA 95321; 209/379-2260; website: www.yosemitecabins.com.

Yosemite Gatehouse Lodge

8. YOSEMITE-MARIPOSA KOA

Every KOA in America should be like the one in Mariposa. Imagine staying in a little log cabin next to a pond with ducks paddling around. Then imagine an easy drive into Yosemite National Park for a tour of nature's greatest showplace. That is exactly what you get here, right down to the ducks.

Luxury rating: 2

Recreation rating: 3

Mariposa, off Highway 140

Yosemite-Mariposa KOA is located in the town of Midpines, about five miles east of Mariposa on Highway 140, in the transition zone where the Central Valley foothills rise into the pine-covered mountains. When you drive into the campground, you will pass a series of drive-in RV sites, a small grocery store, and a swimming pool, until you arrive at a pond with KOA Kamping Kabins perched just up from its shore.

The log-style cabins are little, with a bunk bed on one side and a queen bed on the other. Each cabin has electric heat and a swing, barbecue, and picnic table out front. You will need to bring the rest, including sleeping bags. The lack of asphalt, especially around the cabins, contributes to this KOA's quality setting. In addition, it's also very quiet here at night, and any family who breaks the 10 P.M. quiet time curfew is told to keep it down.

From the KOA, it's about an hour's drive on Highway 140 to reach Yosemite Valley, cruising along the Merced River through the Arch Rock entrance station and down into the valley. It is critical to get an early start to avoid traffic. Even the most popular trails in the valley—Yosemite Falls and Bridalveil Falls—are relatively uncrowded between dawn and 8 A.M. The same is true with Glacier Point until about 9 A.M.

Those interested in California history will enjoy exploring the gold rush–era town of Mariposa (the name means "butterfly" in Spanish). Another option is to spend a day hiking along, fishing in, swimming in, or rafting on the Merced River. In April, the wildflower blooms at Red Hills in the Merced Recreation Area along the Merced River are among the best anywhere in the Sierra foothills. To access this area, drive east to Briceburg and follow the signs to the Bureau of Land Management camping areas.

Facilities: Yosemite-Mariposa KOA has 12 Kamping Kabins, furnished inside with electricity, a bunk bed, a queen bed, and a small table, and outside with a swing, a picnic table, and a barbecue. A restroom with showers is nearby, along with a small store, pay telephone, and swimming pool. At the pond adjacent to the cabins, paddleboats are available. There are also 30 RV spaces with full hookups, 40 sites for tents, and 10 additional sites for tents or RVs. No pets are allowed in cabins.

Bedding: No bedding is provided; bring your own sleeping bag, pillow, and towels.

Reservations and rates: Reservations are recommended (call 800/562-3403). Cabins run $48 for two per night, $5 for each additional person.

Directions: From San Francisco, drive east on I-580 past Livermore into the Central Valley. At the Highway 205/I-580 split, veer south on I-580 and continue about eight miles to Highway 132. Turn east on Highway 132 and drive to Modesto and Highway 99. Turn south on Highway 99 and drive to Merced. At Merced, turn east on Highway 140 and drive to Mariposa. Continue east for 5.5 miles to Midpines and turn left at the Yosemite-Mariposa KOA

Contact: Yosemite-Mariposa KOA, KOA Mariposa, Box 545, Highway 140, Midpines, CA 95345; 209/966-2201; website: www.koa.com. A free map/brochure of Yosemite National Park is provided at park entrance stations as part of the $20 entrance fee.

Yosemite-Mariposa KOA

9. RANCHO BERNARDO

At Rancho Bernardo, they're full of bull and proud of it. You see, this is a 40-acre cattle ranch, and the owner is a former bull rider from way back who'd be happy to tell you about the art of bull riding at the drop of a hat. In addition, the innkeepers, Barney and Kathy Lozares, are perfect hosts: friendly, helpful, and down-to-earth. And their rental facilities are stunningly beautiful, combining modern and rustic elements—you're in for a real treat when you stay here.

Luxury rating: 3

Recreation rating: 3

off Highway 140, near Mariposa

The guest house is a gorgeous, 1,000-square-foot sanctuary of towering vaulted ceilings covered in knotty pine, windows with expansive views of the rolling countryside, hardwood floors with area rugs, and modern kitchenette with refrigerator, microwave, sink, and ceramic tile counters. There's also a sitting area with sleeper sofa, television with VCR, woodstove on a brick hearth, a sleeping loft with plush bedding, and a full-size pool table.

The barn suite has a cozy bedroom with a slightly vaulted knotty pine ceiling and pastel walls, queen-size brass bed with tastefully coordinated bedding, ceiling fan, kitchenette with microwave and refrigerator, private bathroom, television with VCR, and lots of wood accents. The retreat is inviting, bright, and cheerful. If you hear any whinnying during the night, it's not a ghost; it's probably one of the horses that reside downstairs in the barn. Both rentals have air-conditioning, which is a huge bonus, since here in foothill country—at only 1,500 feet in elevation—summers can be smoking hot. You won't be disappointed with these luxurious, spacious, down-home accommodations.

Catheys Valley is secluded, dotted with oak trees, rolling hills, ranches, and short rock walls that were constructed by Chinese laborers during the gold rush. The immigrants were promised the chance of riches in America and instead often found themselves being used virtually as slave labor. The little village of Hornitos is nearby, and history buffs would enjoy seeing the old pioneer church and cemetery, and ruins of the former gold mining town where the bandit Joaquin Murietta was rumored to have hidden out in the 1800s. When we were last there, a sign at the entrance to town proclaimed, "Our town is like heaven to us, so don't drive like hell through it."

Rancho Bernardo is on the route to Yosemite National Park, about a 90-minute drive to Yosemite Valley. Closer to the ranch (a 15-minute drive) is the historic town of Mariposa, full of gold rush–era buildings and museums. For details about the Mariposa area, see the listing for Yosemite-Mariposa KOA Cabins, above.

Facilities: Rancho Bernardo has a guest house and a barn suite with private bathrooms. The facilities have a microwave, a refrigerator, and a sink. A complimentary hearty breakfast is provided, as are coffee, tea, and afternoon sodas and cookies. The barn suite has a woodstove. Barbecues are available on request, and a wraparound deck and picnic area are available. The facilities are not suitable for children. Pets are not allowed. No smoking is permitted.

Bedding: Linens and towels are provided.

Reservations and rates: Reservations are recommended. For two people, the rate is $95 per night for the barn suite and $135 per night for the guest house. Additional persons are $25 per night per person. There is a two-night minimum on holidays. Major credit cards are accepted. Open year-round.

Directions: From Highway 99 in Merced, turn east on Highway 140 and drive to Planada. Continue on Highway 140 for approximately 13 miles to Old Highway. Turn right and drive 2.5 miles to Rancho Bernardo on the left, just after passing the intersection with School House Road.

Contact: Rancho Bernardo Bed and Breakfast, 2617 Old Highway South, P.O. Box 5008, Mariposa, CA 95338; tel./fax 209/966-4511; website: www.ranchobernardobnb.com.

Rancho Bernardo

10. OWL'S NEST

When you pull up to Owl's Nest and see that the cabins are right along Highway 41, you might proceed with a fair amount of apprehension. After all, Owl's Nest is located just a mile from the southern entrance to Yosemite National Park, and the vision of a noisy parade of vehicles might seem like a potential nightmare.

Luxury rating: 3

Recreation rating: 4

Fish Camp, off Highway 41, near Yosemite

Instead, a funny thing happens at Owl's Nest: quiet, peace, and privacy. It seems that come nightfall, the road is suddenly abandoned, with almost nobody at all going up and down that highway to Yosemite.

The A-frame cabins here at Owl's Nest are set at 5,000 feet in elevation outside of Yosemite's Wawona entrance. Two of the cabins, Ponderosa and Christmas Tree, can sleep up to six and are completely furnished, with Christmas Tree providing a fireplace. The other, Tamarack, is a smaller "sleeper cabin" for two with no kitchen.

Horseback rides are available out of Fish Camp. They include scenic rides of an hour or two, along with a five-and-a-half-hour trail ride to Mariposa Big Trees. The same destination takes about 10 minutes by car and is best visited by 8:30 A.M., before the crowds show up. Some of the best day hikes in Yosemite are along the road to Glacier Point; the drive to Glacier Point from Fish Camp is about 50 minutes. Golfing is available in Wawona and Ahwahnee.

Facilities: Owl's Nest has two two-story cabins and one sleeper cabin. All have bathrooms and a deck with a barbecue. Two have kitchens with cookware and utensils, and one has a fireplace. A small grocery store is located nearby. Pets are not permitted.

Bedding: Linens are provided.

Reservations and rates: Reservations are required. Cabin rates are $125 per night for two people, plus $15 for each additional person. The maximum number of people per cabin is six. The sleeper cabin rents for $85 per night for two people. A three-night minimum stay is required in the summer. Credit cards are accepted.

Directions: From Highway 99 in Merced, turn east on Highway 140 and drive to Mariposa. In Mariposa, turn south on Highway 49 and drive 30 miles to Highway 41 at Oakhurst. Turn left on Highway 41 and drive 13 miles to the town of Fish Camp, and look for Owl's Nest on the left side of the road.

Contact: Owl's Nest, P.O. Box 33, Fish Camp, CA 93623; 559/683-3484; website: www.owlsnestlodging.com. A free map/brochure of Yosemite National Park is provided at park entrance stations as part of the $20 entrance fee. Horseback riding rentals are available at Yosemite Trails Pack Station, 559/683-7611.

Owl's Nest

11. THE HOMESTEAD

A unique foothill hideaway, set on 160 acres with upscale accommodations, is what you get at The Homestead. This is an adult-oriented retreat a few miles from Oakhurst in a quiet, private setting amid oaks, natural gardens, and stone walls. One of the unusual benefits is that you can park your horse here for the night as well; horse stalls are available in the stable. Nestled at 2,300 feet in elevation, the facilities consist of a main house, four adobe-and-stone cottages, and a loft room over the stable.

© ERIC ZEPEDA

Luxury rating: 4

Recreation rating: 3

off Highway 49, near Oakhurst

The four hillside cottages were built in 1992 and attest to the benefits of fine craftsmanship and attention to detail. Inside, you'll find Saltillo tile floors, hand-troweled plaster, yellow pine trim, vaulted ceilings, country kitchens, comfortable living rooms with fireplace, ample bathrooms, and romantic bedrooms with a big log bed and an eclectic mix of antique and contemporary furnishings. Outside the 560-square-foot cottages are private patios and comfortable Adirondack chairs.

The little Star Gazing Loft is located above the stable and has a picture window next to the bed. This is ideal for guests traveling with horses, since they can keep an eye on Mr. (or Mrs.) Ed from this vantage point. If you don't care for horses, or sleeping near them, one of the cottages is more suitable for you.

Even though this is a country hideaway a few miles from the nearest town, the innkeepers have ensured that their guests are not deprived of amenities usually found in a larger, more urban establishment. If you want a catered dinner, a massage, or other concierge services, it's no problem. And if you feel like going out for a special meal, the five-star Erna's Elderberry House is just a 10-minute drive down the road in Oakhurst. We were not disappointed with the gourmet food or the atmosphere, although it can get crowded.

When you decide to explore the local area, you'll discover that the southern entrance to Yosemite National Park is 21 miles away. Golfers are in luck, as two courses are nearby. The nine-hole Sierra Meadows at River Creek is less than a five-minute drive from the resort, and Sierra Meadows, an 18-hole course, is six miles away.

Facilities: The Homestead has four cottages with fully equipped kitchens and private baths. Fireplace, television, air-conditioning, and picnic area with gas barbecue are included. Complimentary muffins, fruit, coffee, and tea are provided. Concierge services are available. There are no telephones in the cottages, but a telephone and fax machine are available in the office. The facilities are not suitable for children. Pets are not allowed. No smoking is permitted. One cottage is wheelchair accessible.

Bedding: Linens, towels, and daily maid service are provided.

Reservations and rates: Reservations are recommended. The fee is $149 to $225 per night per cottage, and $115 to $135 per night for the loft. There is a two-night minimum on weekends and a three- to four-night minimum on holidays. Major credit cards are accepted. Open year-round.

Directions: From Oakhurst, drive north on Highway 49 for 4.5 miles to Road 600. Turn left (south) and drive 2.5 miles to The Homestead on the right.

Contact: The Homestead, 41110 Road 600, Ahwahnee, CA 93601; 559/683-0495; website: www.homesteadcottages.com.

The Homestead

12. THE FORKS RESORT

The Forks Resort, Miller's Landing (see listing below), and a real estate agency provide the opportunity for cabin rentals at Bass Lake. These cabins can feel like refuges of peace from the wild water sports and boating activity on Bass Lake.

Luxury rating: 4

Recreation rating: 4

Sierra National Forest, off Highway 41 at Bass Lake

Bass Lake is a long, beautiful lake set in the Sierra foothills—elevation 3,400 feet—that has become a recreation center for boating and water sports. It features five campgrounds, four resorts, and two boat launches. Waterskiing, tubing, personal watercraft riding, fishing, and swimming are all extremely popular. On a hot summer day, you can count on seeing jet boats zooming about, as the roar from their big V-8 engines echoes down the lake. The scene is wild and wet.

Sound like your kind of place? If so, you'll want to book a stay at either The Forks Resort or Miller's Landing. The Forks Resort has some of the most nicely furnished cabin rentals on the lake, whereas Miller's Landing provides a range of inexpensive and rustic to well-furnished ones.

The cabins at The Forks Resort were first built in the '50s and '60s, but have been recently remodeled. Most have knotty pine interiors and are set high above the road with good views. Cabin 5 is popular because it's one of the largest cabins with more amenities, even though it has the worst view. Cabins 6, 7, and 8 are the newest cabins.

How good are they? Good enough that reservations start being made on January 2 for the upcoming summer. Almost every day of the summer fills up. If you want to guarantee yourself a cabin here during summer, then you will have to plan ahead, make your reservations early, and then get ready for the Bass Lake experience.

Facilities: The Forks Resort has 20 one- and two-bedroom cabins with private bathrooms and fully equipped kitchens with microwave. Each cabin has a porch and fireplace. There are no televisions or telephones in the cabins. Laundry facilities, a restaurant, a general store, a full-service marina, and boat rentals are available. The resort is suitable for children. Leashed pets are allowed. No smoking is permitted.

Bedding: Linens and towels are provided.

Reservations and rates: Reservations are recommended. The fee is $80 to $140 per night per cabin, or $500 to $920 per week per cabin. The pet fee is $25 per night per pet. A four-night minimum stay is required from Memorial Day weekend to Labor Day weekend. Major credit cards are accepted. Open April through September.

Directions: From Fresno, drive 50 miles north on Highway 41 to Yosemite Forks. Turn right onto County Road 222 and drive six miles, keeping to the right at each of two Ys in the road; the resort is on the right.

Contact: The Forks Resort, 39150 Road 222, Bass Lake, CA 93604; 559/642-3737; website: www.theforksresort.com.

The Forks Resort

13. MILLER'S LANDING

Miller's Landing has some of the most beautiful chalets imaginable, complete with picture windows and beautiful views of Bass Lake. They also have a series of one- and two-bedroom cabins ideal for those who only need a cold beer to stay happy. Take your pick—for most, it'll work out just fine.

Luxury rating: 3

Recreation rating: 4

*Sierra National Forest,
off Highway 41 at Bass Lake*

Miller's Landing has the largest marina at Bass Lake, the raucous powerboating headquarters of the Sierra foothills. This place can really rock. The high-speed boats dominate the water all summer, the sales of ice and beer are off the charts, and occasionally, folks sleep for a couple of hours each night.

That's where this place comes in. The primitive cabins are basically designed as a place to crash for the night before going back out on the water and doing it all over again. The most primitive one-bedroom cabins here have no piped water inside, just a small refrigerator and stove; a water faucet is available nearby outside the cabins. Most will just set up a camp-like existence in the cabin and use the adjacent facilities at the park's resort and camp if necessary. The most important items, beer and ice, are available nearby. These rustic cabins are small and spaced fairly closed together—about 100 feet apart. They are not winterized and are available only from May 1 to September 15.

For those who require more deluxe accommodations, well, these are available, too. There are several very nice units, including some with lake views and everything a visitor could ask for, like a shower, a bed with fresh sheets, and a good home-cooked meal. The six cabins with lake views are Pentwater, Cabins 1, 9A, 9B, 10A, and 10B. Because cabins 9A, 9B, 10A, and 10B are duplexes, Cabin 1 is the most popular; it's also the most spacious. These cabins have vaulted ceilings, carpeting, breakfast bars, some oak cabinetry, and knotty pine ceilings. The good ones are drop-dead gorgeous.

The nearby marina provides boat rentals, and Miller's Landing is located close to the free Wishon boat ramp.

Facilities: Miller's Landing has 13 cabins ranging from rustic to deluxe. The five rustic cabins have no piped water inside, but a water faucet is located outside. The rustic cabins do not have private bathrooms and linens and towels are not provided; refrigerator, stove, deck, and fire ring are provided. Other cabins have private bathrooms and fully equipped kitchens; linens and towels, a deck, a picnic table, a fire ring, and a woodstove are provided. A bathhouse, laundry facilities, a restaurant, a full-service marina, and boat rentals are available. The cabins are suitable for children. Leashed pets are allowed. Smoking is permitted. One cabin is wheelchair accessible.

Bedding: Linens and towels are provided in some faciltes.

Reservations and rates: Reservations are recommended. The fee is $35 to $170 per night per cabin, and $245 to $1,190 per week. For pets, a $25 cleaning fee is charged. A two-day minimum stay is required, and a one-week minimum during July and August. Major credit cards are accepted.

Directions: From Fresno, drive 50 miles north on Highway 41 to Yosemite Forks. Turn right onto County Road 222 and drive approximately eight miles, keeping to the right at each of two Ys in the road; the resort is on the right.

Contact: Miller's Landing, 37976 Road 222, Wishon, CA 93669; 559/642-3633; website: www.millerslanding.com.

OTHER CABINS AND COTTAGES NEARBY
• The Pines Resort, P.O. Box 109, Bass Lake, CA 93604; 559/642-3121 or 800/350-7463; website: www.basslake.com

Miller's Landing

CHAPTER 11

Sequoia & Kings Canyon

*T*here is no place on earth like the high Sierra, from Mount Whitney north through Sequoia and Kings Canyon National Parks. This is a paradise filled with deep canyons, high peaks, and fantastic natural beauty, and sprinkled with groves of the largest living things in the history of the earth—giant sequoias.

Though the area is primarily known for the national parks, the cabins available span a great variety of settings. The most popular spots, though, are in the vicinity of Sequoia and Kings Canyon National Parks, or on the parks' access roads.

Most of the cabins are historic structures, built more than 60 years ago. If you have high aspirations for luxury, you're better off taking one of the high-end inn rooms at Wuksachi Lodge. Otherwise, get this picture of most of the cabins in focus: historic, rustic, and only modest upgrades for some. Some are even primitive. For many, that's just fine. For others, it's not. One of the most unusual experiences in the area is at Montecito-Sequoia Lodge, which has pretty basic lodging, yet where all meals are provided and where 70 employees direct full days of recreation for visitors. "Like a cruise ship in the forest," as they say.

Sooner or later, everyone will want to see the biggest tree of them all—the General Sherman Tree, estimated to be 2,300 to 2,700 years old with a circumference of 102.6 feet. It is located in the Giant Forest at Sequoia National Park. To stand in front of it is to know true awe. That said, we found the Grant Grove and the Muir Grove even more enchanting.

These are among the highlights of a driving tour through both parks. A must for most is taking in the view from Moro Rock, parking and then making the 300-foot walk up a succession of stairs to reach the 6,725-foot summit. Here you can scan a series of mountain rims and granite peaks, highlighted by the Great Western Divide.

The drive out of Sequoia and into Kings Canyon features rim-of-the-world-type views as you first enter the Kings River canyon. You then descend to the bottom of the canyon, right along the Kings River, and can gaze up at the high glacial-carved canyon walls, and drive all the way out to Cedar Grove, the end of the road. The canyon rises 8,000 feet from the river to Spanish Peak, the deepest canyon in the continental United States.

Crystal Cave is another point of fascination. Among the formations are adjoined crystal columns that look like the sound pipes in the giant organ at the Mormon Tabernacle. Lights are placed strategically for perfect lighting.

This is only a start. Bears, marmot, and deer are abundant and are commonly seen in Sequoia, especially at Dorst Creek Campground. If you drive up to Mineral King and take a hike, it can seem like the marmot capital of the world.

But this region also harbors many wonderful secrets having nothing to do with the national parks. One of them, for instance, is the Muir Trail Ranch near Florence Lake. The ranch is set in the John Muir Wilderness and requires a trip by foot, boat, or horse to reach it. Other unique launch points for trips into the wilderness lie on the eastern Sierra near Bishop: Bishop Creek Lodge, Glacier Lodge, Parchers Resort, Cardinal Village Resort.

On the western slopes of the Sierra, pretty lakes with good trout fishing include Edison, Florence, and Hume Lakes. Hidden spots in Sierra National Forest provide continual fortune hunts, especially up the Dinkey Creek drainage above Courtright Reservoir. On the eastern slopes, a series of small streams offers good vehicle access; here, too, you'll encounter the beautiful Rock Creek Lake, Sabrina and South Lakes, and great wilderness trailheads at the end of almost every road.

The remote Golden Trout Wilderness on the southwest flank of Mt. Whitney is one of the most pristine areas in California. Yet it is lost in the shadow of giant Whitney, elevation 14,495 feet, the highest point in the continental United States, where hiking has become so popular that reservations are required at each trailhead for overnight use, and quotas are enforced to ensure an undisturbed experience for each visitor.

In the Kernville area, there are a series of cabin rentals along the Kern River. Most choose this canyon for one reason: the outstanding white-water rafting and kayaking.

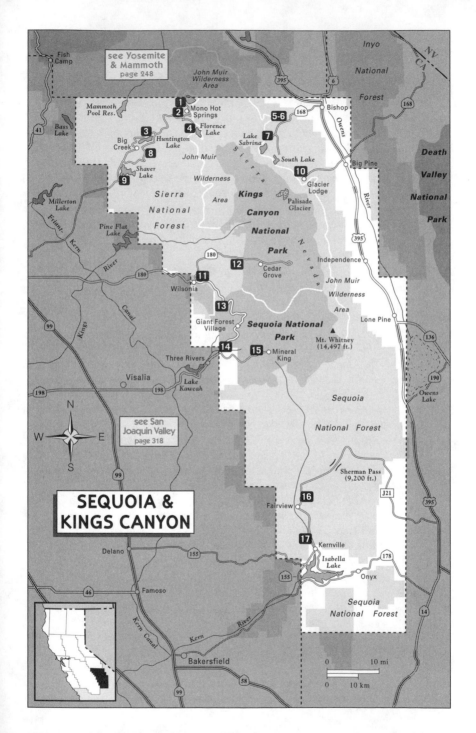

see Yosemite
& Mammoth
page 248

Inyo

National

Forest

NV
CA

Fish
Camp

John Muir
Wilderness
Area

395

6

168

1 Mono Hot
2 Springs

Bishop

168

Owens

5-6

3

4 Florence
Lake

Mammoth
Pool Res.

41

Bass
Lake

Big
Creek

Huntington
Lake

8

Lake
Sabrina

7

South Lake

Death

Valley

National

Park

9

Shaver
Lake

John Muir

Wilderness

Area

10

Glacier
Lodge

Big Pine

Sierra

Millerton
Lake

National

Forest

Kings

Canyon

National

Palisade
Glacier

River

395

Frant-

Kern

Pine Flat
Lake

River

180

Park

Nevada

Independence

715

John Muir

136

180

12

Cedar
Grove

99

Kings

Canal

11

Wilsonia

180

Wilderness

Area

Lone Pine

13

190

Giant Forest
Village

Sequoia National

Park

Mt. Whitney
(14,497 ft.)

Owens
Lake

14

Three Rivers

15

Mineral
King

198

Visalia

Lake
Kaweah

Sequoia

198

see San
Joaquin Valley
page 318

N

W   E

S

National   Forest

Sherman Pass
(9,200 ft.)

**SEQUOIA &
KINGS CANYON**

99

16

J21

395

Fairview

Delano

155

17 Kernville

178

46

Famoso

155

Isabella
Lake

Onyx

Kern

Canal

Kern   River

Sequoia

14

National   Forest

0   10 mi

0   10 km

Bakersfield

99

58

CHAPTER 11
SEQUOIA & KINGS CANYON

1. VERMILION VALLEY RESORT

This is one of the best tent camping destinations in California. You get lakeside accommodations, boat rentals and shuttle service, horseback riding, and all the fishing and hiking you want at an elevation of 7,650 feet. The only downer is that the lake level fluctuates greatly, and you never know how full it's going to be for your trip.

Luxury rating: 1

Recreation rating: 5

Sierra National Forest, off Highway 168 at Lake Edison

The 10 tent cabins have metal frames, twin bunkbeds, wooden floors, decks, picnic tables, and fire rings—much like camping. A communal bathhouse is nearby and you can shower for $2. Cabins 1, 2, and 5 have lake views and are about 30 yards from the lake when it's full. If you don't want to cook, there's a restaurant offering home-cooked meals and Saturday night barbecues. Motel rooms are also available, and some of them have kitchenettes.

Edison Lake is fed by Mono Creek, a cold, pure, and pristine trout stream. A 15-mph speed limit on the lake makes it ideal for those who love to fish, either by boat or from the shore. Some giant brown trout live in this lake, but they aren't easy pickings.

For hiking, explore the great trailhead at the head of the lake that travels up Mono Creek for 2.5 miles to reach the John Muir Trail. To reach the head of the lake, take the water taxi from the resort, which makes two trips a day across the lake and back. The fee is $8 per adult one-way and $15 round-trip; children under age 12 are $5 one-way and $10 round-trip. Refer to the book *Foghorn Outdoors: California Hiking* for details.

Facilities: Vermilion Valley Resort has 10 tent cabins and four motel rooms with kitchenettes. The tent cabins do not have electricity, kitchen facilities, or private bathrooms; a communal bathhouse is available. A small deck, picnic table, gas heater, and fire ring are provided. A restaurant, a store, bait and tackle, a fish cleaning station, a dock, boat rentals, and water taxi are available. The resort is suitable for children. Leashed pets are allowed. Smoking is permitted.

Bedding: Linens and towels are not provided; you must bring your own.

Reservations and rates: Reservations are recommended. The fee is $40 to $45 per night per tent cabin, and $65 to $85 per night for motel rooms. Shower facilities are $2 per day per person. There is no pet fee. There is a two-night minimum on weekends, and a three-night minimum on holidays. Major credit cards are accepted. Open mid-May through October, weather permitting.

Directions: From the town of Shaver Lake, drive north on Highway 168 for 21 miles to Kaiser Pass Road/Forest Road 80. Turn right and drive 16 (narrow and twisting) miles to a fork in the road. Bear left onto Edison Lake Road and drive approximately six miles to the resort at the end of the road.

Contact: Vermilion Valley Resort, P.O. Box 258, Lakeshore, CA 93634; 559/259-4000 (summer) or 559/855-6558 (winter); website: www.edisonlake.com.

Vermillion Valley Resort

2. MONO HOT SPRINGS RESORT

Nobody gets here by accident. People who stay here truly want to be here—no doubt about it. It's one long drive from just about anywhere.

Luxury rating: 2

Recreation rating: 4

Sierra National Forest, off Highway 168 near Huntington Lake

But the payoff for the long, winding drive is significant: a soothing mineral pool, soaking tubs, massages, and cozy cabins. Another big bonus is that you're in a magnificent area set in the Ansel Adams Wilderness and Sierra National Forest.

The cabins range from studios to two-bedrooms, and the rustic cabins are primitive with absolutely no frills. The more deluxe cabins have kitchen facilities and private bathrooms, and some have siding of cobblestone instead of wood. A restaurant is located on the premises and is open for breakfast, lunch, and dinner. The hot springs consist of a small, outside mineral pool and private, enclosed soaking tubs; water temperatures average over 100°F. The day-use fee is $4; massages are available for an extra charge. The hot springs first opened in 1934; the same gentleman has owned and operated the facility for the past 40 years.

There is sensational hiking around here, and a must-do is the popular one-mile hike to Doris Lake for swimming; trout fishing is marginal, since the lake is no longer stocked. Tule Lake is the place to hike to if you want good bass fishing; plan on a fairly easy three-mile round-trip. More stream and lake fishing is available nearby; for details, refer to the guidebook *Foghorn Outdoors: California Fishing.* Other activities include horseback riding and day trips to Lake Edison and Florence Lake, where boat rentals are available.

Facilities: Mono Hot Springs Resort has 15 cabins, some with fully equipped kitchens, private bathrooms, and fireplaces. Central bathrooms are provided. Laundry facilities, a restaurant, and hot springs are on-site. The resort is suitable for children. Leashed pets are permitted. Smoking is permitted.

Bedding: Linens and towels are provided in some of the cabins with an extra fee.

Reservations and rates: Reservations are required. The fee is $45 to $84 per night per cabin. Additional persons are charged $8 per night, and infants are free. The seventh night is half-price. The pet fee is $4 per night per pet. There is a $4 per day per person fee for the use of the hot springs facilities, with special packages and discounts available. There is a three-night minimum on weekends. Major credit cards are accepted. Open mid-May to November.

Directions: From the town of Shaver Lake, drive north on Highway 168 for 21 miles to Kaiser Pass Road/Forest Road 80. Turn right and drive 16 (narrow and twisting) miles to a fork in the road. Bear left onto Edison Lake Road and drive approximately 2.5 miles to the resort.

Contact: Mono Hot Springs Resort, General Delivery, Mono Hot Springs, CA 93642 (summer), or P.O. Box 215, Lakeshore, CA 93634 (winter); 559/325-1710; website: www.monohotsprings.com.

Mono Hot Springs Resort

3. LAKESHORE RESORT

Sailing is king here on four-mile long Huntington Lake, even though there is a wide variety of recreational activities available, ranging from fishing, waterskiing, and swimming to downhill skiing and snowmobiling in winter. However, come June, the sailing regattas begin and continue through August. And that is why you need to reserve a cabin three months in advance for summer.

Luxury rating: 3

Recreation rating: 4

Sierra National Forest, off Highway 168 at Huntington Lake

There are no cookie-cutter cabins here; each one is unique. The cabins were built between the 1920s and 1940s, but they have been updated. They're small and set on an incline, about one block from the lake and some 30 feet from each other. Situated in an old growth forest of ponderosa and tamarack, the cabins have no lake views. The cabins are homey, with quilts on the beds, and some rentals have knotty pine interiors.

Deer Creek runs along the property and fishing is fair for trout. Huntington Lake, at 7,000 feet in elevation, is planted with trout and kokanee salmon during spring and summer, and the fishing is good; refer to the book *Foghorn Outdoors: California Fishing*, for details. A swimming beach is nearby. For those interested in horseback riding, you'll find facilities only about a quarter mile away at D & F Pack Station.

In winter, Sierra Summit Ski Area, 2.5 miles away, offers downhill skiing and a snowboarding hill. You also can snowmobile from your cabin, where 150 miles of trails await.

Facilities: Lakeshore Resort has 26 cabins with private bathrooms and 20 RV sites. Some of the cabins have fully equipped kitchens. A restaurant, a saloon, a banquet room, a general store, bait and tackle, boat slips, boat rentals, and fishing licenses are available. The resort is suitable for children. A maximum of two leashed dogs are allowed; cats are not allowed. No smoking is permitted.

Bedding: Linens and towels are provided, but a discount is available by bringing your own supplies. There is no daily maid service.

Reservations and rates: Reservations are recommended. The fee is $71 to $137 per night per cabin with no linens and towels, and $78 to $150 per night with linens and towels provided. Additional persons are $10 per night. The pet fee is $15 per night per dog. There is a two-night minimum on weekends, and a three-night minimum on holidays. Boat launching fees are $12.50 per day or $82.50 per week. Major credit cards are accepted.

Directions: From the town of Shaver Lake, drive 21 miles north on Highway 168 to Huntington Lake Road. Turn left and drive approximately one mile to the resort on the right.

Contact: Lakeshore Resort, P.O. Box 197, Lakeshore, CA 93634; 559/893-3193; website: www.lakeshoreresort.com.

Lakeshore Resort

4. MUIR TRAIL RANCH

One if by land, two if by sea, and we vote for three by land and sea to get to Muir Trail Ranch. Whether you take the adventurous route by trail and boat or you opt for the longer foot or horse route, you won't soon forget your ambitious trip to the 200-acre Muir Trail Ranch.

Luxury rating: 2

Recreation rating: 5

Sierra National Forest, off Highway 168 near Florence Lake

Your journey begins at Florence Lake. From here, you have the option of taking a water taxi across the lake and then hiking five miles through the John Muir Wilderness to the ranch. Or, you can pack-in by horse or on foot for a total of 10 miles. Some visitors opt to have their belongings packed in, while they boat and hike their way to the ranch.

Once at the ranch, you'll be set up in a tent cabin or log cabin. The eight log cabins come with toilet and sink, whereas the four tent cabins do not. There is a communal bathroom, communal kitchen, hot springs, and a little outdoor café available to all guests.

At Muir Trail Ranch, you have the run of the place in a pristine high-mountain hideaway at over 9,000 feet in elevation. You are surrounded by the John Muir Wilderness and all it has to offer, which includes hiking and riding on your choice of quality trails, or fishing and swimming in any number of lakes and streams. You can make day trips or plan overnight excursions; guides are available.

   And when you return, tuckered out, at the end of the day, you have two enclosed hot spring baths or the small outdoor hot springs pool to relax in, a café to eat at or kitchen to cook in, and your warm sleeping bag to snuggle into. As you gaze at the stars, satisfied smile on your face, you can't help wondering: is this wilderness, or is it heaven? Actually, it's both.

Facilities: Muir Trail Ranch has eight log cabins and four tent cabins and can accommodate groups of up to 15 people; singles, couples, and small groups are welcome on a space available basis. Kitchenette facilities are not provided in the cabins, but a communal kitchen is available. A sink with cold running water and a toilet are provided in each log cabin, but not in the tent cabins. A communal bathroom, hot springs, an outdoor café, a small store with fishing supplies, a fire ring, and horse rentals and guide services are available. The ranch is suitable for children. Pets are not allowed. Smoking is permitted in some of the facilities.

Bedding: Linens and towels are not provided, so bring a sleeping bag and towels.

Reservations and rates: Reservations are required. For stays of one or two nights, the rate is $95 to $125 per night per person, including meals. For stays of a week, the rate is $595 per person, plus $150 to $200 per person for meals. Groups of up to 15 persons may reserve the entire lodge for $8,925, plus meals. Horses can be rented for $50 per day per horse. Credit cards are not accepted. Open June through September.

The water taxi makes two trips a day across Florence Lake and back. The fee is $8 per person one-way and $15 round-trip; children under age 12 are $5 one-way and $10 round-trip.

Directions: From the town of Shaver Lake, drive north on Highway 168 for 21 miles to Kaiser Pass Road/Forest Road 80. Turn right and drive to Florence Lake Road (located two miles south of the town of Mono Hot Springs). Turn right (south) and drive five miles to Florence Lake. Check in at the store and park your vehicle in the trailhead parking lot.

Contact: Muir Trail Ranch, P.O. Box 176, Lakeshore, CA 93634-0176; 209/966-3195; website: www.muirtrailranch.com.

Muir Trail Ranch

5. BISHOP CREEK LODGE

   When spring arrives in the high Sierra, the Bishop Creek Canyon and its environs are transformed into one of the most stellar recreation lands in America. This is the high country, where visitors get a unique mix of glacial-carved granite, lakes the color of gems, great hiking, horseback riding, and good evening fishing for rainbow trout or sometimes a big brown. In the fall, the

Luxury rating: 4

Recreation rating: 5

*Inyo National Forest,
off U.S. 395 near Bishop*

mountain slopes shimmering golden from the turning aspens are unforgettable.

With its furnished cabins, lodge, and facilities, Bishop Creek Lodge makes an excellent headquarters for this adventure. The cabins are built to withstand tough winters, and that means they are very snug in the summer, as well as being equipped with everything you need for a comfortable stay.

For people who need a clean bed for a good night's sleep, this is the place. You will awake ready for some of the best adventures in the high country. The 13 cabins can sleep two to eight people and include kitchens; the rental rate includes a continental breakfast at the lodge. The interiors are clean, modern, and cozy, often finished off with knotty pine siding.

Note that Bishop Creek Lodge is set down the road from Parchers Resort (see below) and features the same recreation options.

Facilities: Bishop Creek Lodge has 13 cabins with fully equipped kitchens and private bathrooms. There is complimentary continental breakfast. A café, a saloon, laundry facilities, a store, bait and tackle, and boat rentals are available. The lodge is suitable for children. Leashed pets are allowed. Smoking is permitted. Some facilities are wheelchair accessible.

Bedding: Linens and towels are provided.

Reservations and rates: Reservations are recommended. The fee is $90 to $205 per night per cabin, and $80 to $190 per night for two or more nights. The seventh night is free. Additional persons are $15 per night per person. There is a two-night minimum and a three-night minimum on holidays. Major credit cards are accepted. Open May through October.

Directions: From Bishop on U.S. 395, turn west on Highway 168 and drive for approximately 13.5 miles to the South Lake turnoff. Turn left on South Lake Road and drive three miles to the lodge on the left.

Contact: Bishop Creek Lodge, 2100 South Lake Road, Bishop, CA 93514; 760/873-4484, fax 760/873-8524.

Bishop Creek Lodge

6. PARCHERS RESORT

Since the early 1900s, Parchers Resort has been a gateway to the high Sierra wilderness, and at 9,200 feet, offers a stellar alpine experience. It's a complete getaway for families, groups, and company retreats.

Luxury rating: 4

Recreation rating: 5

*Inyo National Forest,
off U.S. 395 near Bishop*

Like its friendly neighbor, Bishop Creek Lodge, this lodge features excellent cabin units that are clean, well-furnished, and comfortable. They come with all the goodies: beds, bathrooms with showers, and kitchens, all of which rate high on the comfort scale. The friendly competition between the two adjacent lodges has kept each a quality operation.

Parchers is set on the same road as Bishop Creek Lodge, just a little bit higher on the mountain, and in turn, a little bit closer to nearby South Lake, the centerpiece of the area for outstanding fishing and hiking.

South Lake is set at 9,755 feet and covers 166 acres. It was created by a small dam on the South Fork of Bishop Creek. A good boat ramp is available, popular among owners of trailered aluminum boats, who can launch easily and then troll adjacent to the lake's shore. A 15-mph speed limit is in effect.

In addition, more good lakes lie within a two-hour's hike. A trailhead on the southeast side of the lake leads to a trail that is routed up to Bishop Pass. But get this: the trail forks off, providing routes to three different series of lakes. If you head to the right, you will reach Treasury Lakes after about a 2.8-mile hike, a good day trip. If you head to the left, you will be on the trail that leads to Bishop Pass, in the process passing Bull Lake, Long Lake, Saddlerock Lake, and Bishop Lake. On the way up, you will also pass a turnoff on the left for Ruwau Lake (requiring a short but steep climb), where there are beautifully colored brook trout in the foot-long class. To catch them, cast a Met-L Fly or Panther Martin spinner, black with yellow spots, and get it deep enough so it swims just over the top of the big boulders on the bottom of the lake at the far end.

Facilities: Parcher's Resort has 10 cabins with bathrooms; most have fully equipped kitchens. Complimentary continental breakfast is provided. A small store, bait and tackle, a fish cleaning station, boat rentals at South Lake, and a restaurant (breakfast and lunch only) are available. The resort is suitable for children. Leashed pets are permitted. Smoking is permitted. Two cabins are wheelchair accessible.

Bedding: Linens and towels are provided.

Reservations and rates: Reservations are recommended. The fee is $65 to $145 per night per cabin; the seventh night is free. Additional persons are $15 per night. The pet fee is $10 per night per pet. There is a three-day minimum on holidays. Major credit cards are accepted. Open May through October, weather permitting.

Directions: From Bishop on U.S. 395, turn west on Highway 168 and drive for approximately 13.5 miles to the South Lake turnoff. Turn left on South Lake Road and drive 5.5 miles to the resort on the left.

Contact: Parcher's Resort, 2100 South Lake Road, Bishop, CA 93514; 760/873-4177, fax 760/873-8524; website: www.bishopcreekresorts.com.

OTHER CABINS AND COTTAGES NEARBY

• Paradise Resort, Route 2, Bishop, CA 93514; 760/387-2370; website: www.theparadiseresort.com.

Parcher's Resort

7. CARDINAL VILLAGE RESORT

You'll take a walk through California gold-mining history when you stay at the Cardinal Village Resort, site of a former mining town. The remnants of the mining village date to the late 1800s. Back then, about 100 cabins, a store, and a schoolhouse stood; today only 13 of these original buildings exist, and you can take your pick for lodging.

Luxury rating: 3

Recreation rating: 4

Inyo National Forest, off U.S. 395 near Bishop

The cabins have been painstakingly renovated and named after local high-mountain lakes. They range from the two-person Hungry Packer to the spacious Golden Trout Cabin that sleeps 16. Other cabins include Topsy Turvy, Loch Leven, Moonlight, and Fish Gut. These cabins have fully equipped kitchens and private bathrooms.

The mine is a short walk from the resort. Although the machinery and buildings are no longer around, you can get a look at the old foundations and the head frame of the main shaft. Guided horseback tours of the mine and beyond are available from the Fourth of July weekend into September.

The resort borders Bishop Creek, which is well-stocked with trout, including some native brown trout. The resort's pond is stocked with Alpers trout and rainbow trout. Fishing is available at nearby North Lake, well-known for its awesome aspen groves and towering granite cliffs, and at the more popular Sabrina Lake, the largest of the four lakes in the immediate vicinity of the Bishop Creek drainage. Sabrina Lake has a boat ramp and rentals, as well as some giant Alpers trout and big browns that can keep fishing enthusiasts busy. For details, check out the guidebook *Foghorn Outdoors: California Fishing*.

But there's more to this area than fishing. The hiking nearby is top notch and there are many options. In the summer, the Saturday night barbecue at the resort is extremely popular; it costs $15 (not included in your stay) and you'll need a reservation. In winter, ice-skating is available at the resort's pond.

Facilities: Cardinal Village Resort has 10 cabins with fully equipped kitchens and private bathrooms. A barbecue, a picnic area, a meeting room, a fishing pond, Sunday morning nondenominational church service, a restaurant, and Saturday night barbecue are available. The resort is suitable for children. Pets are not allowed. No smoking is permitted.

Bedding: Linens and towels are not provided; bring your own, or rent them for a small fee.

Reservations and rates: Reservations are recommended. The fee is $75 to $275 per night per cabin; holiday and summer rates are slightly higher. Additional persons are $15 per night per person. Linens can be rented for $5 per stay per person. There is a two-night minimum and a three-night minimum on holidays. Major credit cards are accepted. Open May to October.

Directions: From Bishop on U.S. 395, turn west on Highway 168 and drive for approximately 18 miles to Aspendell and Cardinal Road. Turn right on Cardinal Road and drive .5 mile to the resort at the end of the road.

Contact: Cardinal Village Resort, Route 1, Box A3, Bishop, CA 93514; 760/873-4789; website: www.cardinalvillageresort.com.

Cardinal Village Resort

8. DINKEY CREEK INN AND CHALETS

Luxury rating: 3

Recreation rating: 4

Sierra National Forest, off Highway 168 near Shaver Lake

If you have high demands, trying to find a cabin rental in a beautiful setting can be like playing a game of mission impossible.

Say you want a pretty spot that accommodates families and pets, has a full kitchen and bathroom, won't drain your bank account, and is nice enough for Mom to feel like she's getting a special vacation—and has a variety of activities all year long to keep everyone happy. Trying to find the darned place can ruin your vacation before it's begun. Well, you can stop searching, because we found just the place, and it has every item on the checklist.

At Dinkey Creek Inn and Chalets, you get a modern A-frame chalet with fully equipped kitchen, carpeting, propane heat, and a stunning floor-to-ceiling wall of glass overlooking a large deck and a forest of pine and fir. The chalets are spaced 100 feet or more from each other. They're within 200 yards of Dinkey Creek and a historic, wood-trestle bridge built in 1938, and they're located in the Sierra National Forest.

In winter, you can cross-country ski, snowshoe, or snowmobile from the inn. In the summer, you can fish along Dinkey Creek, which is stocked with trout weekly throughout the summer. Some people come here for the hiking, with most heading 12 miles northeast to the Dinkey Creek Wilderness for hikes to Mystery Lake, South Lake, Rock Lake, and others.

A big bonus here is that your pooch can go on vacation, too. And remember, the café is open for breakfast and lunch only.

Facilities: Dinkey Creek Inn and Chalets has eight chalets that can sleep up to six persons with fully equipped kitchens and private bathrooms. A barbecue, deck, woodstove, and television are provided. A café, a grocery store, bait and tackle, and fishing licenses are available. The inn is suitable for children. Leashed pets are allowed. Smoking is permitted. One cabin is wheelchair accessible.

Bedding: Linens and towels are not provided, so bring your own.

Reservations and rates: Reservations are required. The fee is $85 to $100 per night per chalet during the summer, and $75 to $85 per night during the winter. Additional persons are charged $25 per night per person. The pet fee is $25 per stay for each chalet. Major credit cards are accepted.

Directions: From Fresno, drive north on Highway 168 for approximately 50 miles to the town of Shaver Lake and Dinkey Creek Road. Turn right (east) on Dinkey Creek Road and drive 13 miles to the inn on the right side of the road.

Contact: Dinkey Creek Inn and Chalets, 53861 Dinkey Creek Road, Shaver Lake, CA 93664; 559/841-3435; website: www.dinkeycreek.com.

Dinkey Creek Inn and Chalets

9. SHAVER LAKE LODGE

Staying here in the winter and then venturing back in the summer is like visiting with Dr. Jekyl, then Mr. Hyde. Depending on your frame of mind, in the summer, you will either love it or hate it. The activity level is intense at Shaver Lake all summer, filled with fast boats, water-skiers, and personal watercraft riders.

Since the elevation is 5,370 feet, lower than some of the neighboring lakes, the water is warmer and more appealing for water-contact sports. Spring and early summer fishing is also good because the lake is stocked with trout and kokanee salmon. The closest marina is about 1.5 miles away. Refer to the book *Foghorn Outdoors: California Fishing*, for more information.

Luxury rating: 3

Recreation rating: 3

Sierra National Forest, off Highway 168 at Shaver Lake

In the winter, most visitors use this place as a base for winter sports. For downhill skiers, Sierra Summit Ski Area is about 20 miles north on Highway 168, and several snow parks are even closer for cross-country skiing, snowshoeing, and snowmobiling.

The 21 units are 1930s-era rustic cabins that have been updated a tad and now have carpeting and showers, but no kitchens. Sizes ranging from studios to two-bedrooms are available. They are spaced close together across the road from the lake, and although every cabin has a lake view, the two cabins closest to the lake—with the best views—are Cabins 9 and 10.

The restaurant is open for lunch and dinner, and there is live music on weekends. At press time, the lodge was being sold and it was uncertain if the new owner was making changes.

Facilities: Shaver Lake Lodge has 21 cabins with private bathrooms. There are no kitchen facilities, but some of the rentals have microwaves and refrigerators. A deck or porch is provided, and some cabins have televisions. A restaurant and bar are available. The lodge is suitable for children. Pets are not allowed. Smoking is not permitted.

Bedding: Linens, pillows, blankets, and towels are not provided, so bring your own or rent them from the lodge.

Reservations and rates: Reservations are required. The fee is $55 to $115 per night per cabin. Linens and towels can be rented for $10 per night per cabin. There is a two-night minimum on holidays. Major credit cards are accepted.

Directions: From Fresno, drive north on Highway 168 for approximately 50 miles to Shaver Lake and the lodge on the right, past the town of Shaver Lake.

Contact: Shaver Lake Lodge, 44185 Highway 168, Shaver Lake, CA 93664; 559/841-3326.

Shaver Lake Lodge

10. GLACIER LODGE

Whiners are not welcome here. The owners of Glacier Lodge tell you straight out that if you want to be waited on and have modern conveniences, "look for the Hilton." And since there's no luxury hotel or resort anywhere near here, you'd better zip your lips and smile if you want lodging. The appeal here is the pristine beauty

© KAREN WOLFORD

Luxury rating: 2

Recreation rating: 5

*Inyo National Forest,
off U.S. 395 near Big Pine*

and myriad recreational opportunities available. If you want some phenomenal hiking, you're at the right place. You're next to trailheads that lead into the John Muir Wilderness, with scads of high-mountain lakes and incredible scenery. The Palisades Glacier, the southernmost glacier in the United States, is a few miles from the lodge. You'll see plenty of backpackers here, and the lodge has an RV campground and public showers to accommodate them.

The fishing is pretty good, too. In addition to the lakes accessible by hiking, Big Pine Creek is stocked with 38,200 trout from the Sage Flat Campground to Glacier Lodge during the summer. No, that trout number is not a misprint.

The lodge and cabins are rustic and old, first built in 1917, and you're at the end of the road, surrounded by wilderness at almost 8,000 feet in elevation. Since the lodge generates its own electricity, you can't bring any appliances for safety reasons. The restaurant is closed down, but take-out meals are available at the general store on request. Private guided tours into the wilderness are available, as are pack horses and mules.

After one trip here, the only whining you'll probably do is if you can't get a reservation for your next trip.

Facilities: Glacier Lodge has 12 cabins that can accommodate two to nine people; lodge rooms are also available. Kitchenette facilities are provided in the cabins, but kitchen utensils are limited. The bathrooms have showers. Barbecues are provided and some cabins have decks. There are no televisions or telephones. A children's fishing pond and general store are on-site. The lodge is suitable for children. Leashed pets are allowed. No smoking is permitted. Some facilities are wheelchair accessible.

Bedding: Linens and towels are supplied. There is no daily maid service in the cabins, but towels can be exchanged at the front desk.

Reservations and rates: Reservations are recommended. The fee is $70 to $75 per night per cabin, and there is a two-night minimum. For more than two persons, $15 to $18 per night per person is charged. There is a fee of $15 per night per pet. Major credit cards are accepted, but checks are not allowed. Open April through October.

Directions: From U.S. 395 in Big Pine, turn west on Glacier Lodge Road and drive 11 miles to the lodge.

Contact: Glacier Lodge, P.O. Box 370, Big Pine, CA 93513; 760/938-2837; website: www.jewelofthesierra.com.

Glacier Lodge

11. GRANT GROVE VILLAGE

Places like this were only supposed to be possible in the good old days. But when you walk amid the giant sequoias of the Grant Grove, maybe you'll soon realize these are the good ol' days—right now.

© STEPHANI STIENSTRA

Luxury rating: 2

Recreation rating: 5

Sequoia National Park, off the Generals Highway east of Fresno

Walking around the General Grant tree has a way of making people remember this. It is 1,800 to 2,000 years old, has a circumference of 107 feet, is 267 feet tall, and is set in the Grant Grove, likely the world's most spectacular grove of giant trees. The ideal approach is to get up early in order to hike the short loop trails in the sequoia groves in the morning. At this time, light refracts through the tree limbs and makes for breathtaking scenes, with the magnitude of the girth of the giant sequoias simply breathtaking.

Many people drive long distances and camp to see this phenomenon, but it is much easier to book one of the cabins at the nearby Grant Village. Fifty-one cabins are available, but only nine have bathrooms, heat, and electricity. That means the rest are one step up from camping. But privacy is another benefit, a rare asset in a national park that sees close to one million visitors every summer.

The Cozy Cabins (i.e., the ones with bathroom) were originally constructed in the 1920s, but many are being renovated with modern amenities. Cabins are painted or stained dark brown with white-trimmed windows. The Rustic Cabins have carpeting, insulated walls, and battery-operated lamps (now that's progress!).

Nearby Grant Village features a small store, a gift shop, post office, and visitor center, so it is an ideal launch point for your vacation in Sequoia and Kings Canyon National Parks. The big trees in this area live 30 to 40 times longer than people. The big ones do not die from old age, by insects, nor by fire, but rather from falling over. They sprout not from saplings, but from tiny seeds produced from cones, often aided by fire. In addition to Grant Grove, there are also spectacular groves of sequoias elsewhere in the park at Sherman Grove and Giant Forest (including the world's largest living thing, the Sherman Tree), Redwood Mountain Grove, Muir Grove, Lost Grove, and Converse Basin Grove.

Facilities: Grant Grove Village has nine Cozy Cabins, 23 Rustic Cabins, 19 tent cabins in the summer, and 30 lodge rooms. There are no kitchen facilities. A porch and picnic table are provided, and some cabins have woodstoves. A restaurant, store, and gift shop are available. The lodging is suitable for children. Pets are not allowed. No smoking is permitted. Some facilities are wheelchair accessible.

Bedding: Linens and towels are provided.

Reservations and rates: Reservations are recommended. The fee is $38 to $93 per night per cabin, and lodge rooms are $128 per night. Additional persons are $10 per night per person. Children ages 12 and under are free. Major credit cards are accepted. A $10-per-vehicle national park entrance fee is charged; it's good for seven days.

Directions: From Fresno, drive east on Highway 180 to the Big Stump Entrance Station at Kings Canyon National Park. Continue 1.5 miles to the Y intersection. Bear left on Highway 180 North and drive approximately one mile to Grant Grove Village.

Contact: Kings Canyon Park Service, 5755 East Kings Canyon Road, Suite 101, Fresno, CA 93727; 559/561-3314 or 866/522-6966, fax 559/561-3135; website: www.sequoia-kingscanyon.com.

Grant Grove Village

12. KINGS CANYON LODGE

You can search the Internet and all of the information provided by the national park, and you just plain won't find out about Kings Canyon Lodge. That's because it's not listed, it doesn't advertise, and it purposely doesn't want to be found by the collective masses. So Kings Canyon Lodge remains one of the few national park hideaways in America.

It also means that when every other place is booked in midsummer, you can often call just a week in advance and get yourself a cabin for a national park vacation. "If you're looking for a pool, HBO, and a restaurant, this isn't the place for you," might well be the mantra. Instead, it's the kind of place that caters to people who want to go hiking and have true park experience.

About the only way you find out about Kings Canyon Lodge is to go there. It is located near Yucca Point on the edge of Kings Canyon, and for those who know the area, it is roughly midway on the drive from Grant Grove in Sequoia to Cedar Grove in Kings Canyon. Upon arrival, the first thing you will notice is an antique gas pump out front. It was astonishing to us that it wasn't just for show; it actually works. Turns out it is the oldest double gravity gas pump on earth.

A lot of the place is just like this, a living time capsule. It is the

oldest lodge with cabins in the area, originally built in the 1930s as a fishing and hunting lodge. It has been restored to include bathrooms with showers, paneling, and electricity (the lodge makes its own power with a generator). There is no air-conditioning, no television, and no telephone, and like they say here, "It's like stepping back in time."

Luxury rating: 2

Recreation rating: 4

*Kings Canyon National Park,
off Highway 180 east of Fresno*

Naturally, the feature adventures are heading east up the canyon on the Kings Canyon Scenic Byway. This is the deepest canyon in the continental United States, rising 8,000 feet from the Kings River to Spanish Peak. As you enter the canyon, the landscape is transformed from an oak woodland to sheer granite walls with pyramid-shaped crests that poke holes in the sky. The road edges the canyon, and once, for more than a minute while we drove at 20 mph, a golden eagle glided just above and ahead of us, riding the rising thermals out of the canyon.

The fly fishing and hiking in the canyon is often stellar. Fly fishing with nymphs is excellent by working pockets at the head of the canyon, though large fish are rare. The best trail for views is up to Lookout Peak (challenging and 12 miles), and the best for waterfalls are to Roaring Falls (easy and one-half mile) and Mist Falls (easy and nine miles).

Facilities: Kings Canyon Lodge has 12 cabins of various sizes that include bathrooms with showers and electricity. Televisions, telephones, and air-conditioning are not provided. Smoking and pets are not permitted.

Reservations and rates: Reservations are recommended. Rates range from $69 for a cabin with double bed to $189 for a family cabin that will sleep eight. A $10 per vehicle national park entrance fee is charged and includes a brochure and map; the parking pass is good for seven days.

Directions: From Fresno, drive east on Highway 180 for 55 miles to the Big Stump entrance station at Sequoia National Park. Continue on Highway 180 (do not turn right at Generals Highway) for 17 miles (passing both turnoffs for Hume Lake) to the lodge on the right.

Contact: Kings Canyon Lodge, Kings Canyon National Park, P.O. Box 820, Kings Canyon National Park, CA 93633; 559/335-2405.

Kings Canyon Lodge

13. MONTECITO-SEQUOIA LODGE

Going to Montecito-Sequoia Lodge is like going to camp—only mom and dad go as well. And if mom and dad (or grandma and grandpa) like the idea of camp, then the whole family should have a great time.

Luxury rating: 3

Recreation rating: 5

Giant Sequoia National Monument, on Generals Highway east of Fresno

This is a full-service vacation camp that provides complimentary meals and activities for all ages from sunup to sundown, and a staff of 70 to keep it running smoothly. You can participate in as many activities as you desire. Choices include canoeing, sailing, or waterskiing in a private lake, mountain biking, swimming, horseback riding, fencing, and arts and crafts. During the winter, the emphasis is on cross-country skiing and snowshoeing. You name it, they probably have it.

"It was like being on a cruise ship, only in the forest," said one guest. There are theme nights such as Swing is King, Beach Party, Space Odyssey, Frontier Carnival, and Disco Dance. And each evening there's a campfire and sing-along.

The lodge and camps are enormously popular with families; often several generations will show up together for a family vacation or reunion. The lodge also caters to single parents. For singles and couples looking for lodging in a beautiful setting, we recommend going during the off-season when it's quieter and cheaper.

You'll have a choice of a rustic cabin with central bathhouse, or a lodge room with private bathroom. You don't need kitchen facilities, since buffet meals are provided in the dining room. The cabins are dark brown, boxy structures, with a king or queen bed and bunk beds, electricity, ceiling fans, and woodburning stoves or propane heat. Your fee includes all meals and most activities; horseback riding, mountain biking, waterskiing, and some arts and crafts cost extra. The lodge is situated at 7,500 feet in elevation.

Facilities: Montecito-Sequoia Lodge has 13 cabins and 30 lodge rooms. Complimentary meals and activities are provided. The cabins are heated by woodstove or propane, and do not include kitchen facilities, piped water, or bathrooms; communal bathrooms and showers are available nearby. Lodge rooms have private bathrooms. A heated pool, a spa, and tennis and volleyball courts are on-site. Water sports, winter sports, and a slew of other activities are available. A restaurant, a lounge, laundry facilities, a baby-sitting service, and a small store are available. The facilities are suitable for children. Pets are not allowed. No smoking is permitted. Some facilities are wheelchair accessible.

Reservations and rates: Reservations are recommended. During the summer, the cabin fee is $725 per adult for six nights, $660 for ages 2 to 12, and $100 for children under age two. Saturday night fees during the summer are $69 per person for adults, $39 per person for ages 4 to 12, and $8 per person for ages three and under. Midweek rates during the spring and fall are $55 per night per adult, $35 per night for ages 4 to 12, and $8 per night for ages three and under. Winter weekend rates for two nights are $218 per adult, $178 for ages 12 to 16, and $158 for ages 5 to 11. All meals are included. Call for holiday and other rates; lodge rooms are priced higher. Reservations can be made by calling 800/227-9900 or 650/967-8612, or writing to 2225 Grant Road, Suite 1, Los Altos, CA 94024. A $10-per-vehicle national park entrance fee is charged; the pass is good for seven days.

Directions: From Fresno, drive east on Highway 180 to the Big Stump Entrance Station at Kings Canyon National Park. Continue 1.5 miles to the Y intersection. Turn right (south) on Generals Highway and drive eight miles to the lodge entrance road on the right. Turn right and drive .25 mile to the parking lot.

Contact: Montecito-Sequoia Lodge, 8000 Generals Highway, Box 858, Kings Canyon National Park, CA 93663; 559/565-3388 or 800/227-9900; website: www.mslodge.com.

Montecito-Sequoia Lodge

14. SEQUOIA VILLAGE INN

Sequoia Village Inn sits just beyond the outskirts of Sequoia National Park, literally minutes from the Ash Mountain entrance station. There are many fantastic adventures nearby—not just gazing at the giant sequoias of the famed Giant Forest, as so many newcomers might believe.

First, you need to set up Sequoia Village as your launch point. It offers five cottages and two- and three-bedroom chalets. These are fully furnished, deluxe units, and they make fine vacation accommodations for those who require facilities a clear step above rustic.

Most everyone who stays here is planning a getaway to adjacent Sequoia National Park. But on your drive into Sequoia Village, you may find yourself gawking at the Kaweah River—beautiful and trout-filled—that is ideal for fly-fishing pocket water. Highway 198 runs beside the river for miles, and the road to Mineral Kings provides access to the East Fork Kaweah as well.

Luxury rating: 4

Recreation rating: 4

*Sierra foothills, off Highway 198
near Sequoia National Park*

After you enter the park, the road becomes twisty and your driving gets slower. Instead of trying to make good time, take off your watch and enjoy the drive, stopping at the lookouts to take in the spectacular Castle Rock to the south. The drive slowly rises into the Sierra, eventually entering forest. Suddenly, a few giant trees appear, massive sequoias marked by their giant circumference; they increase in number as you enter the Giant Forest. Soon, you will turn right to witness the General Sherman Tree.

As with the giant trees in the other groves, this tree is best seen at dawn, when no one else is around, so it feels sacred. After all, the General Sherman Tree is the largest living thing on earth, estimated to be 2,300 to 2,700 years old. It has a circumference of 102.6 feet, is 274.9 feet tall, has a 17.5-foot diameter 60 feet above the ground, has a branch with an 8-foot diameter, and grows enough wood each year to create a 60-foot tree.

Other musts are the tour through Crystal Cave and the short and easy hike to the Moro Rock Lookout. Crystal Cave is a marbleized cave, where taking a tour is like walking back to the beginning of time. Among the formations are adjoined crystal columns resembling the sound pipes in the giant organ at the Mormon Tabernacle. Lights are placed strategically for perfect lighting. The cave is two million years old, which is quite young in geologic time for a cave with calcium deposits.

Moro Rock provides one of the most breathtaking views in the Sierra. To get to it, you climb a succession of stairs for about 10 minutes—a 300-foot climb to reach the 6,725-foot summit. From here, the awesome Great Western Divide features prominently in the landscape, yet with a single turn, you can also take in about two-thirds of the park, the rims spiked by tower-like granite crags.

Facilities: Sequoia Village Inn has five cottages, two chalets, and a small suite. The cabins and chalets have fully equipped kitchens, and all rentals have private bathrooms. A microwave and refrigerator are provided in the suite. Televisions, VCRs, microwaves, and telephones are provided, and barbecues are available on request. Some cottages feature a deck, patio, and fireplace. A pool, a spa, laundry facilities, and a continental breakfast are on-site, and a restaurant is across the street. The inn is suitable for children. Leashed pets are allowed. Smoking is permitted in some cabins.

Bedding: Linens and towels are provided.

Reservations and rates: Reservations are recommended. The fee is $79 to $22? per night per cabin. Additional persons are $5 per night per person. There is a three-night minimum on holidays. Major credit cards are accepted. For tours of Crystal Cave, tickets are $8 with discounts for children and seniors; tickets are sold only at the Lodgepole or Foothills visitor centers (559/565-378? or 559/565-3135).

Directions: From Visalia, drive east on Highway 198 to Three Rivers. Continue east for approximately six miles (crossing a bridge) to the inn on the left.

Contact: Sequoia Village Inn, 45971 Sierra Drive, P.O. Box 1014, Three Rivers, CA 93271; 559/561-3652 or 559/561-0410; website: www.sequoiavillageinn.com.

Sequoia Village Inn

15. SILVER CITY MOUNTAIN RESORT

Just like Goldilocks, you'll find a variety of sleeping options at Silver City Mountain Resort: from small to large, from old to new, from primitive to modern. This is a long-time establishment set close to hikers' paradise. And if you're lucky, you might even see three bears (or at least one).

Luxury rating: 3

Recreation rating: 3

Sequoia National Park, off Highway 198 near Mineral King

The resort was built in the 1930s, and the same family has been running the place since then. How's that for tradition? The hiker's hut and the rustic cabins are original and nearly identical to when they were built. Don't expect a lot of extras in these cabins: the hut has a bed and a sink with cold water, and the rustic cabins have a stove (and some even have refrigerators). A central bathroom and shower facilities are close by.

The comfy cabins are a step up from the rustic cabins and include a toilet, a refrigerator, hot and cold water, and two bedrooms that can sleep up to six persons. For deluxe accommodations, rent a new, modern chalet with three bedrooms, fully equipped kitchen, private bathroom, and deck.

The cabins are spaced at least 30 feet apart, set amid pine and cedar cover. Silver Creek runs alongside the resort, and some of the cabins and chalets are situated near the creek, including Cozy Pines, Honeymoon, Rock Cabin, and Alpine Chalet.

The restaurant is open Thursday through Monday only, so if you don't like to cook, make sure you plan your stay accordingly. The resort is known for its "Thanksgiving Dinner," held the second Saturday after Labor Day. It's a traditional, home-cooked turkey feast with all the trimmings, and you need to make reservations to be included.

For a listing of excellent hiking options, refer to *Foghorn Outdoors: California Hiking*. Local fishing prospects include good fly fishing for small trout on the Kaweah River, with catch-and-release fishing regulations in place.

Facilities: Silver City Mountain Resort has 10 cabins and four chalets. Some cabins have kitchens and bathroom facilities; others do not. The chalets have fully equipped kitchens and private bathrooms. All the rentals have a deck, fire ring, and some cooking utensils and supplies. Bring paper towels and tall trash bags. A central bathroom with showers is available. The resort is suitable for children. Pets are not allowed. No smoking is permitted.

Bedding: Linens and towels are not provided, but blankets and pillows are provided, so bring your own sheets, pillow cases, and towels.

Reservations and rates: Reservations are recommended. The fee is $85 to $150 per night for cabins, $70 per night for the hiker's hut, and $200 to $250 per night for chalets. Early and late season discounts are available. There is a two-night minimum for the chalets. Major credit cards are accepted. Open Memorial Day weekend to late October. A $10 national park entrance fee is charged for each vehicle; the pass is good for seven days.

Directions: From Visalia, drive east on Highway 198 to Three Rivers. Continue east for three miles to Mineral King Road. Turn right (east) and drive approximately 23 miles to the resort on the left. The last 23 miles of road are slow and winding; plan on one hour of driving.

Contact: Silver City Mountain Resort, P.O. Box 56, Three Rivers, CA 93271; 559/561-3223 (summer) or 805/528-2730 (winter), fax 805/528 8039 (winter); website: www.silvercityresort.com.

Silver City Mountain Resort

16. ROAD'S END LODGE

If you like rafting, swimming, and fishing, you are in luck, because the major attraction here is access to the Kern River. What most people don't know, though, is that in winter the road into the high country is snowplowed up to six miles from the lodge, providing access to both the nearby town of Johnsondale and a connecting road, which is also plowed. Miles of snowmobiling trails branch out from this area. Therefore, the area near the lodge can be a popular destination spot for snowmobilers, too.

White-water rafting companies are available 16 miles south, and rafting is best in spring and early summer. As the water level subsides, swimming becomes more popular. Fishing is good for rainbow trout; details can be found in the guidebook *Foghorn Outdoors: California Fishing*. There are hiking trails galore within a few miles, and by driving up the road, you are quickly surrounded by giant sequoia trees.

Luxury rating: 3

Recreation rating: 4

Kern River, off Kern River Highway near Kernville

Lake Isabella is 25 miles to the south and is one of the largest freshwater lakes in Southern California. It has the most complete and dynamic array of water sports facilities available. It is a great getaway for waterskiing, powerboating, fishing, and windsurfing.

The cottages are set close to the Kern River, amidst oak trees, at an elevation of 3,600 feet, and range from studios to two-bedrooms. They are painted forest green with beige trim, and most of the 1920s-era cottages have been redecorated recently, but the knotty pine interior is still intact. Riverside Cottage is the most popular rental during the summer because it sits closest to the river and the lodge's sandy beach. For romance, Sunflower Cottage wins hands down because of its rock fireplace and ivy-covered porch.

Facilities: Road's End Lodge has seven cottages that can accommodate up to eight persons, depending on the rental. Most units have fully equipped kitchens and private bathrooms with showers. A fire pit and picnic table are provided, and some rentals have a deck or porch and fireplace. Not included are air-conditioning, televisions, and telephones. A general store, bait and tackle, and fishing licenses are available. The facilities are suitable for children. Pets are not allowed. No smoking is permitted.

Bedding: Linens and towels are provided, but you receive one set only.

Reservations and rates: Reservations are recommended. The fee is $60 to $115 per night. There is a two-night minimum on weekends, and a three-night minimum on holidays. Major credit cards are accepted.

Directions: From Kernville, drive 16 miles north on Sierra Way Road/Kern River Highway to the lodge on both sides of the road.

Contact: Road's End Lodge, P.O. Box 2022, Kernville, CA 93238-2022; 760/376-6562.   *Road's End Lodge*

17. WHISPERING PINES LODGE CABINS

You want easy-to-reach lodging with scads of recreational opportunities available all year long? Then hustle yourself and your fanny pack to Whispering Pines Lodge Cabins, where you can choose between white-water rafting, kayaking, hiking, fishing, swimming, cycling, and—well, you get the picture.

Luxury rating: 3

Recreation rating: 4

Kern River, near Kernville

These cabins are actually suites with common walls; more lodge room than cabin, and packed with amenities. All rentals have at least one king-size bed, and they are situated as close as 100 feet from the Wild and Scenic Kern River. A few of the cabins have fully equipped kitchens, and all rentals have refrigerators and coffeemakers. A complimentary full breakfast is included.

Cabins 105 through 108 are the most popular because they have full river views; you get a glimpse of the river from Cabins 109 through 114. Cabins 114 and 117 do not have fireplaces.

Several rafting companies operate out of Kernville, so it's easy to plan a rafting or kayaking trip. Take your pick of many scenic hiking and cycling trails in the area. You are near the northern shore of Lake Isabella, and for fishing information, refer to the guidebook *Foghorn Outdoors: California Fishing*. And in the winter, cross-country and downhill skiing and snowmobiling are less than an hour away.

Got your bags packed?

Facilities: Whispering Pines Lodge Cabins has 17 cabins with private bathrooms with whirlpool tubs. Some of the cabins have a fully equipped kitchen, fireplace, and deck or porch. Air-conditioning, television, and telephone are provided. A pool is available. Although the lodge can accommodate children, it is more suitable for adults. Pets are not allowed. No smoking is permitted.

Bedding: Linens and towels are provided.

Reservations and rates: Reservations are recommended. The fees are $99 to $159 per night, and breakfast is included. For more than two persons, $20 per night per person is charged. Major credit cards are accepted.

Directions: From Kernville, drive .3 mile north on Sierra Way to the lodge on the left.

Contact: Whispering Pines Lodge Cabins, 13745 Sierra Way, Route 1, Box 41, Kernville, CA 93238; 760/376-3733 or 877/241-4100, fax 760/376-6513; website: www.kernvalley.com/inns.

Whispering Pines Lodge Cabins

APPENDIX

*ADDITIONAL
CABINS AND COTTAGES*

The following real estate agencies also provide rental services for privately owned cabins, homes, and chalets:

Bass Lake Realty, P.O. Box 349, Bass Lake, CA 93604; 559/642-3600; website: www.basslakerealty.com

Bass Lake Vacation Rentals, P.O. Box 507, Bass Lake, CA 93604; 559/642-2211

Bodega Bay & Beyond, 575 Coast Highway 1, P.O. Box 129, Bodega Bay, CA 94923-0129; 800/888-3565 or 707/875-3942; website: www.sonomacoast.com

Clear Lake Vacation Rentals, 1855 South Main Street, Lakeport, CA 95453; 707/263-7188; website: www.clearlakevacations.com

Coast Retreats of Mendocino, P.O. Box 977, Mendocino, CA 95460; 800/859-6260 or 707/937-1121; website: www.coastretreats.com

Coastal Vistas, P.O. Box 413, Bodega Bay, CA 94923; 800/788-4782 or 707/875-3000; website: www.coastalvistas.com

Don Berard Associates, Sea Ranch Vacation Rentals, P.O. Box 604, Gualala, CA 95445; 800/643-8899 or 707/884-3211; website: www.donberard.com

Graeagle Vacation Rentals, P.O. Box 307, Graeagle, CA 96103; 800/836-0269 or 530/836-2500; website: www.graeagleproperties.com

Kendall & Potter, 783 Rio del Mar Boulevard, Suite 7, Aptos, CA 95003; 888/692-5331 or 831/688-3511; website: www.montereycoast.com

Lake Tahoe Reservation Bureau, 599 Tahoe Keys Boulevard, P.O. Box 16584, South Lake Tahoe, CA 96151; 530/544-5397 or 800/698-2463; website: www.tahoevacationguide.com

Lake Valley Properties, 591 Tahoe Keys Boulevard, Cedar Building, D-1, P.O. Box 7405, South Lake Tahoe, CA 96158; 800/634-3397; website: www.lakevalleyproperties.com

McKinney & Assoc. Inc., 2196 Lake Tahoe Boulevard, Suite 1, South Lake Tahoe, CA 96150; 800/748-6857 or 530/542-0557; website: www.stayintahoe.com

Rams Head Realty & Rentals, Inc., 1000 Annapolis Road, P.O. Box 123, The Sea Ranch, CA 95497-0123; 800/785-3455 or 707/785-2427; website: www.ramshead-realty.com

Russian River Vacation Homes, 14080 Mill Street, P.O. Box 418, Guerneville, CA 95446; 800/310-0804 or 707/869-9030; website: www.riverhomes.com

Shoreline Properties, 18200 Old Coast Highway, Fort Bragg, CA 95437; 707/964-1444; website: www.shorelinevacations.com

Sierra Vacation Rentals, 7252 North Lake Boulevard, Suite 101, P.O. Box 37, Carnelian Bay, CA 96140; 800/521-6656 or 530/546-8222; website: www.sierravacations.com

Tahoe Rental Connection, 2241 James Street, Suite 3, South Lake Tahoe, CA 96150; 800/542-2100 or 530/542-2777; website: www.tahoerental connection.com

Vacation Station, Inc., 110 Country Club Drive, P.O. Box 7180, Incline Village, NV 89452; 800/841-7443 or 775/831-3664; website: www.vacation station.com

West Lake Properties, 115 West Lake Boulevard, P.O. Box 1768, Tahoe City, CA 96145; 800/870-8201 or 530/583-0268; website: westlake properties.com

Yosemite West Lodging, Inc., P.O. Box 720, Bass Lake, CA 93604; 559/642-2211; website: www.yosemitewestreservations.com

INFORMATION SERVICES

Amador County Chamber of Commerce and Visitors Bureau, P.O. Box 596, Jackson, CA 95642; 209/223-0350; website: www.amadorcounty chamber.com

Bishop Area Chamber of Commerce and Visitors Bureau, 690 N. Main Street, Bishop, CA 93514; 760/873-8405; website: www.bishopvisitor.com

Calaveras Visitors Bureau, P.O. Box 637, Angels Camp, CA 95222; 800/225-3764 or 209/736-0049; website: www.visitcalaveras.org

Crescent City-Del Norte County Chamber of Commerce, 1001 Front Street, Crescent City, CA 95531; 800/343-8300 or 707/464-3174; website: www.northerncalifornia.net

El Dorado County Chamber of Commerce, 542 Main Street, Placerville, CA 95667; 800/457-6279 or 530/621-5885, website: www.eldorado county.org

Eldorado National Forest Information Center, 3070 Camino Heights Drive, Camino, CA 95709; 530/644-6048; website: www.r5.fs.fed.us /eldorado

Eureka Chamber of Commerce, 2112 Broadway, Eureka, CA 95501; 800/356-6381 or 707/442-3738; website: www.eurekachamber.com

Fort Bragg/Mendocino Coast Chamber of Commerce, P.O. Box 1141, Fort Bragg, CA 95437; 800/726-2780 or 707/961-6300; website: www .mendocinocoast.com

Grass Valley/Nevada County Chamber of Commerce, 248 Mill Street, Grass Valley, CA 95945; 530/273-4667; website: www.gvncchamber.org

Lake Tahoe Basin Management Unit, 870 Emerald Bay Road, Suite 1, South Lake Tahoe, CA 96150; 530/573-2600: website: www.r5.fs .fed.us/ltbmu

Lee Vining Chamber of Commerce, P.O. Box 130, Lee Vining, CA 93541; 760/647-6629; website: www.leevining.com

Mammoth Lakes Visitor Center and Ranger Station, P.O. Box 148, Mammoth Lakes, CA 93546; 760/924-5500; website: www.r5.fs.fed.us/inyo

Mariposa County Chamber of Commerce, P.O. Box 425, Mariposa, CA 95338; 209/966-2456; website: www.mariposa.org

Mono Basin Scenic Area Visitor Center, P.O. Box 429, Lee Vining, CA 93541; 760/647-3044; website: www.r5.fs.fed.us/inyo

Monterey County Convention and Visitors Bureau, P.O. Box 1770, Monterey, CA 93942-1770; 831/649-1770; website: www.montereyinfo.org

Morro Bay Chamber of Commerce and Visitor Center, 880 Main Street, Morro Bay, CA 93442; 800/231-0592 or 805/772-4467; website: www.morrobay.org

Mount Shasta Visitors Bureau, 300 Pine Street, Mount Shasta, CA 96067; 800/397-1519 or 530/926-4865; website: www.mtshasta.com/chamber

Napa Chamber or Commerce, 1556 First Street, Napa, CA 94559; 707/226-7455; website: www.napachamber.org

North Lake Tahoe Chamber of Commerce, 245 North Lake Boulevard, Tahoe City, CA 96145; 530/581-8795; website: www.mytahoevacation.com

Plumas County Visitors Bureau, P.O. Box 4120, Quincy, CA 95971; 800/326-2247 or 530/283-6345; website: www.plumas.ca.us

Shasta Lake Visitor Center, 14250 Holiday Road, Redding, CA 96003; 530/275-1589; website: www.r5.fs.fed.us/shastatrinity

Sonoma Valley Chamber of Commerce, 651-A Broadway, Sonoma, CA 95476; 707/996-1033; website: www.sonomachamber.com

South Lake Tahoe Chamber of Commerce, 3066 Lake Tahoe Boulevard, South Lake Tahoe, CA 96150; 530/541-5255; website: www.tahoeinfo.com

Truckee-Donner Chamber of Commerce, 10065 Donner Pass Road, Truckee, CA 96161; 530/587-2757; website: www.truckee.com

Tuolumne County Visitors Bureau, P.O. Box 4020, Sonora, CA 95370; 800/446-1333 or 209/533-4420; website: www.thegreatunfenced.com

West Marin Chamber of Commerce, P.O. Box 1045, Point Reyes Station, CA 94956; 415/663-9232; website: www.pointreyes.org

Yosemite Sierra Visitors Bureau, 40637 Yosemite Highway 41, Oakhurst, CA 93644; 559/683-4636; website: www.go2yosemite.net

INDEX

KOA Cabins: 8–9; Crystal Crag Lodge: 280–282; Dillon Beach Resort: 224; Dinkey Creek Inn and Chalets: 350–351; Dockside Boat and Bed—San Francisco: 240–241; Dorrington Inn: 171–172; Double Eagle Resort and Spa: 272–273; Eagle Lake RV Park & Cabins: 87–88; Eagle Lake Cabins: 85–86; Echo Lake Chalet: 208–209; Edelweiss Lodge: 275–276; Edgewater Resort: 126–127; Elwell Lakes Lodge: 186–188; Emandal Farm: 110–111; Enright Gulch Cabins: 44–45; Forks Resort, The: 334–335; Four Seasons, The: 271–272; Gables Cedar Creek Inn: 175–176; Glacier Lodge: 352–353; Gold Lake Lodge: 188–189; Gorda Springs Resort: 309–310; Grant Grove Village: 354–355; Gray Eagle Lodge: 185–186; Greenhorn Creek Guest Ranch: 182–183; Hat Creek Resort: 84–85; Haven, The: 269–270; Highland Ranch: 124–125; Hunewill Guest Ranch: 254–255; Indian Beach Resort: 127–128; June Lake Pines Cottages: 270–271; Kay's Silver Lake Resort: 213–214; Kings Canyon Lodge: 355–356; Kit Carson Lodge: 212–213; Knotty Pine Resort: 98–99; KOA Lassen/Shingletown: 88–89; La Playa Hotel Cottages: 297–298; Lake Alpine Lodge and Cabins: 216–217; Lake Berryessa Marine Resort: 143–144; Lake Front Cabins: 268–269; Lake Nacimiento Resort: 312–313; Lake Oroville Floating Camps: 160–161; Lake Pillsbury Resort: 112–113; Lake San Antonio Resorts: 311–312; Lake Siskiyou Resort: 39–40; Lake Tulloch RV Camp and Marina: 322–323; Lakeshore Inn & RV: 59–60; Lakeshore Resort: 344–345; Lakeview Terrace Resort: 63–64; Lassen View Resort: 101–102; Lava Creek Lodge: 79–80; Lazy S Lodge: 205–206; Le

Trianon Resort: 122–123; Little Bear RV Park: 184–185; Little Mount Hoffman Lookout: 76–77; Little Norway Resort: 99–100; Littlefield Ranch Cabins: 68–69; Long Valley Resort: 183–184; Loon Lake Chalet: 200–201; Lundborg Landing: 233–234; Manka's Inverness Lodge: 227–228; Marble Mountain Ranch: 33–34; Mattole River Organic Farm's Country Cabins: 22–23; McAlpine Lake and Park: 296–297; McGovern's Chalets: 94; Meeks Bay Resort and Marina: 198–199; Mill Creek Park: 89–90; Mill Creek Resort: 95–96; Miller's Landing: 335–336; Mission Ranch: 298–299; Mono Hot Springs Resort: 343–344; Mount Shasta Resort: 38–39; Muir Trail Ranch: 345–346; Narrows Lodge Resort, The: 121; Packer Lake Lodge: 189–190; Padilla's Rim Rock Resort: 83–84; Parchers Resort: 348–349; Patrick Creek Lodge: 11; Piety Hill Cottages: 164–165; Pine Acres Blue Lakes Resort: 119–120; Pine-Gri-La: 45–46; Pinecrest Chalet: 252–253; Pinecrest Lake Resort: 251–252; Pinewood Cove: 53–54; Placerville KOA: 167–168; Plumas Pines Resort: 97–98; Redwoods River Resort: 25–26; Richardson Grove RV Park & Family Camp: 24; Ripple Creek Cabins: 42–43; Rippling Waters Resort: 82–83; Rivers Resort, The: 250–251; Riverwalk RV Park: 21–22; Road's End Lodge: 361–362; Robbs Hut: 201–202; Rock Creek Lakes Resort: 286–287; Rock Creek Lodge: 285–286; Rollins Lakeside Inn: 166–167; Sacramento-Metro KOA: 168–169; Sandy Bar Ranch Cabins: 34–35; Sardine Lake Resort: 190–192; Sequoia Village Inn: 358–360; Serenisea Cottages: 131–132; Shaver Lake Lodge: 351–352; Shore House at Lake Tahoe: 193–194; Sierra Shangri-

Hendy Woods State Park: 125
Henry Cowell Redwoods State Park: 294
Heritage House: 105, 116–117
Heritage Land Company: 85
Hetch Hetchy: 247, 256
Highland Ranch: 124–125
hiking: Agate Cove Inn: 113–114; Ahwahnee Cabins: 262–263; Albion River Inn: 117–118; Angora Lakes Resort: 206–207; Auberge du Soleil: 150–151; Bear Basin Lookout & Pierson Cabin: 9–10; Bear River Lake Resort: 214–215; Beaver Creek: 135–136; Best in the West Resort: 46–47; Big Basin Redwoods State Park: 243–244; Big Rock Resort: 274–275; Big Sur Campground and Cabins: 302–303; Big Sur Lodge: 303–304; Bishop Creek Lodge: 346–347; Bishop Pine Lodge: 13–14; Bonanza King Resort: 50–51; Bucks Lake Lodge: 158–159; Burney Mountain Guest Ranch: 81–82; Cabins at Strawberry & Strawberry Inn: 172–173; Camp Marigold Garden Cottages: 12–13; Caples Lake Resort: 211–212; Cardinal Village Resort: 349–350; Carter House Inns: 20–21; Casa Rubio Bed and Breakfast: 7–8; Cave Springs/Dunsmuir Cabins: 41–42; Childs Meadow Resort: 96–97; Clark Creek Lodge: 77–78; Cloverdale KOA: 134; Convict Lake Resort: 282–283; Cotillion Gardens RV Park: 294–295; Cottage Grove Inn: 141–142; Cottage Inn at Lake Tahoe, The: 195–196; Crescent City Redwoods KOA Cabins: 8–9; Crystal Crag Lodge: 280–282; Dancing Coyote Beach: 226; Dillon Beach Resort: 224; Dockside Boat and Bed—Oakland: 242–244; Dockside Boat and Bed—San Francisco: 240–241; Dorrington Inn: 171–172; Double Eagle Resort and Spa: 272–273; Drakesbad Guest Ranch: 91–92; Echo Lake Chalet: 208–209; Edelweiss Lodge:

275–276; Elwell Lakes Lodge: 186–188; Emandal Farm: 110–111; Emerald Forest: 14–15; Enright Gulch Cabins: 44–45; Eureka/Arcata KOA Kamping Kabins: 19; Evergreen Lodge: 256; Four Seasons, The: 271–272; Gerstle Park Inn: 234–236; Girard Ridge Lookout: 48; Glacier Lodge: 352–353; Gold Lake Lodge: 188–189; Gorda Springs Resort: 309–310; Grant Grove Village: 354–355; Gray Eagle Lodge: 185–186; Gray's Retreat and Jasmine Cottage: 229–230; Greenhorn Creek Guest Ranch: 182–183; Hat Creek Resort: 84–85; Haven, The: 269–270; Heritage House: 116–117; Highland Ranch: 124–125; Holly Tree Inn: 228–229; Homestead, The: 333–334; Howard Creek Ranch: 108–109; Huckleberry Springs Country Inn and Spa: 147–148; Hunewill Guest Ranch: 254–255; Indian Springs: 140–141; Inn at Schoolhouse Creek, The: 114–115; Inn at Sugar Pine Ranch: 325–326; June Lake Pines Cottages: 270–271; Kay's Silver Lake Resort: 213–214; Kings Canyon Lodge: 355–356; Kit Carson Lodge: 212–213; KOA Lassen/Shingletown: 88–89; Lake Alpine Lodge and Cabins: 216–217; Lake Front Cabins: 268–269; Lake San Antonio Resorts: 311–312; Lake Siskiyou Resort: 39–40; Lakeview Terrace Resort: 63–64; Lassen View Resort: 101–102; Lava Creek Lodge: 79–80; Lazy S Lodge: 205–206; Lazy Z Resort Cabins: 173–174; Little Bear RV Park: 184–185; Little Mount Hoffman Lookout: 76–77; Littlefield Ranch Cabins: 68–69; Long Valley Resort: 183–184; Loon Lake Chalet: 200–201; Lucia Lodge: 308–309; Malakoff Diggins State Historic Park: 163–164; Manchester Beach KOA: 123–124; Manka's Inverness Lodge: 227–228; Marble Moun-

Notes

Notes

Notes

Notes

Notes

Notes

Notes

AVALON
TRAVEL
publishing

How far will our travel guides take you? As far as you want.

Discover a rhumba-fueled nightspot in Old Havana, explore prehistoric tombs in Ireland, hike beneath California's centuries-old redwoods, or embark on a classic road trip along Route 66. Our guidebooks deliver solidly researched, trip-tested information—minus any generic froth—to help globetrotters or weekend warriors create an adventure uniquely their own.

And we're not just about the printed page. Public television viewers are tuning in to Rick Steves' new travel series, *Rick Steves' Europe*. On the Web, readers can cruise the virtual black top with *Road Trip USA* author Jamie Jensen and learn travel industry secrets from Edward Hasbrouck of *The Practical Nomad*.

In print. On TV. On the Internet.

We supply the information. The rest is up to you.

Avalon Travel Publishing

Something for everyone

www.travelmatters.com

Avalon Travel Publishing guides are available at your favorite book or travel store.

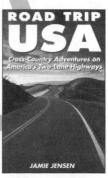

FOGHORN OUTDOORS guides are for campers, hikers, boaters, anglers, bikers, and golfers of all levels of daring and skill. Each guide focuses on a specific U.S. region and contains site descriptions and ratings, driving directions, facilities and fees information, and easy-to-read maps that leave only the task of deciding where to go.

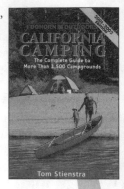

"Foghorn Outdoors has established an ecological conservation standard unmatched by any other publisher."   ~Sierra Club

WWW.FOGHORN.COM

TRAVEL SMART guidebooks are accessible, route-based driving guides focusing on regions throughout the United States and Canada. Special interest tours provide the most practical routes for family fun, outdoor activities, or regional history for a trip of anywhere from two to 22 days. Travel Smarts take the guesswork out of planning a trip by recommending only the most interesting places to eat, stay, and visit.

"One of the few travel series that rates sightseeing attractions. That's a handy feature. It helps to have some guidance so that every minute counts."
~San Diego Union-Tribune

CiTY·SMaRT™ guides are written by local authors with hometown perspectives who have personally selected the best places to eat, shop, sightsee, and simply hang out. The honest, lively, and opinionated advice is perfect for business travelers looking to relax with the locals or for longtime residents looking for something new to do Saturday night.

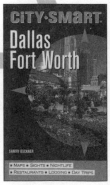